The King Can Do No Wrong

The King Can Do No Wrong

Constitutional Fundamentals, Common Law History, and Crown Liability

MARIE-FRANCE FORTIN

OXFORD
UNIVERSITY PRESS

OXFORD
UNIVERSITY PRESS

Great Clarendon Street, Oxford, OX2 6DP,
United Kingdom

Oxford University Press is a department of the University of Oxford.
It furthers the University's objective of excellence in research, scholarship,
and education by publishing worldwide. Oxford is a registered trade mark of
Oxford University Press in the UK and in certain other countries

Published in the United States of America by Oxford University Press
198 Madison Avenue, New York, NY 10016, United States of America

British Library Cataloguing in Publication Data

Data available

Library of Congress Control Number: 2024931140

ISBN 9780198886914

DOI: 10.1093/9780191994487.001.0001

To Liam, Lorna, and Luke

Preface

The daughter of a loyal and dedicated civil servant, this historical constitutional enquiry into the liability of the government would have come as a surprise even to my younger self. It is in part by following paternal footsteps as a government lawyer, but also by crossing the fence to assist those wronged by the state, that the general confusion surrounding the foundations of the crown's immunity from suit at common law became apparent to me. In my search for more clarity, I was extremely fortunate to have been welcomed again by Queens' College at the University of Cambridge as a PhD student. The completion of this book would not have been possible without the enlightening, thoughtful, and constant guidance, support, and mentorship of my doctoral supervisor, Professor John Allison. The community of Queens' brilliant fellows and their own families made my husband and me feel home amongst friends in the College where we had first met. Queens' College's Day Nursery also proved to be the most wonderful environment for our three children. The guilt I felt at leaving my young toddlers to pursue my own professional interests was allayed by my confidence in the College nursery's marvellous carers. Their warmth and exceptional educating talents, as well as those of Newnham Croft Primary School's teachers, made our Cambridge experience one of our family's happiest times.

I am also extremely grateful to Ms Lesley Dingle, the former Law Librarian at the Squire Law Library, for her time and her unparalleled legal research expertise, as well as to Mrs Alison Hirst, whose kindness and profound mastery of the intricacies of graduate studies policies at the University allowed me to successfully navigate the doctoral stage of my journey while also happily welcoming another child. To the convenors of the research training programme at the Law Faculty, I am very grateful for the opportunity to present an early version of the first chapters of this book, and particularly to Professor Stelios Tofaris for his insightful comments and suggestions, as well as Professors Surabhi Ranganathan and Pippa Rogerson for their helpful advice. Dr Shona Wilson Stark and Professor Alison Young's pioneering Centre for Public Law Lunchtime seminar also allowed me to receive invaluable comments, as did Dr Julia Kelsoe and Dr Emily Gordon's invitation to present at the Centre for English Legal History's seminar series, and Dr Carolina Armenteros's inclusion of my paper for the Monarchy and Modernity Conference. I am also very grateful to Dr Rose Melikan, Professor Peter Cane, Sir John Baker, Dr Joseph Canning, Dr Paul Cavill, Professor David Renders, and the community of my fellow doctoral peers for their time and illuminating discussions during my time in Cambridge. Little candles lit here and there along the way have shone a light on the greater picture I was attempting to draw.

Like *the king can do no wrong* itself, versions of this book have travelled across common law jurisdictions (and mixed legal systems) at various stages of its completion. I am greatly indebted to Dr Sebastian Payne for his perceptive comments on my thesis, as it then was, and on the potential value of my research for other aspects of public law. I will be forever grateful to Professor Jean Leclair, who provided invaluable insight in the early stages of my research and encouragement throughout. I also wish to thank the Université de Montréal's Law Librarian, Ms Stéphanie Pham-Dang, for her time and expertise, and the convenors of the legal research training programme at the Université de Montréal, particularly Professors Violaine Lemay and Michel Morin, for deepening my thinking on public law legal research and methodology. I also very thankful to Professor Timothy Endicott and Raphaël Grenier-Benoit, convenors of the Public Law Discussion Group at the University of Oxford, for an enriching discussion on recent constitutional developments and *the king can do no wrong*. Professor Vanessa MacDonnell's support, mentorship, and help, along with that of Mathieu Tovar-Poitras, in organizing a book workshop at the Public Law Centre of the University of Ottawa have also been exceptional, and resulted in an extraordinary venue where I was immensely privileged to discuss a later version of this book with Professors Pierre Foucher, Kevin Bouchard, Han-Ru Zhou, Peter Oliver, Geneviève Cartier, Terry Skolnik, Sylvia Rich, Philippe Lagassé, Paul Daly, Charles-Maxime Panaccio, and Ghislain Otis, as well as Dr Nessan Akemakou Njinga. Conversations with colleagues, especially Michelle Giroux, Mistrale Goudreau, Sarah Berger-Richardson, Sylvia Rich, and Julie Paquin, have also been very precious to me, and helped me through the first years of teaching (and pandemic)!

My special thanks also to the Centre for Constitutional Studies of the Sutherland School of Law, University College Dublin, and to the convenors of the symposium *New and Emerging Voices in Constitutional Law*, Seána Glennon and Professor Eoin Carolan. Thanks to them, I was able to engage with Irish jurists on Irish legal thinking on *the king can do no wrong*. University College Cork and Trinity College Dublin have also been generous in their support and have provided a home for me as a visiting researcher: I wish to thank the staff in both these Irish institutions' law libraries for their welcoming and helpful assistance.

I am also greatly indebted to my *alma mater*, Université Laval, and its Faculté de droit, where my academic journey began, thanks to Professor Marie-Claire Belleau. It was also where my interest in public law legal history was first piqued, thanks to Professor Emeritus Pierre Issalys, and where this book was presented in its final form to the Centre d'études en droit administratif et constitutionnel, under the auspices of Professors Kevin Bouchard, Monica Popescu, Antoine Pellerin, and Patrick Taillon. It was an immense privilege to present this book to an audience of law students and academics sitting on benches where I had sat more than two decades earlier, and which included members of the government's civil service—a community that guided my first steps on the path to a legal career.

I am still hoping that my mastery of the English language may one day equal Samuel Beckett's mastery of the French language; I may very well still be waiting for Godot, however, and I am therefore very grateful to my copyeditor, Jeremy Langworthy. Bright young minds have greatly helped me enrich the later chapters of this book; I am very thankful to my research assistants, Florence Robert, Aurélie Romy Harchaoui, Joémy Binette, and Milo Hallak, for their diligent work. It has also been a great joy to work with Oxford University Press's project editor, Ms Lindsay Glick, in whose very professional and competent hands this book underwent the last stages of publication.

My most heartfelt thanks go to my husband Paul and to our three children, Liam, Lorna, and Luke. Paul's patience and generosity in reviewing more drafts than one could count, his faith in my project even as we were starting our family, and his support throughout this part of our journey together meant everything. To our children: it is your love, the strength you give me, the laughs we share together, and the immense happiness with which you fill my life that made writing this book possible.

Contents

Table of Cases

AUSTRALIA

CANADA

IRELAND

NEW ZEALAND

UNITED STATES

ENGLAND & UNITED KINGDOM

Table of Statutes

IRELAND

New Zealand

SOUTH AFRICA

UNITED STATES OF AMERICA

Introduction

1 The evolution of *the king can do no wrong*: an overview

The king can do no wrong is a capacious expression, associated in legal thinking with notions as diverse as the king having no legal power to do wrong,[1] the king's perfection and prerogative,[2] the monarch's personal immunity from suit,[3] the crown's immunity from suit,[4] the crown's irresponsibility in tort,[5] ministerial responsibility,[6] sovereign immunity in international law,[7] and the doctrine of crown act of state.[8] *The king can do no wrong* is also confused with the contemporary rule of construction that statutes do not bind the crown,[9] and is said to be the source

[1] William Wade, Christopher Forsyth, and Julian Ghosh, *Administrative Law* (12th edn, OUP 2022) 653.

[2] William Blackstone, *Commentaries on the Laws of England*, vol 1 (facsimile of 1765–1769 1st edn, University of Chicago Press 1979) 238–39.

[3] *Halsbury's Laws of England*, vol 29 (5th edn, LexisNexis 2014) [52]; to Wade and Forsyth, *the king can do no wrong* is to be understood as an immunity from legal process attaching to the crown as a corporation sole, *viz* the king in his political capacity: Wade and Forsyth (n 1) 651.

[4] Peter W Hogg, Patrick Monahan, and Wade K Wright, *Liability of the Crown* (4th edn, Carswell 2011).

[5] Wade and Forsyth (n 1) 654.

[6] Clayton Roberts, *The Growth of Responsible Government in Stuart England* (CUP 1966); Kenneth Pickthorn, *Early Tudor Government: Henry VII* (CUP 1934); Janelle Greenberg, 'Our Grand Maxim of State: "The King Can Do No Wrong"' (1991) 12 Hist Pol Thought 209. Stubbs also associated *the king can do no wrong* with ministerial responsibility, and pointed to the infancy of Henry III (1216–1272) as its starting point: William Stubbs, *The Constitutional History of England, in Its Origin and Development*, vol 2 (reprint of 4th edn, Clarendon Press 1906) 41.

[7] Maurice Sunkin, 'Crown Immunity from Criminal Liability in English Law' [2003] PL 716, 722–23. The two dimensions of crown liability upon which the heuristic model is based in Chapter 1 are also relevant to the law of state immunity: as Diplock LJ noted in *Empson v Smith* [1966] 1 QB 426, 438 (CA), it is 'elementary law that diplomatic immunity is not immunity from legal liability but immunity from suit'.

[8] *Rahmatullah (No 2) v Ministry of Defence and another* (2017) UKSC 1, [2017] AC 649 [16] (Lady Hale).

[9] Anthony Gray, 'Immunity of the Crown from Statute and Suit' [2010] Canb LR 1, 17. For a historical analysis of the evolution of the rule of construction laid down by Lord du Parcq in *Province of Bombay v Municipal Corporation of the City of Bombay* [1947] AC 58—and recently revisited by the Supreme Court of the United Kingdom in *R(on the application of Black) v Secretary of State for Justice* (2017) UKSC 81, [2018] AC 215—see: Harry Street, 'The Effects of Statutes upon the Rights and Liabilities of the Crown' (1948) 7 UTLJ 357; Marie-France Fortin, 'Revisiting the Application of Statutes to the Crown: A Historical Constitutional Approach' (2021) 3 J CommonwL 271.

The King Can Do No Wrong. Marie-France Fortin, Oxford University Press. © Marie-France Fortin 2024.
DOI: 10.1093/9780191994487.003.0001

of various procedural immunities from remedies,[10] such as injunctions,[11] and immunity from execution of judgments.[12]

The king can do no wrong has been attributed varying status, ranging from the legal to the metaphysical. Across the common law world, it has been said to be, among other things, a 'mystical notion',[13] a 'dogma',[14] an 'article of faith',[15] a 'precept',[16] an 'ancient' 'doctrine',[17] 'an old slogan of the common law',[18] a 'principle',[19] a 'constitutional principle',[20] an 'obscure constitutional principle',[21] and—to famed English constitutional law scholar AV Dicey—'a law of the constitution'.[22] *The king can do no wrong* is also referred to as a 'maxim'[23]—sometimes said to be 'ancient and fundamental'[24]—or combining both the legal status of a 'maxim' and that of a 'legal fiction' at common law.[25] The concept has also been associated with the notion of 'sovereign immunity' in the United States, and from there the American notion sometimes crosses the border over to Canada.[26] *The king can do no wrong* has been called by Irish judges and scholars an 'English feudal concept'[27] and an 'idea' from which is derived an 'ancient prerogative immunity from suit'.[28] The mysticism surrounding *the king can do no wrong* and the belief that it finds its legal origins in

[10] Peter W Hogg and Patrick Monahan, *Liability of the Crown* (3rd edn, Carswell 2000) 152; see also Hogg, Monahan, and Wright (n 4) for the various procedural immunities benefitting the crown.

[11] *M v Home Office* [1994] 1 AC 377 (HL) 407–08 (Lord Woolf).

[12] Daniel Mockle and HR Eddy, *Immunity from Execution* (Law Reform Commission of Canada 1987).

[13] JWF Allison, *A Continental Distinction in the Common Law: A Historical and Comparative Perspective on English Public Law* (revised edn, OUP 2000) 107.

[14] Stuart Anderson, 'Public Law' in WR Cornish and others (eds), *The Oxford History of the Laws of England*, vol XI (OUP 2010) 376.

[15] Edwin Borchard, 'Government Liability in Tort' (1924) 34 YLJ 1, 3.

[16] Paul Craig, *Administrative Law* (7th edn, Sweet & Maxwell 2012) 902.

[17] *Matthews v Ministry of Defence* (2003) UKHL 4, [2003] 1 AC 1163 [19] (Lord Bingham); Peter Cane, *Controlling Administrative Power* (CUP 2016) 402.

[18] Timothy Endicott, *Administrative Law* (5th edn, OUP 2021) 553.

[19] *M v Home Office* (n 11) 408 (Lord Wolf); *Rahmatullah* (n 8) [16] (Lady Hale); Sir John Baker, *The Reinvention of Magna Carta 1216–1616* (CUP 2017) 45, 150.

[20] See also Grégoire Webber, 'Loyal Opposition and the Political Constitution' (2017) 37 OJLS 357, 363.

[21] See the editorial note to the annotated report of the case of *Adams v Naylor* (1946) AC 543, 2 All ER 241 (HL) 242.

[22] AV Dicey, *Lectures Introductory to the Study of the Law of the Constitution: The Oxford Edition of Dicey*, vol 1 (JWF Allison ed, OUP 2013) 21.

[23] *Tobin v The Queen* (1864) 16 CB NS 310, 354–55 (143 ER 1148) (Erle CJ); *Feather v The Queen* (1865) 6 B&S 257, 295 (122 ER 1191) (Cockburn CJ); William Edward Hearn, *The Government of England: Its Structure and Its Development* (2nd edn, Robertson 1886) 20; Dicey (n 22) 21.

[24] Blackstone (n 2) 238.

[25] *R v Eldorado Nuclear Ltd; R v Uranium Canada Ltd* [1983] 2 SCR 551, 564 (Dickson J).

[26] See Chapter 6; on the use of the notion of sovereign immunity in Canadian legal thinking, see eg Bruce Feldthusen, 'Public Authority Immunity from Negligence Liability: Uncertain, Unnecessary, and Unjustified' (2013) 92 Can Bar Rev 211, 227.

[27] *Byrne v Ireland* [1972] 1 IR 241, 265.

[28] John M Kelly, 'Hidden Treasure and the Constitution' (1988) 10 DULJ 5, 7. On Irish legal thinking's understanding of *the king can do no wrong*, see Chapter 6.

English feudal times are part of the lore across the common law world—and old myths die hard.

Despite the confusion surrounding *the king can do no wrong*, it has been the object of only a few studies. It has been considered by historians of political thought and political scientists of the seventeenth century.[29] There have been concise discussions of *the king can do no wrong* in the work of legal historians.[30] It has appeared briefly in public lawyers' work and in important cases.[31] Eighteenth- and nineteenth-century thinkers' understandings of *the king can do no wrong* have been interpreted in connection with the concept of the state in British legal thinking.[32] Past scholarly pieces from across the common law world have focussed on the availability of remedies—including the petition of right—from a historical perspective, on crown liability from tort and contract law perspectives, and on the liability of public officials.[33] But there are no comprehensive studies of the historical evolution of *the king can do no wrong* in legal thinking and of its consequences for our understanding of crown liability.

[29] Roberts (n 6); Greenberg (n 6); Joyce Lee Malcolm, 'Doing No Wrong: Law, Liberty, and the Constraint of Kings' (1999) 38 J Brit Stud 161.

[30] See eg Ludwik Ehrlich, 'Proceedings against the Crown (1216–1377)' in Paul Vinogradoff (ed), *Oxford Studies in Social and Legal History*, vol 6 (Clarendon Press 1921) 14, 42–49, 70; Baker (n 19) 45.

[31] See eg *M v Home Office* (n 11) 395 (Lord Templeman), 407–08 (Lord Woolf); Christopher Vincenzi, *Crown Powers, Subjects and Citizens* (Pinter 1998) 203; Stephen Sedley, 'The Crown in Its Own Courts' in Christopher F Forsyth and Ivan Hare (eds), *The Golden Metwand and the Crooked Cord: Essays in Honour of Sir William Wade QC* (OUP 1999); Maurice Sunkin and Sebastian Payne (eds), *The Nature of the Crown: A Legal and Political Analysis* (OUP 1999); Mads Andenas and Duncan Fairgrieve, 'Reforming Crown Immunity: The Comparative Law Perspective' [2003] PL 730; Sunkin (n 7) 723–24; Janet McLean, *Searching for the State in British Legal Thought: Competing Conceptions of the Public Sphere* (CUP 2012); Wade and Forsyth (n 1) 652–54; Paul Craig, *Administrative Law* (9th edn, Sweet & Maxwell 2021) 907; Endicott (n 18) 553.

[32] McLean (n 31).

[33] See eg WS Holdsworth, 'The History of Remedies against the Crown I' (1922) 38 LQR 141; Louis L Jaffe, 'Suits against Governments and Officers: Sovereign Immunity' (1963) 77 Harv L Rev 1; Carol Harlow, *Compensation and Government Torts* (Sweet & Maxwell 1982); David Cohen, 'Thinking about the State: Law Reform and the Crown in Canada' (1986) 24 Osgoode Hall LJ 379; David Cohen, 'Suing the State' (1990) 40 UTLJ 630; Sue Arrowsmith, *Civil Liability and Public Authorities* (Earlsgate 1992); Bruce Feldthusen, 'The Recovery of Pure Economic Loss in Canada: Proximity, Justice, Rationality and Chaos' (1996) 24 Man LJ 1; Bruce Feldthusen, 'Failure to Confer Discretionary Public Benefits: The Case for Complete Negligence Immunity' (1997) 5 Tort L Rev 17; Susan Kneebone, *Tort Liability of Public Authorities* (LBC Information Services 1998); Tom Cornford, 'Legal Remedies against the Crown before and after M' in Maurice Sunkin and Sebastian Payne (eds), *The Nature of the Crown: A Legal and Political Analysis* (OUP 1999); Carol Harlow, *State Liability: Tort Law and Beyond* (OUP 2004); Janet McLean, 'The Crown in Contract and Administrative Law' (2004) 24 OJLS 129, 144–45; Hogg, Monahan, and Wright (n 4) 32, 152; Bruce Feldthusen, 'Simplifying Canadian Negligence Action against Public Authorities—or Maybe Not' (2012) 20 Tort L Rev 176; Feldthusen (n 26); Jasmine van Schouwen, 'The King Can Still Do No Wrong: A Critical Perspective on the Crown's Private Law Duty of Care in Canada' (2016) 24 Tort L Rev 159. For comparative analyses, see eg Carol Harlow, 'Fault Liability in French and English Public Law' (1976) 39 MLR 516; Basil Markesinis (ed), *Tortious Liability of Statutory Bodies: A Comparative Look at Five Cases* (Hart Publishing 1999); John Bell and AW Bradley (eds), *Governmental Liability: A Comparative Study* (United Kingdom National Committee of Comparative Law 1991); Duncan Fairgrieve, *State Liability in Tort: A Comparative Law Study* (OUP 2003).

The lack of clarity in legal thinking in relation to a concept understood as an ancient maxim of the common law and a law of the constitution still has significant consequences today. *The king can do no wrong* is not merely a harmless medieval relic (it is, in fact, not medieval, as is explained in Chapters 2 and 3). When conjured by modern-day governments, *the king can do no wrong* still has the effect of shielding them at common law from liability before the courts (how central government departments came to benefit from that royal shield over the course of the nineteenth century is explored in Chapter 4, and the enduring consequences for the current law of crown liability are exposed in Chapter 5). As I recount in further detail in Chapters 5 and 6, that spell was only partially broken by statutory interventions in England, Canada, and the United States; it was defeated progressively by statutory and judicial inroads in Australia; and it was definitively lifted by the Supreme Court of Ireland[34] more than fifty years ago.

Prior to nineteenth- and early twentieth-century English courts' interpretation of *the king can do no wrong* and of their conception of it in relation to the ambiguous notion of 'crown', the king had been conceived of as capable of doing wrong since medieval times in English legal thinking. A wrong could even be attributed to him until the constitutional pact of the seventeenth century and the Glorious Revolution of 1688, after which the king's ministers and servants became liable in lieu of the monarch for executing the king's wrongful commands. The spirit of the constitutional pact of the seventeenth century, whereby the king was granted immunity from suit in exchange for every minister's, servant's, and other instrument's liability, was lost in the nineteenth century when English courts interpreted *the king can do no wrong* to mean that there can be no wrong in the king. No wrongful deed or order was to be attributed to the king: this nineteenth-century understanding of *the king can do no wrong* was subsequently extended to the ambiguous notion of crown, resulting in *the crown can do no wrong* at the turn of the twentieth century.

As famed English legal historian Maitland wrote in the early days of the twentieth century, the use of the word 'crown' to refer to the government or the state more broadly was then but a recent phenomenon.[35] The word appeared in the context of cases where the monarch or public officials were sued from the middle of the nineteenth century onward, as the governmental apparatus as we now know it was developing.[36] The judicial (mis)construction of the notion of crown was spurred in part by the revival of the petition of right—a remedial procedure to sue the king dating to the fourteenth century, the origins of which are discussed in Chapter 2. The petition of right was famously resorted to on three occasions: in 1840, by the Speaker of the House of Commons whose belongings were ravaged in the fire of the

[34] *Byrne v Ireland* (n 27).
[35] FW Maitland, 'The Crown as Corporation' (1901) 17 LQR 131, 139.
[36] See Chapter 4.

palace of Westminster—a fire which had been set off by negligent crown servants of the Commissioners of Woods and Forests;[37] by the estate of the owner of a boat destroyed in 1862 by a captain of the royal navy on the erroneous assumption that the ship was involved in the slave trade;[38] and by an inventor whose patented process to build ships was usurped by Commissioners in the office of the Lord High Admiral of the United Kingdom.[39] The three petitions were presented to the courts to no avail, and the petitioners left empty-handed: English courts denied that the petition of right was available against the sovereign, Queen Victoria. The monarch could not be petitioned to remedy a wrong on the ground that *the king can do no wrong* (see Chapter 4). If one was to be sued for the tortious conduct, it had to be the individual wrongdoing crown servants.

In the courts' interpretation of *the king can do no wrong* in the context of petition of right cases against the monarch personally in the nineteenth century, the crown was understood as a corporation sole of one person, the king. But the notion of crown also came to be understood, over the course of the nineteenth and early twentieth centuries, as the growing governmental apparatus that was slowly centralized and taking shape in Whitehall. Blackstone, writing his famous *Commentaries on the Laws of England* in the eighteenth century, could still describe offices in the medieval sense as 'incorporeal hereditaments': charges of a proprietary nature bought by individuals to acquire 'a right to exercise a public or private employment'.[40] But the situation evolved thereafter. Governmental administration in England slowly departed from the medieval model of personal, proprietary, officeholders. A more modern, hierarchical, salaried, and departmentalized civil service under the direction of ministers of the crown came to replace medieval officeholders,[41] but the law of governmental liability was simultaneously developed on the old foundations of individual officers' and crown servants' personal liability. The crown became conceived of as a corporation of many—a corporation aggregate. The nineteenth-century understanding of *the king can do no wrong*—the absence of liability for a wrong insofar as the king is personally concerned—was extended to the crown understood as government departments and became *the crown can do no wrong* (see Chapter 4). Government departments were shielded from liability under the guise of the crown, erstwhile a single person, the king. Only the individual crown servants charged with executing governmental orders remained liable.

[37] *Viscount Canterbury v Attorney General* (1843) 1 Ph 306.

[38] *Tobin v The Queen* (n 23).

[39] *Feather v The Queen* (n 23).

[40] Blackstone added that 'a man may have an estate in them either to him and his heirs, or for life, of for a term of years, or during pleasure only': William Blackstone, *Commentaries on the Laws of England*, vol 2 (facsimile of 1765–1769 1st edn, University of Chicago Press 1979) 36, cited in Paul D Finn, *Law and Government in Colonial Australia* (OUP 1987) 9.

[41] Finn (n 40) 9–10, 14–15.

2 The problem with the confusion surrounding *the king can do no wrong*

The enduring mysticism—Maitland might have written 'cover for ignorance'[42]—surrounding *the king can do no wrong* create important incoherences in the realm of public law. From fundamental divergences in administrative and constitutional law on the one hand and the law of crown liability on the other, to the impossibility of obtaining compensation for certain kinds of governmental wrongs, and the differing conceptual bases governing the liability of public authorities and that of the central government understood as the crown (or, in America, the sovereign), *the king can do no wrong* is still believed to be heard clinking medieval chains which it never possessed.[43]

2.1 A constitutional incoherence in public law: judicial review *vs* crown liability

The direct liability in tort of statutory public authorities such as the Commissioners of the Board of the Mersey Docks and Harbour—which was established in the landmark eponymous case[44]—was not to befall government departments, protected by the 'shield of the crown'.[45] Government departments were instead considered to be the 'crown', and therefore immune from suit on the grounds that *the crown can do no wrong*. Public authorities and local governments are liable at common law, whereas central government departments conceived of as the crown are not. In the realm of judicial review, since the seminal *GCHQ* case, the source of the power exercised—derived either from statutory authority or the prerogative—is immaterial.[46] In contrast, in the realm of tortious liability of public bodies—either statutory public authorities or central governmental departments—a parallel

[42] FW Maitland, *The Constitutional History of England* (reprint of 1908 1st edn, CUP 1911) 418.

[43] See *United Australia Ltd v Barclays Bank Ltd* [1941] AC 1 (HL) 29 (Lord Atkin): 'When these ghosts of the past stand in the path of justice clanking their medieval chains the proper course for the judge is to pass through them undeterred.'

[44] *Mersey Docks Trustees v Gibbs* (1866) 1 LR 93 (HL).

[45] *Mersey Docks Trustees v Cameron* (1864) 11 HLC 443, 508 (Lord Cranworth). The two *Mersey Docks* cases 'finally established that the Crown's privileges are confined to the Crown in a direct and personal sense, and to those authorities of the central government which have a close connection with the Crown': Geoffrey Sawer, 'Shield of the Crown Revisited' (1958) 1 Melb ULR 137, 137. Following the *Mersey Docks* cases and the dichotomy between statutory public bodies and the crown understood as central government, the reason behind the creation of statutory corporate bodies with the capacity to sue and be sued was to put the crown on a level playing field with other commercial actors when fulfilling commercial endeavours: Bradley Selway, 'The Source and Nature of the Liability in Tort of Australian Governments' (2002) 10 Tort L Rev 14, 17. The survival of the doctrine is criticized: Janina Boughey, Ellen Rock, and Greg Weeks, *Government Liability: Principles and Remedies* (LexisNexis Butterworths 2019) 47–50.

[46] *Council of Civil Service Unions v Minister for the Civil Service* (1985) AC 374, 400 (Lord Tullybelton), 407 (Lord Scarman), 410 (Lord Diplock), 417 (Lord Roskill).

conclusion to the one reached in *GCHQ* has not yet been drawn. The source of a public authority's existence—either statutory or emanating from the crown—still matters because *the crown can do no wrong*. As Street put it more than half a century ago, 'Why should the Crown as an administrative unit be treated differently from other public bodies? Until our law relating to public authorities is homogeneous, it will remain a legitimate target for volleys of criticism.'[47]

The confusion surrounding *the king can do no wrong* also has made it more difficult to elaborate a notion of the 'crown', due in part to the perceived need to conceive of the crown as a corporation sole to limit the scope of the immunities generated by the concept.[48] The lack of a clear notion of the crown has in turn given rise to a flawed conception of the immunities of the crown and whom they should benefit.[49] The confusion is such that the notion of crown differs in the realm of judicial review from that of crown liability.[50]

The issue of the differentiated treatment granted to government departments in the realm of crown liability became all the more salient at the end of the twentieth century, once ministers and their government departments were expressly excluded from the notion of crown in the seminal case of *M v Home Office*, and could not shield themselves from the courts' jurisdiction under the cover of the crown.[51]

In *M v Home Office*, a minister of the crown was held in contempt for having disregarded the court's order by wrongfully deporting an asylum seeker, and the liability of crown officials in judicial review proceedings was at issue. Following the Lords' decision in *M v Home Office*, in the realm of administrative law, the notion of crown excludes ministers, government departments, and all other crown servants, who are all subject to judicial review. But Lord Woolf made clear that the confusion surrounding *the king can do no wrong* in legal thinking and the use of history in invoking it to support the crown's immunity were not at issue in that seminal case.[52] The confusion surrounding the contours of the notion of the 'crown' which benefits from an immunity from suit at common law remains, fuelled by the uncertainty as to the historical evolution of legal thinking that led to the passing of the king's personal immunity from suit to the whole governmental apparatus.

[47] Harry Street, *Governmental Liability: A Comparative Study* (CUP 1953) 40.

[48] William Wade, 'The Crown, Ministers and Officials: Legal Status and Liability' in Maurice Sunkin and Sebastian Payne (eds), *The Nature of the Crown: A Legal and Political Analysis* (OUP 1999); Wade and Forsyth (n 1) 35–39, 651. cf Martin Loughlin, 'The State, the Crown and the Law' in Maurice Sunkin and Sebastian Payne (eds), *The Nature of the Crown: A Legal and Political Analysis* (OUP 1999) 75.

[49] JDB Mitchell, 'The Causes and Effects of the Absence of a System of Public Law in the United Kingdom' [1965] PL 95, 113–15; Adam Tomkins, 'Crown Privileges' in Sebastian Payne and Maurice Sunkin (eds), *The Nature of the Crown: A Legal and Political Analysis* (OUP 1999) 175–76; Allison (n 13) 80–81; Richard Rawlings and Carol Harlow, *Law and Administration* (3rd edn, CUP 2009) 9–10. 'The conceptual rationale underlying the doctrine of Crown immunity is obscure': *Eldorado Nuclear* (n 25) 558 (Dickson J).

[50] See Chapter 5.

[51] *M v Home Office* (n 11).

[52] ibid 408.

In the realm of judicial review, therefore, both the crown and *the king can do no wrong* are understood again in light of the seventeenth-century understanding that the monarch is personally immune from suit and that all others—ministers, servants, and all other instruments of the king—are to be liable instead. Following *Miller 2*, that constitutional understanding of *the king can do no wrong* as enshrining the king's personal immunity on the one hand and ministerial responsibility on the other is also resounding in the realm of the prerogative: the monarch is not to be held liable for following the Prime Minister's unlawful advice to prorogue Parliament.[53] While administrative law and constitutional law have benefitted from clarity in reducing the contours of the crown to that of the person of the monarch, the historical foundations of the law of crown liability remain shrouded in mystery. The result is an 'extension of the shield of the Crown to what might more fitly be described as the public government of the country',[54] including government departments and crown corporations.

The extension of the shield of the sovereign's immunity has also occurred in the United States, where the confusion surrounding the identity of the sovereign in the American republic has led to competing claims to the title between the people, the states, and the federal government. By contrast, in Ireland—also a republic—sovereignty clearly resides with the people alone under the constitution. Irish courts' ruling that the Constitution of the Republic of Ireland is incompatible with the survival of *the king can do no wrong* understood as governmental immunity from suit offers a stark contrast with American legal thinking on sovereign immunity, and interesting parallels with more recent Australian judicial developments, which are discussed in Chapter 6.

2.2 Dicey's ghost: dominance of individual officers' liability and absence of direct liability of the crown

The consequences of the current persistent confusion surrounding *the king can do no wrong* in legal thinking include the absence of direct liability of government departments at common law for a tort. The absence of direct governmental liability, as I explain in Chapter 4, is due in part to nineteenth- and early twentieth-century English courts' interpretation of *the king can do no wrong* and, of their conception of it in relation to the ambiguous notion of 'crown'. Dicey's exposition on the rule of law and its lasting legacy, a usual suspect, also plays an important part in our current understanding of the law of crown liability.

53 *R(Miller) v Prime Minister* (2019) UKSC 41 (*Miller 2*); Marie-France Fortin, 'Rule of Law, Parliamentary Sovereignty and Executive Accountability in English Legal Thinking: The Recent Revival of The King Can Do No Wrong' (2022) 44 J Const Hist 43.

54 *Mersey Docks Trustees v Cameron* (n 45) 508 (Lord Cranworth); see Chapter 4, section 3.3.

An individual crown servant's liability before the courts is an important feature of English law, as evidenced by the seminal case of *Entick v Carrington*, dating to the eighteenth century.[55] But, after nineteenth-century petition of right cases where the courts ruled that the king could not be sued to in tort, the tortious liability of individual officials subsequently became integral to Dicey's notion of equality before the law and his interpretation of *the king can do no wrong* (see Chapter 4).[56] The liability of individual wrongdoing officials according to the ordinary law of tort became the foundation of the law of crown liability, and remains so to this day, even under the relevant crown proceedings legislation—in England, Canada, and New Zealand (see Chapter 5). Except for the crown's liability in relation to occupier and employer's duties,[57] the crown is not directly liable in tort in these jurisdictions:[58] '[The Act] does not work by making the state a potential tortfeasor: it works by making the Crown vicariously liable for the tort of its servants'.[59]

The Federal Tort Claims Act (FTCA), enacted by the American Congress in 1946, is based on a similar conceptual foundation to the English, Canadian, and New Zealand legislation in providing for indirect liability. It waives partially the United Sates' sovereign immunity by allowing a private party to sue the United States vicariously, before federal courts, to obtain compensation for damages caused by specified torts of employees of the federal government.[60] The situation now differs in Australia—except for the state of Victoria—since the end of the twentieth century, when the High Court interpreted the relevant legislation as lifting the procedural bar to suing the crown directly in tort, as opposed to suing it vicariously for the tort committed by its servant[61] (see Chapter 6). Nevertheless,

[55] *Entick v Carrington* (1765) EWHC KB J98, (1765) 2 Wilson KB 275, (1765) 19 St Tr 1030.

[56] Dicey (n 22) 21, 100, 123.

[57] In English law, under the Crown Proceedings Act 1947 (10 & 11 Geo VI c 44) (CPA), s 2(1)(b), (c); in Canadian federal law, under the Crown Liability Act (SC 1952–53, c 30), now the Crown Liability and Proceedings Act (RSC 1985, c C-50), s 3(a)ii, (b)ii; in New Zealand, under the Crown Proceedings Act 1950, s 6(1)(b), (c).

[58] Loughlin (n 48); Andenas and Fairgrieve (n 31) 732–33; Sunkin (n 7) 724; Tom Cornford, *Towards a Public Law of Tort* (Ashgate 2008) 10; McLean (n 31) 226–32; Mark Aronson, Matthew Groves, and Greg Weeks, *Judicial Review of Administrative Action and Government Liability* (6th edn, Lawbook Co 2017) 1092–94; Mark Elliott and Jason Varuhas, *Administrative Law: Text and Materials* (5th edn, OUP 2017) 587.

[59] *Chagos Islanders v Attorney General* (2004) EWCA Civ 997, [20] (Sedley LJ).

[60] The FTCA (28 USC §§ 1346, 2671–80) was adopted as part of the Congressional Reorganization Act 1946, c 753 (60 Stat 812). In *Bivens v Six Unknown Agents of the Federal Bureau of Narcotics* (1971) 403 US 388, individual federal officers' personal liability for constitutional torts (violations of the Fourth Amendment) was also recognized by the Supreme Court: see Janet McLean, 'The Crown in the Courts' in Linda Pearson, Michael Taggart, and Carol Harlow (eds), *Administrative Law in a Changing State* (Hart Publishing 2008) 161, 175. Although the federal government is not vicariously liable for the constitutional torts of its employees as it is under the FTCA, empirical analysis of successful *Bivens* claims against one federal agency shows that the federal government itself compensates the victims—or negotiates the substitution of a *Bivens* claim for an FTCA claim—and that individual federal employees' personal contribution is in fact minimal: James E Pfander, Alexander A Reinert, and Joanna C Schwartz, 'The Myth of Personal Liability: Who Pays When Bivens Claims Succeed' (2020) 72 Stan L Rev 561.

[61] *Commonwealth v Mewett* (1997) 191 CLR 471, where the High Court interpreted s 64 of the Judiciary Act 1903 (Cth): Aronson, Groves, and Weeks (n 58) 1093.

legislative innovations which occurred from the middle of the nineteenth century in South Australia, Queensland, and New South Wales, although influential in New Zealand and South Africa,[62] were initially hampered by colonial courts' reliance on more conservative English case law.[63] English courts' influence on Australian and Canadian legal thinking—to varying degrees—during most of the twentieth century is a common feature of both jurisdictions: the study of the historical evolution of *the king can do no wrong* in common law legal thinking therefore crosses national boundaries. In Ireland, a different path was taken following independence and the birth of the republic: *the king can do no wrong* was found to be incompatible with the constitution and the crown's immunity from suit was completely removed, rendering moot the distinction between direct and indirect liability of the state, as is further explained in Chapter 6.

The consequences of the absence of direct liability of the crown—or, in America, of the government—became tragically clear in the midst of the Second World War. On the afternoon of 8 August 1942, three children were running after a stray tennis ball on a sandhill off the coast of England. The fence and warning signs surrounding what was in fact a minefield had been poorly maintained and were buried in the sand. One child triggered a mine and died instantly; another was left injured. The nominal defendant was an army officer of the Royal Engineers, who was designated by the crown with the understanding that public funds would cover the cost of the award against him, should the action succeed. He appeared in fact 'neither to have been at the top nor the bottom of the ladder of responsibility'.[64] The absence of an individual wrongdoing crown servant was fatal to a claim in tort for 'such a claim cannot be made directly against the Crown'.[65] It was the impossibility of suing the crown directly for its negligent maintenance of its land as an occupier,[66] for its fault as an employer, or vicariously for the negligence of its servants, which prompted the UK Parliament to adopt the Crown Proceedings Act 1947, upon which is modelled Canadian legislation at the federal and many provincial levels, as well as New Zealand's and the Australian state of Victoria's.[67] But, as previously mentioned, the government is not otherwise directly liable in tort in these common law systems.

The consequences of the absence of the crown's direct liability in tort are now particularly salient in relation to institutional or systemic failures, which are

[62] Mark Leeming, 'The Liability of the Government under the Constitution' (1998) 17(3) Aust Bar Rev 214, 216: in New Zealand, The Crown Redress Act 1871, 35 Vict 49; The Crown Redress Act 1877, 41 Vict 39; The Crown Suits Act 1881, 45 Vict 8; and in South Africa, the Crown Liabilities Act 1888, Cape Act No 37.

[63] Finn (n 40) 141–66.

[64] *Adams v Naylor* (n 21) 245 (Lord Thankerton).

[65] ibid 244 (Viscount Simon). See also *Royster v Cavey* [1947] KB 204 (CA).

[66] *Adams v Naylor* (n 21) 246 (Lord Utwatt).

[67] Hogg, Monahan, and Wright (n 4) 154–59; Boughey, Rock, and Weeks (n 45) 45. On the Canadian federal legislation, see Chapter 5.

perhaps more common in a complex modern society.[68] The crown is not directly liable in negligence, even under the relevant crown proceedings legislation, therefore there can be no compensation for 'institutional inertia' or 'institutional indifference'.[69] There is no 'institutional liability': a government department is not liable in tort for its 'own sins in not having a proper structure in place' or in 'having an inadequate system which in itself has created a breach of duty of care on the part of the Department itself'.[70] Because it is assumed that *the king can do no wrong* means that, at common law, the crown is not liable, the crown is immune from institutional liability as result. For example, a wrongly convicted individual whose repeated applications for mercy are denied or ignored by successive ministers over a lengthy period of time cannot obtain compensation from the crown by claiming that there was 'one continuous fault that subsumed the individual actions of the successive Ministers'.[71] She must instead point to 'the individual conduct of each of the successive Ministers acting in his or her capacity as a servant of the . . . Crown'.[72]

The crown's vicarious liability in tort created by crown proceedings legislation in various common law jurisdictions[73] operates in such a way that 'the crown is (vicariously) liable for a tort only if one of its servants is also liable'.[74] The absence of direct liability at common law can also prove to be problematic, therefore, when a specific wrongdoer cannot be identified.[75] Indeed, it was the impossibility, for the injured person, of identifying the wrongdoing crown servant which had led to the governmental practice of identifying a nominated defendant prior to the adoption of the Crown Proceedings Act 1947: 'Otherwise', as the House of Lords explained, 'the plaintiff could in many cases not commence his action at all'.[76] The governmental practice of identifying a nominated defendant to allow a case to proceed

[68] See eg *Beggs v Scottish Ministers* (2005) SC 342 (Court of Session Inner House First Division); *Morgan v Ministry of Justice* (2010) EWHC 2248 (QB), (2010) All ER (D) 117 (Sep) [43]–[52]; *Hinse v Canada (Attorney General)* [2015] 2 SCR 621 [92]; Sunkin (n 7) 724; Hogg, Monahan, and Wright (n 4) 182–87.

[69] *Hinse* (n 68) [92]. The concept is also aptly referred to as 'institutional immunity', as opposed to personal liability: Paul Scott, *The National Security Constitution* (Hart Publishing 2018) 267.

[70] Stuart Anderson, '"Grave Injustice", "Despotic Privilege": The Insecure Foundations of Crown Liability for Torts in New Zealand' (2009) 12 Otago L Rev 1, 4.

[71] *Hinse* (n 68) [92].

[72] ibid.

[73] In English law, under the CPA, s 2(1)(a); in Canadian federal law, under the Crown Liability and Proceedings Act, s 3(a)i, (b)i; in New Zealand, under the Crown Proceedings Act 1950, s 6(1)(a). Note, however, that the Supreme Court of New Zealand has implied that the crown could be directly liable in tort as a result of s 27(3) of the Bill of Rights Act 1990: *Couch v Attorney-General (No2)* (2010) 3 NZLR 149, 184, 210–22, 213–14, 227–28; *Commissioner of Inland Revenue v Chesterfields Preschools Ltd* (2013) 2 NZLR 679, 715–17: see Aronson, Groves, and Weeks (n 58) 1172.

[74] Anderson (n 70) 4.

[75] See *Hinse* (n 68); Sunkin (n 7) 724; Hogg, Monahan, and Wright (n 4) 182–87; McLean (n 31) 230.

[76] *Adams v Naylor* (n 21) 244 (Viscount Simon). See Glanville Williams, *Crown Proceedings: An Account of Civil Proceedings by and Against the Crown as Affected by the Crown Proceedings Act, 1947* (Stevens 1948) 17–19; Leeming (n 62) 216: 'there could be no recourse by a plaintiff who did not know the identity of the servant by whom the tort had been committed, or whose only cause of action was directly against the Crown (such as in cases of occupier's liability)'.

was abandoned after the adoption of the Act. Perhaps the practice was thought to have been rendered superfluous by Parliament's intervention and the newly established vicarious liability of the crown for the wrongful acts of its servants. But crown proceedings legislation providing for crown liability in tort—other than the crown's liability as an occupier—is still grounded in the commission of a tort by an individual crown servant in England, Canada, New Zealand, and the Australian state of Victoria, and in the commission of a tort by a federal government employee in the United States. If the individual crown servant owes no duty of care to the plaintiff, is otherwise not at fault, or cannot be identified, the vicarious liability of the crown for its servant also falls. Governments are now highly departmentalized, decentralized, and staffed by numerous civil servants with a variety of expertise. Vicarious liability grounded in the wrongful conduct of an identifiable individual civil servant can hardly encompass all possible wrongs committed by the government as a whole, especially in complex matters spanning a long period of time and involving many government departments and divisions within those departments.

The issue of being able to identify the wrongdoing crown servant whose tortious conduct inflicted damages on the plaintiff therefore remains a live one, as I discuss in Chapter 5. In the absence of identifiable individual tortfeasors, the crown retains its immunity at common law—a judicial immunity resulting from nineteenth-century English courts' understanding of *the king can do no wrong*, which I retrace in Chapter 4. As for the American government, it retains its sovereign immunity on different conceptual grounds, which I explore in Chapter 6.

Similarly, although these instances are now rare,[77] there can be no injunction or order against the crown when the power is not conferred on a minister in her own name.[78] Even when Parliament has intervened to subject the government—confused with the 'crown'—to ordinary law in the realm of civil liability, the courts remain under the interpretive influence of *the king can do no wrong*. The 'residual privileges and immunities' under current crown proceedings legislation and the hypothetical possibility that Parliament could repeal such legislation—thereby reviving *the king can do no wrong* and the crown's immunity from suit at common law—have been alluded to in order to narrowly interpret the scope of crown proceedings legislation.[79] *The king can do no wrong*'s potency is such that even Parliamentary sovereignty cannot truly overcome it. When the crown's immunity from suit at common law—understood as founded in *the king can do no wrong*—is put into abeyance, the mere possibility of its future resurgence following statutory

[77] William Wade, 'Injunctive Relief against the Crown and Ministers' (1991) 107 LQR 4, 5.

[78] CPA, s 21(1)(a); *M v Home Office* (n 11) 413 (Lord Woolf).

[79] *Canada (Attorney General) v Thouin* [2017] 2 SCR 184, [23]. See also, in the Australian context, *Commonwealth v Mewett* (1997) 191 CLR 471, 502–03 (Dawson J, concurring) discussing the scope of s 64 of the Judiciary Act and how that provision is 'inherently susceptible to alteration'; see also *Georgiadis v Australian and Overseas Telecommunications Corporation* (1994) 179 CLR 297, 305–06 (Mason CJ, Deane and Gaudron JJ); 325–26 (McHugh J, dissenting).

repeal is enough to lead the courts to interpret strictly the scope of crown liability legislation.

2.3 Sovereign immunity and the migration of the policy-operation distinction

The mysticism surrounding *the king can do no wrong* still exerts its effects over the legal mind even in America, where it was reborn under the republican guise of sovereign immunity. As I explain further in Chapter 6, in American legal thinking, sovereign immunity is grounded in the notion that the sovereign is above the law and therefore immune from suit. The theoretical foundations of sovereign immunity differ from that of crown immunity in English legal thinking, where the king has historically been subject to law and bound not to do wrong. But the result is currently similar due to nineteenth-century English developments: in the absence of statutory intervention, both the American sovereign and the crown are now immune from suit at common law.

In America, Congress has waived the federal government's sovereign immunity in relation to the taking of property—including takings under the Fifth Amendment[80]—for breach of contract,[81] for discriminatory employment practices,[82] and, as mentioned previously, for specified torts of federal employees under the FTCA.[83] But sovereign immunity is the default rule. The discretionary function exception under the FTCA, for instance, has the effect, when it applies, of simply reverting the law back to sovereign immunity. The exception is triggered, and sovereign immunity applies, when a plaintiff's damages were caused by 'the exercise or performance or the failure to exercise or perform a discretionary function or duty on the part of a federal agency or an employee of the Government' within the meaning of 28 USC § 2680(a), also known as the discretionary function exception. Perhaps the most staggering example of the application of that exception to the FTCA and the ensuing resurgence of sovereign immunity occurred in 1953 in *Dalehite*, the case which gave rise to the policy-operation distinction.[84] On 16 and

80 Under the 1887 Tucker Act (28 USC § 1346), which granted an extended jurisdiction to the Court of Claims—established by Congress in 1855 (10 Stat 612)—to hear claims 'founded either upon the Constitution, or any Act of Congress, or any regulation of an executive department, or upon any express or implied contract with the United States, or for liquidated or unliquidated damages in cases not sounding in tort' (§ 1346 a(2)). The exclusion of actions in tort from the ambit of the jurisdiction of the Court of Claims was emphasized by the Supreme Court in *Gibbons v US* (1868) 75 US 269, 275 (Miller J). See Leeming (n 62) 232–33.

81 Contract Disputes Act 1978 (41 USC §§ 7101–09).

82 Under Chapter 21 of the US Code, titled Civil Rights (42 USC § 2000e–16).

83 FTCA (n 60). Other statutory claims are also available; see George C Sisk, 'The Inevitability of Federal Sovereign Immunity' (2010) 55 Vill L Rev 899, 922–23.

84 *Dalehite v US* (1953) 346 US 15, 42 (Reed J): 'The decisions held culpable were all responsibly made at a planning, rather than operational, level and involved considerations more or less important to the practicability of the Government's fertilizer program.'

17 April 1947, hundreds of tons of ammonium nitrate fertilizer caught fire in the port of Texas City. The fire that began on the morning of 16 April on board the SS Beauchamp, moored in the port of the city, set in motion a chain reaction of explosions and fires in the port and adjoining ships that sent shockwaves and caused destruction across the city over two days. The inferno and carnage that ensued killed more than 500 people and injured more than 3,000 others. Hundreds of suits were filed against the United States under the FTCA, culminating with the Supreme Court's decision in *Dalehite*. As the dissenting judges explained, the fertilizer was 'manufactured in Government-owned plants at the Government's order and to its specifications', and, when tragedy struck, the fertilizer 'was being shipped at (the government's) direction as part of its program of foreign aid' in the aftermath of the Second World War.[85] Far from being an 'act of God', the disaster 'was caused by forces set in motion by the Government, completely controlled or controllable by it'.[86] Yet a majority of the justices held that the American government was not liable under the FTCA, because the negligence of its employees occurred in the exercise of a discretionary power, and not at the operational level. The majority's conclusion in *Dalehite* resulted in a resumption of sovereign immunity, and led the dissenters to conclude that 'the ancient and discredited doctrine that "The King can do no wrong" has not been uprooted; it has merely been amended to read, "The King can do only little wrongs"'.[87] Understandings of *the king can do no wrong* and their historical evolution and relationship with sovereign immunity in American legal thinking are further explored in Chapter 6.

The policy-operation distinction elaborated in *Dalehite* under the discretionary function exception of the FTCA was subsequently abandoned by the American Supreme Court,[88] but it migrated with success to other common law jurisdictions.[89] The distinction was adopted in the United Kingdom by the House of Lords[90] before it was abandoned at the end of the twentieth

[85] *Dalehite* (n 84) 48 (Jackson J, dissenting).

[86] ibid.

[87] ibid 60 (Jackson J, dissenting). The public outrage that followed the Supreme Court's ruling led Congress to enact compensatory legislation for the bereaved families: Sisk (n 83) 922.

[88] *US v Gaubert* (1991) 499 US 315. In *US v Varig Airlines* (1984) 467 US 797, 811–12 (Burger CJ), the Court recognized that its reading of the FTCA 'admittedly has not followed a straight line', but it did not yet 'accept the supposition that *Dalehite* no longer represents a valid interpretation of the discretionary function exception'.

[89] The precise temporal and geographical origins of the policy-operation distinction are debatable: it was alluded to it in the earlier English case of *East Suffolk Rivers Catchment Board v Kent* [1941] AC 74 (HL); Craig (n 31) 912. *East Suffolk Rivers* was later cited to with approval in *Dalehite* (n 84) 36. But contemporary English legal thinking appears to reject the idea that the distinction originated in England, and associates it instead with American law: Paul Craig, 'Negligence in the Exercise of a Statutory Power' (1978) 94 LQR 428, 442–47 (tracing the origins of the dichotomy to the later American case, *Dalehite*); *Robinson v Chief Constable of West Yorkshire Police* [2018] UKSC 4, [38] (Lord Reed): '[*Anns*] added to the confusion by importing public law concepts, and the American distinction between policy and operational decisions'.

[90] *Anns v Merton London Borough Council* [1978] AC 728. Although *Dalehite* was not cited in *Anns*, Lord Wilberforce referred in his speech to American law and cited *Indian Towing Co Inc v US* (1955) 350 US 61; Aronson, Groves, and Weeks (n 58) 1116. *Anns* followed *Home Office v Dorset Yacht Co Ltd*

century.[91] It continues to endure, albeit modified, in other parts of the Commonwealth, such as Canada[92] and Australia[93]—the latter having also adopted an equivalent to the American discretionary function exception, the independent discretionary function principle.[94] But regardless of the debates on the policy-operation distinction's merits or whether the distinction remains relevant or not in various common law jurisdictions, the foundations of the law of governmental liability remain sovereign immunity and crown immunity at common law. Although the policy-operation distinction or its successors—including the concept of justiciability—govern both the law of public authority liability and that of crown liability in determining whether there was a duty of care, they act only as a second layer insofar as central government is concerned. Since the turn of the twentieth century and *the crown can do no wrong*, the crown understood as central government is thought to be immune from suit, and liable only if legislation allows for it to be sued. If a plaintiff's claim does not fit the contours of crown proceedings

[1970] AC 1004, where the Lords distinguished the Home Office's policy behind the borstal system from the operation of the system itself in recognizing a new duty of care in negligence. See SH Bailey and MJ Bowman, 'The Policy/Operational Dichotomy—A Cuckoo in the Nest' (1986) 45 CLJ 430.

[91] *Murphy v Brentwood District Council* [1991] 1 AC 398; *X (Minors) v Bedfordshire County Council* [1995] 2 AC 633. The policy-operation dichotomy was highly criticized, and decisions of the Supreme Court of Canada were cited as illustrations of its shortcomings in *Stovin v Wise* [1996] AC 923, 955 (Lord Hoffmann). The concept of justiciability was adopted instead in English law; on the justiciability test and its applications to various circumstances involving public authorities in English law—including education, social, health, and police and emergency services—see Duncan Fairgrieve and Daniel Squires, *The Negligence Liability of Public Authorities* (2nd edn, OUP 2019) 23–70.

[92] *Kamloops (City) v Nielsen* [1984] 2 SCR 2; *Just v British Columbia* [1989] 2 SCR 1228; *Nelson (City) v Marchi* 2021 SCC 41. The Supreme Court of Canada has also heavily borrowed from its American counterpart's reasoning in *Gaubert* (n 88) in defining core governmental policy decisions protected from suit as 'decisions as to a course or principle of action that are based on public policy considerations, such as economic, social and political factors, provided they are neither irrational nor taken in bad faith': *R v Imperial Tobacco Canada Ltd* [2011] 3 SCR 45, [90] (McLachlin CJ).

[93] The distinction was adopted in *Sutherland Shire Council v Heyman* (1985) 157 CLR 424, but was subsequently criticized in *Pyrenees Shire Council v Day* (1998) 192 CLR 330, 393–94 (Gummow J) for its unhelpfulness, and in *Romeo v Conservation Commission (NT)* (1998) 192 CLR 431, 484 (Kirby J) for the paucity of legal authority on the distinction in Australia. The distinction was reframed as an issue of core policy in *Crimmins v Stevedoring Industry Finance Committee* (1999) 200 CLR 1, 36–39, 50–51 (McHugh J); *Graham Barclay Oysters* (2002) 211 CLR 540, 664 (Callinan J): see Mark Aronson, 'Government Liability in Negligence' (2008) 32 Melb ULR 44, 54–55. On the Australian judicial debates on the *Anns* test and its legacy, see Aronson, Groves, and Weeks (n 58) 1116–18; Christian Witting, 'Tort Law, Policy and the High Court of Australia' (2007) 31 Melb ULR 569.

[94] *Enever v The King* (1906) 3 CLR 969; *Little v Commonwealth* (1947) 75 CLR 94; *Cubillo v Commonwealth [No 2]* (2000) 103 FCR 1, 336–39 (O'Loughlin J); Susan Kneebone, 'The Independent Discretionary Function Principle and Public Officers' (1990) 16 Monash ULR 184. On the relationship between English law (where the discretionary function exception was abolished with the adoption of the CPA 1947, s 2(3)), American law (where it remains grounded in the FTCA), and Australian law (where the exception was developed by judges after crown immunity was abolished by statute, before and after federation), see Joachim Dietrich and Iain Field, 'Statute and Theories of Vicarious Liability' (2019) 43 Melb ULR 515, 535. On the 'policy defence' restoring immunity for policy decisions advocated for by the review panel chaired by the Hon David Ipp QC, Panel of Eminent Persons ('Ipp Committee'), *Review of the Law of Negligence: Final Report* (Commonwealth of Australia, 2002), see Aronson (n 93); Justine Bell-James and Kit Barker, 'Public Authority Liability for Negligence in the Post-IPP Era: Sceptical Reflections on the "Policy Defence"' (2016) 40 Melb ULR 1.

legislation, immunity prevails on the basis—it is believed—that the crown is immune at common law because *the king can do no wrong*. The underlying assumption that the crown is not liable at common law may even colour a court's findings that a policy decision was at play and, therefore, that the crown's immunity should remain, or that policy arguments negate the recognition of a new duty of care.

3 Uncovering *the king can do no wrong*: a historical constitutional approach

This book's aim is twofold. The first aim is to fill the gap and clear the confusion in legal constitutional scholarship on *the king can do no wrong* by studying its evolution in legal thinking. Assertions and hypotheses—notably those of Laski, Holdsworth, Borchard, Street, Keir and Lawson, and Harlow[95]—about the historical evolution of *the king can do no wrong* in legal thinking will be scrutinized. The second aim is to build on this book's study of the concept and its evolution in legal thinking to revisit and shed light on our current understanding of crown liability.

The evolution of *the king can do no wrong* in legal thinking has been studied in this book by relying on sources of a legal nature, such as judicial decisions, legislation, legal commentaries and treatises, and other orthodox legal sources.[96] The aim in studying key texts, including court judgments and legal treatises, has been to trace the use of the phrase *the king can do no wrong* across time. The approach is decidedly more doctrinal and differs, therefore, from the contextual approach recently adopted in the field of public law history, where 'texts are read against the constitutional background that gives them meaning'.[97] This book spans instead cases and the work of legal authors where *the king can do no wrong* featured or with which it was subsequently associated in English legal thinking, such as the work attributed to Bracton. The method is similar to that of the Cambridge historians of ideas, among whom is Skinner: it has been assumed that 'the best method' to confidently grasp past legal thinkers' understanding of *the king can do no wrong* is to study how those words were invoked and discussed by them, although from a legal doctrinal standpoint.[98] Among the authors studied, Coke, Hale, Blackstone,

[95] Harold J Laski, 'The Responsibility of the State in England' (1919) 32 Harv L Rev 447, 448; WS Holdsworth, *A History of English Law*, vol 3 (3rd edn, Methuen 1923) 462, 465–66; Edwin Borchard, 'Governmental Responsibility in Tort, VI' (1926) 36 YLJ 1, 30–31; Harry Street, 'Crown Proceedings Act, 1947' (1948) 11 MLR 129; David L Keir and FH Lawson, *Cases in Constitutional Law* (FH Lawson and DJ Bentley eds, 6th edn, Clarendon Press 1979) 72; Harlow, *Compensation and Government Torts* (n 33) 17–18.

[96] The authors of *The Oxford History of the Laws of England* were applauded for relying on similar sources, although their understanding of the law which was their subject of enquiry was broader: Janet McLean, 'Ideologies in Law Time: "The Oxford History of the Laws of England"' (2013) 38 L & Soc Inquiry 746, 748.

[97] Thomas Poole, *Reason of State: Law, Prerogative and Empire* (CUP 2015) 7.

[98] Quentin Skinner, 'A Genealogy of the Modern State' (2009) 162 Proceedings of the British Academy 325, 325.

and Dicey are also conventionally identified as significant in common law legal thinking.[99] Others—such as Finch, Paley, or Hearn—may not be as widely remembered today but their treatises had a non-negligible popularity and their discussion of *the king can do no wrong* is therefore pertinent to the study of its evolution in legal thinking.

The king can do no wrong is significant to both constitutional law and theory,[100] which themselves often touch upon the realm of political theory.[101] Enquiry into the evolution of a legal concept is not alien to that of ideas as intellectual products. However, given the 'complexities involved in making such connections between the general social and intellectual history and the legal history',[102] caution has been exerted not to draw conclusions of direct causal relationship between dominant philosophical ideas during a given era—such as those of Bodin or Hobbes—and the evolution of legal thinking. The analysis of the evolution of *the king can do no wrong* in legal thinking in this book therefore corresponds more to the intellectual history of a legal concept as the history of the development of a legal concept found in legal doctrine or theory[103] than to the historical method in public law where the history of public law is understood as a historico-political discourse.[104]

My approach was also informed in part by the criticism of the common law as having failed to develop a process for reaching a satisfactory understanding of the past and for structuring the use of history in the development of legal norms.[105] I also took into consideration the view that the dominant document-based best-evidence approach of legal historians—most famously Maitland[106]—and its focus

[99] FW Maitland, *The Collected Papers*, vol 2 (HAL Fisher ed, CUP 1911) 418; SA De Smith, *Judicial Review of Administrative Action* (1st edn, Stevens 1959) 270; AWB Simpson, 'The Rise and Fall of the Legal Treatise: Legal Principles and the Forms of Legal Literature' (1981) 48 U Chi LR 632.

[100] cf TRS Allan, *Law, Liberty, and Justice: The Legal Foundations of British Constitutionalism* (Clarendon Press 1993) 3; Allan sees no meaningful distinction between the two.

[101] See Geoffrey Marshall, *Constitutional Theory* (first published 1971, OUP 1980) 1. Debates between legal theorists as to the necessity of political theory in public law legal thinking are discussed in McLean (n 60). McLean herself has suggested that lawyers and judges are ill-equipped 'to bring together the legal, the political and the metaphysical' in thinking of the state, and that their theory of it 'is impoverished indeed': Janet McLean, 'Personality and Public Law Doctrine' (1999) 49 UTLJ 123, 146, 149. She has also noted, however, that 'so far as the legal responsibility of the state is concerned, contemporary political theory appears to be struggling as much as legal theory to give meaning to political practice': McLean (n 60) 176. Without weighing in on these controversies, I adopt the view that cases brought against the crown or crown officials are often not propitious to the development of sophisticated theories of the state. As such, the evolution of the notion of crown in English legal thinking is discussed in this book insofar as it is relevant to the study of *the king can do no wrong* and its consequences for our understanding of the law of crown liability.

[102] McLean (n 96) 748.

[103] Assaf Likhovski, 'The Intellectual History of Law' in Markus D Dubber and Christopher L Tomlins (eds), *The Oxford Handbook of Legal History* (OUP 2018) 151. See also Baker (n 19) x.

[104] Martin Loughlin, 'The Historical Method in Public Law' in Markus D Dubber and Christopher L Tomlins (eds), *The Oxford Handbook of Legal History* (OUP 2018) 992.

[105] Bradley Selway, 'Of Kings and Officers: The Judicial Development of Public Law' (2005) 33 FL Rev 187, 238.

[106] FW Maitland, *The Collected Papers*, vol 1 (HAL Fisher ed, CUP 1911) 48–97; JH Baker, 'Why the History of English Law Has Not Been Finished' (2000) 59 CLJ 62, 63–64; JWF Allison, *The English Historical Constitution: Continuity, Change and European Effects* (CUP 2007) 19–20.

on evidence of the past is far too nuanced, detailed, and complex to serve constitutional purposes.[107] As the orthodox[108] approach to legal history is understood as the study of the past for its own sake and not in aid of the needs of the present,[109] that approach was not followed in this book because I aimed precisely to inform our understanding of the evolution of *the king can do no wrong* in legal thinking in order to revisit our current understanding of crown liability in constitutional theory. My method is not, however, completely divorced from Maitland's approach to constitutional history,[110] interpreted as the mastery of the genesis of our legal concepts and their intellectual production across time to understand our current constitutional arrangements.[111] The tracing of the evolution of *the king can do no wrong* here is closer to the intellectual history of legal ideas, which seeks to place legal ideas in their historical context, trace their influence over time, and to 'defamiliarize' current ideas to allow for suggestions of reform.[112]

Given my aims of studying the historical evolution of *the king can do no wrong* in legal thinking with a view to shedding new light on our current understanding of crown liability and suggesting reforms, a historical constitutional approach is more apt.[113] In line with this approach, the study of *the king can do no wrong*, in Chapters 2, 3, and 4, demonstrates continuity and change in connection with the understandings of this concept in the history of English[114] legal thinking since

[107] Allison (n 106) 19–20; Mathias Reimann, 'Historical Jurisprudence' in Markus D Dubber and Christopher L Tomlins (eds), *The Oxford Handbook of Legal History* (OUP 2018) 405, 417.

[108] Or 'purist' approach: Reimann (n 107) 416–17. For an alternative description of the traditional, dominant, school of legal history as 'internal' to law as opposed to 'external' legal history drawing from other disciplines, including sociology, see Russell Sandberg, *Subversive Legal History: A Manifesto for the Future of Legal Education* (Routledge 2021) 21–41.

[109] Baker (n 106) 64; JWF Allison, 'History to Understand, and History to Reform, English Public Law' (2013) 72 CLJ 526, 527–28; Joshua Getzler, 'Personality and Capacity: Lessons from Legal History' in Tim Bonyhady (ed), *Finn's Law: An Australian Justice* (The Federation Press 2016) 154; Russel Sandberg, *A Historical Introduction to English Law: Genesis of the Common Law* (CUP 2023) 2. We are, of course, greatly indebted to legal historians' invaluable work in uncovering and making accessible primary sources, as I hope is obvious throughout Chapter 2.

[110] FW Maitland, *The Constitutional History of England* (CUP 1963) 537–39.

[111] McLean (n 31) 1, 12; Getzler (n 109) 154; John Hudson, 'Maitland and Austin, Legal History and Legal Thought in the Late Nineteenth Century' in Mark Godfrey (ed), *Law and Authority in British Legal History, 1200–1900* (CUP 2016) 304, 321. Hudson, in particular, emphasizes both the importance of legal historical development to understanding present law and the importance of historical specificity in Maitland's thought.

[112] Reimann (n 107); Likhovski (n 103) 151. It is different, however, from historical jurisprudence understood as the study of the historical evolution of legal thinking in relation to law; see Kevin Bouchard, *Constitutionnalisme et common law dans la pensée juridique anglo-américaine* (Classiques Garnier 2021); Geoffrey Samuel, *Rethinking Historical Jurisprudence* (Edward Elgar Publishing 2022).

[113] Allison (n 106); see also McLean (n 31); Richard Gordon, '*Entick v Carrington* [1765] Revisited: All the King's Horses' in Satvinder Juss and Maurice Sunkin (eds), *Landmark Cases in Public Law* (Hart Publishing 2017).

[114] Allison (n 106) 16, 20. The focus is placed on English law specifically because, despite the union of England and Scotland in 1707, English law on crown immunity from suit in delict was not adopted in Scottish law until 1897: JR Philip, 'The Crown as Litigant in Scotland' (1928) 40 Jurid Rev 238, 245. That is not to say that Scottish law—and the Scotland Act 1998 in particular—cannot offer valuable insights in relation to the notions of crown, king, ministers, executive, and government: see McLean (n 60) 180–81. Scotland's Crown Suits Act 1857, c 44, is also illuminating: it predated changes brought about by

the late Middle Ages. While past and present understandings of *the king can do no wrong* in legal thinking do not specifically pertain to forms of government or their normative historical account's constitutional significance, they do relate to a constitutional arrangement from the past that has both continued and changed,[115] as is explored in Chapters 5 and 6.

The approach adopted in this book is also 'constitutional' in the sense that *the king can do no wrong* and its evolution in legal thinking in relation to crown liability for a legal wrong is the primary object of study. The focus of the study is not the history of remedies and whether they would be available in light of our current concept of tort.[116] In studying the evolution of *the king can do no wrong* in legal thinking, the caution associated with a historical constitutional approach has also been adopted to avoid anachronisms. As will be shown, the analysis of its evolution in legal thinking—especially in nineteenth-century cases on the petition of right—shows that the concept became associated with the absence of the king's liability for a tort in the nineteenth century. However, referring to the concept of 'tort' would be misleading for periods preceding the nineteenth century.[117] The term 'tort' was not always a technical term and in the Middle Ages, it 'denoted any kind of legal injury and is best translated as "wrong"'.[118] Until the sixteenth century, tort and wrong overlapped in meaning.[119] The idea of a 'wrong' in the Tudor era was 'perhaps the broadest and least well-defined concept in the common law' and 'came to encompass failures to perform undertakings or to pay debts'.[120] A wrong encompassed a breach of contract and a comparison with our current concept of tort would, as a consequence, be 'doomed to mislead'.[121] The use of the word 'tort' in

English courts' reinterpretation of *the king can do no wrong* and the law of governmental liability from the second half of the nineteenth century (see Chapter 4). The Act clearly distinguished under s 1 between the queen, the crown, and public departments, and even defined the latter under s 4; see *Smith v Lord Advocate* (1932) SLT 374, 378–79 (Lord MacKay). The understanding of the law of crown liability in the Scottish context, viewed from a historical perspective, can perhaps be described as closer to what I define in this book as the Bractonian, seventeenth-century constitutional understanding of *the king can do no wrong*. Nineteenth-century English courts' departure from that constitutional understanding is in stark contrast and, as a result, 'the constitutional law of the northern part of the United Kingdom is irreconcilable with the theory that the Crown can do no wrong': Sedley (n 31) 263.

115 Allison (n 106) 19.

116 For such historical studies on remedies, see eg Holdsworth (n 33); Street (n 47) 1–24; for remedies against the crown generally, authoritative references include Hogg, Monahan, and Wright (n 4); Boughey, Rock, and Weeks (n 45).

117 Selway (n 105) 196; Cane (n 17) 371.

118 Sir John Baker, *An Introduction to English Legal History* (5th edn, OUP 2019) 427.

119 ibid.

120 JH Baker, *Oxford History of the Laws of England*, vol 6 (OUP 2003) 753.

121 ibid. Moreover, early English law's action of trespass—an equivalent to the Roman action for wrongs—covered 'a range of disparate situations with at first no common core': David Ibbetson, '*Iniuria*, Roman and English' in Eric Descheemaeker and Helen Scott (eds), *Iniuria and the Common Law*, vol 9 (Hart Publishing 2013) 34. 'The word "trespass" meant no more than "wrong", and its legal use had no predetermined boundaries': David Ibbetson, *A Historical Introduction to the Law of Obligations* (OUP 1999) 14; the broad concepts of wrongdoing and of the causation of loss were prevalent: 13–17, 39–43, 63–70.

studying the understandings of *the king can do no wrong* in legal thinking would also not be apt because the term is often taken to imply the availability of an ordinary remedy against a wrongdoer. As will be discussed in this book, an action in the ordinary sense was not available against the king but the attribution of a wrong to the king was another issue and a subject could sue to the king by petition of right. To use our current concept of 'tort' as a guide in studying the understandings of *the king can do no wrong* in legal thinking would not only be anachronistic, it would also unduly narrow the focus of the enquiry. Throughout history, *the king can do no wrong* appeared in different areas of the law—land law, rule of construction of statutes, constitutional theory, and, since the nineteenth century, as is reflected in Dicey's work, crown immunity from suit. As Maitland advised in relation to the study of constitutional history, almost all departments of law became of constitutional importance at one time or another.[122] Similarly, focussing solely on the concept of tort in studying *the king can do no wrong* would lead to the exclusion of essential material in understanding its evolution in legal thinking.[123] Therefore, in studying *the king can do no wrong* in legal thinking, the term 'wrong' has been preferred in order not to unduly narrow the study of the evolution of the concept and to avoid anachronisms. A wrong refers to legal wrongs—acts or omissions contrary to law—in contrast with moral wrongs.

My perspective in retracing the evolution of *the king can do no wrong* is also 'constitutional', as it relates to executive accountability before the courts. *The king can do no wrong*, given its longevity and near ubiquity, is perhaps unique in allowing us to retrace how constitutional thinking evolved by bringing into focus the different understandings that were ascribed to it throughout various historical periods. As would do an archaeologist or a geologist, uncovering *the king can do no wrong* is akin to discovering 'new layers being added over more ancient ones' as 'new understandings were added to the layers of older understandings, which retained their relevance'.[124] The evolution of constitutional thinking in relation to *the king can do no wrong* and executive accountability, for instance, can support a historically-informed view of the constitution built on a triad composed of (1) the king's personal immunity, (2) his ministers' political accountability before Parliament, and (3) his ministers' and servants' legal liability before the courts, as *Miller 1* and *Miller 2* recently illustrated.[125]

The heuristic model elaborated in the first chapter of this book to facilitate the analysis of the historical evolution of *the king can do no wrong* in legal thinking is

[122] Maitland (n 110) 538.

[123] In the twelfth century, for instance, there was no action for damages and no indication that the king's court would eventually develop the modern law of tort: John H Beale, 'Introduction' in Ranulf de Glanville, *A Translation of Glanville* (John Beames ed, Byrne 1900) xix.

[124] Fortin (n 53) 44–45.

[125] ibid; *R(Miller) v Secretary of State for Exiting the European Union* (2017) UKSC 5 (*Miller 1*); *Miller 2* (n 53).

based on the premise that crown liability has two dimensions: a substantive one—the king's capacity to do wrong—and a procedural one—his amenability to justice. Crown liability is therefore understood in this book as involving two dimensions—an understanding found in the literature across the common law world.[126] The first, substantive dimension of crown liability is the crown's capacity to do wrong—the possibility of ascribing a wrong to the crown. The second, procedural dimension of crown liability is the crown's amenability to justice for a wrong. The model is also based on the observation that three notions associated with *the king can do no wrong*—the king's status in relation to law, his perfection, and his immunity from suit—indicate how the king's capacity to do wrong and his amenability to justice, the two dimensions of crown liability, were understood in legal thinking in given historical periods.

In this book I analyse *the king can do no wrong* in legal thinking from a historical constitutional perspective in order to revisit our understanding of crown liability for a wrong now understood as tortious liability. My approach is normative only to the extent that claims as to the historical foundations of the law governing crown liability should be consistent with that history. If *the king can do no wrong* is invoked as a historically grounded basis for the crown's absolute immunity from suit at common law, the study of the history of the understandings of the concept in legal thinking should support that claim.

My aim with this book is to retrace the evolution of the understandings of *the king can do no wrong*, to assess the historical constitutional validity of the claim that the crown is immune at common law because of that ancient, feudal, mystical, concept. Once the footsteps (or the absence thereof) are retraced, the paths taken revisited, and the forks in the road located in relation to the evolution of *the king can do no wrong* in legal thinking, a better light can be shone on the field of crown (or governmental) immunity. The shadow of confusion surrounding the notion of the crown will also be partly enlightened. *The king can do no wrong* now commonly believed to be a feudal maxim embodying royal irresponsibility is in fact—as I will explain in Chapter 4—of a more recent Victorian vintage. In the Middle Ages, the English king was subject to law, bound to do justice, and to remedy a wrong (see Chapter 2). Medieval constitutional thinking to the effect that the king was not entitled to do wrong was reflected in understandings of *the king can do no wrong* which led to parliamentary monarchy in the seventeenth century (explored in Chapter 3). The medieval and seventeenth-century constitutional understandings of *the king can do no wrong* still underpin the constitutional arrangement whereby the royal prerogative is subject to parliamentary sovereignty, and they are the foundations of ministerial responsibility and of ministers' and crown servants' liability before the courts.

[126] See Chapter 1.

As the object of the enquiry is the evolution of the understanding of *the king can do no wrong* in legal thinking, the focus of the analysis has been put on legal authors' and the courts'—and individual judges'—understanding of the words. As a result, attention has been paid to the understanding of *the king can do no wrong* in cases where it featured, even if crown liability was not directly at issue or where the concept was referred to in *obiter*. The approach thus differs from the common lawyer's traditional doctrinal approach to cases. Emphasis has not been put on the facts of the cases or the matter in dispute where they were not material to the understanding of *the king can do no wrong*. However, seminal cases on crown liability and sovereign immunity receive a more extensive treatment.

The penultimate chapter of this book includes a case study of the consequences for the Crown Proceedings Act 1947—and acts modelled on it across the common law world—of revisiting our understanding of crown liability by adopting a historical constitutional approach. Although the confusion in legal thinking surrounding *the king can do no wrong* also has consequences for state liability at international law, the crown's criminal irresponsibility, and possibly for judicial review and the honour of the crown and Indigenous peoples, they are aspects of the crown's liability which exceed the scope of this book.[127]

In the last chapter, Chapter 6, I turn to the evolution of *the king can do no wrong* in other common law jurisdictions, where it also features in legal thinking. The purpose of the necessarily brief comparative examination is threefold: first, to enlighten understandings of *the king can do no wrong* in each jurisdiction and how these understandings relate to, or depart from, *the king can do no wrong* as it has been understood in English legal thinking; second, to explore how current understandings of *the king can do no wrong* in the selected jurisdictions can inform a better understanding of the law of crown liability in the common law world; and third, to determine the extent to which the heuristic model developed for a historical analysis of one jurisdiction in Chapter 1 can also be useful to a historical comparative study. The comparison in Chapter 6 includes American, Irish, and Australian legal thinking on *the king can do no wrong* because there have been exchanges of ideas between the three jurisdictions on the issue of governmental liability over the course of the twentieth century. American, Irish, and Australian perspectives on *the king can do no wrong* are also sufficiently different from English legal thinking to offer enriching contrasting viewpoints. *The king can do no wrong* is conceived of as being akin to a shared common law heritage—allowing for aspects of the model elaborated in this book for the purposes of a historical

[127] On the crown's criminal responsibility and *the king can do no wrong*, see Glanville Llewelyn Williams, *Criminal Law* (Stevens 1961) para 257; Sunkin (n 7) 720; Malcolm Barrett, 'Prosecuting the Crown' (2002) 4 Notre Dame L Rev 39. On *the king can do no wrong* and crown liability in regard to Indigenous peoples in Australia, Canada, and the United States, see Ros Kidd, 'The Revolutionary Potential of Walsh's Law' (2006) 31 Alt LJ 137.

enquiry to be used in analysing the concept comparatively in different jurisdictions.[128] But understandings of *the king can do no wrong* in English legal thinking were either inherited (as in Canada), rejected (as in Ireland and Australia), or exchanged for different theoretical underpinnings (as in the United States) across the former empire.

The king can do no wrong is conceived of as a tenet of constitutional law. Yet there have been different understandings of *the king can do no wrong* in legal thinking since the seventeenth century. This book seeks to demonstrate that revisiting crown liability in legal thinking can be achieved by adopting a historical constitutional approach to this well-known yet multifaceted law of the constitution that is *the king can do no wrong*. As a law of the constitution, *the king can do no wrong* means that the king is capable of doing wrong, but that he benefits from an immunity from suit which was granted to him—and to the person of the king only—in exchange for his ministers', servants', and all other instruments' liability, including that of government departments.

To facilitate the analysis of the historical evolution of *the king can do no wrong*, a heuristic model of crown liability is elaborated in Chapter 1 based on the different understandings of the concept. Guided by the heuristic model presented in Chapter 1, the evolution of *the king can do no wrong* in legal thinking is traced through the late Middle Ages and Tudor eras (Chapter 2), the constitutional struggles of the seventeenth century (Chapter 3), and lastly, since Blackstone (Chapter 4). In Chapter 5, the law of crown liability in England and in Canada is revisited in light of the historical evolution of *the king can do no wrong* in English legal thinking, and the current constitutional differences in understandings of *the king can do no wrong* in the realm of judicial review, liability of public authorities, and crown liability are highlighted. The probing of the historical and constitutional foundations of the law of crown liability is complemented in Chapter 6 by a comparison of the understanding of *the king can do no wrong*, its evolution, and its implication for governmental liability and constitutional theory in the United States, Ireland, and Australia.

[128] Historical legal analysis can be conceived of as a form of comparative analysis, as both can lead to reforms upon discovering how things were (in the past) or are (in another jurisdiction) done differently: Sandberg (n 108) 12–13.

1

Understandings of *The King Can Do No Wrong* in Legal Thinking and Heuristic Model of Crown Liability Derived from Them

1 Overview of the chapter

This chapter begins with an analysis of the understandings of *the king can do no wrong* in legal thinking. As will be demonstrated in the second section of this chapter, surveying the understandings of *the king can do no wrong* in legal thinking is a means to a heuristic model. The heuristic model will, in turn, facilitate the study of the historical evolution of *the king can do no wrong* in legal thinking in Chapters 2, 3, and 4.

2 Understandings of *the king can do no wrong*

The ambiguity to which *the king can do no wrong* lends itself has been noted by legal authors of the twentieth and twenty-first centuries. It can be understood as whatever the king does is legally right or as the king is not entitled to do wrong, or yet again as the king is capable of committing a wrong or as the king is incapable of committing a wrong.[1] Recently, three 'common understandings' of *the king can do no wrong* have been identified: the king is incapable of thinking or doing wrong,

[1] Ludwik Ehrlich, 'Proceedings against the Crown (1216–1377)' in Paul Vinogradoff (ed), *Oxford Studies in Social and Legal History*, vol 6 (Clarendon Press 1921) 42; Edwin Borchard, 'Government Liability in Tort' (1924) 34 YLJ 1, 2; Edwin Borchard, 'Governmental Responsibility in Tort, VI' (1926) 36 YLJ 1, 22; Louis L Jaffe, 'Suits against Governments and Officers: Sovereign Immunity' (1963) 77 Harv L Rev 1, 3–4; Adam Tomkins, 'Crown Privileges' in Maurice Sunkin and Sebastian Payne (eds), *The Nature of the Crown: A Legal and Political Analysis* (OUP 1999) 189–90; Tom Cornford, 'Legal Remedies against the Crown before and after M' in Maurice Sunkin and Sebastian Payne (eds), *The Nature of the Crown: A Legal and Political Analysis* (OUP 1999) 235; Maurice Sunkin, 'Crown Immunity from Criminal Liability in English Law' [2003] PL 716, 720; Sir John Baker, *The Reinvention of Magna Carta 1216–1616* (CUP 2017) 45.

The King Can Do No Wrong. Marie-France Fortin, Oxford University Press. © Marie-France Fortin 2024.
DOI: 10.1093/9780191994487.003.0002

the king has no legal power to do wrong, and the king is immune from legal process,[2] but at least four others can be identified. The understandings of *the king can do no wrong* are discussed in this section. It is important to distinguish the understandings of *the king can do no wrong* because the phrase is used indiscriminately and the understandings can be contradictory.

2.1 The king is immune from suit

That *the king can do no wrong* means the king's immunity from suit is a view widely held. Maitland understood it as the king cannot be sued or prosecuted.[3] So did Dicey, Vinogradoff, Laski, Brazier, Wade, and Lord Templeman in *M v Home Office*.[4] Keir and Lawson and Wade have attributed to *the king can do no wrong* the meaning of crown immunity from suit.[5]

Harlow—relying on Maitland—and Sunkin have grounded the understanding of *the king can do no wrong* as immunity from suit in the historical fact that the king as feudal lord could not be sued in his courts.[6] On the other hand, Loughlin has rejected the king's feudal privilege not to be sued in his own courts as the basis for the understanding of *the king can do no wrong* and has hypothesized that *the king can do no wrong* understood as the king's immunity from suit is rooted in the idea that the prerogative must be exercised for the good of the people, the king's role as fountain of justice, his perfection and incapacity to do wrong, and his status as above the law.[7]

[2] Tomkins (n 1) 176.

[3] FW Maitland, *The Constitutional History of England* (CUP 1963) 100, 195, 482; Frederick Pollock and FW Maitland, *The History of English Law before the Time of Edward I*, vol 1 (2nd, reissued edn, CUP 1968) 515–18.

[4] AV Dicey, *Lectures Introductory to the Study of the Law of the Constitution: The Oxford Edition of Dicey*, vol 1 (JWF Allison ed, OUP 2013) 21; Paul Vinogradoff, 'Some Problems of Public Law: I' (1924) 12 CLR 348, 350; Harold J Laski, 'The Responsibility of the State in England' (1919) 32 Harv L Rev 447, 447–48; Rodney Brazier, 'Constitutional Reform and the Crown' in Maurice Sunkin and Sebastian Payne (eds), *The Nature of the Crown: A Legal and Political Analysis* (OUP 1999) 345–46; *M v Home Office* [1994] 1 AC 377 (HL) 395.

[5] David L Keir and FH Lawson, *Cases in Constitutional Law* (FH Lawson and DJ Bentley eds, 6th edn, Clarendon Press 1979) 97; William Wade, 'The Crown, Ministers and Officials: Legal Status and Liability' in Maurice Sunkin and Sebastian Payne (eds), *The Nature of the Crown: A Legal and Political Analysis* (OUP 1999) 24–25.

[6] Carol Harlow, *Compensation and Government Torts* (Sweet & Maxwell 1982); Sunkin, 'Crown Immunity from Criminal Liability' (n 1) 720. See also JH Morgan, 'Remedies against the Crown' in Gleeson E Robinson, *Public Authorities and Legal Liability* (University of London Press 1925) v, xviii–xix.

[7] Martin Loughlin, 'The State, the Crown and the Law' in Maurice Sunkin and Sebastian Payne (eds), *The Nature of the Crown: A Legal and Political Analysis* (OUP 1999) 60; Martin Loughlin, *Foundations of Public Law* (OUP 2010) 26. See also *Halsbury's Laws of England*, vol 29 (5th edn, LexisNexis 2014) [52].

2.2 The king is perfect and is incapable of doing wrong

That the king is perfect and incapable of doing wrong has been another understanding of *the king can do no wrong* in legal thinking since Blackstone.[8] In the late eighteenth and early nineteenth centuries, it conveyed the sense of the king as a 'moral exemplar', a 'legal paragon' whose will is to uphold the law and ensure that right be done to his subjects.[9] The king—being perfect and a moral exemplar—was harmed, along with his subjects, when his officials acted wrongfully.[10] The romantic view of the king wishing only the good of his people as the understanding of *the king can do no wrong* could lead to two contradictory versions of the constitution. Either the king is perfect and his ministers are liable in his stead—leading to a shift of responsibilities from the king to his advisers—or the king's perfection and goodwill justify his involvement in the conduct of public affairs.[11]

The understanding of the *king can do no wrong* as the perfect king incapable of acting unlawfully is not an ordinary immunity.[12] The immunity conferred on the king on this understanding of *the king can do no wrong* is not procedural but rather grounded in a conception of a king to whom extra-natural attributes are ascribed. The king, being perfect, is both physically and mentally incapable of committing a wrong and is consequently immune from suit because of that perfection.

The understanding of *the king can do no wrong* as the king is perfect and thereby incapable of doing wrong implies that the king is inviolable. He cannot be sued because he is infallible. The king's infallibility commands logically his immunity from suit—if the king is perfect and incapable of doing wrong, he cannot consequently be sued. For instance, it was the king's perfection that was accepted as the ground for *the king can do no wrong* understood as the monarch's absolute immunity from liability in a recent decision where the queen's former Lieutenant Governor was prosecuted for fraud in Canada.[13]

The king's incapacity to do wrong is not always associated with the notion of the king's perfection. The king's incapacity to do wrong is also said to be a fiction, or a presumption that the king is incapable of doing wrong; he is 'deemed incapable of acting unlawfully'.[14] As will be shown in Chapter 4, that the king cannot be

[8] William Blackstone, *Commentaries on the Laws of England*, vol 1 (facsimile of 1765–1769 1st edn, University of Chicago Press 1979) 238–39; Joseph Chitty, *A Treatise on the Law of the Prerogatives of the Crown* (Butterworth & Son 1820) 5; Robert Dorsey Watkins, *The State as a Party Litigant* (Johns Hopkins Press 1927) 39; Cornford (n 1) 235; Rodney Brazier, 'Royal Incapacity and Constitutional Continuity: The Regent and Counsellors of State' (2005) 65 CLJ 352, 353; *Halsbury's Laws of England* (n 7) [52]; Joshua Getzler, 'Personality and Capacity: Lessons from Legal History' in Tim Bonyhady (ed), *Finn's Law: An Australian Justice* (The Federation Press 2016) 152, 170.

[9] Janet McLean, *Searching for the State in British Legal Thought: Competing Conceptions of the Public Sphere* (CUP 2012) 26–27, 209–10.

[10] ibid 27.

[11] Denis Baranger, *Parlementarisme des origines* (Presses Universitaires de France 1999) 61–62.

[12] Janet McLean, 'The Crown in Contract and Administrative Law' (2004) 24 OJLS 129, 143–44.

[13] *Trudel Thibault v R* (2012) QCCA 2212 [9]–[11].

[14] Cornford (n 1) 235.

presumed to have concurred in a wrong is a recent understanding of *the king can do no wrong.*

2.3 Whatever the king does is legal

Keir and Lawson have argued that after the Middle Ages, *the king can do no wrong* came to be understood as 'whatever the king does is right', a change they attributed to Royalists in the seventeenth century.[15] That in law the king does not do wrong because he is above the law is associated with theocratic kingship and the Stuart kings. [16]

That *the king can do no wrong* can be understood as either 'it is not unlawful if the King did it'—a Royalist understanding—or 'if it was unlawful, it was not the King who did it'—an understanding associated, post Glorious Revolution, with ministerial responsibility—was recently remarked upon and traced in *The King v Speyer.*[17] Yet it appears that Lord Reading understood *the king can do no wrong* in that case as the courts having no power over the sovereign.[18] To Avory J in *The King v Speyer, the king can do no wrong* was to be understood as the king being personally, in his natural capacity, not amenable to justice but also as the king being under the law and therefore not entitled to sanction an unlawful act.[19] *The King v Speyer* does not appear therefore to be an illustration of *the king can do no wrong* understood as everything the king does is legal or that an unlawful act cannot be the king's, but seems rather to be a (typically confusing) example of *the king can do no wrong* understood as the king's personal immunity from suit. It is a procedural understanding and is distinct from *the king can do no wrong* understood at a substantive level as everything the king does is lawful. The king's personal immunity from suit is also distinct from the fiction that the king did not commit the unlawful act at issue and was advised by evil councillors, although the latter fiction is often resorted to as a justification for the king's personal immunity.[20]

The understanding of *the king can do no wrong* as whatever is done by the king is legal can now be seen extended to the crown[21]—*the crown can do no wrong.*[22] A similar understanding is that *the king can do no wrong* means immunity of the crown from legal process because it is beyond law's reach, and not subject to a

[15] Keir and Lawson (n 5) 72, 98.

[16] Loughlin, *Foundations* (n 7) 26, 258.

[17] Timothy Endicott, *Administrative Law* (5th edn, OUP 2021) 552–54. *The King v Speyer* [1916] 1 KB 595.

[18] *The King v Speyer* (n 17) 610 (Reading CJ).

[19] ibid 619 (Avory J). See Chapter 4, section 3.3.4.

[20] Watkins (n 8) 39.

[21] Or denied the crown: Stephen Sedley, 'The Crown in Its Own Courts' in Christopher F Forsyth and Ivan Hare (eds), *The Golden Metwand and the Crooked Cord: Essays in Honour of Sir William Wade QC* (OUP 1999) 261–62.

[22] Cornford (n 1) 236.

different category of law such as public law.[23] Therefore, although one could presume *the king can do no wrong* understood as everything the king does is legal to have become obsolete after the Glorious Revolution, that understanding of *the king can do no wrong* is still relevant and referred to in connection with crown immunity from suit.[24]

The king can do no wrong understood as everything the king does is legal knows another variant, found in Hearn's work, and is grounded in the strict procedures and rules which ensure that the king's acts are lawful:

> Every official act of the Crown must be done in the manner prescribed by law. Every such act so done is lawful. Every act done under the colour of Royal authority, but not in the proper manner, is not an official act of the Crown. . . . Thus no injury, no legal wrong, can be done by the King, because all his official acts are done in accordance with law, and because no unlawful act can be recognized as an act of the Crown.[25]

Hearn cited the medieval treatise known as Bracton's—discussed in Chapter 2—to support his definition of *the king can do no wrong*. Hearn's thesis that the king cannot do wrong because procedural rules bind the king's actions 'in his official character' can also be found in sixteenth-century cases where the king's two bodies featured, and where the king was found to be bound by procedures developed in the Middle Ages to preserve the crown from a spendthrift monarch (see Chapter 2, section 2.2.3).[26]

2.4 The king is not entitled to do wrong

The king can do no wrong is also understood in legal thinking as the king being capable of doing wrong but not being entitled to do wrong. If the king does commit a wrong, it cannot be an act committed by the king as king, because it exceeds his jurisdiction—the king, by law, is only entitled to act lawfully.

That *the king can do no wrong* is to be understood as the king having no legal power to do wrong is the view taken by Jaffe, Wade and Forsyth, Craig, Baker, and Weeks—the king's powers were derived from the law and it did not allow him to exceed them.[27] Lord Woolf in *M v Home Office* also appeared to subscribe to that

[23] JWF Allison, *A Continental Distinction in the Common Law: A Historical and Comparative Perspective on English Public Law* (revised edn, OUP 2000) 177–78.

[24] Sunkin, 'Crown Immunity from Criminal Liability' (n 1) 720.

[25] William Edward Hearn, *The Government of England: Its Structure and Its Development* (1st edn, Robertson 1867) 20.

[26] ibid.

[27] Jaffe (n 1) 4; William Wade, Christopher Forsyth, and Julian Ghosh, *Administrative Law* (12th edn, OUP 2022) 652–53; Paul Craig, *Administrative Law* (9th edn, Sweet & Maxwell 2021) 907; Baker (n 1) 45. Note that Weeks, for instance, adopts a procedure-based view that the king was not

understanding.[28] Wade and Forsyth and Baker have argued that *the king can do no wrong* had very little to do with the king's procedural immunity from suit.[29] Wade and Forsyth have traced the principle that the law does not allow the king to do wrong to Bracton while Baker made a connection with Magna Carta.[30] The understanding of *the king can do no wrong* as the king is not entitled to do wrong is referred to in this book as the Bractonian understanding of the concept.

2.5 The king's wrongful acts or orders are void and cannot serve as a defence

In legal thinking, *the king can do no wrong* is also understood as the impossibility for the king's servant to claim as a defence that the wrongful act was committed pursuant to a command from the king. *The king can do no wrong* understood as the king's wrongful acts and commands are void but that his ministers and servants are liable for them is exemplified by Hale's reasoning in the seventeenth century, and also figure in Hearn's work from the nineteenth century.[31] As will be further discussed in Chapter 3, *the king can do no wrong* understood as the king's wrongful commands are void also implies the Bractonian understanding of the concept as the king is not entitled to do wrong.

As will be discussed in this book, the implication of *the king can do no wrong* that servants can be sued for a wrong committed following the wrongful orders of the king can be traced at least to the seventeenth century. However, as will be discussed in Chapter 4, the fiction that the wrong committed by the king 'disappears' insofar as the king is concerned but that the wrongful act does not cease to exist for ministers and servants was a product of nineteenth-century judicial decisions. That understanding of *the king can do no wrong* can be described as a 'conundrum of the Crown ordering wrongful acts that ex hypothesi must have been non-wrongful qua the Crown, a special kind of damnum sine injuria'.[32] Chrimes and Keir and

entitled to do wrong because he 'could not refuse to redress wrongs', instead of a substantive-based understanding that the king was not entitled by the law to do wrong: Greg Weeks, *Soft Law and Public Authorities: Remedies and Reform* (Hart Publishing 2016) 182; see also Janina Boughey, Ellen Rock, and Greg Weeks, *Government Liability: Principles and Remedies* (LexisNexis Butterworths 2019) 44–45.

[28] *M v Home Office* (n 4) 408.

[29] Wade and Forsyth (n 27) 652–53; Baker (n 1) 45. However, Wade himself also shared the view held by Maitland and Harlow that *the king can do no wrong* was connected to the king's feudal privilege not to be sued in his own courts: Wade (n 5) 24–25; Maitland (n 3) 100; Harlow (n 6) 17–18.

[30] Baker (n 1) 45.

[31] Sir Matthew Hale, *On the Law of Nature, Reason, and Common Law: Selected Jurisprudential Writings* (Gerald Postema ed, OUP 2017) 221–22; Hearn (n 25) 21–22: 'Since no unlawful act is the act of the Crown, no command to do any such act can be a command of the Crown. No person therefore doing any unlawful act under colour of the Royal authority can shelter himself from the penal or other consequences of his act under the protection of that pretended command.'

[32] Getzler (n 8) 172.

Lawson, in addition to the understanding of *the king can do no wrong* as the crown's immunity from suit, have also adopted the understanding that a wrong done by the king is presumed not to have been done by him.[33] As will be discussed in this book, that the king is presumed not to have done or authorized the wrong can also be explained by reference to the second understanding of *the king can do no wrong* identified above, namely that the king is perfect.

2.6 Imputed ministerial responsibility: legal and political accountability of the king's ministers

The king can do no wrong is understood in legal thinking as 'if an evil act is done, it, though emanating from the king personally, will be imputed to his ministers, for whose acts the king is in no way responsible'.[34] That understanding of *the king can do no wrong*, as Maitland and Loughlin have noted, refers to the king's ministers and servants' legal liability before the courts as well as the former's political liability before Parliament.[35] Maitland and Loughlin therefore understood *the king can do no wrong* as the king's immunity from suit and that that understanding is 'coupled with ministerial responsibility' as another understanding of the concept.[36] Maitland emphasized that ministers are not only accountable before Parliament, but that ministerial responsibility also means that ministers are responsible before the courts of law for exceeding their lawful authority. The fact that the act was an official act, even the highest act of state, offers no justification.[37]

The king can do no wrong is therefore understood in legal thinking as ministers' political responsibility before Parliament and the king's ministers and servants' legal liability before the courts. Political scientists and historians of political thought associate *the king can do no wrong* primarily with the former understanding of ministerial responsibility—ministers' political responsibility.[38] This understanding of ministerial responsibility—as opposed to their and other servants' legal liability—may contribute to explain why some authors have traced *the*

[33] SB Chrimes, *English Constitutional History* (3rd edn, OUP 1965) 18; Keir and Lawson (n 5) 97–98.

[34] Earl William Jowitt, *Jowitt's Dictionary of English Law*, vol 2 (Daniel Greenberg ed, 4th edn, Sweet & Maxwell 2015) 2119.

[35] Maitland (n 3) 195–96; Loughlin, *Foundations* (n 7) 255–56.

[36] Maitland (n 3) 484; Loughlin, *Foundations* (n 7) 255–56, 263.

[37] Maitland (n 3) 484.

[38] David Ogg, *England in the Reign of Charles II* (Clarendon Press 1934) 452–54; Clayton Roberts, *The Growth of Responsible Government in Stuart England* (CUP 1966) 4–10, 115; Janelle Greenberg, 'Our Grand Maxim of State: "The King Can Do No Wrong"' (1991) 12 Hist Pol Thought 209; Joyce Lee Malcolm, 'Doing No Wrong: Law, Liberty, and the Constraint of Kings' (1999) 38 J Brit Stud 161; Loughlin, *Foundations* (n 7) 255–56.

king can do no wrong to the minority of Henry III, without however demonstrating its use during that period.[39]

Ministerial responsibility is a concept often confused with that of responsible government. While both ministerial responsibility and responsible government can refer to ministers' political responsibility before Parliament, ministerial responsibility in legal thinking can also include ministers' and civil servants' legal liability before the courts, as is evidenced by Dicey's writings.[40]

2.7 The king does nothing, therefore he cannot do wrong

Lastly, *the king can do no wrong* is understood to refer to the view that the king no longer exercises governmental control.[41] The king exercises only what Bagehot called the 'dignified parts' of the constitution and cannot do wrong because he is advised, directed, and controlled when exercising his prerogative powers.[42] Loughlin traces to Blackstone in the eighteenth century *the king can do no wrong* understood as the king can only act lawfully because he does so according to a set of official processes which commands the confidence of Parliament.[43] That understanding of *the king can do no wrong* as the king is constrained by predetermined and burdensome procedures could, however, be conceived of as having older, medieval origins.[44] More bluntly, *the king can do no wrong* conveys the more recent nineteenth- and twentieth-century idea that the king cannot do wrong because the king is little more than a figurehead.[45]

This last understanding of *the king can do no wrong* also implies an immunity for the king. As the king does little anymore and is advised by his ministers when exercising his prerogative powers, the king should not be held liable for decisions made in his name, but without his participation in the making of the decisions. The immunity in fact stems from the fact that ministers act on behalf of the king and that the latter should not be held liable for decisions made by the ministers. The immunity applies therefore only to the king, not to the ministers who decide

[39] William Stubbs, *The Constitutional History of England, in Its Origin and Development*, vol 2 (reprint of 4th edn, Clarendon Press 1906) 41; William Reynell Anson, *The Law and Custom of the Constitution*, vol 2 part 1 (A Berriedale Keith ed, 4th edn, Clarendon Press 1935) 20.

[40] Dicey (n 4) 178–79.

[41] Roberts (n 38) 395; Guy I Seidman, 'The Origins of Accountability' (2005) 49 St Louis ULJ 393, 468.

[42] Walter Bagehot, *Bagehot: The English Constitution* (Paul Smith ed, CUP 2001) 5–8, 143; Baranger (n 11) 64, 184–85; Loughlin, 'State, Crown and Law' (n 7) 58.

[43] Martin Loughlin, *The Idea of Public Law* (OUP 2003) 24, citing Blackstone (n 8) 239; Greenberg (n 38).

[44] The medieval king, for instance, could only act by matter of record: Baker (n 1) 45–46. Even the development of the doctrine of the king's two bodies and of the notion of the perfection of the king's body politic in the fifteenth century did not exempt the king from having to follow the more onerous procedures applicable to the king: see Chapter 2, section 2.2.3.

[45] Watkins (n 8) 192.

in his name. A revival of this understanding of *the king can do no wrong* is implicit in the United Kingdom Supreme Court's decision in *Miller 2*. The Supreme Court held that the Prime Minister's advice to the late queen to prorogue Parliament was unreasonable and unlawful, but the Court avoided laying any blame at the feet of the monarch:

> We know that in approving the prorogation, Her Majesty was acting on the advice of the Prime Minister. We do not know what conversation passed between them when he gave her that advice. We do not know what conversation, if any, passed between the assembled Privy Counsellors before or after the meeting. We do not know what the Queen was told and cannot draw any conclusions about it.[46]

2.8 Conclusion

As was shown in this section, different understandings of *the king can do no wrong* are adopted in legal thinking. However, the different understandings of the concept and the implications of those differences are not clearly acknowledged.[47] Moreover, distinct understandings of *the king can do no wrong* can be contradictory. For instance, 'the king's unlawful command is not a valid defence' is an understanding of *the king can do no wrong* which implies that the king is capable of doing wrong—although not entitled to do so—and is therefore not logically compatible with the understanding of the concept as the king is perfect and incapable of doing wrong. *The king can do no wrong* as the king is not entitled to do wrong is also superfluous if it is understood as the king is perfect and incapable of doing wrong.

The distinct understandings of *the king can do no wrong* in legal thinking have led to confusion. Hence this book's aim to study the historical evolution of the different understandings of *the king can do no wrong* in legal thinking in order to shed new light on our current understanding of crown liability.

3 Heuristic model of crown liability

In light of the understandings of *the king can do no wrong* explained above, a heuristic model of crown liability has been elaborated for the purposes of this book. The model facilitates the study of the evolution of the understandings of *the king can do no wrong* in legal thinking to shed new light on our current understanding of crown

[46] *R(Miller) v Prime Minister* (2019) UKSC 41 (*Miller 2*) [15]; Marie-France Fortin, 'Rule of Law, Parliamentary Sovereignty and Executive Accountability in English Legal Thinking: The Recent Revival of The King Can Do No Wrong' (2022) 44 J Const Hist 43.

[47] For a recognition of some of the various understandings of *the king can do no wrong*, see Watkins (n 8) 39–40; McLean (n 12) 143–44.

liability by guiding this study with the three notions associated with *the king can do no wrong* and two dimensions of crown liability—procedural and substantive.

The heuristic model in this book has not been elaborated in the abstract with predetermined criteria. The objective has not been to design an ideal model and apply it to different understandings of *the king can do no wrong* in legal thinking to assess whether normative criteria were met throughout history. Instead, the model has been elaborated based on the various understandings of *the king can do no wrong* in legal thinking listed in this chapter to facilitate the analysis of the concept in various historical periods in order to shed light on crown liability in legal thinking. The model is a means to facilitate as encompassing an analysis of the sources where *the king can do no wrong* features as possible; the model itself is not the objective of the analysis.[48]

As a result, the model has been elaborated based on the premise that crown liability has two dimensions, influenced by three notions associated with *the king can do no wrong*. The two dimensions identified with crown liability and the three notions, which are discussed in this section, have been evident throughout the enquiry into the understandings of *the king can do no wrong* in legal thinking. The model therefore serves as a heuristic tool to better analyse the evolution of the understandings of the concept in legal thinking for various historical periods by focussing on the three notions, which in turn point to the status of the two dimensions of crown liability for these periods. The analysis of the understandings of *the king can do no wrong* in legal thinking throughout various historical periods and their meaning for crown liability—based on the three notions and two dimensions captured by the model—in Chapters 2, 3, and 4, in turn sheds new light on current legal thinking in relation to crown liability in Chapter 5—thereby allowing suggestions of reform—including in other jurisdictions, explored in Chapter 6.

3.1 Two dimensions

The heuristic model developed in the book is based on the idea that there are two dimensions to crown liability—a substantive and a procedural dimension. Crown liability in this book refers therefore to both the king's status as being legally obligated or not—whether the king is conceived of as subject to law and capable of acting unlawfully—and to the king's status as being accountable or not—whether the king is conceived of as amenable to judicial process. The heuristic model in this book is therefore based on the substantive dimension of crown liability, understood as the king's capacity to do wrong, and the procedural dimension of crown liability, understood as his amenability to justice.

[48] See, for a similar treatment of the uses of a heuristic model in the context of a historical-comparative jurisprudential analysis, Allison (n 23) 32–33.

That crown liability has two dimensions finds support in an analysis of the understandings of *the king can do no wrong* in legal thinking. As appears from the first section of this chapter, there are understandings of *the king can do no wrong*—such as the king's immunity from suit, the king's wrongful acts or commands do not constitute a defence, and ministerial responsibility—which relate to the procedural dimension of crown liability and whether the king is amenable to justice or not. Other understandings—such as the king is perfect and incapable of doing wrong, whatever the king does is legal, the king is not entitled to do wrong, and the king's wrongful commands are void—relate to the substantive dimension of the king's liability, whether the king is capable of doing wrong or not. The idea that there are two dimensions to crown liability will be familiar to Australian jurists, as is further discussed in Chapter 6.

That there are two dimensions to crown liability is also evident in case law and in legal literature. In *Matthews v Ministry of Defence*, Lord Hope of Craighead noted that 'the crown's protection from liability is grounded on two rules of law, the substantive rule of law that *the king can do no wrong* and the procedural rule that the king cannot be sued in his own courts'.[49] A similar distinction between the king cannot be sued in his own courts and *the king can do no wrong* was also made in *Mulcahy* by Neill LJ[50] and the two rules were also referred to by counsel in *M v Home Office*.[51]

Jaffe[52] also noted a distinction between the immunity of the sovereign from suit, which he called 'sovereign immunity', and the sovereign's capacity to violate or not the law, which he referred to as 'the King can do no wrong'. Jaffe considered the two notions of the king's immunity from suit and the king's legal status in relation to law to be independent. His brief observations highlight how there are two distinct dimensions to crown liability.

The two dimensions of crown liability—procedural and substantive—also feature in Harlow's thinking about *the king can do no wrong*. To Harlow, the 'procedural maxim' that *the king can do no wrong* is grounded in the king's feudal privilege not to be sued in his courts[53] and is reflected in section 21 of the Crown Proceedings Act 1947 and the common law rule that mandamus does not lie against the crown.[54] *The king can do no wrong* as an 'ancient procedural maxim', Harlow has argued, would have changed meaning in the seventeenth century to be understood as the king cannot be guilty of torts or crimes.[55] From a procedural maxim, *the king can do no wrong* would have become the principle that the king cannot be held liable.

[49] *Matthews v Ministry of Defence* (2003) UKHL 4, [2003] 1 AC 1163 [54].
[50] *Mulcahy v Ministry of Defence* [1996] QB 732 (CA) 740.
[51] *M v Home Office* (n 4) 407 (Lord Woolf).
[52] Jaffe (n 1) 4.
[53] Harlow (n 6); see also Sunkin, 'Crown Immunity from Criminal Liability' (n 1) 720.
[54] Harlow (n 6) 17.
[55] ibid 17–18.

Harlow's account was not based on a historical enquiry and the evolution over time of the understanding of *the king can do no wrong* traced in this book differs in part from hers, but the model elaborated here is based on the same premise that there are two dimensions to crown liability—procedural and substantive.

Cornford has also adopted the view that 'two basic doctrines governed the legal position of the Crown at common law', *the king can do no wrong*—the king is incapable of acting unlawfully—and the king cannot be sued in his own courts.[56] McLean has equally noted that 'crown immunity' can be understood in at least two different senses. The first sense is that the king cannot be sued in his own courts and the second is that *the king can do no wrong*.[57] In the first sense, McLean explained, the king is subject to law but there can be no enforcement mechanism against him. In the second sense, *the king can do no wrong* has two contradictory meanings; it can mean either that the king is constrained because he is not entitled to do wrong or that the king is perfect and is therefore incapable of doing wrong.[58] In that latter meaning, McLean has argued, *the king can do no wrong* is not an ordinary immunity but the result of the attribute of perfection given to the king for the political purposes of withdrawing the king from the ambit of the law.[59] McLean therefore conceived of two types of immunity in relation to crown liability: a procedural immunity from suit (the king cannot be sued in his own court) and the status of the crown as a pre-legal entity to whom the law does not apply—a substantive immunity.

In constitutional theory today, the king is thought incapable of committing a wrong (substantive dimension) and not answerable before justice (procedural dimension). Both dimensions were present, for instance, in Chrimes's definition of *the king can do no wrong*—'The King cannot be sued or held legally responsible'.[60] It will be shown in this book that the two dimensions of crown liability—capacity to do wrong and amenability to justice of the king—have been differently interpreted throughout the ages and that the distinction between the two has not always been understood. In fact, 'the actionable liability of the Crown for tort . . . is a subject upon which the distinction between procedure and substantive law has never been steadily maintained, at all events in the manner in which the Crown's immunity has been stated and explained'.[61]

In short, the heuristic model in this book is based on the premise that there are two dimensions to crown liability—the king's capacity to commit a wrong and the king's amenability to justice. The premise that crown liability can be understood as

[56] Cornford (n 1) 235. See also Harrison Moore, 'Liability for Acts of Public Servants' (1907) 23 LQR 12, 14; Laski (n 4) 447–48; Bradley Selway, 'Of Kings and Officers: The Judicial Development of Public Law' (2005) 33 FL Rev 187, 207; Wade and Forsyth (n 27) 653.

[57] McLean (n 12) 143–44.

[58] ibid.

[59] ibid; Allison (n 23) 177–79.

[60] Chrimes (n 33) 18.

[61] *Werrin v The Commonwealth* (1938) 59 CLR 150, 167 (Dixon J).

having two dimensions is derived from the understandings of *the king can do no wrong* in legal thinking and in cases and public law literature. The king's capacity to do wrong relates to the substantive dimension of crown liability and the king's amenability to justice concerns the procedural dimension.

3.2 Three notions

In light of the various understandings of *the king can do no wrong* listed above, the heuristic model in the book has been elaborated based on the proposition that there are three notions—identified from analysis of sources—influencing the two dimensions of crown liability. The three notions associated with *the king can do no wrong* point to the status of the two dimensions of crown liability.

The three notions evident in the understandings of *the king can do no wrong* listed in the first section of this chapter are the king's legal status in relation to law (whether the king is conceived as under or above the law), the perfection of the king (whether king is conceived as perfect or not), and the king's immunity from suit (whether king is immune from suit or not). That the king is under the law—or not—is a notion which can be associated with the king not being entitled to do wrong, whatever the king does is legal, and the king's wrongful commands are void. The notion of perfection of the king can be associated with the king is incapable of doing wrong. The notion of immunity from suit can be associated with the first understanding of *the king can do no wrong* listed above.

As to the first notion—the king's status in relation to law—it is not the purpose of this book to analyse the constitutional position of the king as a whole throughout history. The scope of such an inquiry would far exceed that of this book. The notion is rather intended to encapsulate the king's status in relation to law in connection with his capacity to do wrong—the first dimension of the model. The notion of the king's status in relation to law serves a functional analytical purpose and is analysed in connection with the other notions. The second notion, the perfection of the king, refers to the monarch's infallibility in legal thinking. The third notion, the king's immunity from suit, relates to the king's immunity from ordinary actions and other procedures.

The three notions are incorporated in the heuristic model in this book to analyse the evolution of *the king can do no wrong* in legal thinking and therefore allow a better understanding of the two dimensions of crown liability throughout history—the king's capacity to do wrong and amenability to justice. The variability of the combination of the three notions influences the two dimensions of crown liability. The ordering of the three notions does not have an impact on the analysis: the way notion 2 is interpreted—whether the king was conceived as perfect or not—does not depend on the way notions 1 and 3 are interpreted. The ordering of the notions is not relevant in determining how the two dimensions of crown liability were conceived in legal thinking. If, for example, the king was conceived of as not being perfect in legal thinking, he was logically capable of doing wrong. The king's capacity to do wrong, however, was also dependent on his status in relation to law. If the king was imperfect but above the law, his capacity to do wrong was negated because he was not subject to law and could not therefore commit a wrong in the eye of the law. If the king was subject to law and not conceived of as perfect, he was capable of doing a wrong. As for the procedural dimension of crown liability—whether the king was amenable to justice—it can be understood by studying the notion of the king's immunity from suit, supplemented by the study of the availability of other remedies against the king.[62]

It will be demonstrated throughout this book how the three notions were conceived of in legal thinking considering the understandings of the *king can do no wrong*.

Finally, the analysis of the understandings of *the king can do no wrong* drawn from the sources for this book allows us to conclude that three notions can be associated with these understandings. The three notions—the king's status in relation to law, the perfection of the king, and the king's immunity from suit—influence the two dimensions of crown liability. It will be further demonstrated in the following chapters that a study of the evolution of the understandings of *the king can do no wrong* in legal thinking guided by the model—which entails an analysis of the three notions: the king's status in relation to law, his perfection, and his immunity from suit—can enlighten how the two dimensions of crown liability—the king's capacity to do wrong and amenability to justice—were understood historically. The way the three notions interact in legal scholars' writings and in cases where *the king can do no wrong* was invoked or discussed allows us to understand better how the king's capacity to do wrong (whether the king is capable of committing a wrong) and the king's amenability to justice (the king's immunity from suit and other legal remedies) were understood—or forgotten—over time.

[62] In some instances, the vocabulary used in this book and the model developed for the purpose of investigating the evolution of *the king can do no wrong* in legal thinking can be explained in relation to Hohfeld's definition of the legal terms he identified and the correlative and opposite relationships they convey: see Wesley Hohfeld, *Fundamental Legal Conceptions as Applied in Judicial Reasoning* (W Cook ed, Yale UP 1923). For instance, the king being referred to as being 'not entitled to do wrong' in this book would translate in Hohfeldian terms as 'disabled' to do wrong because he was not given the 'power'—the jurisdiction—to do wrong. However, in other cases, a Hohfeldian vocabulary could risk being ahistorical. The Hohfeldian jural opposites 'immunity' and 'liability', do not translate to the model: 'liability' in this book is also understood as the king's capacity to do wrong—the possibility of ascribing a wrong to the crown. Immunity from suit does correspond to an individual's 'disability' to sue the king by ordinary action, but the individual—as will be shown—could use other remedies. The king's capacity to do wrong—whether the king is conceived of as being capable of doing wrong—is analysed regardless of the subject's capacity to sue the king. Moreover, in the context of the first dimension of this book's model, it is the relationship between the king and the law itself which is the object of the enquiry, and that relationship differs from Hohfeld's theory understood as resting on the premise that legal conceptions were 'conceptions about relationships between people, and that the words which expressed these conceptions functioned by referring to these relationships': AWB Simpson, *Legal Theory and Legal History: Essays on the Common Law* (Hambledon 1987) 350.

3.3 Limitations of the model

The heuristic model outlined in this chapter does not result in mathematical precision. For instance, where the king is under the law (notion 1) and not perfect (notion 2), it would be possible to conclude that the king is not immune from suit (notion 3). However, the model is used to understand *the king can do no wrong* in a historical context. The model is not used in vacuum. It is used to grasp how *the king can do no wrong* was understood during a given historical period in light of the model's three notions but other factors can contribute to shift the understanding of the two dimensions of crown liability in legal thinking. For example, the king may have been under the law (notion 1), not perfect (notion 2), and could therefore have been found not to be immune from suit (notion 3) but external considerations may have influenced the understanding of the procedural dimensions of crown liability—such as medieval theological imperatives to the effect that the king had no superior but God. When used to interpret *the king can do no wrong* in a historical context, the possible outcomes identified by the model are therefore contingent on other past factors external to the model.

4 Conclusion: analysis of crown liability through the evolution of *the king can do no wrong*

In summary, the analysis of the evolution of the understandings of *the king can do no wrong* in legal thinking is facilitated in this book by the model, which is based on the premise that there are two dimensions to crown liability, a substantive and a procedural one. The substantive dimension of crown liability—the king's capacity to do wrong—is influenced by the notions of the king's status in relation to law and the notion of perfection of the king. The procedural dimension of crown liability—the king's amenability to justice—is influenced by the notion of the king's immunity from suit and includes the availability of remedies such as the petition of right. Therefore, the two dimensions of crown liability are influenced by three notions—the king's status in relation to law, the king's perfection, and the king's immunity from suit. The hypothesis submitted in this book is that the study of the evolution in legal thinking of the understandings of *the king can do no wrong*—facilitated by relying on the model's three notions—can shed new light on our understanding of crown liability in its two dimensions and how that understanding evolved in legal thinking over time.

2
The King Can Do No Wrong in The Late Medieval and Tudor Periods

1 Overview of the chapter

Traditionally in scholarly writing, *the king can do no wrong* is traced back to medieval England[1] and the first written record of this now well-known maxim is said to date to the end of the fifteenth century.[2] Borchard[3] and Laski[4] have hypothesized—and Keir and Lawson have assumed[5]—that the original medieval understanding of *the king can do no wrong* changed from a conception of limitation of the king's power to one of a blanket immunity under the Tudors' despotism.[6] In this chapter, it will be demonstrated that although *the king can do no wrong* understood as the king is not entitled to do wrong can be traced back to Bracton, *the king can do no wrong* itself was coined in legal literature at the turn of the seventeenth century, and was given pride of place in Edward Coke's work, fundamental to the history of the common law.

[1] Edwin Borchard, 'Government Liability in Tort' (1924) 34 YLJ 1, 2–3; Ludwik Ehrlich, 'Proceedings against the Crown (1216–1377)' in Paul Vinogradoff (ed), *Oxford Studies in Social and Legal History*, vol 6 (Clarendon Press 1921) 42; David E Engdahl, 'Immunity and Accountability for Positive Governmental Wrongs' (1972) 44 U Colo L Rev 1, 2–3; WS Holdsworth, 'The History of Remedies against the Crown I' (1922) 38 LQR 141, 143–46; Frederick Pollock and FW Maitland, *The History of English Law Before the Time of Edward I*, vol 1 (2nd, reissued edn, CUP 1968) 515; Robert Dorsey Watkins, *The State as a Party Litigant* (Johns Hopkins Press 1927) 4–11.

[2] (1483) YB Trin 1 Edw V, fo 8a, pl 13; SB Chrimes, *English Constitutional Ideas in the Fifteenth Century* (CUP 1936) 45; WS Holdsworth, *A History of English Law*, vol 5 (1st edn, Methuen 1924) 466; Kenneth Pickthorn, *Early Tudor Government: Henry VII* (CUP 1934) 162; Clayton Roberts, *The Growth of Responsible Government in Stuart England* (CUP 1966) 4; Sir John Baker, *The Reinvention of Magna Carta 1216–1616* (CUP 2017) 45.

[3] Edwin Borchard, 'Governmental Responsibility in Tort, VI' (1926) 36 YLJ 1, 30–31.

[4] Harold J Laski, 'The Responsibility of the State in England' (1919) 32 Harv L Rev 447, 448.

[5] David L Keir and FH Lawson, *Cases in Constitutional Law* (FH Lawson and DJ Bentley eds, 6th edn, Clarendon Press 1979) 72.

[6] Watkins also appears to point to the Tudor era and the emergence of the concept of sovereignty as the turning point: Watkins (n 1) 11. Holdsworth did not recognize that the Bractonian understanding of *the king can do no wrong* conveyed a limitation on the king not to do wrong. He posited instead that *the king can do no wrong* originally meant, at the end of the fifteenth century, that the king could not be sued for a wrong and came to mean in the sixteenth century that the king could not be sued and his agents were liable instead: Holdsworth (n 1) 154.

The King Can Do No Wrong. Marie-France Fortin, Oxford University Press. © Marie-France Fortin 2024.
DOI: 10.1093/9780191994487.003.0003

2 Three notions underlying the king's liability

The objectives in this section are twofold. The first objective is to identify the understanding of *the king can do no wrong* as the king is not entitled to do wrong in one of the major legal treatises of the late Middle Ages—known as Bracton—and in cases from the late medieval and Tudor periods. The second objective is to trace the development of the three notions of this book's heuristic model—the king's legal status in relation to law, his perfection, and his immunity from suit—which related to *the king can do no wrong* from the late Middle Ages to the Tudor era and underpinned the two dimensions of crown liability.

2.1 The king's status in relation to law

The writing in the first half of the thirteenth century of the *Treatise on the Laws of England*,[7] known as Bracton's,[8] constituted the main general legal treatise of importance before Coke. As will be demonstrated in this section, Bracton's treatise reflected the contemporary understanding—evidenced in 1215 with Magna Carta[9] and King John's infamous reign—that the king was capable of doing wrong but that he was subject to law and not entitled to do wrong. English kings after the Conquest were never absolute rulers in the context of feudal relationships between the king and his tenants-in-chief and Bracton's writings reflect that situation.[10] Bracton's treatise is also relevant because jurists of the early modern period regained interest

[7] Henry de Bracton, *Bracton on the Laws and Customs of England*, vol 2 (George Edward Woodbine ed, Samuel E Thorne tr, Belknap Press of Harvard UP 1968).

[8] The treatise was authored and edited by justices of the royal courts, including Henry de Bratton (Bracton) himself, between the 1220s and 1260s: Thomas J McSweeney, *Priests of the Law: Roman Law and the Making of the Common Law's First Professionals* (OUP 2019). For ease of reference, 'Bracton' or 'Bracton's treatise' is used to identify the text originally titled *De legibus et consuetudinibus Angliae*. Henry de Bracton, *Bracton on the Laws and Customs of England*, vol 3 (George Edward Woodbine ed, Samuel E Thorne tr, Belknap Press of Harvard UP 1977) v–vi; xxxiii–lii. The authorship of the treatise has been contested but it is now generally accepted that Bracton was at least in possession of the text, whatever state it was then in, before it was edited by a redactor, and that Bracton himself contributed to the editing process: JH Baker, 'Bracton, Henry De' in AWB Simpson (ed), *Biographical Dictionary of the Common Law* (Butterworths 1984); Paul Brand, 'The Age of Bracton' in John Hudson (ed), *The History of English Law: Centenary Essays on 'Pollock and Maitland'* (OUP 1996); David Crook, 'Raleigh, William of (d 1250)', *Oxford Dictionary of National Biography* (online edn, January 2008, OUP 2004) <http://www.oxforddnb.com/view/article/23042> accessed 30 June 2019; Paul Brand, 'The Date and Authorship of *Bracton*: A Response' (2010) 31 JL H 217; Serge Dauchy and others (eds), *The Formation and Transmission of Western Legal Culture* (Springer International Publishing 2016) 32; Nicholas Vincent, 'Henry of Bratton (*Alias* Bracton)' in Mark Hill and RH Helmholz (eds), *Great Christian Jurists in English History* (CUP 2017) 39–42.

[9] See cl 61, which expressly provided for the enforcement of the charter by twenty-five barons were the king to commit wrongful acts: 'if we or our justiciary or our bailiffs or any of our servants offend against anyone one in any way, or transgress any of the articles of peace or security': JC Holt, *Magna Carta* (3rd edn, CUP 2015) 395.

[10] Eleanor Constance Lodge and Gladys A Thornton (eds), *English Constitutional Documents* (CUP 1935) 1–2.

in it—as is evidenced by the publication of a printed version in 1559—and frequently referred to it.[11]

Central to Bracton's theory of kingship was that the king was under God and the law because the law makes the king. That the king was limited in his rule is evidenced by Bracton's folios 107–07b, which show that being God's vicar did not give the king absolute perfection or authority: 'For the king, since he is the minister and vicar of God on earth, can do nothing save what he can do *de jure*' and 'His power is that of *jus* not *injuria*'.[12] Bracton also states, in what appears to be a paradoxical statement, that the king has no superior in his realm.[13] He had to maintain and administer the law, a duty imposed on him by his coronation oath, his duty as feudal overlord, and the absence of any other superior. The meaning of law in the late Middle Ages, the status of the king as under the law, and the absence of a superior above him, as well the king's duty to administer justice, will be studied in turn. Their relationship with *the king can do no wrong* understood in the Bractonian sense as the king is not entitled to do wrong will be explained.

2.1.1 Bracton's theory of kingship

The king's status in relation to law constitutes one of the notions of the model attaching to *the king can do no wrong*. As Ehrlich explains in his seminal study of proceedings against the crown in the thirteenth and fourteenth centuries, the king was not entitled to do wrong, meaning violating a right.[14] *The king can do no wrong*—the maxim was not yet coined—'meant, that the king must not, was not allowed, not entitled, to do wrong; his acts, if against the law, were not legal acts, but *iniuriae*, wrongs'.[15] An analysis of Bracton's work in this section demonstrates the validity of Ehrlich's claim. The ideas in Bracton's treatise that the king was under the law, that a wrong was attributed to the king, and that his jurisdiction did not include the power to do wrong will be analysed in turn, as will the conceptual difficulty that arose from the absence of a superior above the king.

2.1.1.1 The king is under the law

As was explained in Chapter 1, the notion of the king's status in relation to law—which is part of this book's heuristic model—is not to be understood as the king's status as a whole as under the law, but his status as under the law for a wrong.[16] It

[11] DEC Yale, 'Some Later Uses of Bracton' in Samuel E Thorne and Morris S Arnold (eds), *On the Laws and Customs of England: Essays in Honor of Samuel E Thorne* (University of North Carolina Press 1981); Michael Lobban, *A History of the Philosophy of Law in the Common Law World, 1600–1900*, vol 8 (E Pattaro ed, Springer 2007) 3.

[12] Bracton, vol 2 (n 7) 305–06.

[13] ibid 33, 157.

[14] Ehrlich (n 1) 42, 127–28; Baker (n 2) 45.

[15] Ehrlich (n 1) 42.

[16] Kantorowicz eg has argued that although the notion of 'positive' law in Bracton probably had a larger meaning than it did on the Continent, the prerogative was excluded from its ambit. The rights of the crown, or *res quasi sacrae*, were also not subject to prescription and were inalienable: Ernst

was clear to Bracton that a wrong could be imputed to the king and it was still the case in the fourteenth century.[17]

In Bracton's time the king was subject to the law and obligations to administer the law were imposed on him, although the king could not be coerced into fulfilling them. The notion that the king was subject to law was accepted in England from the thirteenth century.[18] That the king is subject to law was later reiterated by Fortescue, who was said to represent prevalent theories in the fifteenth century.[19] Although he did not refer to Bracton's treatise,[20] Fortescue emphasized—as had Bracton—the king's duty to rule in accordance with the law, as he held his power from the law that created him.[21] Coke in *Prohibitions del Roy*[22] and Blackstone in his *Commentaries*[23] later argued that the king's status as under the law is a fundamental principle of English law. That the king is subject to law raises, however, the issue of characterizing the concept of 'law' when Bracton's treatise was written.

The concept of 'law', even today, is the subject of academic debate. It is not to be expected that it should be any clearer in a medieval context. As Maitland observed, in the time of Bracton 'Our English lawyers have no philosophy of law, nor have they pursued very far the question, How does law, or a law, come into being?'[24] The absence of an effort to rationalize law was further evidenced by the absence of a distinction between legal rules (*lex*) and law (*ius*), and the two Latin terms were used interchangeably.[25] The ambiguity in relation to the concept of law was evidenced by the indiscriminate use of the words *lex*, *ius*, and *iustitita* in medieval texts. 'Law' in the Middle Ages could mean either justice or positive law.[26] Divine law, natural law, the law of nations (*ius gentium*), and positive law were all referred to by commentators in the Middle Ages.[27] Arguments have been made that the king in Bracton was under not only divine law but also under positive law. For instance, while he argued that the law Bracton was subjecting the king to was the 'Law of the land',[28] Kantorowicz emphasized that the meaning of 'law' the king was bound to

H Kantorowicz, *The King's Two Bodies, A Study in Medieval Political Theology* (first published 1957, Princeton UP 2016) 165–67.

[17] Ehrlich (n 1) 42, 43, 53, 127.
[18] ibid 40–43, 70; Holdsworth (n 1) 144.
[19] Chrimes (n 2) 306; FW Maitland, *The Constitutional History of England* (CUP 1963) 199.
[20] Interest in Bracton's work was at its lowest in the fifteenth century: Chrimes (n 2) 324.
[21] John Fortescue, *On the Laws and Governance of England* (Shelley Lockwood ed, CUP 1997) 48.
[22] (1607) 12 Co Rep 63 at 65, quoting Bracton: 'quod Rex non debet esse sub homine, sed sub Deo et lege'.
[23] William Blackstone, *Commentaries on the Laws of England*, vol 1 (facsimile of 1765–1769 1st edn, University of Chicago Press 1979) 232.
[24] Pollock and Maitland (n 1) 174.
[25] ibid.
[26] Ehrlich (n 1) 113.
[27] Kenneth Pennington, *The Prince and the Law, 1200–1600: Sovereignty and Rights in the Western Legal Tradition* (University of California Press 1993) 120; Gaines Post, 'Bracton on Kingship' (1967) 42 Tul L Rev 519, 523, 545–53.
[28] Kantorowicz (n 16) 147.

observe in Bracton was comprised of, but was also more encompassing than only, 'Natural Law' or the 'law of Reason'.[29] Tierney argued that there was not in Bracton a distinction between divine and natural law on the one hand and positive law on the other: the law Bracton said the king was under was the 'real complicated earthy law of England'.[30] Postema also understands Bracton as subjecting the king to the common law of England and not merely to natural or divine law.[31]

That English law was unwritten did not alter its status: English feudal society considered unwritten law—customs and conventions—as providing overriding governing principles.[32] Glanvill, writing before Bracton and relying on Roman law sources, was of the opinion that the laws of England were *leges* even if they were unwritten, as even the prince's will is *lex*.[33] Bracton recognized the value of usage and that it can confer to custom the status of *lex*.[34] He equally accepted that English unwritten laws were *leges*.[35] While other Western European thinkers of that period thought the prince subject to divine and natural law but transcending positive law thanks to his *potestas absoluta*,[36] Bracton appeared to believe that the king was subject to the unwritten English positive law and not solely to divine and natural law.

Bracton stated that the king is under God and the law, and that it is the law that makes the king, under the following folios: 5b ('The king must not be under man but under God and under the law, because law makes the king'), 34 ('The king has a superior, namely, God. Also the law by which he is made king'), 55b ('He in whose power it is to cause the laws, customs, and assises provided, approved and sworn in his realm to be observed by his people, ought himself to observe them in his own person'), and 107–07b ('For the king, since he is the minister and vicar of God on earth, can do nothing save what he can do *de jure* . . . His power is that of *jus*, not *injuria*').[37]

2.1.1.2 Attribution of a wrong to the king

In addition to the king being under the law, Bracton also stated that the king can commit a wrong. For instance, in folio 34 Bracton set out that 'one may say that the king has committed an *injuria*, and thus charge him with amending it'—*injuria*

[29] ibid 147–49.

[30] Brian Tierney, 'Bracton on Government' (1963) 38 Speculum 295, 304.

[31] Sir Matthew Hale, *On the Law of Nature, Reason, and Common Law: Selected Jurisprudential Writings* (Gerald Postema ed, OUP 2017) xxiv–xxv.

[32] Paul Vinogradoff (ed), *Oxford Studies in Social and Legal History*, vol 6 (Clarendon Press 1921) iii; FW Maitland, *Selected Passages from the Works of Bracton and Azo* (Quaritch 1894) 11.

[33] GDG Hall, *The Treatise on the Laws and Customs of the Realm of England, Commonly Called Glanvill* (Nelson 1965) 2.

[34] Bracton, vol 2 (n 7) 22.

[35] ibid 19.

[36] Pennington (n 27) 120.

[37] Bracton, vol 2 (n 7) 33, 110, 166, and 305–06.

meaning a legal wrong.[38] Similarly, Bracton in folios 368–69 explained that if the king learned that he had been deceived by false representations, but nonetheless persisted in supporting the wrongful party (in the context of these folios, a tenant), then 'the *injuria* from then on it will be the *injuria* of the king himself'.[39] In folio 5, Bracton set out that it can be asked of the king 'that he correct and amend his act', implying again that the king was capable of committing a wrong.[40] That the king was capable of committing a wrong and that his subject could ask him to amend his *injuria*, for instance when the king granted something to one the 'prejudice of the liberties of others', also featured in folios 56b[41] and 34: 'one may say that the king has committed an *injuria*, and thus charge him with amending it, lest he and the justices fall into the judgement of the living God because of it'.[42] Lastly, that the king was not considered to be perfect or divine but was thought a simple man capable of being deceived is apparent from folio 369: 'for the king may be deceived since he is a man, but God can never be deceived since he is God'.[43]

Folio 171b is another instance where Bracton described a wrong as having been committed by the king. Bracton stated there that in the case of a remedy of assize (an assize of 'novel disseisin') where the defendant has received seisin following the king's or the king's officers' disseisin of the plaintiff, the action must fall as no action may lie against the king (diseisin was akin to the dispossession of one's free tenement without judgment). In such a case the king is the original 'disseisor', the first and principal disseisor, and the defendant to whom the property was transferred another principal.[44] While the absence of a recourse against the king will be discussed further in section 2.3, the emphasis here is on folio 171b as it indicates that in such a situation, the *injuria* is to be attributed to the king:

[38] To Richardson, the term *injuria* referred to the breach of a right and the cause of a right of action, in addition to referring to pleas of the crown for breach of the king's peace: HG Richardson, *Bracton: The Problem of His Text* (Selden Society 1965) 51.

[39] Henry de Bracton, *Bracton on the Laws and Customs of England*, vol 4 (George Edward Woodbine ed, Samuel E Thorne tr, Belknap Press of Harvard UP 1977) 159.

[40] Bracton, vol 2 (n 7) 33.

[41] ibid 169.

[42] ibid 110. Cases from the thirteenth century also demonstrate that a party, eg the king's grantee, could not benefit from the king's wrongful disseisin: see pl 769, 1106, and 1108 in FW Maitland, *Bracton's Note Book: A Collection of Cases Decided in the King's Courts during the Reign of Henry the Third*, vols 1–3 (reprint of 1887 edn, CUP 2010) 586–88 (vol 2), 123–28 (vol 3).

[43] Bracton, vol 4 (n 39) 159.

[44] On the concept of seisin in medieval land law and on the assize of novel disseisin, which appeared under Henry II, perhaps in 1166, see Donald W Sutherland, *The Assize of Novel Disseisin* (Clarendon Press 1973); AWB Simpson, *A History of the Land Law* (2nd edn, Clarendon Press 1986) 28–33, 37–44. For a discussion of actions against the king via a third party, see Ralph V Turner, *The King and His Courts: The Role of John and Henry III in the Administration of Justice, 1199–1240* (Cornell UP 1968) 253; Ralph V Turner, 'The Royal Courts Treat Disseizin by The King: John and Henry III, 1199–1240' (1968) 12 Am J Leg Hist 1. Turner notes that assizes of novel disseisin were heard from time to time by royal judges, who either dismissed them or referred them to the king for his judgment, as was the procedure laid down by Bracton in fo 171b.

> But if another is in seisin by the act and disseisin of the prince, . . . he has not done so alone but with another, that is, with the prince, and . . . the person of the prince may be brought in, to the extent that he amend his deed, or the *injuria* will clearly fall upon him. . . . from then on the act and the *injuria* will be on the head of the lord king, . . . and from then on he can if he wishes amend his act, compelled, so to speak by the law, which, since he is subject to it, he ought faithfully to observe.[45]

Similar language attributing fault to the king is found under folio 204, where it is further explained that the action must fall against the other principal disseisor, to whom the king gave seisin following his disseisin, as he cannot answer without the principal disseisor, the king, with whom he committed the wrong.[46]

Relying on pleadings recorded during the reign of Edward III, Holdsworth noted that 'in 1342–1343 there was no hesitation in imputing a wrong to the king'.[47] A study of the judiciary under King John and King Henry III in the twelfth and thirteenth centuries also allowed an author to conclude that 'justices knew that the king was a man who could do wrong. From time to time, they witnessed the king's anger; for example, he closed his courts to certain suitors because of ill will toward them.'[48] Ehrlich similarly noted that lawyers of the thirteenth century did not hesitate to say that the king had committed a wrong—either himself or through his servants—including a wrongful disseisin, 'the wrong which we should consider the one most corresponding with a modern tort'.[49] That the *injuria* was recognized as the king's meant that legal wrongs committed by the king or by his officers acting in his name were attributed to the king: the king could do wrong and the presumption was that the wrongful act was the king's act.[50] A legal wrong included the violation of a subject's right.[51] The king could not do an *injuria* in the sense that the king was not allowed, not entitled to do a legal wrong: the king was under the law and 'ought' not to do wrong.[52]

2.1.1.3 The king's jurisdiction

That the wrong was the king's is clear from folios 34, 171b, 204, and 368–69, discussed in section 2.1.1.2. Folios 368–69 could, however, be construed as introducing a distinction between *injuria* and deed, and can be read to imply that although the *injuria* is the king's, if the king's deed is wrongful, then the deed is not

45 Bracton, vol 3 (n 8) 43.

46 ibid 118; Turner, 'Disseizin by the King' (n 44) 12.

47 (1343) YB Hil 17 Edw III, RS, fo 164, pl 34; Holdsworth (n 2) 465.

48 Ralph V Turner, *The English Judiciary in the Age of Glanvill and Bracton, c1176–1239* (CUP 1985) 275.

49 Ehrlich (n 1) 14.

50 ibid 26, 127; Holdsworth (n 2) 465; Borchard (n 3) 22.

51 Ehrlich (n 1) 42.

52 Bracton, vol 2 (n 7) 305.

the king's. Although it is not the king's, the deed cannot be revoked without the king's consent.[53]

Although the understanding that a wrongful deed is not the king's is similar to two understandings of *the king can do no wrong*—that the king cannot commit a wrong because the king is perfect, or that the king cannot be sued for a wrong because he can do no wrong in law—there are two substantial differences. First, in Bracton's work, the wrong was the king's to begin with. Bracton's initial premise—that the king has committed the wrong—is diametrically opposed to the Blackstonian understanding of *the king can do no wrong* that the king cannot be conceived to have committed or even to have thought a wrong.[54] In Bracton's theory, the wrong is the king's to begin with—'the injuria will fall on the king'. As will be discussed in Chapter 4, in cases decided since the nineteenth century, the wrong is never attributed to the king.[55] Second, Bracton, after setting out that the deed is not the king's if it is wrongful, then adds that the same deed can be questioned and judged. Bracton's conclusion is again diametrically opposed to the conclusion drawn in the nineteenth century that the king's wrongful act at common law cannot give rise to a remedy.[56]

That the deed was deemed not to be the king's if it was wrongful, whereas a wrong could be attributed to the king may appear to be paradoxical. The paradox can be resolved by reference to Bracton's statement that the king, when committing a wrong, is exceeding his jurisdiction (which is limited to *jus*, and does not extend to *injuria*). If the king exceeds his jurisdiction and commits a wrong, he can therefore have his act judged. It is precisely because the wrongful deed is deemed not to be the king's that it can be judged: it would otherwise be impossible, as the king has no superior. The notion that the wrongful deed is not the king's—although the wrong is attributed to the king—serves the purpose of allowing redress to be had against the king. The king committed the wrong but because it exceeded his power as king, it was not an act that a king can commit. As the wrong was not an act that the king was entitled to commit, it fell beyond the scope of kingly deeds and thereby was not immune from scrutiny. Baldus similarly thought that when the king went against the *dignitas* of his office, his actions were void.[57] The king's jurisdiction derived from the right to discharge his office and his acts could not

[53] Bracton, vol 4 (n 39) 159.

[54] William Blackstone gave prominence to the notion of perfection of the king in the eighteenth century: see Chapter 4, Section 2.1. That *the king can do no wrong* meant that the king is capable of committing a wrong and is diametrically opposed to its more recent meaning that the king is incapable of committing a wrong was noted by Borchard (n 1) 2; Ehrlich (n 1) 42; Louis L Jaffe, 'Suits against Governments and Officers: Sovereign Immunity' (1963) 77 Harv L Rev 1, 3–4; Tom Cornford, 'Legal Remedies against the Crown before and after M' in Maurice Sunkin and Sebastian Payne (eds), *The Nature of the Crown: A Legal and Political Analysis* (OUP 1999) 235; Maurice Sunkin, 'Crown Immunity from Criminal Liability in English Law' [2003] PL 716, 720.

[55] See Chapter 4, section 3.3.1.

[56] *Feather v The Queen* (1865) 6 B&S 257, 295 (122 ER 1191) (Cockburn CJ).

[57] Guido Rossi, 'Baldus and the Limits of Representation' (2018) 86 Leg Hist Rev 55, 77.

be imputed to the crown when they could not derive from the crown.[58] Only the rightful acts of a king benefited from the absence of a superior above the king. The study of folios 368–69 therefore allows us to expand on the many ideas found in Bracton's treatise, namely the king's 'jurisdiction',[59] his position in relation to law, and the absence of a superior above him.

The passage about the wrongful deed of the king has an echo, first, in folios 107–07b, where Bracton clearly stated that the king is *rex* inasmuch as he rules well.[60] Bracton expounded the idea that the king was not authorized to commit a wrong in folio 107, where he stated that the king, being God's vicar on earth, was king only inasmuch as he ruled according to the law: 'the king . . . can do nothing save what he can do *de jure*' and '[h]is power is that of *jus*, not *injuria*'.[61] The king was perceived as doing the devil's work when acting according to the power of *injuria* and achieving God's work when acting with the power of *jus*.[62] If he did not, his acts were consequently not those of a king. Folios 368–69 therefore provide an illustration of the limits of the king's 'jurisdiction': if the act was wrongful, it was not the king's, because it exceeded his power to act *de jure*.

The first part of folios 107–07b relates to the power of the king, his jurisdiction. It does not speak to his status in relation to law. In fact, Bracton made clear later in folios 107–07b, following the passage on the king being *rex* only from ruling according to justice, that the king was subject to law.[63]

The law which protected the subjects' rights was a limitation on the king's jurisdiction.[64] Holdsworth, in his famous *A History of English Law*, argued that to restrict the king's jurisdiction to act according to law did not constitute a limitation of the king's power, because 'Incapacity to err is the mark of the Deity'.[65] Holdsworth's interpretation, however, does not accord with Bracton's theory: it is clear from Bracton's writings that he conceived of the king as being capable of doing wrong and even of choosing to do wrong. That the king in such circumstances would be doing the devil's work in Bracton's thinking highlights the fact that he did not

[58] ibid 79.

[59] Bracton himself did not classify these ideas. In addition, there was not in medieval times a clear distinction between the king's 'jurisdiction', his legislative power, and his executive powers: Tierney (n 30) 307–08; Ewart Lewis, 'King above Law? "Quod Principi Placuit" in Bracton' (1964) 39 Speculum 240, 266; cf Charles Howard McIlwain, *Constitutionalism, Ancient and Modern* (revised edn, Cornell UP 1947) 76; Kantorowicz (n 16) 148; Martin Loughlin, 'The State, the Crown and the Law' in Maurice Sunkin and Sebastian Payne (eds), *The Nature of the Crown: A Legal and Political Analysis* (OUP 1999) 49–51.

[60] Blecker also made a connection between fos 107 and 368–69 in Michael Blecker, 'The King's Partners in Bracton' (1984) 96 Studi Senesi 66, 94–95.

[61] Bracton, vol 2 (n 7) 305–06.

[62] A parallel can be drawn here with the extent of the king's power to legislate as identified by Tierney: Tierney (n 30) 305–06.

[63] Bracton, vol 2 (n 7) 305–06.

[64] Gaines Post, *Studies in Medieval Legal Thought: Public Law and the State, 1100–1322* (Princeton UP 1964) 321.

[65] WS Holdsworth, *A History of English Law*, vol 2 (3rd edn, Methuen 1923) 253.

consider the king to be of divine perfection. The king could decide to do wrong, but in so doing he exceeded the power given to him by God and the law. Bracton's statement that the king must act according to law constituted a limitation of the king's jurisdiction.

2.1.2 Tudor era

Although *the king can do no wrong* could not be found in its exact form as an expression in cases of the sixteenth century, the understanding in the late Middle Ages—that the king was not entitled to do wrong—can be found in various sources. It appears for instance in the case of *Duke of Buckingham v Bishop of Winchester*, where it is reasoned that the king cannot deny any man justice, as that would 'do him wrong'.[66]

The Bractonian understanding of *the king can do no wrong*—that the king is not entitled to do wrong—can also be found in a note from Spelman dating to 1509.[67] Commenting on what is presumably a reading at the Inns of Court, Spelman noted that the king could not be a disseisor and discussed the fiction that he automatically lost possession when he had no legal right to it. Spelman hypothesized that if the prince was a disseisor upon his accession to the throne, he lost possession of the land that had been wrongfully taken when becoming king. Spelman's understanding of the maxim that the king cannot be a disseisor and the fiction that he automatically lost possession if land was held wrongly demonstrates that legal thinking was still to the effect that the king was not entitled to do wrong. That the king could not be a disseisor was still interpreted in the early sixteenth century as it originally was in the late Middle Ages. It meant a special limitation on the king's jurisdiction—it restricted the acts the king could commit to lawful acts.

The case of *Willion v Berkley* in 1562 constitutes the next prominent use of the Bractonian understanding of *the king can do no wrong* in reports of the sixteenth century. In that seminal case, Plowden reported that the defendants' counsel argued that 'every discontinuance is a wrong, which the king cannot do'.[68] Brown J also ruled in *Willion v Berkley* that the king was not entitled to do wrong: 'for the King cannot do any wrong, nor will his prerogative be any warrant to him to do an injury to another'.[69]

The issue in *Willion v Berkley* was whether the king was bound by an act, *De Donis Conditionalibus*, which attempted to prevent the donee—and his heirs—from alienating the land granted to them by the donor and to ensure that the donor's will was to be followed and that the land would pass to the donee's issue. In *Willion v Berkley*, the land had been gifted by the donor to the king and to his male

[66] (1515) Pasch King's Council in John Caryll, *Reports of Cases by John Caryll*, vol 2 (JH Baker ed, Selden Society 1999) 670.

[67] John Spelman, *The Reports of Sir John Spelman*, vol 1 (JH Baker ed, Selden Society 1977) 172.

[68] *Willion v Berkley* (1562) 1 Plowden 223, 233.

[69] ibid 246.

issue. Brown J ruled that it was a wrong for the king to make an alienation in fee to another person than his male heirs as was the will of the donor. The effect of an alienation to another party was to prevent the land from reverting to the donor or his issues. The king was not authorized to do such a wrong:

> [F]or such alienation would have been a wrong in another person, and so should it have been in the King, if it were adjudged an alienation in fee, and therefore he could not do it, for the King cannot do any wrong, nor will his prerogative be any warrant to him to do an injury to another.
>
> ...
>
> And he that will maintain that the King is in a degree to make such alienation, must at the same time maintain that the King may do wrong, and that the law suffers him to do wrong, which none can maintain; and it is a difficult argument to prove that a statute, which restrains men generally from doing wrong, leaves the King at liberty to do wrong.[70]

Although Brown J did not use the exact words *the king can do no wrong*, the phrasing is very similar and is used to convey the Bractonian understanding that the king is not entitled to do wrong. In relation to the king's liability, Brown J also found that 'if the King kills a man, there is no remedy in the law, and yet it is not well done'.[71] The king was capable of killing a man but it remained a wrong. Although there was no remedy—the petition of right, although it had a large scope of application, would not have covered personal bodily injury caused by the king[72]—Brown J conceived of the king's killing as a wrong and attributed it to the king. The understanding of *the king can do no wrong* was the same in *Willion v Berkley* as it was in Bracton. The king was thought of as capable of committing a wrong and the wrong was attributed to the king.

It was also held in *Willion v Berkley* that the king's prerogative did not apply to exempt him or to favour him when it was found after a petition that the king was not entitled to land and was holding it wrongly. Dyer CJ argued that in such a case of restitution to the rightful owner, when it was found that the king did wrong in holding another's land, 'words shall be taken most strongly against the king, and his prerogative shall not hold place, nor shall he be favoured more than another person'.[73] Dyer CJ's words in *Willion v Berkley* echoed Bracton's statement that the king 'ought to be the last, or almost so' to receive justice when he is a plaintiff.[74] In fact, Dyer CJ's speech to the effect that words should be interpreted most strongly against the king constituted a stronger stance on the understanding that *the king*

70 ibid 246, 248 (Brown J).
71 ibid 247.
72 See Ludwik Ehrlich, 'Petitions of Right' (1929) 45 LQR 60.
73 *Willion v Berkley* (n 68) 252.
74 Bracton, vol 2 (n 7) 33.

can do no wrong than Bracton's. That the king was not entitled to do wrong—he was only entitled to act *de jure*—can be found in Bracton's. Bracton denied any favour to the king, but only in cases where the king was a plaintiff.[75] On the other hand, Dyer CJ also denied any favour to the king when the king was a defendant in the context of a petition, having acted wrongfully. That the king was not entitled to do wrong received an even broader application in Dyer CJ's words in *Willion v Berkley* than it did in Bracton's.

In short, the Bractonian understanding that the king is not entitled to do wrong—which featured notably in Plowden's reports of *Willion v Berkley* and *Nichols Case*[76]—remained unchanged in the sixteenth century, contrary to the view of Borchard, Laski, Keir, and Lawson reported in the introduction to this chapter.

2.2 Perfection of the king

English kings were not considered to be perfect in the Middle Ages. The king as a Christ-like figure is characteristic of this period,[77] but English jurists of the Middle Ages were said to be 'less messianically minded'[78] than Continental glossators. Already in the twelfth century, theocratic kingship based on a Christ-like king was the reminiscence of an already bygone era.[79] It represented an even more remote period at the time Bracton's treatise was written in the thirteenth century. Bracton did not consider Henry III—or any English king—to be descended from the heavens to rule in God's stead.[80]

To Kantorowicz, the dual nature of the king, both human and divine—*persona mixta* or *gemina persona*—in the Middle Ages marked a duality between spiritual and temporal capacities of the king.[81] It did not, in Kantorowicz's opinion, mark a distinction between a natural body and a politic one. Kantorowicz saw no direct relationship between the medieval duality of the king and the Tudor kings' two bodies.[82] There remained between the Christ-like king of the Middle Ages and the Tudor king's two bodies a 'perplexing physiological difference'.[83] There was not in the Year Books any reference to the king's two bodies either.[84]

As will be demonstrated in this section, the notion of perfection of the body politic of the king, when it was developed during the Tudor era, was tied to the

[75] ibid.
[76] *Nichols v Nichols* (1576) 2 Plowden 477, 487.
[77] Kantorowicz (n 16) 45; Martin Loughlin, *Foundations of Public Law* (OUP 2010) 41–42.
[78] Kantorowicz (n 16) 147.
[79] ibid 44–46; Loughlin (n 77) 41.
[80] Kantorowicz (n 16) 147.
[81] ibid 45.
[82] ibid.
[83] ibid 46. On the other hand, Loughlin identified the *gemina persona* of the Middle Ages as the precursor of the famed sixteenth-century doctrine of the two bodies of the king: Loughlin (n 77) 41–42.
[84] FW Maitland, 'The Crown as Corporation' (1901) 17 LQR 131, 134.

doctrine of the king's two bodies. In this section, a different perspective to Kantorowicz's is adopted in relation to the doctrine of the king's two bodies. The perspective Kantorowicz adopted in his seminal study *The King's Two Bodies* was to demonstrate the theological groundings of the doctrine of the king's two bodies.[85] Consequently, the emphasis in his description of the two bodies of the king was on the theological influences that can be traced in the concept of two bodies and perfection of the body politic.[86] An internal legal perspective is adopted in this section to analyse legal sources during the Tudor era, especially cases reported by Plowden.[87] As the approach is to focus primarily on legal sources and legal thinking, the analysis of the doctrine of the king's two bodies in the case of the *Dutchy of Lancaster* and *Willion v Berkley* differ from Kantorowicz's. Costanzo, reviewing Kantorowicz's work on the king's two bodies, would have liked the author to expand more on the practical use Tudor jurists made of the fiction to secure 'private and public rights, privileges, and prerogatives in public law'.[88] My aim is to answer part of Costanzo's wish by drawing conclusions about the doctrine of the king's two bodies and the notion of perfection of the king in relation to *the king can do no wrong*.

Fortescue's thinking in relation to the notion of perfection of the king is presented briefly first, and its similarity to Bracton's thinking is also put into focus. The second section then turns to the doctrine of the king's two bodies as it was developed in the Elizabethan period and its relationship with the notion of perfection. The third section looks at the doctrine's impact on our understanding of *the king can do no wrong*.

2.2.1 Fortescue and the political king's perfection

Both Maitland and Kantorowicz saw the cases reported by Plowden as the starting point for the theory of the king's two bodies; Kantorowicz and Loughlin also argued that hints of the theory could be found in Fortescue's writings. To Kantorowicz, the religious grounding for the perfection of the king's body politic was manifest

[85] Kantorowicz (n 16) 8–9; Conrad Leyser, 'Introduction' in ibid xix–xx. See also William Chester Jordan's preface to the 1997 reprint of the 1957 edition, xxv–xxvi.

[86] Kantorowicz, for instance, submitted that Fortescue's allusion to the perfection of angels—devoid of infirmities and old age—influenced the notion of the perfection of the king's body politic: Kantorowicz (n 16) 8–9. cf Paul Raffield, *Shakespeare's Imaginary Constitution: Late-Elizabethan Politics and the Theatre of Law* (Hart Publishing 2010) 89, 92.

[87] On criticism of Kantorowicz's work when it was published and the more recent criticism of his treatment of Plowden, see: Norman F Cantor, 'Review, The King's Two Bodies: A Study in Political Theology' (1958) 64 Am Hist Rev 81; Ewart Lewis, 'Review, The King's Two Bodies: A Study in Medieval Political Theology' (1958) 73 Pol Sci Q 453; Joseph F Costanzo, 'Review, The King's Two Bodies: A Study in Medieval Political Theology' (1959) 321 Annals Am Acad Pol & Soc Sci 203; David Norbrook, 'The Emperor's New Body? Richard II, Ernst Kantorowicz, and the Politics of Shakespeare Criticism' (1996) 10 Textual Practice 329; Lorna Hutson, 'Not the King's Two Bodies: Reading the Body Politic in Shakespeare's Henry IV, Parts 1 and 2' in Victoria Ann Kahn and Lorna Hutson (eds), *Rhetoric and Law in Early Modern Europe* (Yale UP 2001).

[88] Costanzo (n 87) 204.

in Fortescue's work and may well have inspired Tudor lawyers in developing the theory of the king's two bodies.[89] On closer inspection, however, Fortescue's work shows a similitude with Bracton's. His writings certainly allude to defects, impotency, and divine perfection, but they do not lend themselves easily to supporting the notion of a perfect king who is entitled to do wrong. Rather, Fortescue's king did not have the power to do wrong.

Fortescue's theory in *On the Governance of England*, was that there were two kings: the king ruling royally and the king ruling politically:

> [T]he power of the two kings [the king ruling royally and the king ruling politically] is equal since the power by which one of them is free to do wrong does not increase his freedom, just as to be able to be ill or to die is not power, but is rather to be deemed impotency because of the deprivation involved. For, as Boethius said, 'There is no power unless for good' so that to be able to do evil, as the king reigning royally can more freely do than the king ruling his people politically, diminishes rather than increases his power. For the holy spirits who, already confirmed in glory, are unable to sin, are more powerful than we, who with a free rein take delight in any deed.[90]

In England, according to Fortescue, the king was ruling both politically and royally. While the king ruling royally was all-powerful, Fortescue was adamant that the political king he devised should not be conceived of as limited; the fact that the king was not entitled to do wrong therefore had to be addressed, and Fortescue rebranded the capacity to do wrong as a 'nonpower' or 'impotence'.[91] The king being free of the impotence that is the power of doing wrong, he was presented as delivered from the 'nonpower' of sin. Fortescue's metaphysical conception of the king's perfection was devised to hide the fact that the English king was not entitled to do wrong.

The excerpt Kantorowicz relied on in support of his argument that Fortescue's king was of divine perfection—like the 'angels'—is the following, taken from *Governance of England*:

> Just as it is no power to be able to sin, and to do ill, or to be able to be sick, or to grow old, or for a man to be able to hurt himself. For all these powers come of impotency. And therefore they may properly be called non-powers. Wherefore the

[89] Maitland (n 84); Kantorowicz (n 16) 7–8; Loughlin (n 59) 52.

[90] Fortescue (n 21) 23–24.

[91] 'This is a very significant part of Fortescue's theory; it is important that the "political" nature of the monarchy should not be seen to reduce the power of the king or to place limitations on it, therefore Fortescue employs the notion of "nonpower" or "impotence". Power to sin is not power but impotence, therefore the king's inability to err, makes him more divine than human, he is perfectly free and all-powerful (*Praise*, ch. xiv, p. 24; *Governance*, chs 6 and 19, pp. 95, 122; *Nature*, Appendix A)': Shelley Lockwood, 'Introduction' in ibid xxix.

> holy spirits and angels, who are not able to sin, grow old, be sick, or hurt themselves have more power than we, who may harm ourselves with all these defects. So the king's power is greater, in that he may not put from himself possessions necessary for his own sustenance, than if he might put them from himself, and alienate the same to his own hurt and harm.[92]

Lockwood, in the introduction to his edition of Fortescue's work, interprets this passage of Fortescue's *Governance of England* to mean that the king 'becomes character *angelicus*'.[93] But as Lockwood also explains, 'as king, he does not have the capacity or power to sin, he has his power for good and good alone, good being defined as the common good'.[94]

On closer inspection, the king's divine-like perfection is not what Fortescue implied in the excerpted passage. The reference to holy spirits did not mean that Fortescue's king was of divine perfection and therefore did not commit wrong. Rather, this excerpt from Fortescue's *Governance of England* is to the effect that limitations on the king were not limitations because he did not have the power to do wrong to begin with. He was, like the angels, deprived of the power to do wrong. Angels are incapable of doing wrong, and the English king is not entrusted with the power to do wrong. As a result, says Fortescue, the English king is, like the angels, but not for the same reason, free of the impotence of doing wrong.

As in Bracton's treatise, Fortescue also treats the notion of an absence of the king's power to do wrong as a non-power. While Bracton says that the king acts as minister of the devil and is not a king when he does not act lawfully,[95] Fortescue says that the king ruling politically—or royally and politically, as in England—does not have the power to do wrong.

In *In the Praise of the Laws of England* and *On the Governance of England*, Fortescue does not make an analogy between the king ruling politically and divine entities to support the argument that the king is divinely perfect and incapable of doing wrong. A closer reading of the relevant passages shows that Fortescue's two kings—the king ruling royally and the king ruling politically—have the same amount of power. It is not the case that the king ruling politically is divine-like while the king ruling royally is not divine-like because he is free to do wrong. Neither are divine-like. The king ruling royally has the power to act wrongly while the king ruling politically does not have that power. But the absence of the power to do wrong does not mean that the king ruling politically has less power. Fortescue submits that because such a power to do wrong is a non-power, the absence of it does not result in a lessening of the political king's power.

92 ibid 95.
93 'Introduction' in ibid xxix.
94 ibid.
95 *Bracton*, vol 2 (n 7) 305–06.

In summary, Fortescue's objective in relying on an analogy with divine entities is that just as divine entities are not less powerful because they cannot sin, so the king ruling politically is not less powerful because he does not have the power to do wrong. Fortescue was answering the criticism that his theory imposed limits on the king by arguing that for the king not to have the power to do wrong is not a limit imposed on him, for doing wrong is not a power, it is an impotency.[96] While the holy spirits and angels are unable to sin because they are perfect and do not have impotencies, Fortescue argues that the king ruling politically is, by analogy, also more powerful than the king ruling royally because the former is not entrusted with the 'non-power' or 'impotency' of doing wrong. Such an interpretation of Fortescue's argument is validated by the exposition of his argument in *On The Nature of the Law of Nature*, where he makes the same argument as can be found in *In the Praise of the Laws of England* and *On the Governance of England*, but without resorting to an analogy with angels or other divine manifestations:

> But let not the Royal Law (Lex Regia) on that account exalt itself, thinking itself freer or more powerful than the Political Law (Lege Politico), or its king freer or more powerful than a king governing the people politically, seeing that the ability to sin does not belong to power, but is a dangerous impotence and slavery, as in the case of privation of sight or the ability to be ignorant of virtue. . . . Wherefore to be able to sin is not power or liberty, no more than to be able to grow old or rotten, nor can he who is powerful to sin be called absolutely powerful, on account of the contrary quality contained in the adjunct, no more than a dead man can be called absolutely a man.[97]

The crux of Fortescue's theory is the negative nature of the power to do wrong: it is a non-power. Fortescue's argument is in essence similar to Bracton's theory. In Bracton's treatise, the king's jurisdiction does not extend to doing wrong: acts committed by the king as king can only be lawful, not wrongful.[98] It is not a limit imposed on the king not to recognize in him a power to do wrong, for the reason that, in Bracton's mind, it is not part of a king's jurisdiction. It is equally not a limit imposed on the king not to recognize in him a power to do wrong, for the reason that, in Fortescue's mind, it is a non-power. There was not, in Fortescue's work, the notion that the king was incapable of doing wrong because of his divine perfection. Fortescue did not submit that the king was, like the angels, devoid of infirmities or of old age. He was only devoid of the power to do wrong. It may have suited Elizabethan jurists to argue that the perfection of the king's body politic had its roots in Fortescue's work. But if that were the case and if the sixteenth-century

[96] Lockwood, 'Introduction' in Fortescue (n 21) xxix.
[97] Fortescue (n 21) 133–34.
[98] See section 2.1.1.

metaphysiological notion of the perfection of the body politic of the king devoid of infirmities was inspired by Fortescue's work, it was a considerable alteration of his argument.

2.2.2 Perfection and the two bodies of the king

The focus of this section is the state of legal thinking in relation to the king's perfection in the Tudor era. It will be demonstrated how the notion of perfection of the king could be found early in the reign of Henry VII. It was further developed by Elizabethan jurists along with the doctrine of the two bodies of the king.

The notion of the perfection of the king can be found in a case of 1485, where the judges decided that the attainder Richard III had issued against Henry VII—then Henry Tudor—was voided by Henry VII taking on the royal dignity of becoming king.[99] By taking on the office of kingship—the royal dignity—Henry VII voided all disabilities he might have been attainted with.[100] It could therefore be argued that at the beginning of Henry VII's reign, there was an early indication that the notion of perfection attached to the royal dignity of kingship. The royal dignity, or office of kingship, was, for instance, immortal (*dignitas non moritur*).[101] In 1485, it was thought that it could also 'perfect' defects affecting the king.

In that case of 1485, Huse CJ set out that the king could not arrest anyone for suspicion of treason or felony because, if the arrest was wrongful, the injured party could not have an action against the king given that the king may not be sued. Huse CJ's remarks appear to be unrelated to the issue before the court, the attainder of Henry VII. But it may be that Huse CJ's speech in the case of 1485 was not purely coincidental and that it acted as a reminder of the Bractonian understanding that *the king can do no wrong*—the king is not entitled to do wrong. While the court opined that the dignity of kingship cured the attainder of the king, Huse CJ may have subtly wished to qualify that perfecting effect by restating that the king was not entitled to do wrong. The interpretation that Huse CJ reaffirmed that the king is not entitled to do wrong finds support in the fact that he demonstrated again his independence of mind the following year. In 1486, Huse CJ refused to give the king a preliminary opinion on a treason case, insisting instead that it should be properly adjudicated before the court.[102] It was also Huse CJ who had ruled in *Baker's Case* that the king could not change issue (ie the nature of his pleading) as that would wrong a subject.[103] *Baker's Case* was subsequently frequently referred to as illustrating the idea that the king's prerogative cannot be used to do wrong. Huse CJ's reasons can be interpreted as an attempt to limit the perfecting effect of the

[99] (1485) YB Mich 1 Hen VII, fo 4b, pl 5.

[100] ibid.

[101] Kantorowicz (n 16) 383–400.

[102] *R v Strafford* (1486) YB Trin 1 Hen VII, fo 25, pl 1; Sir John Baker, *An Introduction to English Legal History* (5th edn, OUP 2019) 178.

[103] (1473) YB Pasch 13 Edw IV, fo 8a, pl 1.

dignity of kingship. The perfection of the king's dignity—the office of kingship—did not entail that the king was entitled to do wrong.

While there is evidence of a notion of perfection of the king at the beginning of Henry VII's reign, there was no further application of the perfecting effect of the king's dignity until the reign of Elizabeth I. By the 1536 Act of 28 Hen VIII c 17, for instance, it was provided in anticipation of Edward VI's minority and regency that statutes made before his twenty-fourth birthday could be abolished. Such provision is evidence that the doctrine of the two bodies of the king was not yet part of legal thinking. Had it been otherwise, the concept of the king's body politic perfecting his body natural so that the king was never underage would have run contrary to the act of 1536. The perfecting effect of the body politic so that the king was never underage would have conflicted with providing for the future king's inability to assent to statutes during his minority.

The notion of perfection became apparent in legal thinking along with the doctrine of the king's two bodies during Elizabeth I's reign. In the Middle Ages, the realm was often conceived of as a body corporate, with the king at its head.[104] Such a notion of the realm as a body corporate, or body politic, could still be found in the early Tudor era. There was in 1521 a *dictum* to the effect that the body politic was like a natural body, kept together by the law, and that the king and the realm were together a body politic.[105] Therefore, there was still in 1521 use of the medieval concept of 'body politic'; referring to society as a natural body. The realm conceived of as a body politic with the king as its head can even be found in the Act in Restraint of Appeals to Rome 1533, where the king is the 'supreme head . . . unto whom a body politic, compact of all sorts and degrees of people' is bound.[106] The notion of the realm as a body politic—ubiquitous throughout Europe—had no connection with the notion of the king's two bodies,[107] which only took root in England.[108] In addition, the fact that the body politic in the Act in Restraint of Appeals 1533 was likened to a natural body—with the king as the head and the realm as the body—shows that the two types of body, natural and politic, were not treated as distinct. On the contrary, the realm was a body politic likened to a body natural. That the kingdom was a 'body politic'—and therefore a corporation aggregate of many with the king as the head[109]—could still be found in notes of a case

[104] Kantorowicz (n 16) 225; Post (n 64) 318–19; Lockwood, 'Introduction' in Fortescue (n 21) xxvi.

[105] *R v Buckingham*, Port's Notebook, Notes Taken in the Inner Temple and Westminster Hall, note 75 in John Port, *The Notebook of Sir John Port* (JH Baker ed, Selden Society 1986) 125.

[106] Paul L Hughes and Robert F Fries (eds), *Crown and Parliament in Tudor-Stuart England: A Documentary Constitutional History, 1485–1714*, vol 1 (GP Putnam's Sons 1959) 39.

[107] Marie Axton, *The Queen's Two Bodies: Drama and the Elizabethan Succession* (Royal Historical Society 1977) 12.

[108] Kantorowicz (n 16) 447.

[109] *King's College, Cambridge v Hekker*, Trin 1519–Mich 1520 (CP), Hil 1522 (KB, decision in error) in JH Baker (ed), *Year Books of Henry VIII: 12–14 Henry VIII, 1520–1523* (Selden Society 2002) 69, 71–2 (Broke J), 101 (Fyneux CJ).

dating back to 1534.[110] The concept of the king having two distinct bodies was not yet to be found in legal thinking in the early sixteenth century.

The doctrine that the king has two bodies, one natural, the other politic and devoid of infirmities, has rightly been attributed to cases reported by Plowden during Elizabeth I's reign.[111] It may have had theological influences[112] and led eventually to further 'metaphysiological non-sense' in relation to, among other things, the king's incapacity and immortality.[113] Importantly for the purposes of our study of *the king can do no wrong* and the king's capacity to do wrong and amenability to justice, the notion of perfection of the king that was elaborated in the Tudor era had, as will be shown in Chapters 3 and 4, an important impact on later understandings of *the king can do no wrong* in legal thinking.

The first allusion to the two bodies of the king featured in the 1555 case of *Hill v Grange*.[114] *Hill v Grange* was reported by Plowden a few years before the 1561 case *Dutchy of Lancaster* and the 1562 case *Willion v Berkley*. Plowden reported as follows *Hill v Grange*:

> [T]he King is a body politic, and when an Act says, *the King*, or says, *we*, it is always spoken in the person of him as King, and in his dignity royal, and therefore it includes all those who enjoy his function.[115]

Three out of four judges in *Hill v Grange* ruled in that case that the word 'king' in the act included the king's heirs and successors. *Hill v Grange* demonstrates that a separation was maintained between the body natural of the king and his body politic. Only the body politic was incorporated with the king's dignity, his immortal office, thereby rendering it also perpetual.[116] The king's body natural, however, was still subject to death. 'Death' became 'demise' so as to signal that the king's body politic—incorporated with the king's eternal office, or 'dignity'—continued seamlessly to live on. At the demise of the king, the eternal office became incarnated by the new king in his body natural.[117]

The doctrine of the king's two bodies was further developed in the cases of the *Dutchy of Lancaster* in 1561[118] and *Willion v Berkley* in 1562.[119] To explain the

[110] Anonymous note on a case in the Common Pleas, Mich 1534 in JH Baker (ed), *Reports of Cases from the Time of King Henry VIII*, vol 2 (Selden Society 2004) 431.

[111] Maitland (n 84) 134; Kantorowicz (n 16) 7. The doctrine of the king's two bodies was not, therefore, a medieval doctrine; cf JG Allen, 'The Office of the Crown' (2018) 77 CLJ 298, 301.

[112] Kantorowicz (n 16) 16, 19, 445–46.

[113] Maitland (n 84) 135.

[114] *Hill v Grange* (1555) 1 Plowden 163.

[115] ibid 176.

[116] JWF Allison, *The English Historical Constitution: Continuity, Change and European Effects* (CUP 2007) 51–52.

[117] *Hill v Grange* (n 114) 177–7a.

[118] *Case of the Dutchy of Lancaster* (1561) 1 Plowden 212.

[119] *Willion v Berkley* (n 68).

doctrine of the king's two bodies in English legal thinking, Kantorowicz indiscriminately collated the arguments of the plaintiffs, the defendants, and the dissenting judge in *Willion v Berkley*.[120] Kantorowicz also relied heavily on arguments made by Serjeants Southcote and Harper in *Willion v Berkley* and erroneously called them 'Justices'[121] (as appears from Plowden's report, Southcote and Harper were not judges, but counsel for the defendants).[122] Although Brown J and Dyer CJ did find in favour of the defendants in *Willion v Berkley*, the arguments of the defendants in their pleadings were not authoritative and were not adopted by the majority judges. Kantorowicz also relied on passages from Weston J's reasons in the case of *Willion v Berkley* to support his account of the doctrine of the king's two bodies.[123] But Weston J's reasons were contrary to Southcote and Harper's arguments in the same case. Moreover, Weston J dissented in *Willion v Berkley* as the majority judges, Brown and Dyer, did not concur with his reasons.

That the two bodies of the king are conjoined and that the body politic perfects the body natural is apparent from the pleadings of plaintiff's counsel in *Willion v Berkley*: 'the body natural and the body politic are consolidated into one, and the body politic wipes away every imperfection of the other with which it is consolidated'.[124] Brown J in *Willion v Berkley* opined that the estate the king held in his body natural in that case was changed by the act passed by Parliament. As a result, the king had to take the estate at issue with the conditions that were attached to it.[125] In that case, the statute *De Donis Conditionalibus* was passed to prevent donees from barring the reversion of the land that was given to them and their issue and to avoid frustrating the donor's will that the land should pass—by intestate succession—to the donee's issue. Brown J found that the king could not be allowed by his prerogative to modify the estate and avoid the condition that the statute attached to it. Brown J ruled that for the king to modify the estate by his prerogative and give it to another would amount to doing wrong, which the king was not entitled to do.[126]

Similar language in relation to the conjunction of the king's two bodies—natural and politic—can be found in the unanimous opinion of the judges and serjeants in the case of *Dutchy of Lancaster*:

> For the King has in him two bodies, *viz.* a body natural and a body politic. His body natural (if it be considered in itself) is a body mortal, subject to all infirmities that come by nature or accident, to the imbecility of infancy or old age, and

[120] Kantorowicz (n 16) 12.
[121] ibid 13. Kantorowicz's mistake was also noted by Raffield (n 86) 95.
[122] *Willion v Berkley* (n 68) 229, 234–35.
[123] Kantorowicz (n 16) 12.
[124] *Willion v Berkley* (n 68) 238.
[125] ibid 245, 248.
[126] ibid 248 (Brown J).

> to the like defects that happen to the natural bodies of other people. But his body politic is . . . utterly void of infancy, and old age, and other natural defects and imbecilities, which the body natural is subject to, and for this cause, what the King does in his body politic, cannot be invalidated or frustrated by any disability in his natural body.
>
> . . .
>
> So that he has a body natural . . . and a body politic together indivisible, and these two bodies are incorporated in one person, and make one body and not divers. . . . So that the body natural, by the conjunction of the body politic to it, (which body politic contains the office, government, and majesty royal) is magnified, . . . for his body politic, which is annexed to his body natural, takes away the imbecility of his body natural, and draws the body natural, which is the lesser, and all the effects thereof to itself, which is the greater . . . [127]

The Duchy of Lancaster had been severed from the crown but it was held by a unanimous court in the case of the *Dutchy of Lancaster* that nonage could not be argued against the king in relation to his possessions in the duchy because the king's body politic and body natural are indivisible, and the king's body politic perfects the body natural so that the king can never be underage. Even if the king possessed duchy lands in his personal capacity and not as of his crown, the perfecting effect of the body politic extended to his body natural. In section 2.2.3, the interaction between this perfecting effect and the king's capacity to do wrong is analysed.

In short, an early indication of the notion of perfection curing the king's disabilities appeared early in the reign of Henry VII. The notion of the king's perfection was then developed in English legal thinking in the middle of the sixteenth century, along with the doctrine of the king's two bodies—one natural and the other politic and perfect. The Tudor era marked an important development in legal thinking—not only was a duality developed in relation to the king's two bodies, but the perfection of the body politic transcended the body natural. As will be shown in Chapters 3, 4, and 5, the duality of the king's bodies and the notion of perfection of the king remain important features of legal thinking.

2.2.3 The king's two bodies and *the king can do no wrong*

The focus of this section are the cases reported by Plowden in which the doctrine of the king's two bodies was elaborated, particularly the case of the *Dutchy of Lancaster* and *Willion v Berkley*. It will be demonstrated how the notion of perfection attaching to the body politic of the king was not to be used to place the king above the law or to allow him to do wrong. Lastly, it will be shown that *Sir Thomas Wroth's Case*,[128] reported by Plowden later in the Tudor era, confirmed that the

[127] *Dutchy of Lancaster* (n 118) 213.

[128] *Sir Thomas Wroth's Case* (1572) 2 Plowden 452.

doctrine of the two bodies of the king was not to be resorted to in order to inflict a wrong on the king's subject.

Raffield has argued that Plowden's reports of the case of the *Dutchy of Lancaster* and, even more so, *Willion v Berkley*, demonstrate judges' use of the doctrine of the king's two bodies to ensure the constitutional principle of a limited monarchy, curtail the king's prerogative, and 'restrict the application of the king's mystical body politic'.[129] In the same vein, the argument submitted in this section is that an important concern in the judges' elaboration of the doctrine of the king's two bodies was to maintain the Bractonian understanding that the king was not entitled to do wrong—*the king can do no wrong*. It will be shown in this section how the Bractonian understanding of *the king can do no wrong* as the king being under the law and not perfect, although immune from suit, was maintained in legal thinking, even as the notion of perfection of the king's body politic was developing.

To explain the doctrine of the king's two bodies when it originated in English legal thinking in the Tudor era, Kantorowicz relied simultaneously on the dissenting judge's reasons and the defendants' arguments in *Willion v Berkley*. He did not rely, as a common lawyer would, on the authoritative parts of the decision. Had he done so, he would have noted that Brown J and Dyer CJ, who decided the case of the *Dutchy of Lancaster*[130] in November 1561 along with a unanimous court, were then the two majority judges in the 1562 case of *Willion v Berkley*. Although they acknowledged that the body natural of the king was perfected by the body politic following *Dutchy of Lancaster*, Brown J and Dyer CJ tellingly avoided the notion of perfection of the king in their speeches on the application of a statute to the monarch in *Willion v Berkley*.[131]

Serjeants for the plaintiffs in *Willion v Berkley*, although their arguments were not retained by Brown J and Dyer CJ in that case, were also serjeants for the queen in the case of the *Dutchy of Lancaster*. The decision in the case of the *Dutchy of Lancaster* was rendered by a unanimous court—including Brown J and Dyer CJ—and the reasons given were very similar to the arguments of the plaintiffs in *Willion v Berkley*. At first glance, the case of *Willion v Berkley* may appear to constitute a reversal of the ruling in the *Dutchy of Lancaster* of 1561. Raffield, who has also noted the short length of time between the two cases, argued that the doctrine that the king's body natural was subsumed by the body politic was rejected in *Willion v*

[129] Raffield (n 86) 96; Paul Raffield, 'The Monarchical Republic, Constitutionality, and the Legal Profession' in Lorna Hutson (ed), *The Oxford Handbook of English Law and Literature, 1500–1700* (OUP 2017) 178–79.

[130] *Dutchy of Lancaster* (n 118) 222. Plowden's report of the case implied that Elizabeth I repeatedly demanded her judges to reconsider her case: Axton (n 107) 17. By order of the queen, the case was argued again in 1562, but the judges reached the same conclusion they had in November 1561: (n 118) 223.

[131] Following the judges' opinions delivered during the arguments in 1562, judgment was rendered in November of 1563: *Willion v Berkley* (n 68) 252.

Berkley.[132] It is submitted here that there was no outright rejection of the doctrine of the king's two bodies in *Willion v Berkley*. The doctrine that the king has two bodies was acknowledged by the majority judges.[133] It was decided that the king could hold things in his body natural separately from his body politic. It was also decided that the king's body politic did not alter the nature of the estate held.[134] The king's prerogative was found not to apply in that case because the statute was remedying a wrong at common law.[135] To Brown and Dyer JJ in *Willion v Berkley*, allowing the prerogative in that case to shield the king from the ambit of the act would have been tantamount to allowing the king to commit a wrong, which he could not do.[136]

The case of *Willion v Berkley*, decided a few months after that of the *Dutchy of Lancaster*, shows that the doctrine of the king's two bodies could not be used to defeat the Bractonian understanding that *the king can do no wrong*. It is clear from that case that the notion of perfection of the king's body politic could not be resorted to in order to circumvent the Bractonian understanding that the king is not entitled to do wrong. Weston J, dissenting in *Willion v Berkley*, opined that special favour was granted to the king by the law because he is the cause and origin of it.[137] His reasoning was flatly rejected by Brown J and Dyer CJ. Brown J was adamant in his speech in *Willion v Berkley* that the king cannot do wrong, that his prerogative will not suffer him to do wrong, and that his prerogative could not alter the estate held by the king.[138] With regard to the king's status in relation to law in *Willion v Berkley*, Raffield has noted that: 'In the majority judgments of Dyer CJ and Anthony Brown J (finding for the defendant), the Bractonian principle of a king subject to the law was firmly restated.'[139] In both cases reported by Plowden, the doctrine of the king's two bodies—and the notion of perfection attaching to the king's body politic—were not to be resorted to in order to allow the king to do wrong.

Even in the case of the *Dutchy of Lancaster*, the effect of the doctrine of the king's two bodies was that the queen was held to the lease that her brother had made while still underage. That Tudor judges held the queen to an act made by her infant brother Edward VI is significant. That the king could claim that he was underage or, to the contrary, that he was always of age depending on the circumstances is apparent from the Year Books.[140] However, to claim that the king

[132] Raffield, 'Monarchical Republic' (n 129) 179. Raffield had previously argued that the doctrine of the king's two bodies was not rejected in *Willion v Berkley*: Raffield, *Shakespeare's Imaginary Constitution* (n 86) 98.
[133] *Willion v Berkley* (n 68) 245 (Brown J), 250 (Dyer CJ).
[134] ibid 246 (Brown J).
[135] ibid 251–52 (Dyer CJ).
[136] ibid 248 (Brown J), 251–52 (Dyer CJ).
[137] ibid 242–43 (Weston J, dissenting).
[138] ibid 246, 248 (Brown J).
[139] Raffield (n 86) 98.
[140] Baker (n 2) 6.

became almost another person when he became king,[141] in a manner that ran contrary to the king's interests, was not argued by a party opposing the king.[142] The case of the *Dutchy of Lancaster* therefore marked an important development as judges resorted to the doctrine of the king's two bodies to rule that Edward VI was always of age because of his body politic, even if that went against Elizabeth I's interests as his successor.

In addition, in the *Dutchy of Lancaster*, a unanimous court found that even private things which belong to the king must be dealt with according to the special formalities which the king is required to meet in relation to his possessions as king.[143] In the case of the *Dutchy of Lancaster*, the judges found that the body natural was conjoined with the body politic, so that the course of things possessed by the king in his body natural are changed by the king's body politic. As a result, it was held that formalities and procedures required of things held by the king in his body politic also applied to things held in his body natural.[144] If the king had a right of entry in relation to his private possessions prior to becoming king, he lost that right once he became king. He had to proceed instead by matter of record.[145] In short, the more onerous procedural requirements that were imposed on the king also applied in relation to his private possessions.

It was decided unanimously in the *Dutchy of Lancaster* that the prerogatives that the law attributed to the king—including the prerogative never to be underage[146]—were found to apply even in relation to land of the Duchy of Lancaster which the king held in his body natural.[147] Yet a close reading of the two cases shows a continuity in the thinking of the judges.

The crux of the court's argument in *Dutchy of Lancaster* was that defects of the king's natural body 'shall not blemish or defeat the acts or suits which he does or pursues in his body politic'.[148] The main concern in *Dutchy of Lancaster* was not that the body politic should entitle the king to do wrong, or to be above the law. That point was to be settled a few months later in *Willion v Berkley*, where Brown J and Dyer CJ's speeches were to the effect that the doctrine of the two bodies of the king could not be resorted to in order to entitle the king to wrong another and to claim to be above the law. Rather, the main concern in the case of the *Dutchy of Lancaster* was to ensure that the king's minority or other physical or mental infirmities were not to be used as justifications to undermine the king's acts. The queen

[141] William Illingworth (ed), *Placita de Quo Warranto Temporibus Edw I, II & III* (Printed by George Eyre and Andrew Strahan 1818) 429–30.

[142] Pollock and Maitland (n 1) 524.

[143] *Dutchy of Lancaster* (n 118) 213.

[144] ibid.

[145] ibid 214.

[146] ibid 216.

[147] ibid 216.

[148] ibid 213.

herself in the case of the *Dutchy of Lancaster* was not allowed to rely on a previous king's natural 'defects' to avoid being bound by his actions. In *Dutchy of Lancaster*, the monarch—unlike ordinary persons—could not use a predecessor's defects to avoid being bound by legal obligations.

Further, the court's point in the *Dutchy of Lancaster* in asserting that the bodies are conjoined was to ensure that special formalities and procedural requirements imposed on the king be respected even in relation to his private possessions. That reasoning is in line with the majority judges' thinking in *Willion v Berkley* that the king is subject to law and not entitled to do wrong.

The ruling in the case of *Willion v Berkley* was not contrary to the ruling in the *Dutchy of Lancaster*. As Brown J and Dyer CJ found in *Willion v Berkley*, the court—including Brown J, Dyer CJ, and Weston J—unanimously agreed in the *Dutchy of Lancaster* that the king can inherit land in his body natural, to the exclusion of his body politic.[149]

The case of the *Dutchy of Lancaster* was to the effect that the king could not avoid his legal obligations. The court decided in that case that Elizabeth I could not use the infancy of her brother, Edward VI, to avoid being bound by a lease made by the latter when he was not yet of age.[150] That the doctrine of the king's body politic and its perfection was flattering to the Tudor queen may have been a cunning way to avoid her displeasure at the effect of the decision, which was to hold her to the lease. The court in the *Dutchy of Lancaster* applied the doctrine of the king's two bodies to restrict the king's privileges. Even if the body politic 'draws the body natural, which is lesser, and all the effects thereof to itself',[151] the judges qualified that statement. For instance, when land descended to the king in his body natural, it became subject to the restrictions imposed on the king in his body politic. The prince who had land passed on to him in his body natural had then to act in relation to that land by matter of record once he became king. He also had to go through an office to prove his title instead of having a simple right of entry on the land like an ordinary person.[152] The restrictions which were developed during the Middle Ages in relation to the manner in which the king could exercise his rights were maintained. The king could not avoid those restrictions by arguing that things held in his newly found body natural were not subject to legal requirements and procedures which applied to the king prior to the elaboration of the doctrine of the king's two bodies.

By ruling that the body natural was perfected by the body politic in the case of the *Dutchy of Lancaster*, Brown J and Dyer CJ's reasoning demonstrates that the doctrine of the king's two bodies could not be used to allow the king to do

149 ibid 214.
150 ibid 217.
151 ibid 214.
152 ibid 214.

wrong and avoid his obligations. Dyer CJ, Brown J, and Weston J in the case of the *Dutchy of Lancaster*, along with the same serjeants who had argued for the losing plaintiffs in *Willion v Berkley* in the spring of 1561, delivered a unanimous decision in November 1561. Even Weston J subscribed to the view in the *Dutchy of Lancaster* that the queen was not to avoid her obligations, nor to avoid the procedural requirements and formalities required by her position as queen, even in relation to her private possessions. The case of *Willion v Berkley*, decided a few months after that of the *Dutchy of Lancaster*, shows that the doctrine of the king's two bodies—and therefore the perfection of his body politic—was not used to defeat the Bractonian understanding that *the king can do no wrong*.[153] The majority in *Willion v Berkley*, while they acknowledged the doctrine of the king's two bodies, did not accept that the idea that the king's perfect body politic draws to it the body natural could allow the king to avoid the law. In both cases, the doctrine of the king's two bodies subjected the king to law, even more so than an ordinary person who could claim minority. The perfection of the king's body politic did not alter the Bractonian understanding that *the king can do no wrong*—the king is not entitled to do wrong.

Sir Thomas Wroth's Case,[154] a later case dating to 1573, also reported by Plowden, is further evidence that the doctrine of the two bodies of the king was not to be used to do wrong to a subject. In that case, Sir Thomas Wroth had been granted by Henry VIII an annuity for his services as Usher of the Privy-Chamber to Prince Edward—the future Edward VI. Judges in that case referred to the doctrine of the two bodies of the king in a manner that was consistent with the explanation given in *Dutchy of Lancaster* and *Willion v Berkley*. As Plowden reported in *Wroth's Case*, the Barons of the Exchequer opined that the services to be provided by Wroth to the prince were not to be rendered to his body natural only. Unlike a physician tending to the king's body natural, Wroth's services as Usher of the Privy-Chamber were not solely related to the king's body natural. Wroth's services had to be performed to a higher degree by more honourable ministers when Edward became king because they related to the king's body politic.[155] When the prince became Edward VI, he left the lower estate of prince and was elevated to the dignity—or the office—of kingship. Wroth was thereby discharged by law from rendering his services.[156] The capaciousness of the doctrine of the two bodies of the king is such that judges in *Wroth's Case* could have decided either in favour of Wroth or not. They could have found that it was the body natural of the king that was to receive Wroth's

[153] cf Greenberg, who argued that the maxim *the king can do no wrong* meant immunity from suit, was elaborated in connection with the king's two bodies in Plowden's reports, and applied to both the king's bodies so as to put him above the law: Janelle Greenberg, 'Our Grand Maxim of State: "The King Can Do No Wrong"' (1991) 12 Hist Pol Thought 209, 215.

[154] *Wroth's Case* (n 128).

[155] ibid 456.

[156] ibid 456.

services. Had Wroth's services been considered to attach to the king's body natural, he would have been discharged upon the death of Edward VI. Conversely, the judges in *Wroth's Case* could have decided that the services, because they were to be rendered to the king's body politic—which is immortal—were never discharged and that Wroth was to be paid his annuities in arrears. Ultimately, they decided that it was in his body politic that Henry VIII granted the annuity to Thomas Wroth.[157] Because the king's body politic never dies, Wroth was found to hold the annuity for the duration of his life. Annuities in arrears and for the future were commanded to be paid to Wroth.[158] *Wroth's Case* therefore constitutes another instance where the doctrine of the two bodies of the king was interpreted in a way that did not wrong the king's subject. The doctrine of the two bodies of the king was in fact interpreted by the Barons of the Exchequer in *Wroth's Case* in the manner most beneficial for Sir Thomas Wroth.

In summary, an analysis of cases in Plowden's reports show that an explanation can be given for what appears to be a sudden change of mind on Brown J and Dyer CJ's part in the case of *Willion v Berkley*. In fact, Brown J and Dyer CJ did acknowledge in *Willion v Berkley* the doctrine of the king's two bodies and they recognized that the name 'king' included the natural body of the king.[159] But they also limited the effects of the doctrine of the two bodies of the king that had been elaborated in the *Dutchy of Lancaster*. The effect of their ruling was that the body politic of the king could not entitle him to do wrong, nor could it render the king above the law. Weston J's argument in *Willion v Berkley* that the king was above the law was not adopted. The perfection of the body politic of the king was not to be used to argue that the king was above the law or that he was entitled to do wrong to his subjects.

In conclusion, the king's perfection—one of the three notions I identify as having been associated with *the king can do no wrong* at various points throughout history—emerged along with the doctrine of the king's two bodies during the Tudor period, but it was not determinative in relation to the substantive dimension of crown liability—the king's capacity to do wrong. As Maitland suggested, lawyers in the Tudors' reign may have been prone to flatter the ego of their king with the doctrine of the king's two bodies, but that doctrine also contained the limits that had gradually been imposed on the king's lawful power.[160] A study of Plowden's reports proves Maitland right: the perfection of the king's body politic was not a ground that was relied on by Tudor lawyers in relation to the king's capacity to do wrong or to change the Bractonian understanding of *the king can do no wrong* that the king is not entitled to do wrong.

157 ibid 457.
158 ibid 458.
159 *Willion v Berkley* (n 68) 244–45 (Brown J), 250 (Dyer CJ).
160 Pollock and Maitland (n 1) 512.

2.3 Immunity from suit

As was discussed in section 2.1.1.2, in the late Middle Ages, a wrong was attributed to the king himself. Bracton did not indicate how a redress against the king's wrong should be given.[161] It has been argued that Bracton's 'contradictory' statement that the king is under God and the law, but has no superior in his realm, leaves unanswered the 'critical question'[162] of determining how justice is to be attained if the king knows of no superior. However, to consider the issue of a lack of remedy to be critical is anachronistic if it is premised on a rule-of-law conception of liability that is alien to medieval thinking. It is not anachronistic, however, if the lack of remedy is looked at from the perspective of the king's royal and feudal duty to administer justice, addressed in this section.

The king's feudal privilege not to be sued in his own courts and the absence of a writ against him were counteracted by the emergence of the petition of right and the possibility for the king to assume liability for the fault of his agents, which are both examined below.

There were no enforcement mechanisms when the king exceeded his jurisdiction to act according to law. That the king had no superior was another idea in Bracton's writings at the end of folio 369; in folio 52, 'the king has no equal, no neighbour, no superior';[163] and in folio 5b 'The king has no equal within his realm, nor *a fortiori* a superior, because he would then be subject to those subjected to him. . . . No one may presume to question his acts, much less contravene them.'[164]

It flows from such an absence of a superior over the king that even a wrongful deed of the king—although not his because it exceeds his power—cannot be corrected without the king's consent.[165] The end of folio 369 constitutes an illustration of the impossibility of correcting the king's wrong without his approval. There has been much scholarly debate around what Bracton meant by the absence of a superior and how it acted as a qualification to the king's status as under the law. The main arguments advanced to solve the inconsistencies in Bracton's theory of kingship were made at a theoretical level and aimed to achieve an interpretation of Bracton's text that could be intellectually satisfying and logical by attempting to reconcile the king's status as under the law with the absence of a superior.[166] The

[161] Ehrlich (n 1) 43.
[162] Loughlin (n 77) 40.
[163] Bracton, vol 2 (n 7) 157.
[164] ibid 33.
[165] See section 2.1.1.3.
[166] See eg Maitland (n 32); Paul Vinogradoff, 'The Text of Bracton' in HAL Fisher (ed), *The Collected Papers of Paul Vinogradoff*, vol 1 (Clarendon Press 1928); Hermann Kantorowicz, *Bractonian Problems* (Jackson, Son & Company 1941); Fritz Schulz, 'Bracton on Kingship' (1945) 60 Eng Hist Rev 136; Tierney (n 30); Lewis (n 59); Post (n 27); Blecker (n 60); Cary J Nederman, 'Bracton on Kingship Revisited' (1984) 5 Hist Pol Thought 61.

use of Roman law in Bracton was highlighted;[167] parallels were drawn between the English king and the Roman emperor's and Christ's voluntary submission to the law.[168] The submission to the law in the king's coronation oath was noted,[169] as well as his duty to obey the law,[170] and the moral aspect of the king's submission to the law was later emphasized.[171] It was also argued that Bracton's king was under the law unequivocally.[172] The role of the king's barons in restraining an unbridled king[173] and the role of the council of magnates in enacting law[174] were given prominence. The *lex regia* that made the Roman emperor was likened to the law that made the king and under which he remained, yet the king was above the positive law, which he could make.[175] To Kantorowicz, the king was both under the law and 'above and beyond' it.[176] Pennington has adopted a practical view on the issue of the contradiction between the king as under the law and yet having no superior, resigning himself to the idea that 'we cannot know, and never will know, what Bracton meant' by his statement in folio 5b (borrowed from Roman law) on the absence of a superior over the king.[177] The king was above the law in the sense that he had no superior to enforce the law against him. That statement, however, does not relate so much to the status of the king in relation to law itself and to the substantive dimension of crown liability pertaining to the king's capacity to do wrong. That there was no superior above the king but God and the law pertains rather to the absence of legal enforcement mechanisms against the king—the procedural dimension of crown liability in our model.

In summary, the theory was that the king was under the law, but there was no enforcement mechanism to 'make this theory a practical reality'.[178] Tierney has argued that the availability of the right to sue the crown is not essential in a constitutional system of government, as the lack of a right of action was only remedied

[167] SJT Miller, 'The Position of the King in Bracton and Beaumanoir' (1956) 31 Speculum 263. On the relationship between Roman law, canon law, and medieval thinking on kingship, see also Harold J Berman, *Law and Revolution: The Formation of the Western Legal Tradition* (CUP 1983); Anna Grzymała-Busse, *Sacred Foundations: The Religious and Medieval Roots of the European State* (Princeton UP 2023) 113–43. On the role Roman law played in the development of the common law more generally, see eg Paul Brand, *The Making of the Common Law* (Hambledon Press 1992); McSweeney (n 8).

[168] Schulz (n 166); Kantorowicz (n 16) 156; Alan Cromartie, *The Constitutionalist Revolution: An Essay on the History of England, 1450–1642* (CUP 2006) 16.

[169] Post (n 27).

[170] Tierney (n 30).

[171] Nederman (n 166); Jeffrey Goldsworthy, *The Sovereignty of Parliament: History and Philosophy* (first published 1999, OUP 2004) 24.

[172] Lewis (n 59).

[173] Blecker (n 60).

[174] Kantorowicz (n 16) 151–52.

[175] ibid 150–51.

[176] ibid 147.

[177] Pennington (n 27) 93.

[178] Charles Howard McIlwain, *The Growth of Political Thought in the West: From the Greeks to the End of the Middle Ages* (Macmillan 1932) 197; Joseph Canning, *A History of Medieval Political Thought, 300–1450* (Routledge 1996) 25; HG Richardson and GO Sayles, *The Governance of Mediaeval England from the Conquest to Magna Carta* (Edinburgh UP 1963) 145.

in England with the Crown Proceedings Act 1947.[179] Tierney's argument supports the idea in this book that the king's position in relation to law and the ability or not to sue the king are two separate notions.

There may be flaws in the logic of Bracton's treatise and gaps in the construction of the text, which has been termed 'paradoxical reasoning',[180] but we have been warned against expecting perfection in logic or consistency from authors of past eras and against attempting to address all such possible logical failures.[181] English jurists of the medieval period, including Glanvill and Bracton, were constrained by 'limitations of thought'[182] and the theories predominant in their time, 'but they felt uneasy about the lack of limitations' imposed on the king.[183] Tierney has also pointed out the difficulty facing the authors of Bracton's treatise in compiling a significant body of English law according to a Roman-inspired structure. The degree of difficulty was increased by the confusion surrounding the notion of kingship and the duality of the king's role as feudal ruler and God's chosen one.[184]

The paradox in Bracton's text between the king's position under the law but with no superior above him but God may not be satisfactorily resolved from a logical point of view, especially a current one. That is no surprise, given that not only was the text written by many, but also that in medieval times God's punishment on the Day of Judgement was satisfactory reparation. That medieval thinkers did not clearly separate legal, moral, and religious duties[185] may also have contributed to the acceptance of divine retribution as satisfactory.

In conclusion, two ideas expounded by Bracton—the king's jurisdiction and the absence of a superior—came into play throughout his treatise, as folios 368–69 exemplify. But the ideas relating to the king's jurisdiction and the absence of an equal in his realm did not alter the other fundamental idea set out by Bracton that the king was under the law or the fact that an *injuria*—a wrong—could be his. The absence of a superior to correct the king's wrong did not make the king's violation of the laws lawful. It only meant that there was no legal enforcement of the king's duty to observe the law.[186] As a result, the king, being under the law, was capable of committing a wrong. The fact that Bracton had to resort in folios 368–69 to the king's wrongful deed as not being 'his' because it exceeded his jurisdiction highlights the fact that the king was capable of doing wrong in the first place. Consequently, the medieval king was not thought of as being perfect. He could do wrong, and although there was no enforcement mechanism against him at the time Bracton

[179] Tierney (n 30) 306.
[180] Loughlin (n 59) 49.
[181] Quentin Skinner, *Visions of Politics*, vol 1 (CUP 2002) 67–68.
[182] Kantorowicz (n 16) 144.
[183] Turner (n 48) 269.
[184] Tierney (n 30) 316–17.
[185] Maitland (n 19) 101.
[186] Tierney (n 30) 301, 303, 309.

wrote his treatise, the petition of right was developed thereafter to allow a wronged subject to sue to the king.

2.3.1 Royal duty to administer justice

It was the duty of any feudal lord to administer justice.[187] The king was a sovereign lord and as a consequence he 'owed a duty of justice to everyone'.[188] The king's royal duties, along with the preservation of the rights of the crown and the maintenance of order, included the obligation to administer and dispense justice.[189] As Bracton set out, 'To this end is a king made and chosen, that he do justice to all men',[190] 'for it is the king's duty to provide an adequate remedy to repress every wrong'.[191] In Bracton's mind, the king had a duty to redress his wrong or the wrong committed by his command.[192]

The king's duty to administer justice was also grounded in his coronation oath: the king's refusal to do justice was a violation of the king's coronation oath to observe and maintain the law and it attracted the punishment of God.[193] The duty to administer and deliver justice was also to be imposed legally on the king by Magna Carta 1215 (cl 39),[194] which constituted an undertaking by the king to administer the law and not to delay justice and right to a subject.[195]

The king's obligations in Bracton's theory of kingship were laid out in folio 107, entitled 'For what purpose a king is created; of ordinary jurisdiction', where Bracton stated that the king, being God's vicar, had the obligation to do justice in his realm.[196]

The king's duty to render justice and correct a wrong was also expressed in folio 369: 'he is bound to dispense justice to all men'.[197] In the context of the king choosing to commit a wrong in folio 369 by supporting a tenant who has unlawfully obtained seisin, either the king renders judgment or he 'imposes the necessity of rendering judgment upon his justices'.[198] It illustrates that 'law' implied a

[187] FM Stenton, *The First Century of English Feudalism, 1066–1166* (1st edn, Clarendon Press 1932) 44.

[188] TFT Plucknett, *Legislation of Edward I* (Clarendon Press 1949) 30.

[189] Fritz Kern, *Kingship and Law in the Middle Ages* (SB Chrimes tr, Blackwell 1948) 75–77; David Carpenter, *The Struggle for Mastery: Britain, 1066–1284* (Allen Lane 2003) 467; Loughlin (n 77) 25. While Kern asserted that the coronation oath did not create a duty to administer justice that was not otherwise imposed on the king, Post argued the opposite: Post (n 27) 521, 527, 534.

[190] Bracton, vol 2 (n 7) 305.

[191] Bracton, vol 4 (n 39) 289.

[192] Ehrlich (n 1) 43.

[193] Post (n 27).

[194] Clause 39 of Magna Carta (1215) read: 'No free man is to be taken or imprisoned or disseised or outlawed or exiled or in any way ruined, nor will we go or send against him, except by the lawful judgment of his peers or by the law of the land': Holt (n 9) 389.

[195] Ehrlich (n 1) 49; Walter Ullmann, *Principles of Government and Politics in the Middle Ages* (Methuen 1961) 170–71. To Ullmann, Magna Carta signalled the weakening of the theocratic basis of kingship and conversely, the increased importance of the feudal-based aspect of kingship.

[196] Bracton, vol 2 (n 7) 305.

[197] Bracton, vol 4 (n 39) 159.

[198] ibid.

distinction between right and wrong, and required that a wrong be remedied,[199] and that the obligation to correct a wrong extended to the king himself, who had a duty to redress a wrong made by him or his royal officials.[200]

In summary, even if the king had no superior, an obligation was imposed on him to correct a wrong and render justice, at least in theory.

2.3.2 Feudal privilege not to be sued

One of the feudal privileges was that a feudal lord could not be sued in his own court.[201] The king being a feudal lord also benefitted from this privilege. However, his 'accidental'[202] position as *overlord* resulted in there being no lord over him before whose courts he could be answerable. The king had no equal in his realm and could not therefore be adjudged by his peers.[203]

The extent to which Roman law inspired Bracton in his theorization of English kingship and royal rule in relation to law was debated: Tierney, for instance, argued that Bracton's thinking in relation to political issues in his treatise was based on Roman and canon law sources, and not feudal law.[204] But the feudal privileges consequent on the king's overlordship were not contested: even Tierney recognized that the king was half feudal private lord, half divine ruler.[205] That the medieval king, 'every inch a man',[206] was essentially a feudal overlord and that his privileges derived mainly from his coincidental position at the apex of a pyramid of relationships was Maitland's position.[207] Whether feudalism was central to the organization of medieval society[208] throughout the Middle Ages or not, the point we are concerned with is rather that the king's privileges were rooted in feudal law. The king's immunity from the jurisdiction of his courts was purely personal.[209]

The king had purely personal privileges, derived from his status as feudal overlord. The distinction between political theories in relation to kingship and the feudal privileges of the king illustrate that the king's status in relation to law on the

199 Bracton, vol 2 (n 7) 305.

200 Ehrlich (n 1) 43; Peter Cane, *Controlling Administrative Power* (CUP 2016) 371.

201 Baker (n 2) 48. Milsom noted that before 1200, the lord's court was the only court where his tenants could seek justice: SFC Milsom, *The Legal Framework of English Feudalism: The Maitland Lectures Given in 1972* (CUP 1976) 11.

202 Pollock and Maitland (n 1) 518.

203 (1348) YB Hil 22 Edw III, fo 3, pl 25.

204 Tierney (n 30) 314.

205 ibid 316–17. Ullmann's interpretation of fo 107 and *quod principi placuit* was also based on the idea that Bracton attempted a reconciliation of feudal and theocratic kingship: Ullmann (n 195) 176–77.

206 Maitland (n 84) 132.

207 Pollock and Maitland (n 1) 518; see also Holdsworth (n 2) 459, 465; John F Reinhardt, 'The Status of the Crown in the Time of Bracton' (1943) 17 Temple LQ 242, 270; Miller (n 167) 265; Turner, 'Disseizin by the King' (n 44) 1.

208 See eg Marc Bloch, *Feudal Society* (LA Manyon tr, Routledge & Kegan Paul 1961); Stenton (n 187); Ullmann (n 195) 24, 182; Milsom (n 201).

209 Borchard (n 1) 4; Paul Vinogradoff, 'Constitutional History and the Year Books', *The Collected Papers of Paul Vinogradoff*, vol 1 (Clarendon Press 1928) 200; Maurice Sunkin and Sebastian Payne (eds), *The Nature of the Crown: A Legal and Political Analysis* (OUP 1999) 3–5; Loughlin (n 59) 47–48.

one hand and his procedural immunity from suit on the other hand are two different notions. Yet the two notions both relate to *the king can do no wrong*.

2.3.3 Absence of writs against the king and the petition of right

As we have seen, Bracton made clear that the king was considered to be subject to law and that a wrong could be imputed to him.[210] Moreover, the king was treated as an ordinary party, whether he was a defendant or plaintiff, and in Bracton's words 'ought to be the last, or almost so' to receive justice when a plaintiff.[211] Turner has demonstrated that there was not in Bracton's time, under Henry III, an independent judiciary. When the king was a defendant, only cases which were instigated by powerful barons or where a fine had been paid were in fact advanced, and matters were referred by the judges to the king for his judgment.[212] Later, under Edward II and Edward III, however, where the king was a plaintiff the claim was to be governed by the law.[213]

According to Bracton, no writ ran against the king.[214] The suggestion that the king could not issue a writ against himself has often been relied on to explain the absence of such an action against the king.[215] There are a number of references to be found in the Year Books that indicate that there were, prior to Edward I's reign, writs against the king. The earliest dates back to 1307.[216] One reference in particular is made by Wilby J to a writ issued against King Henry III, and a description of it is given.[217] This particular reference has been cited by Archbold[218] and Comyns[219] as an indication that a writ could be issued against the king before Edward I's reign, but many have doubted the validity of it, including those writing as early as Staunford[220] and later Hale, Maitland, and Holdsworth.[221] Allen also traced later references to the existence of a writ against the king.[222] Holdsworth

[210] Bracton, vol 2 (n 7) 33, 169; Bracton, vol 3 (n 8) 43.

[211] Bracton, vol 2 (n 7) 33.

[212] Turner (n 48) 251, 270.

[213] Ehrlich (n 1) 118, 120.

[214] Bracton, vol 2 (n 7) 33.

[215] Ehrlich (n 1) 24. For an earlier example, see Brooke's sixteenth-century abridgment: 'Peticion et monstrans de droit' in Robert Brooke, *La Graunde Abridgement* (Tottell 1573) 134.

[216] (1307) YB Pasch 35 Edw I, RS, pl 2 [467]–[471].

[217] (1350) YB Trin 24 Edw III, fos 55b–56a, pl 40.

[218] John Frederick Archbold, *A Digest of the Law Relative to Pleading and Evidence in Actions Real, Personal, and Mixed* (2nd edn, J Butterworth and Son 1839) 5.

[219] John Comyns, *A Digest of the Laws of England* (Anthony Hammond ed, 5th edn, Butterworth 1822) 'Action'.

[220] William Staunford, *An Exposicion of the Kinges Prerogative* (Printed in Fleet Street by Richard Tottel 1583) 42–42b.

[221] Matthew Hale, *The Prerogatives of the King*, vol 92 (DEC Yale ed, Selden Society 1976) 14; Pollock and Maitland (n 1) 516; Holdsworth (n 1) 146; see also Ehrlich (n 1) 25. Clode listed the references to the writ but did not weigh in on the controversy: Walter Clode, *The Law and Practice of Petition of Right under the Petitions of Right Act, 1860* (Clowes 1887) 2–4.

[222] John Allen, *Inquiry into the Rise of and Growth of Prerogative in England* (Longman, Brown, Green, and Longmans 1849) 190–91. Allen recounted that mentions of a writ against the king prior to the reign of Edward I were made in (1348) YB Hil 22 Edw III (n 203) and (1369) YB Trin 43 Edw III, fos 21b–22b, pl 12.

argued that until the beginning of the fourteenth century, the petition of right was procedurally similar to an ordinary action, hence the reference to the existence of a writ against the king prior to the reign of Edward I.[223] For the reason that the king could not issue a writ against himself, but also that if it had been possible, kings would have been submerged by suits against them, Maitland and others have rejected as historically inaccurate those later references to a writ against the king.[224] Nevertheless, references to the existence of a writ against the king in the pleadings of lawyers under the reigns of Edward I and Edward III—and the apparent credence the judges lent to such assertions—indicate that the notion that the king was under the law was widely accepted.[225] The current understandings of *the king can do no wrong* as the king is immune from suit and that he cannot be sued because of his incapacity to do wrong was not yet part of the law.

In folios 5b and 170,[226] Bracton stated that only a 'petition' was available as against the king. The word 'petition' in Bracton's treatise meant generally a request, or demand, and did not refer specifically to the petition of right as a procedure.[227] Although there were petitions by the barons to initiate reforms and legislation prior to 1272, these were extraordinary instances.[228] The routine use of private petitions of right in written form by the king's subjects to state their grievances against actions by the king's servants and ask the king for reparation became common only upon the accession of Edward I.[229] Bracton, therefore, could not have referred to private petitions of right as a remedy as they were not yet in use in England at the time his treatise was written, under the reign of Henry III.[230]

It was Edward I who instituted the petition of right as a common remedy[231] and there is evidence of private petitions of right for Edward I's first Parliament.[232] Evidence that the petition of right was available as against the king is also apparent from a proclamation made in the Parliament of 1341 to the effect that if the king, his ministers, or another person committed wrongs, subjects should petition the king to obtain redress.[233] In 1348, Edward III's order that he should be sued to by

[223] Holdsworth (n 1) 144–46.

[224] Ehrlich (n 1) 24–25; WS Holdsworth, *A History of English Law*, vol 9 (1st edn, Methuen 1926) 12; Watkins (n 1) 6–7; Maitland (n 19) 100; Pollock and Maitland (n 1) 516.

[225] Holdsworth (n 2) 465; Watkins (n 1) 5.

[226] Bracton, vol 2 (n 7) 33; Bracton, vol 3 (n 8) 43. Folio 170, under the title 'Against whom the assise lies and in what way one falls into the assise' reads: 'If it is the prince or king or another who has no superior except God, the remedy by assise will not lie against him; there will only be opportunity for a petition, that he correct and amend his act.'

[227] Ehrlich (n 1) 44–45.

[228] Brand, 'The Making of the Common Law' (n 167) 326–33; Paul Brand, 'Petitions and Parliament in the Reign of Edward I' in Linda Clark (ed), *Parchment and People: Parliament in the Middle Ages* (Edinburgh UP 2004) 14.

[229] Brand, 'Petitions and Parliament' (n 228) 14.

[230] Ehrlich (n 1) 22.

[231] ibid 84, 95; Jaffe (n 54) 5; Brand, 'Petitions and Parliament' (n 228) 14–16. See also Borchard (n 3) 23–30; Holdsworth (n 1); Watkins (n 1) 16–31.

[232] Brand, 'Petitions and Parliament' (n 228) 15–17.

[233] (1341) (15 Edw III) 2 RP 127 n 5 *in fine*.

petition was acknowledged by Thorp CJ,[234] who added that the king could only be adjudged by himself or by his justices.[235] There was, therefore, judicial recognition that a claim against the king could be adjudicated by his judges through the petition of right.

The petition of right gave the king's subjects the opportunity to have a remedy against their king. That remedial procedure had to be strictly observed.[236] In a decision of 1351, under the reign of Edward III, the judges clearly stated that the king could only be sued to by petition.[237] For that reason, they did not allow the king to intervene in favour of the defendant in a case that had been instituted by a writ. The judges reasoned that although the king voluntarily chose to intervene in support of the defendant—who was granted aid of the king in a previous proceeding—the king may choose not to intervene in another case. Because it could not be the law that the king automatically intervenes for every ordinary person, the judges did not allow him to intervene. They also reasoned that they could not have rendered their decision on the case without consulting the king, an unusual procedure in a case that was instituted by a writ. Their opinion that the king could not be received in that action shows not only that the craft of legal reasoning in the fourteenth century was far from lacking, but also offers an illustration of the importance of procedure, and of the petition of right, in the mind of English medieval lawyers.

The creation of the petition of right may be related to a late medieval concept of fair process. Pennington has demonstrated the creation in the late thirteenth century of a notion of fair process—absolute norms protecting the subject's rights to trial—even against Continental princes' *potestas absoluta*.[238] The doctrine evolved in the second half of the thirteenth century so that such an absolute right to trial included matters relating to property rights, which one could not be deprived of without a trial.[239] One of Edward III's charters was even revoked by the Court of Chancery in 1341–42 because its grant was done 'to the damage of him and others without due process of law'.[240] Likewise, it was suggested in the Court of Chancery a few years before that 'the King never ought to record except by due process'.[241] While these later Continental theories could not have influenced the writers of Bracton's treatise in the first half of the thirteenth century, the petition of right was nevertheless asserted under Edward III's reign in the second half of the fourteenth

[234] The king was not 'sued' because he could not be taken to court to appear before his judges by ordinary action, hence the terms 'sued to' to convey that the king was petitioned to remedy his wrong.

[235] (1348) YB Hil 22 Edw III (n 203).

[236] For a description of the procedure, see Maitland (n 19) 224; Peter W Hogg, Patrick Monahan, and Wade K Wright, *Liability of the Crown* (4th edn, Carswell 2011) 5; Baker (n 2) 43–44.

[237] (1351) YB Mich 25 Edw III, fo 91a, pl 1.

[238] Pennington (n 27) 121.

[239] ibid 154.

[240] (1341–42) YB Hil 16 Edw III, RS 109–110, pl 38 and YB Mich 17 Edw III, fo 59, pl 58, in Luke Owen Pike, *Year Books of the Reign of King Edward the Third*, vol 7 (CUP 2012) 108–10.

[241] (1339) YB Hil 13 Edw III, RS 97–101, pl 12 in Luke Owen Pike, *Year Books of the Reign of King Edward the Third*, vol 2 (CUP 2012) 100.

century in a context in which the doctrine of due process was developing and which may have contributed to its promulgation. Baker has noted that in 1354, the term 'due process' was not new and was shared between the Continent and England,[242] and has identified 'due process legislation' under the reigns of Edward III and Henry IV.[243] Although fair process in the second half of the fourteenth century in England had a limited meaning, it nevertheless did prohibit arbitrary treatment of the king's subjects.[244] In short, the petition of right emerged in a context in which fair process was developing.

The increased importance of fair process in the second half of the thirteenth century may have contributed to the fact that the petition of right was not conceived of as a remedy as of grace on the king's part, but as a necessary procedure to have the king answer for his wrong and that of his officials,[245] as was mandated by his duty to correct a wrong and his position under the law. The petition of right was distinct from petitions as of grace: the petition of right was an action 'for right', which necessitated the king's involvement, and which was determined according to positive law.[246]

The petition of right was not originally meant to be of limited use; it was 'recognized as the general and normal remedy'.[247] Most law and litigation in the Middle Ages related to property—especially of land—and feudal relations.[248] The availability of the petition of right as a remedy against the king in relation to matters relating to the property of land—and in particular regarding wrongful disseisin, the wrong which most resembled a modern 'tort'[249]—implied that the general state of the law in the Middle Ages was that there was a remedy against the king for a wrong.[250] Through the petition of right, a direct recourse to the king was available in relation to wrongs which would today qualify as torts.

In addition to the petition of right, the king could be directly the subject of a claim in a recourse of *monstrans de droit* and could be made the subject of a defence by way of a *traverse of office* in a claim for property. In the Middle Ages, a subject could have resort to *monstrans de droit* to show that they had proper title. It was common practice then for a procedural enquiry to take place to establish the

242 Baker (n 2) 40–41.

243 JH Baker, *The Reports of Sir John Spelman*, vol 2 (Selden Society 1978) 71, n 4.

244 It later became associated with Magna Carta: Baker (n 2) 40–41.

245 Cane (n 200) 371.

246 Ehrlich (n 1) 96–97; Holdsworth (n 224) 14–15; Jaffe (n 54) 5; Cane (n 200) 371. Blackstone, in his *Commentaries*, made a historically inaccurate statement when he said that the petition of right was a remedy as of grace: Engdahl (n 1) 5; Blackstone, vol 1 (n 23) 236. See Chapter 4, section 3.3.

247 Holdsworth (n 1) 145; Holdsworth (n 224) 9.

248 Holdsworth (n 1) 151–52; Bloch (n 208) 360; Maitland (n 19) 23–24; Walter Ullmann, *Law and Politics in the Middle Ages: An Introduction to the Sources of Medieval Political Ideas* (Cornell UP 1975) 172. See also WS Holdsworth, 'The History of the Treatment of "Choses" in Action by the Common Law' (1920) 33 Harv L Rev 997.

249 Ehrlich (n 1) 14.

250 See *Robert de Clifton's Case* 18 Edw III 3 RP; *Gervais de Clifton* (1348) YB 22 Edw III, fo 5, pl 12.

veracity of allegations and claims to titles in the pleadings. *Traverse of office* could also be resorted to in medieval times when it was found during an enquiry into the facts that a king's tenant had transferred possession of the land without the king's permission, or where it was found that the party had a title and there was an issue with the king's title. In short, the procedure of *monstrans de droit* could be used at an inquisition into a dispute relating to the king's title or that of the king's tenant—allowing the subject to show further facts establishing her own rights—while *traverse of office* allowed the subject to contest the facts found.[251] Chapter 29 of the 1225 version of Magna Carta was also invoked in defence by subjects who questioned the king's rights before the courts (the 1225 charter was a slimmed down version of the 1215 original version of Magna Carta; it was granted by Henry III and was later conceived of as confirmed by parliamentary legislation).[252]

Petitions other than the petition of right understood as a judicial process could also be made by wronged subjects to seek 'legislative justice' in Parliament, as well as 'administrative justice' before the King's Council, often by invoking Magna Carta and the prohibition it imposed on the king and his officers no to deprive one of one's liberty.[253] In fact, petitions were presented in Parliament in the thirteenth century,[254] and from there they were transferred to the Chancellor, the Exchequer, or the appropriate court of justice, failing which a special commission was created.[255] From the fourteenth century, the practice of presenting a petition of right to the Chancellor to sue to the king was established.[256] Following the king's endorsement of the petition by fiat, if the facts were found to be true by a commission created for the purpose of investigating their veracity, the matter was sent back to the Chancery and, after the king's plea in response, the record was sent to courts

[251] 34 Edw III c 14; 36 Edw III St 1 c 13. *Monstrans de droit* and *traverse of office* were heard in Chancery and, when facts were contested, the matter was sent to trial in the King's Bench: Baker (n 2) 43–44. They were given a broadened scope by Parliament in 1548: 2 & 3 Edw VI c 8. See also *Conyngesby and Mallom v Regem* (1509) Case 438 in Caryll (n 66) 595, 599–602; *Sir George Reynel's Case* (1612) 9 Co Rep 95a; WS Holdsworth, 'The History of Remedies Against the Crown I' (1922) 38 LQR 141, 149, 158–59, 160, 162; William Reynell Anson, *The Law and Custom of the Constitution*, vol 2 part 2 (A Berriedale Keith ed, 4th edn, Clarendon Press 1935) 334.

[252] Baker (n 2) 6–8, 42, 44. Chapter 29 of the 1225 charter provided that 'No free man shall in future be arrested or imprisoned or disseised of his freehold, liberties or free customs, or outlawed or exiled or victimised in any other way, neither will we attack him or send anyone to attack him, except by the lawful judgment of his peers or by the law of the land. To no one will we sell, to no one will we refuse or delay right or justice.'

[253] ibid 48–49.

[254] The submission of written petitions to Parliament as a practice integral to the governing of the realm can be attributed to the reign of Edward I: Brand, 'Petitions and Parliament' (n 228).

[255] A first reform of the petitions occurred from the end of the thirteenth century, under the reign of Edward I, with the Statute of Petitions (1273) 8 Edw 1, and the Ordinance of Petitions (1280) 12 Edw 1, which transferred petitions presented in Parliament to the Chancellor, the Exchequer, and the Justices directly. Under Richard II, the remaining petitions in Parliament were reclassified as Bills of Parliament (which eventually became Acts of Parliament), Bills of Council (which eventually fell under the jurisdiction of the Court of Chancery, the Privy Council, and the Star Chamber), and Bills of Grace (which concerned the petition of right understood as a recourse to sue to the king, presented to the Chancellor from the fourteenth century): Clode (n 221) 13–19.

[256] FW Maitland, *The Constitutional History of England* (reprint of 1908 1st edn, CUP 1911) 224.

of law for adjudication.[257] As for other petitions presented in Parliament which did not pertain to claims against the king, they were eventually conceived of as parliamentary proceedings. To Edward Coke for example, famed common lawyer writing in the early seventeenth century, there were four sorts of proceedings in Parliament: by bill, judicature, petition of grace, and petition of right.[258] The petition of right presented in Parliament aimed to seek redress from the king, but in relation to claims which were often of a political nature. Famous instances of such petitions presented to the English king as requests and political demands include the Petition of Right presented to King Charles I in 1628, and the Petition presented to King George III in 1774 by the members of the First Continental Congress held in Philadelphia.[259] Petitions of a political nature and petitions to ask for the king's grace presented to Parliament or to the king differed from the petition of right understood as a judicial process before the courts to obtain redress when a subject's legal rights were infringed.

In summary, although the king could not be sued because of his feudal privilege not to be sued in his own courts and because there was no superior above him, he was nevertheless amenable to judicial process. Remedies were made available to the king's subjects, the most important of which was the general remedy of the petition of right. The petition of right was available if the plaintiff could show that he had suffered a wrong that the law recognized and that an ordinary writ would have been available if that wrong had been inflicted by an ordinary person and not by the king.[260]

As in the late Middle Ages, the petition of right in the Tudor era provided a way of circumventing the king's immunity from suit. The petition of right was conceived of as a residual remedy,[261] as of right,[262] to ensure that there was a recourse when a party could not have a *monstrans de droit*, a traverse of office, or a *scire facias* against the king.[263] A reading from the early 1500s shows that jurists conceived of the other remedies granted to the king's subjects to be exercised against the king—including the traverse of office and the *monstrans de droit*—to have been

[257] Clode (n 221) 10–13. Petitions of right were sent to the King's Bench, but petitions could also be presented in the Exchequer, as in the sixteenth-century cases of *Sir Henry Nevill's Case* (1570) 1 Plowden 377 and *Sir Thomas Wroth's Case* (n 128). The petition abated if the commissioners found the facts alleged in it to be untrue: Staunford (n 220) 77b.

[258] Elizabeth Read Foster, 'Petitions and the Petition of Right' (1974) 14 J Brit Stud 21, 21. For a discussion of writs of grace in parliamentary petitions and their relationship to the modern-day prerogative writs, see SA De Smith, 'The Prerogative Writs' (1951) 11 CLJ 40, 42–43.

[259] The English Bill of Rights of 1688 also guarantees the right to present a petition to the king: Bill of Rights 1688, 1 Will & Mar c 2, sess 2.

[260] Holdsworth (n 1) 156; Holdsworth (n 224) 17.

[261] See *Parkhurst v Prior of Lewes* (c1523–38) in Spelman (n 67) 15.

[262] Staunford (n 220) 'Petition of Right' fo 72b.

[263] *The Earl of Northumberland's Case* (1463) YB Mich 3 Edw IV, fo 24, pl 19, confirmed in *Multon v Coveney* (1575) Pasch 17 Eliz (CP) in James Dyer, *Reports from the Lost Notebooks of Sir James Dyer*, vol 2 (JH Baker ed, Selden Society 1994) 329, 331. See also Note from a reading of Richard Hesketh, Gray's Inn (c1515) in Spelman (n 67) 213; Caryll (n 66) 702.

elaborated to circumvent the long delays associated with the petition of right and ensure that they could rely on efficient remedies against the sovereign.[264]

The traverse of office given by statute was thought to be a better remedy than the petition of right.[265] It could be resorted to when it was found by office (ie an enquiry into the facts to establish the veracity of a claim) that a king's tenant has alienated property without his leave,[266] or where it was found by an office that the party had a title and there was an issue with that of the king or a king's tenant.[267] As the *monstrans de droit* and the traverse of office were speedier procedures than the petition of right, they superseded it in the sixteenth and seventeenth centuries.[268]

However, reporters in the sixteenth century still discussed the petition of right in their notes and it can also be found in their reports. Legal thinking was to the effect that the king was bound by right to grant a petition of right.[269] If the king took possession of someone's property, that person had for their only remedy a petition of right.[270] Similarly, the king could only be divested of fee simple by a petition to him.[271]

It was thought in the Tudor era that 'the law wills that whoever does wrong should be punished'[272] and that 'wherever a man has any wrong or damage the law gives him a remedy, and that is by way of an action'.[273] Under the reign of Henry VIII, the creation by Parliament of the courts of Augmentation,[274] Wards,[275] and Surveyors[276] also included the creation of new remedies made available to the subject as against the king in these courts. The petition of right was still perceived as a substitute for an action against the king, as can be discerned from a note by

264 Note from a reading, probably in Gray's Inn (c1504–09) in Spelman (n 67) 172.

265 Note 96 (1492) Hil (KB) (where plaintiff traversed the office given by the king relating to a wardship and a farm) in John Caryll, *Reports of Cases by John Caryll*, vol 1 (JH Baker ed, Selden Society 1998) 85–86.

266 *Conyngesby and Mallom v Regem* (1509) Case 438 in Caryll (n 66) 599–603.

267 34 Edw III c 14.

268 Holdsworth (n 1) 163; Borchard (n 3) 30–31. *Monstrans de droit* and traverse of office later fell into disuse from the latter part of the seventeenth century but, like the petition of right, they were said to 'have been recognised and acknowledged for many centuries' and to remain available as the proceedings that 'must be resorted to, if any dispute arises' against the crown as late as the first half of the nineteenth century: *R v Powell* (1841) 1 QB 352, 363 (Lord Denman) (113 ER 1166, 1171); see also *Doe v Roe* (1841) 8 M & W 579, 582 (Alderson B) (151 ER 1169) (Exch).

269 *Marmyon v Baldwyn* (1527) Mich (Exch) (Englefield JCP) in JH Baker (ed), *Reports of Cases from the Time of King Henry VIII*, vol 1 (Selden Society 2003) 64. See also a fifteenth-century reading, probably in Lincoln's Inn (c1455/60) in Baker (n 2) 253.

270 *The Serjeants' Case* (1531) Mich 23 Hen VIII (CP) William Yelverton's Notebook in Baker (n 110) 296.

271 *A Case Argued in the Inner Temple* (c1533) Reports of Caryll Junior, note 12, in Baker (n 110) 373–74.

272 *Burgh v Potkyn* (1522) Mich 14 Hen VIII (CP) (Brudenell CJ) in Baker (n 109) 134.

273 *Fyloll v Assheleygh* (1520) Trin 12 Hen VIII (Newport and Newdgate) in Baker (n 109) 14.

274 Act for the Establishing of the Court of Augmentations 1536, 27 Hen VIII c 27.

275 The Erection of the Court of Wards, and the Names and Several Duties of the Officers Thereof, in the Governance of the King's Wards, and their Estates 1540, 32 Hen VIII c 46.

276 The Erection of the Court of Surveyors of the King's Lands, the Names of the Officers There, and their Authority 1541, 33 Hen VIII c 39, s LVIII.

Caryll Junior,[277] where he explained that if a lord could have had no action against a common person, consequently the lord cannot have a petition to the king either, because the petition stands as a substitute for an action. That the petition of right against the king still stood as the equivalent of an action between common persons is made clear in that note by Caryll Junior, writing during the reign of Henry VIII:

> Therefore he [the lord] cannot have a petition, for that is in lieu of his action, and he has no action in this case. Also a petition is in lieu of a writ of right, and here he has no right until he enters.[278]

Although it was impossible to have a writ against the king in the Tudor era, it appears that legal thinking was still to the effect that the petition of right and other recourses fulfilled an equivalent function, so that the king would answer for a wrong.

2.3.4 Responsibility of the king's officers and servants in the Middle Ages and Tudor era

The responsibility of the king's agent was not yet individual in the late Middle Ages. Wrongful acts committed by agents of the king were attributed to the king, and the latter could decide to assume liability himself.[279] The recourse against an official of the king was therefore not automatic; the king had to consent to the suit against his official instead of choosing to claim as his own the official's act done in his name.

Bracton explained that a negligent sheriff who failed to fulfil the king's writ to attach a party to the detriment of the other party remained at the mercy of the king. A writ could be issued against the negligent sheriff ordering him to attach the party as he had been asked. Should the sheriff refuse to obey that second writ or a third one to the same effect, he faced amercement and contempt of court at the king's will.[280] A recourse for damages by the party against the negligent sheriff was not contemplated.

The Second Statute of Westminster[281] in its chapter 39—the Execution of Process Act 1285[282]—sets out remedies for the king's subjects against his sheriffs. The Execution of Process Act can at first glance appear to enshrine the personal liability of officials. It provides the king's subjects with a remedy against a wrongdoing sheriff, including damages.[283] The act also provided for the punishment of the sheriff by the king's justices and ultimately by the king himself.[284]

277 Reports of John Caryll Junior, Inner Temple, note 28 in Baker (n 110) 383.

278 ibid.

279 Ehrlich (n 1) 28–29, 129. Ehrlich explains that under the reign of Henry III, officials were punished in the Exchequer for violating their duties against the king, but also for wrongs done to private individuals. The individual responsibility of the officials was hampered by the king's privileges, but the king could waive the privilege, and the official then became liable in the ordinary way: ibid 29.

280 Folios 441–42, Bracton, vol 4 (n 39) 369–70.

281 Statute of Westminster II 1285, 13 Edw I St 1.

282 Execution of Process Act, 1285, 13 Edw I St 1 c 39.

283 ibid ss 8, 18.

284 ibid s 20.

Such emphasis on the king's sheriffs' personal liability could appear to vindicate Dicey's emphasis on the officials' liability as a core aspect of the rule of law. However, the king's officials' liability had to be provided for by statute, as appears clearly from the preamble of the Execution of Process Act 1285:

> WHEREAS of late our Lord the King . . . considering that divers of this Realm were disherited, by Reason that in many Cases, where Remedy should have been had, there was none provided by him nor his Predecessors, ordained certain Statutes right necessary and profitable for his Realm . . . thereupon did provide certain Acts, as shall appear here following.[285]

The common law did not provide the king's subjects with a remedy against the king's officials. As is apparent from the preamble and the act and from the fact that the Execution of Process Act creates a remedy that was previously non-existent, the king's subjects were remediless at common law against the king's agents' wrongful acts. In cases where the sheriff failed to execute the king's command or did not return with the full compensation to be paid to the plaintiff debtor, the latter was left without any remedy at common law. As the preamble of the Execution of Process Act 1285 indicates, the king's subjects were in a state of 'oppression' prior to Edward I's legislation. Indeed, the writ of action on the case was not yet in existence.[286] In short, there was no liability of the king's officials at common law. By enacting the Execution of Process Act 1285 and inviting his subjects to sue to him by petition, the king was acting in conformity with Bracton's statement that 'it is the king's duty to provide an adequate remedy to repress every wrong'.[287]

King Edward I's enactment of the Execution of Process Act 1285 must not be interpreted as confirmation that the king was completely immune from any form of remedy. As was noted in section 2.3.3, Edward I instituted the petition of right and recorded copies of petitions can be found for the year 1278. Moreover, the proclamation in the Parliament of 1341 in Edward III's reign that the subjects can submit a petition to the king for his agents' wrongs also illustrates that medieval English kings did not create remedies against their agents to the exclusion of their own responsibility: 'And it was also openly said to everyone that each person who felt himself aggrieved by the king or his officers or by others should put forward a petition, and they shall have good and suitable remedy.'[288]

[285] ibid.

[286] Action on the case did not originate from the *consimili casu* provision of the Statute of Westminster II 1285, 13 Edw I St I c 24, but rather resulted from later development of the common law in the late fourteenth and fifteenth centuries: TFT Plucknett, 'Case and Statute of Westminster II' (1931) 31 Colum LR 778; Elizabeth Jean Dix, 'The Origins of the Action of Trespass on the Case' (1937) 46 Yale LJ 1142; SFC Milsom, *Historical Foundations of the Common Law* (2nd edn, Butterworths 1981) 410.

[287] Folio 414b, Bracton, vol 4 (n 39) 289.

[288] (1341) (15 Edw III) 2 RP 127, note 5 *in fine* (memb 5), 'Edward III: April 1341' in Chris Given-Wilson and others (eds), *Parliament Rolls of Medieval England* (Woodbridge, 2005), *British History*

The Execution of Process Act was adopted in 1285 as part of the Second Statute of Westminster to tackle the maliciousness and corruption of the king's sheriffs. When such maliciousness was found, the sheriff was to be punished and charged with compensating the plaintiff. The reforming aspect of the Execution of Process Act and its aim to address the sheriffs' corruption is apparent from the text of the act. That the king felt bound to redress the situation is also apparent from the act itself. The king's honour in connection with his officials' wrongdoing is expressly referred to: a deceitful sheriff shall be 'punished as a Disheritor of our Lord the King and his Crown' as 'lying' sheriffs who 'make false returns' act 'much to the Dishonour of the King'. The issue the act is set to reform is presented as obstruction to justice caused by the fact 'that Sheriffs do not return Writs original and judicial; (2) and also for that they make false Returns unto the King's Writs'. The sheriffs are also warned by the act not to act wrongfully: 'let the Sheriffs beware from henceforth, for such Manner of Answers redound much to the Dishonour of the King'.

The Execution of Process Act was not enacted to create liability and a remedy against all of the king's officers. The act was adopted as remedial legislation to address the issue of the corruption of the king's sheriffs and it changed the common law only insofar as the king's corrupt sheriffs were concerned. Personal liability of the king's agents was not the common law rule.

The privilege not to be sued at common law belonged only to the king. If his lower agent was sued before the Court of the Exchequer on the basis of that privilege, the king could decide to waive the privilege and see his agent answerable before an ordinary court, which Edward I came gradually to do.[289] Only lower servants were amenable to suit before the Court of the Exchequer under Edward I, but all agents could be complained of to the king himself.[290] The rule under Edward II and III became more general: although agents were still not to be sued before ordinary courts, they were to be brought to suit either before an *ad hoc* court or the Court of the Exchequer.[291]

The king's agents being responsible to the king, a suit against them had both a disciplinary component—which could lead to punishment of the official—and also redress for the aggrieved party.[292] A recourse to the petition of right could then be had by the aggrieved party to obtain reparation from the king.[293]

When agents were to answer for their acts before the Court of Exchequer, the fact that the unlawful act was due to an order of the king was considered to be a

Online <http://www.british-history.ac.uk/no-series/parliament-rolls-medieval/april-1341> accessed 5 February 2018.

[289] Ehrlich (n 1) 111.
[290] ibid.
[291] ibid 153.
[292] ibid 111.
[293] ibid 200.

good justification, at least as late as the reign of Edward III.[294] However, there is evidence from a case of 1334, under the reign of Edward III, that the defence that the king's agent was simply following orders from a superior was controversial.[295] In that case, a woman had been arrested by the marshal for having fled the king's household and her custody was given to the gaoler. It appears from the discussion recorded in the Year Book that the argument had been made in favour of the defendant gaoler that he should always accept custody of prisoners so as to follow the orders of his king. While some justices appear to agree that wrong should not be attributed to the gaoler, the final determination of the case is not clear.[296] Twentieth-century discoveries in the plea rolls in the king's courts for the fourteenth century also show that the validity of a defence to the effect that an order had been issued from a higher authority was a controversial issue.[297] In one case, the court found in favour of the plaintiff who had been wrongfully arrested, even if the order had been given to the king's bailiff by the sheriff.[298] In another case, the mayor of London was sued for false imprisonment and the sufficiency of the warrant issued by the Council and treasurer was questioned.[299] Although the issue was not settled, the fact that the mayor was sued and the competence of authorities was questioned shows that there was no established and generalized immunity from suit for officials.[300] But nor was there full liability either: in two cases involving the Statute of Malborough, for instance, there was a discussion of the king's[301] and the queen's[302] agents' status as differing from that of common persons.

In summary, the king's agents in the Middle Ages were initially subject only to the jurisdiction of special courts and could rely on the defence of having followed the king's unlawful order to exonerate themselves until the reign of Edward III. The House of Lords in *M v Home Office* omitted to mention this first stage in the notion of *the king can do no wrong*, stating instead that from the thirteenth to the fifteenth centuries: 'The corollary was that the King's servants could not rely on royal orders as a defence, even where they in fact acted on royal authority.' [303] That officials could in fact invoke as a valid defence the unlawful order of the king was the reverse

[294] ibid 129, 200.
[295] (1333) YB Trin 7 Edw III, fo 23b, pl 1.
[296] One may presume that the court found in favour of the woman, as the court declared itself willing to help her, seeing that 'she was poor and was not represented by counsel'.
[297] Morris S Arnold, *Select Cases of Trespass from the King's Courts, 1307–1399*, vol 1 (Selden Society 1985) xxxvi–xxxvii.
[298] *Thomas Wenlock v Roger de Drayton*, case no 4.13, ibid 52.
[299] KB 27/229 m 78d (1317).
[300] Arnold (n 297) xxxvii; nightwatchmen were especially at risk of being sued: xxxviii–xxxix.
[301] *Strode v Ergleys et al* (1311) YB Hil 5 Edw II, pl 26 in William Craddock Bolland, *Year Book of Edward II (1311–1312)* (Selden Society 1915) 119.
[302] (1356) YB Hil 30 Edw III fo 5, unnumbered plea.
[303] *M v Home Office* [1994] 1 AC 377, 389–90. Such historical analysis also throws doubt on Miller J's observation in the United States Supreme Court that 'no government has ever held itself liable to individuals for the misfeasance, laches or unauthorized exercise of power by its officers or agents': *Gibbons v United States* (1868) 75 US 269, 274.

of the position developed in modern times and expounded by Dicey, that all officials must be brought to justice before ordinary courts and judged according to the common law.[304] There was the possibility for medieval servants to rely on the unlawfulness of their sovereign's command to avoid justice. Such result is the opposite of the doctrine developed in the nineteenth century that liability must instead lie on the king's officers personally. Since the seventeenth century and predominantly with Dicey's influence, *the king can do no wrong* stands for the idea that the king's wrongful command is void in law and that liability must rest with the king's ministers and officials.[305] The current understanding of *the king can do no wrong*—the king's officials cannot rely on the king's unlawful command as a defence—is different from that of the Middle Ages, where the king's agents could exonerate themselves by arguing that they were following the king's unlawful orders.

As far as agents' liability for acts done in pursuance of their functions as the king's servants is concerned, the king's vicarious amenability to judicial process was limited in the late Middle Ages. The king's limited vicarious amenability to judicial process in that period was nevertheless compensated for by the fact that the king could assume direct liability for the acts of his agents, a possibility that has since been largely lost with regard to the wrongs of crown servants. With the adoption of crown proceedings legislation in the twentieth century, a reverse situation to that prevailing in the late Middle Ages was created: vicarious liability for the wrong of a crown servant is now the predominant feature of the law of crown liability.

The findings recounted so far in this chapter in relation to the theory of kingship and the remedies available against the king in the Middle Ages allow us to trace the development of two distinct notions—the king under the law and his immunity from suit—which distinctly underpinned the *king can do no wrong* at the end of the fifteenth century. The *king can do no wrong* was not yet the idea that the king is perfect and as such is incapable of doing wrong. As a result, the two dimensions of *the king can do no wrong*—the liability of the king (his capacity to commit a wrong) and his overall amenability to judicial process—were both important features of the medieval understanding that *the king can do no wrong*.

2.3.4.1 Tudor developments: interaction between the king's liability and that of his officials

The king's subjects did not have remedies at common law against the king's agents in the Middle Ages and late Middle Ages. The enactment of the Execution of Process Act 1285 created a remedy only as against the king's sheriffs.[306] As in the

[304] AV Dicey, *Lectures Introductory to the Study of the Law of the Constitution: The Oxford Edition of Dicey*, vol 1 (JWF Allison ed, OUP 2013) 100–01.

[305] See eg *Tobin v The Queen* (1864) 16 CB NS 310, 354 (143 ER 1148, 1165).

[306] Statute of Westminster II 1285, 13 Edw I St 1 c 39.

late Middle Ages, it was not possible in the Tudor era to have an ordinary action against the king but it was possible to have a petition of right against the king as well as an action against his officials.[307] Cases in relation to officials' liability in the Tudor era all relate to the king's sheriffs', under-sheriffs', and bailiffs' liability.

Officers sued by aggrieved individuals could pray aid of the king to help them for having executed his commands. Aid prayer was eventually denied, but evidence of such aid in legal literature dates to Coke's era.[308]

It was impossible in the Tudor era to have a third-party action against the king (aid of him by way of voucher). However, it was possible for the king's sheriff to ask aid of the monarch when he was sued for a wrong: when a king's sheriff or bailiff was sued pursuant to the king's lawful command, they could ask the help of the king by way of an aid prayer.[309] For instance, if a lawful act was done for the king, such as a bailiff taking a horse for the king, it was considered to be right that the king's official be aided.[310] Likewise, a sheriff appointed by the king and an under-sheriff appointed by the former could both ask aid of the king in a writ against them when they acted for the king.[311]

Procedure-wise, in a case of aid prayer, a delay would ensue once the case was initiated before it could be heard in the next assize. There is also mention of the opportunity to speak with the king in the meantime:

> By an aid prayer in assize the suit is not put off without day but the parties shall have a day at the next assize, and in the mean time may sue to the king and interplead with the king in Chancery; and, if he does not come at the next assize, it is discontinued and the party shall be reattached.[312]

If he does not come at the next assize, however, the procedure in aid prayer is discontinued and the party is reattached to the original case, according to Caryll's note. Dyer equally reported a case where the queen's agents, who were sued for having trespassed on a citizen of York by taking a piece of cloth for payment of a toll, prayed aid of the queen and a consultation with the queen followed prior to proceeding to judgment. The queen accepted the citizen of York's claim that a charter made during the reign of Richard I exempted all citizens of York from

[307] *King's College, Cambridge v Hekker* (1522) Mich 14 Hen VIII (King's Bench) (Fyneux CJ) in Baker (n 109) 101.

[308] See Chapter 3, section 3.3.2.

[309] *Bedyll v Copwode*, between (1510) (Trin) and (1511) (Pash), Exchequer of Pleas (Fitzherbert), E13/187, mm 5, 6d, from an anonymous report 'En temps Hen VIII' (1510–1535) in Baker, *Cases from Henry VIII* (n 269) 10. See also (1499) Mich 15 Hen VII, fo 17a, pl 11, where the bailiff was sued in trespass for taking goods. The plaintiff was holding of the king a manor of the Duchy of Lancaster and the bailiff in that case seized the goods for rent in arrears to the service of the king.

[310] *Bedyll v Copwode* in Baker, *Cases from Henry VIII* (n 269) 10.

[311] ibid.

[312] Reports of John Caryll Junior, note 45 in Baker (n 110) 389.

toll throughout the realm, and the defendants then had to answer formally the plaintiff's suit.[313]

However, it also appears from a reading at the Inns of court in 1529 on the subject of the king's officers that if the king ordered an unlawful thing, his officer could not always rely on the king's order to exonerate himself, and certainly not if that order was not in writing.[314]

Two observations can be made in relation to that reading of 1529. First, it shows that the state of the law in relation to officers' liability evolved. An officer under the reigns of Edward II and Edward III could invoke the king's order as a defence and the king could still assume liability. Similarly, it appears that in the middle of the fifteenth century, bailiffs, serjeants, and other of the king's officers could still plead the order of the king as justification for their unlawful act committed by the king's command.[315] But discussions identified in the plea rolls for the fifteenth century show that there was a controversy in legal circles as to the validity of defences based on the fact that orders were given from higher authorities in cases of trespass.[316] That it was thought in 1529 that an officer could invoke the king's order as a defence only if that order was in writing narrows down the possibility for the king's officer of being exonerated. It is in line with a case from 1438 noted by Fitzherbert: a command from the king can constitute a valid plea in defence if made in writing.[317] Whereas defences claiming that the order had been given from a higher competent authority had been rejected on certain occasions in the fifteenth century, it appears from that reading from 1529 that the accepted rule was now that laid down in 1438: that if the order was given in writing, the defence was valid.

Second, that the order of the king was characterized as being 'void' in 1529 is an important development. In *Cavendish's Case* in the reign of Elizabeth I,[318] judges who had refused to obey the queen's unlawful command argued that they did not have to obey it because it was contrary to the laws of the land. The principle that the king was not entitled to do wrong and that his wrongful acts were consequently not those of a king had been established since Bracton. Bracton laid down the jurisdiction of the king, and it extended only to lawful acts. The conclusion that the king's wrongful orders are void is in keeping with Bracton's theory of kingship. However, the fact that the king's order was void if wrongful did not lead in the sixteenth century to the conclusion that no remedies could be had against the king: the petition of right was still considered to be a remedy equivalent to an ordinary action.

313 Anon (1576–78) in Dyer (n 263) 357.
314 Baker (n 2) 106.
315 See (1460) YB Mich 39 Hen VI, fo 17, pl 21; Chrimes (n 2) 54.
316 See Arnold (n 297).
317 *Monstrauns* (1438) Trin 16 Hen VI in Anthony Fitzherbert, *La Graunde Abridgement*, vol 2 (Tottel 1577) 83.
318 *Cavendish's Case*, 1 And 152, 155 (123 ER 403).

In short, the fact that the king's official could not exonerate himself by relying on a void, unwritten order, did not imply in the sixteenth century that the king was correlatively absolutely immune from all forms of legal recourses. The reading from 1529 cannot be said to represent the later, seventeenth-century understanding of *the king can do no wrong* which can be found in Hale's work and which was given prominence in the nineteenth-century cases of *Tobin* and *Feather*, discussed in subsequent chapters.[319] In those much later cases, it was held that a wrongful order from the king is void and cannot be attributed to the king, negating the possibility of a remedy against the king—including the petition of right. Following those nineteenth-century cases, the sole recourse to be had in tort was in the form of an action against the official personally. That more recent, Victorian understanding of *the king can do no wrong*—there can be no wrong in the king—is materially different from that held in the sixteenth century.

2.3.4.2 Tudor developments: personal liability of the king's sheriffs and judges

During the Tudor era, the king's sheriffs and even his judges were also subject to the prohibition not to do wrong embodied by *the king can do no wrong*. Sheriffs could be sued for a wrong committed by them in the exercise of their function, as many cases for that period demonstrate.[320]

A party 'condemned in debt, trespass, or similar actions' was remanded to the sheriff's custody pending execution. It was considered to be a common law rule that if the condemned party escaped from custody, the aggrieved other party could have an action in debt against the sheriff who let her escape.[321] The aggrieved party could also have a remedy against a sheriff who wrongly released defendants who could not be recovered.[322] An aggrieved party could also have an action and recover damages against a sheriff in certain cases of false returns; the sheriff was not liable when the return was not solely based on his knowledge, for instance when it was directed by the oath of twelve men and where the sheriff was bound to return as they had found.[323] Similarly, a party could have a writ of trespass against a sheriff who returned less than he took from the defendant, or who returned nothing.[324] It was not possible to traverse the sheriff's return in a case of rescue where the person arrested was illegally freed, but a writ of deceit could be had against the sheriff if the allegation that there had been a rescue was 'not good and true'.[325] A sheriff could

[319] See Chapter 3 for a discussion of Matthew Hale's understanding of *the king can do no wrong*, and see Chapters 4 and 5 on the nineteenth-century cases on the petition of right and their subsequent influence on legal thinking in relation to crown liability.

[320] John Hales' reading (Gray's Inn, 1514), Gray's Inn, MS25 fo 295; *Corbet v Marsham* (1512) KB27/1005, m 87v, cited in Baker (n 243) 91.

[321] Roger Yorke's Notebook, note 198 in Baker, *Cases from Henry VIII* (n 269) 164–65.

[322] Anonymous Reports, note 22, (1520) Mich King's Bench and Common Pleas in ibid 41.

[323] *Pulteney v Andrewe* (1511) Pash Common Pleas in ibid 14.

[324] Yorke's Notebook, note 260 in ibid 189–90.

[325] Port's Notebook, Notes Taken in the Inner Temple and Westminster Hall, note 71, (1523 or 1524) (King's Bench) in John Port, *The Notebook of Sir John Port* (JH Baker ed, Selden Society 1986) 122.

also be sued by a creditor, and damages recovered, if the sheriff took the goods of the debtor arrested for felony before he was attainted.[326] If a juror was found to be older than the legal limit to serve on the jury, the court could not hear the challenge as it had to take the jury as it was returned by the sheriff. But the juror could have a remedy against the sheriff.[327] A lord could also have an action against a sheriff who did not ask for his consent before serving a process within specific exempted areas ('liberties').[328]

Judges could also be found liable. If a court was without jurisdiction and the sheriff acted against the defendant in an action on trespass on the justices' direction, both the justices and the sheriff were considered to be trespassers. The justices were found to be trespassing in awarding the process on which they had no jurisdiction and the sheriff, their servant, was also a trespasser for the reason that 'he shall not be in a better condition than his master'.[329] Similarly, 'if a judge of the King's Bench awarded a grand *cape* in plea of land, and the sheriff takes the land into the king's hand, there the judge and the sheriff are disseisors'.[330] Judges and sheriffs were also considered to be wrongdoers in the case of judges of the Common Bench exceeding their power in sentencing to death a person condemned of felony.[331]

That judges were considered to be wrongdoers under certain circumstances in the sixteenth century can be explained by the fact that justices were conceived of as the king's servants, the king being fount of justice. Findings of judges' liability were, however, more nuanced than for the king's sheriffs. Already in the sixteenth century, there was a controversy as to whether or not judges were punishable when they acted as judges. For instance, Yelverton noted that judges were not punishable when they acted 'as judge'.[332]

Similar language in support of complete judicial immunity for judicial acts committed by justices of the peace could be found in the fifteenth century.[333] But Caryll Junior reported contrary arguments. He noted that it was said on the one hand that if a justice of the peace removes a person from possession by force when that person had a right to it by statute, the justice had no warrant and was therefore a wrongdoer who could be punished like any other common person. Others said,

See also Port's note 15 in his 'Notes form the Readings in the Inner Temple 1493–1503' in ibid, '*The Notebook of Sir John Port*' 146.

[326] (1554) Trin, King's Bench, Dalison's Reports, case 11 in William Dalison, *The Reports of William Dalison: 1552–1558* (JH Baker ed, Selden Society 2007) 76.

[327] Yelverton's Notebook, note 93 (*c*1545–50), Common Pleas in Baker (n 110) 357.

[328] *Bailiffs and Burgesses of Shrewsbury v Vernon* (1526) Mich Common Pleas, Yorke's Notebook, note 413 in Baker, *Cases from Henry VIII* (n 269) 239.

[329] Yelverton's Notebook, note 21 (1529–30) in Baker (n 110) 322.

[330] ibid. A grand *cape* was a writ to recover possession of land.

[331] ibid.

[332] ibid.

[333] (1472) Mich 12 Edw IV, fos 18a–18b, pl 23; (1484) Mich 2 Ric III, fos 9b–11a, pl 22.

on the other hand, that because the judge was to be the judge of that person's act, he thereby had jurisdiction. If the judge removes the person from possession as a judge in such a case, where the person had lawful possession, he is excused for doing so because his wrongdoing is grounded in the judge's lack of knowledge of the law. Caryll Junior also noted that a judge was not liable for wrongly giving a judgment that someone be hanged when that person should not have been.[334] An argument was emerging that when a judge was acting in his jurisdiction, but made a mistake in law, he was not punishable because his wrongdoing was 'merely a lack of knowledge'.[335]

In summary, if an official of the king was sued, he could pray aid to the king. A delay ensued until the next assize and there was an opportunity to speak to the king in the meantime. If the aid prayer was discontinued, the party was reattached[336]—the case was sent back to proceed as it was before the aid prayer was initiated. The king could not issue a protection to exempt his agent from the proceedings against the latter except in limited circumstances. For example, the king could grant a protection where an agent had to be sent abroad on the king's service. However, even the king's command that the agent be under his protection by his 'royal prerogative, which we will not have disputed' was set aside by judges when it did not meet statutory requirements at the end of the fifteenth[337] and beginning of the sixteenth centuries.[338] Such protections increased in number towards the middle of the sixteenth century, and though there are some instances where judges were reluctant to adjudicate on their validity,[339] the court came to quash them formally in 1581.[340] The king's agent could therefore be sued personally, and could have aid of the king, but could generally not be exempted by the king's protection. The Tudor era was marked by an increased number of cases relating to the king's officials' liability, including that of judges. The king's officials—like their master, the king himself—were not entitled to do wrong. But the king's immunity from suit was not absolute: the petition of right and other remedies were available as against the king and were thought equivalent to ordinary actions. A subject could therefore have recourse to a petition of right against the king or—eventually—an ordinary action against his servant.

[334] Reports of Caryll Junior, note 47 in Baker (n 110) 390.

[335] ibid. See also (1484) Mich 2 Ric III, fos 9b–11a, pl 22. For a discussion of when judgments were void and voidable, see Yorke's Notebook, note 258 in Baker, *Cases from Henry VIII* (n 269) 187.

[336] On the effect of reattachment, see (1520) Mich *Walker v Robynson*, KB 27/1030, m 26 'Anonymous Reports—En temps Henry VIII', note 34 in Baker, *Cases from Henry VIII* (n 269) 49–50.

[337] *Devykke v Halman* (1495) 11 Henry VII, CP 40/934, m 124 referred to in JH Baker, 'Introduction' in James Dyer, *Reports from the Lost Notebooks of Sir James Dyer*, vol 1 (JH Baker ed, Selden Society 1994) lxxxiv, 153.

[338] *Isaac v Camden* (1515) CP 40/1010, m 66d, referred to in ibid lxxxiv.

[339] See eg *Alcock v Hitchcock* (1572) Mich, Common Pleas, ibid 152.

[340] ibid lxxxiv–lxxxv; *Warram's Case* (1587) Moo KB 239, 72 ER 553.

3 Coining of *the king can do no wrong*

In this section, cases where statements resembling *the king can do no wrong* were made, as well as cases traditionally identified as the first recorded occurrences of the phrase, will be analysed. It will be demonstrated, first, that although fifteenth-century expressions now taken to resemble *the king can do no wrong* could hardly be construed as a reference to Bracton's text, the cases where they can be found show that the general legal understanding was the Bractonian one that the king was not entitled to do wrong. Second, the significance of the petition of right as a remedy available to a subject wronged by the king in those cases will be analysed.

I will then turn to Edward Coke's role in coining *the king can do no wrong* by giving the phrase pride of place, in different languages, at the turn of the seventeenth century. Coke, a towering figure of the common law, was as much a late sixteenth-century Tudor lawyer versed in Bracton's work as an early seventeenth-century common lawyer and Parliamentarian. He was a figure of constitutional change anchored in continuity—much like *the king can do no wrong* he coined.

3.1 Fifteenth-century developments: the king cannot be a wrongdoer

Traditionally, the first recorded appearance of *the king can do no wrong* has been said to date back to 1483.[341] However, the coining of *the king can do no wrong* is not to be found in that case. In 1937, Rogers translated the 1559 Tottel edition of that excerpt of the Year Books as follows:

> [N]ote that it was said on the same day in the Chancery . . . , and agreed by all the Judges and Serjeants being there . . . that the king could not be said to be one who committed wrong, because if one would disseise another to the use of the king, where the king had no right, the king could not be said to be a disseisor.[342]

Rogers's translation of this case of 1483 should be read in light of earlier cases of 1457, 1463, and 1464, reported in the Year Books, where it is said that the king cannot be said to be a disseisor, but that when he commits disseisin, the disseised can sue him by petition.[343] Similar reasoning can be found in a case of 1467, where it was argued that the king cannot have possession if he obtained the land wrongfully, on the basis that 'the king ought to take no land from anyone'.[344] In cases of

[341] (1483) YB Trin 1 Edw V, fo 8a, pl 13; Ehrlich (n 1) 139; Holdsworth (n 2) 466; Pickthorn (n 2) 162; Roberts (n 2) 4, 7; Greenberg (n 153) 209; Baker (n 2) 45.

[342] Harvard Law Library MS 1329, fo 48, pl 13, <https://www.bu.edu/phpbin/lawyearbooks/display.php?id = 21049> accessed 12 December 2017.

[343] (1457) YB Trin 35 Hen VI, fos 60a–63b, pl 1; *The Earl of Northumberland's Case* (n 263); (1464) YB Mich 4 Edw IV, fo 25b, pl 3.

[344] (1467) YB Mich 7 Edw 4, fos 16b–18a, 17 (Fairfax sjt), pl 11.

wrongful disseisin of the subject, the title remained with the subject.[345] In all the cases listed where it was said that the king cannot be a disseisor, although the king is not called a disseisor, the notion of a wrong having been committed was maintained and the wrong—the disseisin—did not disappear. Regular proceedings were not available to the ousted subject, who could not sue the king directly before the king's judges and who instead had to sue to the king by petition. In the cases where it is said that the king cannot be a disseisor, the claim via petition, although procedurally different, appears to be considered to be of similar remedial effect to an ordinary action available against an ordinary person.

Nevertheless, the case of 1483, translated by Rogers, marks a transition. In place of the previous notion that the king cannot be called disseisor, it was now stated that he cannot be said to be one who committed a wrong. There was a broadening of the language that had so far been confined to land law and disseisin and to the king's status as disseisor. From the legal fiction that the king automatically lost possession when he was without right to seisin and was presumed to always be a possessor in good faith was formulated the idea that he could not be said to be a disseisor, and ultimately that the king cannot be said to have committed a wrong.

Ehrlich[346] and Holdsworth[347] reported that there was not yet in 1457 a defined position as to the king's capacity to commit a wrong. They submit that both positions were argued.[348] Yet a closer reading of the case of 1457 shows that the judges agreed that the king could do a wrong, even if he could not be called a disseisor. The reasons why the king cannot be called a disseisor vary in the judges' speeches in that case, but they relate to procedural technicalities that do not go to the king's incapacity to commit a wrong. In fact, it appears that the reason why the king could not be called a disseisor was that there was no ordinary action available against him. The term 'disseisor', as is apparent from the judges' discourse, implied that a writ was available to the disseised. As there was no such ordinary remedy against the king, he could not be called a disseisor. For instance, Danvers JCP found that 'the king can wrong a man as another man can do, and against him I shall have reparation by way of petition as I would have against another man by way of action'.[349] It also appears from Moyle's speech that the king cannot be said to be a disseisor, but that he is capable of doing a wrong.[350] To illustrate his argument that the king

[345] ibid.

[346] Ehrlich (n 1) 139, fn 4.

[347] Holdsworth (n 2) 466.

[348] (1457) YB Trin 35 Hen VI, fos 60a–63b, pl 1. Although the case contains interesting discussions on the king's capacity to commit a wrong, the outcome of the case seemed to turn rather on the issue of whether a general statute on usurpation, Statute of Westminster II 1285, 13 Edw I St 1 c 25, could be said to apply to the king or not.

[349] (1457) YB Trin 35 Hen VI, fos 60a, 62, pl 1. The excerpts from that case in this section can be found, with an English translation, at <https://www.bu.edu/phpbin/lawyearbooks/display.php?id = 19169> accessed 1 December 2017. I read the original old French and adjusted the translation of the excerpts when necessary.

[350] (1457) YB Trin 35 Hen VI, fos 60a, 61, pl 1.

cannot be a disseisor, Moyle hypothesized that if the king entered on someone's land and ousted him without title, the ousted person could occupy the land and not answer for the profits because the king cannot wrongfully gain seisin of the land. Moyle's hypothesis showed how the king could do a wrong, but how that would not then affect the aggrieved party since the king needed a title to oust the person. The primary consideration of the procedural rule or the remedy—the need for the king to act by title or the availability of the petition of right instead of an ordinary writ—appeared yet again to dictate whether the king could be called a disseisor.

A similar primacy of the remedy available in relation to the idea that the king cannot be a disseisor can be discerned from Ashton JCP's speech. Ashton explained that the king was not to be called a disseisor because no action could be brought against him, only a petition. Ashton then reasoned that a petition to the king in that case was in the same nature as an assize against another person: 'I will sue him by a petition in the nature of an assize and by it I will have a remedy as I would have had by way of assize against another person: thus I think of the remedy as if I had by assize against another person.'[351] Consequently, to Ashton, there was a remedy available against the king as there was against another person and the outcome was similar, but the nature of the procedure differed. The fact that the king could not be called a disseisor was mandated by the absence of a normal recourse of assize against the king. The impossibility of calling the king a disseisor was merely a procedural distinction, given that the petition amounted to an equivalent remedy in Ashton's reasoning. The impossibility of calling the king a disseisor did not go to the king's capacity to commit a wrong: the king was capable of committing a wrong but was not entitled to do so.

Similar reasoning to the effect that the king, when he committed disseisin, could not be called a disseisor but that he could nevertheless be sued to by petition was apparent from the two other cases dating back to 1463 and 1464 mentioned at the beginning of this section,[352] as well as the 1407 *Knotting's Case*.[353]

An illustration that the king was still considered capable of committing a wrong can be found in the Year Books as late as the year 1485.[354] Huse CJ's speech in *obiter* in that case was that the king could not arrest a subject for treason or felony because if he were to commit a wrong (*tort*) by doing so, it would deprive the subject of a remedy, given that no recourse could be had against the king in such cases. Holdsworth opined that Huse CJ's rule was a practical rule.[355] The rule was practical because it implied that the king was capable of doing wrong—although he was

[351] (1457) YB Trin 35 Hen VI, fos 60a, 61, pl 1.

[352] See n 343.

[353] (1407) YB Mich 9 Hen IV, fo 4, pl 17, in which Gascoigne CJ would have allowed an action which was ultimately denied by Hankford J, who claimed that the king could not be a disseisor and therefore that the petition of right was the appropriate remedy: M Hemmant (ed), *Select Cases in the Exchequer Chamber before All the Justices of England, 1377–1461* (Quaritch 1933) 5.

[354] (1485) YB Mich 1 Hen VII, fo 4b, pl 5.

[355] Holdsworth (n 2) 465–66.

not entitled to—but that he should not do wrong, as that would wrong a subject and leave him without a remedy.

The full excerpt of Huse CJ's reasoning was to the effect that the king, unlike his lieges,[356] cannot arrest a subject, because it would deprive that subject of a remedy. That the king's lieges could arrest a person, because that person would not then be deprived of a remedy against the king's liege if the arrest was wrongful, shows that the feudal privilege that a lord cannot be sued in his own courts appears to be the basis of Huse CJ's reasoning. His statement clearly highlights the importance of the availability of a remedy for the subject, as did previous cases in the Year Books. At the end of the fifteenth century, the reasoning as illustrated by Huse CJ's speech was that the king—as other feudal lords—was not incapable of committing a wrong, but that he must not commit a wrong when the subject would have no remedy.

To Holdsworth, Huse CJ's reasoning showed that *the king can do no wrong* was rooted in the feudal privilege that the king could not be sued in his own courts.[357] Holdsworth also believed *the king can do no wrong* meant that the king is incapable of doing wrong and to encapsulate the concept of ministerial responsibility.[358] But Holdsworth's argument that Huse CJ associated *the king can do no wrong* with the king's immunity from suit in his own courts is anachronistic: it is based on the current understanding that *the king can do no wrong* means immunity from suit and ministerial responsibility. What Huse CJ's reasoning illustrated was rather that the Bractonian understanding that the king was not entitled to do wrong was to be interpreted in conjunction with the fact that the king had a feudal privilege not to be sued in his own courts. In order to prevent the king's feudal immunity from circumventing the understanding that the king was not entitled to do wrong, Huse CJ reasoned that the king was not entitled to do certain things to begin with. The primacy of the understanding that the king was not entitled to do wrong was apparent. To ensure that the king did not do wrong to a subject in cases where the subject would have no remedy, Huse CJ insisted that the king simply could not do certain acts. The crux of Huse CJ's speech was that the king could not do a wrong in the sense that he was not entitled to do a wrong. That the king was not entitled to do

[356] The relevant excerpt is translated as follows: 'the king cannot arrest a man on suspicion of treason or felony, as his other lieges may, because if he does wrong the party cannot have an action', in Baker (n 2) 46.

[357] Holdsworth (n 2) 462. cf Baker (n 2) 45: Baker argues—rightly—that the feudal rule that the king cannot be sued in his own courts had no connection with *the king can do no wrong*. To Street—in an uncharacteristically erroneous interpretation—Huse CJ's decision was that there was no petition of right for a 'pure tort', and the decision then led to *the king can do no wrong* in the sixteenth century: Harry Street, 'Tort Liability of the State: The Federal Tort Claims Act and the Crown Proceedings Act' (1948–49) 47 Mich L Rev 341, 341. But Huse CJ did not mention the petition of right in his decision. Moreover, Huse CJ could not have ruled, as Street surmised, that the petition of right was not available for a 'pure tort': the law of tort as we know it underwent major developments over the course of nineteenth century and could not have been the law Huse CJ was acquainted with in 1485. Holdsworth and Street confused *the king can do no wrong* with the king's feudal privilege not to be sued in his own courts, but the two are distinct.

[358] WS Holdsworth, *A History of English Law*, vol 3 (3rd edn, Methuen 1923) 465–66.

wrong was paramount and Huse CJ's aim was to ensure that the Bractonian understanding that *the king can do no wrong* was not thwarted by the feudal privilege of immunity from suit in the king's own courts. In Huse CJ's speech, that the king cannot do a wrong did not mean immunity from suit or that the king was incapable of doing wrong; it meant that the king was not entitled to do wrong.

Also of importance in demonstrating that the king was still conceived of as being capable of committing a wrong at the end of the fifteenth century is the 1473 case in the Court of Exchequer later reported as *Baker's Case*.[359] It was held in that case that the king could not delay procedures by changing his issue (ie what had been pleaded earlier in defence) in a suit in which he was defendant, on the basis that the king by his prerogative cannot do wrong to another.[360] The understanding that the king's prerogative can only be used for the good of the people also figured later during the Tudor era in *Willion v Berkley*.[361] As Baker argues, the sixteenth-century rule that the king's prerogative can only be used for the good of the people can be conceived of as an application of *the king can do no wrong* taken as a limitation of the king's power.[362]

In summary, at the end of the fifteenth century, the expression that the king cannot be said to be one who did wrong did not mean that the king was incapable of committing a wrong. Rather, there was a distinction between the king's capacity to commit a wrong and the king's immunity from suit. That the king's immunity from suit could be overcome by the availability of the petition of right was significant in fifteenth-century cases. When the petition of right was not available, the king was simply not allowed to commit the act, as Huse CJ's *obiter* of 1485 demonstrates.

To conclude, fifteenth-century statements which, in hindsight, resembled *the king can do no wrong*, were uttered at a time where Bracton's treatise was at its lowest popularity and in a context where lawyers did not think about law in terms of overarching legal theories. It has been advanced that Bracton's treatise's importance among contemporaries persisted for 100 years and then declined in the fourteenth and fifteenth centuries[363] before it regained its previous status late in the fifteenth century and in the sixteenth and seventeenth centuries.[364] The indifference of fourteenth- and fifteenth-century jurists to Romanist legal theory and, conversely, their marked emphasis on maxims and procedure, has been said to have led them to lose sight of founding principles.[365] For instance, there were occurrences in pleadings

[359] (1473) YB Pasch 13 Edw IV, fo 8a pl 1.

[360] For a similar reasoning to the effect that the king can change issue only when that does not inflict damage to the other party, see (1470) Mich 49 Hen VI note 20 (Billing CJ) in N Neilson, *Year Books of Edward IV*, vol 47 (Selden Society 1930) 146.

[361] *Willion v Berkley* (n 68) 246 (Brown J), see section 2.2.3.

[362] Baker (n 2) 150.

[363] Yale (n 11) 383; Dauchy and others (n 8) 33.

[364] JH Baker, *Oxford History of the Laws of England*, vol 6 (OUP 2003) 22–23; Ian Williams, 'A Medieval Book and Early-Modern Law: Bracton's Authority and Application in the Common Law c. 1550–1640' (2011) 79 Leg Hist Rev 47, 59–60.

[365] Holdsworth (n 65) 287; Yale (n 11) 383.

and in the texts of the Inns of Court of statements to the effect that the king was above the law, in flagrant contradiction of Bracton's theory of kingship, discussed in section 2.1.1.[366] By the fifteenth century, English practitioners received lectures at the Inns of Court,[367] but these readings were not aimed at teaching law as an overarching system[368] and there was no mention of Bracton in them before the end of the fifteenth century.[369] There is no evidence that the fifteenth-century expressions—the king cannot be a disseisor or a wrongdoer—which resembled *the king can do no wrong*, were references to Bracton. Nevertheless, when statements resembling *the king can do no wrong* appeared in the fifteenth century, they still conveyed the understanding found in Bracton that the king was not entitled to do wrong. The fifteenth-century expressions did not convey the current understandings of *the king can do no wrong* that the king is incapable of doing wrong or that his ministers are to be held accountable in his stead. An analysis of the cases where early statements resembling *the king can do no wrong* can be found demonstrates that fifteenth-century cases reflected the Bractonian understanding that the king was not entitled to do wrong—the king was thought capable of committing a wrong and amenable to justice via the petition of right.

3.2 Coke's coining of *the king can do no wrong*

The coining of the now well-known words *the king can do no wrong* is not to be found in legal literature and cases until the seventeenth century. *The king can do no wrong* in its exact form can be traced to John Davies's submissions to Parliament in November 1601 in the context of debates in the House of Commons on a bill against monopolies. Davies made a connection between the maxim *the king can do no wrong* and the impossibility for the king to be a disseisor.[370] The king's attorney, in one of the other first recorded occurrences of the exact words *the king can do no wrong*, also made a connection between *the king can do no wrong* and the notion in land law that the king cannot be a disseisor when he submitted to the House of Lords 'It is a Maxim in our Law, that the King can do no wrong. Therefore the King can gain no land by disseisin.'[371] Ehrlich posited that the medieval notion, in relation to disseisin in the thirteenth and fourteenth centuries, that the king automatically lost possession when he did not have a right to the land was an application of the understanding that the king was not entitled to do wrong.[372]

366 Baker (n 2) 86.
367 Dauchy and others (n 8) 16.
368 Margaret McGlynn, *The Royal Prerogative and the Learning of the Inns of Court* (CUP 2003) 22.
369 Yale (n 11) 384.
370 William Cobbett, *The Parliamentary History of England*, vol 1 (printed by TC Hansard for Longman et al 1806) 931; on the king being a disseisor, see section 3.1.
371 *Journal of the House of Lords*, vols 3 (1620–28) (His Majesty's Stationery Office 1767) <https://www.british-history.ac.uk/lords-jrnl/vol3/pp745-763> accessed 18 May 2018.
372 Ehrlich (n 1) 60–64, 139–40.

The king can do no wrong also featured prominently in Edward Coke's work. Coke is a towering figure in the history of the common law, having acted as Attorney General to Elizabeth I and James I and VI, before becoming Chief Justice of the Court of Common Pleas and later of the King's Bench.[373] He was a key actor during the transition between the Tudor era and that of the constitutional struggles of the seventeenth century. He decided and wrote reports of seminal cases—including *Prohibitions del Roy* and *The Case of Proclamation*—which are now conceived of as the foundations of English constitutional law.[374] Coke famously recounted having confronted King James I by telling him that the power to administer justice was no longer his to exercise personally. Coke allegedly quoted Bracton to support his position that the king was subject to law.[375] It is doubtful that the encounter truly occurred,[376] but Coke's reliance on the work of Bracton and the Bractonian understanding that the king is subject to law and is therefore not entitled by it to do wrong was at the core of Coke's thinking on *the king can do no wrong*, as is further explained in Chapter 3. Coke was subsequently discharged from his role as Chief Justice and became a prominent Parliamentarian. Coke is perhaps the embodiment of continuity and change in constitutional thinking: Bractonian elements of medieval thinking were retained as the prerogative to administer justice and to legislate was passed on to courts and to Parliament in the seventeenth century. His reports of cases and the institutes of English law he wrote are still referred to today in monographs and cases—the coining of the more recent *R(Miller) v Prime Minister (No. 2)* as *The Case of Prorogation* is an illustration of his enduring constitutional legacy.[377]

Understood as the king is not entitled to do wrong, *the king can do no wrong* was applied by Coke in cases relating to the king's wrongful grants and to the application of statutes to the king. In the 1585 *Knight's Case*, reported by Coke in his reports published in 1605, it was found that the king's prerogative could not do wrong to another and that the king could not change the law by his prerogative.[378] In the *Case of Alton Woods*, Coke, then Attorney General for Elizabeth I, argued for the queen in the Court of the Exchequer in 1595 and before the Exchequer Chamber upon a writ of error in 1601. Moore reported the first decision of the Exchequer and noted Coke's submission that 'le Roy fairoit tort qu'il ne poit faire

[373] See Allan D Boyer, 'Coke, Sir Edward' in *Oxford Dictionary of National Biography* (OUP 2004) <https://doi-org.proxy.bib.uottawa.ca/10.1093/ref:odnb/5826> accessed 1 November 2023.

[374] *Prohibitions del Roy* (1607) 12 Co Rep 63; *The Case of Proclamation* (1610) 12 Co Rep 74. cf Adam Tomkins, *Public Law* (OUP 2003) 54–58, who questions their constitutional significance.

[375] '[T]he King was greatly offended, and said, that then he should be under the law, which was treason to affirm, as he said; to which I said that Bracton saith *Quod rex non debet esse sub homine sed sub Deo et lege*.': *Prohibitions del Roy* (n 374) 65.

[376] Roland G Usher, 'James I and Sir Edward Coke' (1903) 18 Eng Hist Rev 664.

[377] *R(Miller) v Prime Minister* (2019) UKSC 41.

[378] 5 Co Rep 54b, 56a. The publication dates of Coke's reports are taken from JH Baker, 'Coke's Note-Books and the Sources of His Reports' (1972) 30 CLJ 59. Moore reported the case to similar effect: (1585) Moo KB 199, 204 (72 ER 530).

[the king would do wrong, which he cannot do]'.[379] Coke himself reported only his argument before the Exchequer Chamber but also recounted having argued that 'the king's patent cannot do a wrong' and that 'the King cannot do wrong, nor would his prerogative warrant him to do an injury to another'.[380]

In 1607, in the *Case of the King's Prerogative in Saltpetre*, published in the twelfth part of Coke's reports in 1658, Coke found that for the king's agents to cut timber on a subject's land 'would tend to the disinheritance of the subject, which the King by prerogative cannot do; for the King (as it is said in our books) cannot do any wrong'.[381] In the 1615 *Magdalen College Case*, published the same year in the eleventh part of his reports, Coke reported that 'the King being God's lieutenant cannot do a wrong, *Solum Rex hoc non potest facere, quod non potest injuste agere*'.[382] 'The king being God's lieutenant cannot doe wrong' also figures in the Second Part of Coke's *Institutes*,[383] which was probably written before 1628,[384] although published in 1642. The maxim appeared in its exact form—'the king can do no wrong'—in Coke's *Commentary upon Littleton*, published in 1628.[385] As is discussed in further detail in Chapter 3, Coke's Bractonian understanding that the king was subject to law was at the core of his coining of *the king can do no wrong* in the early seventeenth century.

4 Conclusion: the king's capacity to do wrong and amenability to justice in the late Middle Ages and Tudor era

The understanding that the king was not entitled to do wrong—*the king can do no wrong*—was developed in the late Middle Ages as evidenced by Bracton's writings. Traditionally, *the king can do no wrong* as a maxim is said to have first appeared in 1483, out of a legal presumption created in land law in relation to the king's disseisin. That presumption of good faith and the automatic loss of possession of the king when it was found that he had no right to seisin was devised to prevent a wrong from being attributed to the king by the operation of the law. During the fifteenth century, the presumption that the king was always a possessor in good faith led to statements to the effect that 'the king cannot be a disseisor', 'the king cannot be a tortfeasor', 'the king cannot be a wrongdoer', and 'the king cannot be said to be one who did a wrong'. *The king can do no wrong* as a maxim did not appear in the fifteenth century. The fifteenth-century statements to the effect that the king

379 *Welshes Case* (1595–96) Moo KB 413, 416 (72 ER 664).
380 *Case of Alton Woods* (1600) 1 Co Rep 40b, 44b, 45a.
381 (1607) 12 Co Rep 12, 12.
382 *Case of the Master and Fellows of Magdalen College in Cambridge* (1615) 11 Co Rep 66, 72.
383 2 Co Inst 681.
384 Baker (n 378) 77–78.
385 Co Lit 19b.

cannot be a disseisor, tortfeasor, or wrongdoer were in all likelihood not references to Bracton's text. They were nevertheless in accordance with the Bractonian understanding that the king is not entitled to do wrong.

The king can do no wrong as an expression was coined in the Tudors' reign, by Plowden and Coke, and still conveyed the Bractonian understanding that the king is not entitled to do wrong. It did not refer, contrary to Holdsworth's belief, to the king's feudal privilege not to be sued in his own courts.[386] He was fallible and could do wrong, but because the highest courts were his courts, he was not answerable before them.[387]

The medieval king was under the law. His feudal position as overlord prevented any writ from being issued against him because of the feudal privilege that a feudal lord could not be sued in his own courts. However, the petition of right was established to allow aggrieved parties to claim justice from the king, who was bound to administer it and correct a wrong, whether it was his or that of his officials.

Therefore, of the three notions relating to *the king can do no wrong*—the king's status in relation to law, perfection of the king, and immunity from suit—only two were at play during the late Middle Ages. The fact that these two notions can be conceived of as independent is illustrated by Bracton's treatise, which laid out that the king was under the law, but that he had no superior but God and that no writ ran against him. What various authors have considered to be a paradox in Bracton's text—the king was under the law yet there could be no remedy against him—in fact highlights the distinction between two notions: the king's legal status in relation to law and his immunity from suit.

The dominant notions that the king was under the law and that the petition of right was a remedy available against the king both contributed to shape the two dimensions—substantive and procedural—of crown liability. They led to the recognition that the king was liable, in the sense that he was capable of committing a wrong, and that he was amenable to justice. That the king was capable of committing a wrong is clearly evidenced in Bracton's treatise and is apparent from cases dating up to the end of the fifteenth century. As for the petition of right, it was conceived of as fulfilling the same functions as an ordinary writ. Moreover, it was available in relation to disseisin, the most important tort at the time. When a recourse was not available against the king, he was prohibited from committing a wrong for that very reason, as the aggrieved subject would then be left without a remedy. In short, the two dimensions of crown liability for that period were that the king was capable of committing a wrong (substantive dimension) and that he was answerable to justice (procedural dimension).

The king's capacity to commit a wrong—the first dimension associated in this book's model with crown liability—was acknowledged in legal thinking in the late

[386] Holdsworth (n 2) 462; Watkins (n 1) 7; Ehrlich (n 1) 42; Baker (n 2) 45.
[387] Ehrlich (n 1) 24; Watkins (n 1) 10.

Middle Ages. As is evidenced by Bracton's treatise, the king was capable of doing a wrong, and such a wrong was attributed to him. Bracton stated that the king was under the law and that 'the king, since he is the minister and vicar of God on earth, can do nothing save what he can do *de jure*', and that 'what one is bound by virtue of his office to forbid to others, he ought not to do himself'.[388] Although benefitting from various procedural advantages putting him in a more favourable position than ordinary litigants, the king remained, like his subjects, under the law. Even the doctrine of the king's two bodies and the notion of perfection of the king's body politic in the Tudor era did not alter legal thinking in relation to the king's capacity to do wrong and the Bractonian understanding that the king was not entitled to do wrong.

The absence of a superior and the duty to render justice, however, impacted the second dimension of crown liability—the king's amenability to judicial process. Although the king benefitted from an immunity from suit, the petition of right and other recourses filled the gap to allow subjects to have remedies when they were wronged, even under the formidable Tudors.

In summary, a study of *the king can do no wrong* from the later medieval period demonstrates that the Bractonian understanding that the king is not entitled to do wrong was still current under the Tudors and was understood as such by Coke, who attributed it to Bracton.[389] An analysis of cases from that period—especially the case of the *Dutchy of Lancaster*[390] and *Willion v Berkley*[391] reported by Plowden—demonstrates that Borchard, Laski, Watkins, and Keir and Lawson's hypothesis that the meaning of *the king can do no wrong* changed during the Tudor era was manifestly unfounded.[392] Prior to the constitutional settlement reached in the aftermath of the constitutional struggles of the seventeenth century and the Glorious Revolution, the king was capable of doing wrong in legal thinking (substantive dimension) and was amenable to judicial process even if immune from ordinary action (procedural dimension).

[388] Bracton, vol 2 (n 7) 305.
[389] Baker (n 2) 323.
[390] *Dutchy of Lancaster* (n 118).
[391] *Willion v Berkley* (n 68).
[392] Laski (n 4) 448; Borchard (n 3) 30–31; Watkins (n 1) 11; Keir and Lawson (n 5) 72.

3

The King Can Do No Wrong During The Constitutional Struggles of the Seventeenth Century

1 Overview of the chapter

The current understandings of *the king can do no wrong* can all be found, as will be shown, in the seventeenth century. While *the king can do no wrong* still conveyed the Bractonian understanding that the king is not entitled to do wrong in early seventeenth-century cases and in Coke's work, the conflict opposing Royalists and Parliamentarians over the course of that century led to varied—sometimes opposed—understandings of *the king can do no wrong*. At the end of the century, the dominant understanding of *the king can do no wrong* in legal thinking—reflected in Hale's work—was that the king's wrongful commands are void and that his ministers and servants must be sued instead.

2 Understandings of *the king can do no wrong*

The seventeenth-century constitutional struggles in England have been the subject of voluminous study by historians of political thought. They have shown that Parliamentarians claimed that the king was not entitled to do wrong and that an even more radical view was that he should be punished if he did.[1] Royalists—who were, like Parliamentarians, not a homogeneous group[2]—ascribed various interpretations to *the king can do no wrong*. Almost all divine-right theorists, while they believed in the divine right of the king and that the king's authority originated in God, adopted the view that the king's power was limited to ruling according to law.[3]

[1] John Milton, 'Pro Populo Anglicano Defensio (1651)' in Martin Dzelzainis (ed), *Political Writings* (Claire Gruzelier tr, CUP 1991) 212–14; Glenn Burgess, *British Political Thought, 1500–1660: The Politics of the Post-Reformation* (Palgrave Macmillan 2009) 328.

[2] Jeffrey Goldsworthy, *The Sovereignty of Parliament: History and Philosophy* (first published 1999, OUP 2004) 63.

[3] Margaret Judson, *The Crisis of the Constitution: An Essay in Constitutional and Political Thought in England, 1603–1645* (1st edn, Rutgers UP 1949) 20; Glenn Burgess, 'The Divine Right of Kings

The King Can Do No Wrong. Marie-France Fortin, Oxford University Press. © Marie-France Fortin 2024.
DOI: 10.1093/9780191994487.003.0004

Most Royalists believed that the king was limited in his rule by the law—including positive law—and had to act lawfully.[4] For many Royalists, the king was only under the directive power of the law.[5] Such was the case of Matthew Hale, as will be discussed further in this chapter. Moderate Royalists believed that the law guaranteed rights to the subjects as it guaranteed allegiance to the king.[6] They argued that the king is incapable of doing wrong and his agents must be sued instead.[7] The king's incapacity to do wrong was explained by the notion of perfection of the king: the king was thought to be assisted by divine wisdom.[8] Being therefore perfected by divine assistance, he was incapable of doing wrong. The more radical[9] Royalist interpretation of *the king can do no wrong*—which has been termed the 'Stuart version'[10]—was similar to the Continental theory of absolutism and rested on *the king can do no wrong* understood as everything the king does is lawful, a view which Charles I himself conveyed at his trial.[11] In the same vein, *the king can do no wrong* was also said by Berkley J—a Royalist judge who found for the king in the *Ship-Money Case*—to ground the king's supreme majesty and his absolute prerogatives, including that of dispensing with laws.[12] Understood previously in the Bractonian sense as not entitling the king to do wrong, *the king can do no wrong* became in Berkeley J's opinion a maxim grounding the king's unlimited prerogative. In the same case, Finch CJ—who also found for the king—interpreted *the king can do no wrong* as 'it cannot be suspected that the King would do any thing against law and the publick good of the kingdom'.[13] However, the most common Royalist view in

Reconsidered' (1992) 107 Eng Hist Rev 837, 847; Glenn Burgess, *Absolute Monarchy and the Stuart Constitution* (Yale UP 1996) 122. Another school of thought associates divine right with absolutism understood in the Austinian sense as the king above the law: John Neville Figgis, *The Divine Right of Kings* (2nd edn, CUP 1914); JP Sommerville, *Royalists and Patriots: Politics and Ideology in England 1603–1640* (2nd edn, Longman 1999).

[4] Burgess, *Absolute Monarchy* (n 3) 22, 49, 70, 98.

[5] Goldsworthy (n 2) 83.

[6] Burgess (n 1) 206.

[7] ibid 211–12. See eg David Jenkins, '*Lex Terrae*' in *The Works of that Grave and Learned Lawyer Judge Jenkins* (printed for I Gyles 1648) 17, 41.

[8] Judson (n 3) 20–21, 180; Goldsworthy (n 2) 79–80.

[9] William Epstein, 'Judge David Jenkins and the Great Civil War' (1982) 3 JLH 187, 188, 193.

[10] David L Keir and FH Lawson, *Cases in Constitutional Law* (FH Lawson and DJ Bentley eds, 6th edn, Clarendon Press 1979) 72.

[11] Charles I indeed argued that he 'derived his dignity from the Supreme Majesty of Heaven' and did not need to shelter himself under *the king can do no wrong*, a 'general maxim, which guards every English monarch, even the least deserving', for his actions were justified: William Cobbett (ed), *The Parliamentary Debates*, vol 3 (printed by TC Hansard for Longman et al 1808) 1261. That everything the king does is lawful because the king is the law could also be found in some Royalist judges' reasons: Judson (n 3) 137.

[12] *R v Hampden* (1637) 3 How St Tr 825, 1098–99 (Berkley J) (the *Ship-Money Case*): Francis Hargrave and others, *A Complete Collection of State Trials and Proceedings for High Treason and Other Crimes and Misdemeanors*, vol 3 (printed by TC Hansard for Longman et al 1816).

[13] John Rushworth, 'Concerning Ship-Money' in *Historical Collections of Private Passages of State*, vol 3 (1639–40) (D Browne 1721) 233 <https://www.british-history.ac.uk/rushworth-papers/vol3> accessed 9 October 2018.

the lead-up to the 1640s was that the king's wrongful acts were void[14] but that the king could never have intended them and must have been misled by his advisers—who were to be sued instead.[15]

Although the Parliamentarians were triumphant in securing sovereignty in Parliament, the Royalists' interpretations of *the king can do no wrong* prevailed. Two reasons explain why the Royalists' interpretations of *the king can do no wrong* were preferred following the Restoration and the Glorious Revolution.

First, after the regicide and post Glorious Revolution, the accepted view was that the potentially fatal consequences of separating the two bodies of the king—his body natural from his body politic—were to be avoided.[16] The king's martyrdom acted as a powerful catalyst for the development of ministerial responsibility and the king's immunity from suit.[17] A constitutional settlement was reached that left behind feudal elements such as the king's divine right and the subjects' passive obedience[18] but that, for the sake of stability, did not do away with the monarch.[19] The trauma caused by the regicide led to the protection of the king in the constitutional order becoming an objective of primary importance after the Protectorate. Conceiving of the king as perfect and incapable of doing wrong or considering the king's wrongful orders to be void—both Royalist interpretations of *the king can do no wrong*—allowed England to secure peace and safeguard the king's role within the constitution. Considering the king to be irresponsible prevented the king being tainted by wrongdoing.[20] The preservation of the king's person was an obvious objective in associating *the king can do no wrong* with ministerial responsibility, as is evident from the following answer of 1681 to Charles II dissolving Parliament:

> Our laws have taken care to make the king always dear to his people, and to preserve his person sacred in their esteem, by wisely preventing him from appearing as author of any thing which may be unacceptable to them. It is therefore that he doth not execute any considerable act of power, till it be first debated and resolved in council, because then it is the counsellors must answer for the advice they give, and are punishable for such orders as are irregular and illegal. Nor can his ministers justify any unlawful action under the colour of the king's commands, since all

[14] Such was the view held by Sir Roger Twysden, a moderate Royalist writing in the 1640s, and by Glanville, a Royalist Speaker in the Short Parliament: Burgess, *Absolute Monarchy* (n 3) 142–43, 147; Sommerville (n 3) 75–76.

[15] Sommerville (n 3) 75–76; Goldsworthy (n 2) 82.

[16] Janelle Greenberg, 'Our Grand Maxim of State: "The King Can Do No Wrong"' (1991) 12 Hist Pol Thought 209, 220–22; Denis Baranger, *Écrire la constitution non écrite: une introduction au droit politique britannique* (Presses universitaires de France 2008) 203.

[17] Clayton Roberts, *The Growth of Responsible Government in Stuart England* (CUP 1966) 131–34; Greenberg (n 16) 201, 212.

[18] Baranger (n 16) 203.

[19] Greenberg (n 16) 228.

[20] Joyce Lee Malcolm, 'Doing No Wrong: Law, Liberty, and the Constraint of Kings' (1999) 38 J Brit Stud 161, 170.

> his commands, that are contrary to law, are void; which is the true reason of that well known maxim, 'That the king can do no wrong'.[21]

Second, considering the king to be perfect or his wrongful orders to be void allowed for liability to fall on the king's ministers' and servants' heads instead—also an element of the Royalists' interpretations of *the king can do no wrong*. The Royalists' interpretations allowed the country to reach the objective of securing the king's role in the constitutional order while providing for accountability through the king's ministers' responsibility before Parliament and his agents' liability before his courts. The Royalists' interpretations allowed the king to be shielded from any liability[22] while ensuring that his ministers and agents remained accountable before Parliament and before the courts.

The Royalists' interpretations of *the king can do no wrong* still prevail today. *The king can do no wrong* is currently used to refer indiscriminately to ministerial responsibility, to the king's perfection and incapacity in law to do wrong, to the fiction that the king's wrongful acts are void and that his ministers and servants must be sued in his stead, and, finally, to the king's immunity from suit generally.[23]

Although *the king can do no wrong* has been the subject of little study by modern scholars—especially constitutional historians[24]—political scientists have discussed the use of the maxim for political ends in seventeenth-century England.[25] However, historians of political thought, such as Roberts, Greenberg, and Malcolm, associate *the king can do no wrong* primarily with ministerial responsibility.[26]

Roberts rightly pointed out that the maxim was not heard in the twelfth and thirteenth centuries and traces the first occurrence of *the king can do no wrong* as an expression in 1483.[27] As was demonstrated in Chapter 2, *the king can do no wrong* understood as the king was not entitled to do wrong can be traced back to Bracton's treatise in the thirteenth century—although not the maxim. Roberts, however, associated *the king can do no wrong* with ministerial responsibility.[28] Roberts attached three principles to *the king can do no wrong*—the king cannot act himself, his servant should refuse to execute an unlawful act, and she cannot plead

[21] Sir William Jones, 'A Just and Modest Vindication of the Proceedings of the Two Last Parliaments of King Charles II' in William Cobbett (ed), *The Parliamentary Debates*, vol 4 (printed by TC Hansard for Longman et al 1808) cxxxv.

[22] Anson acknowledged that an important element of *the king can do no wrong* understood as ministerial responsibility was constitutional stability and protecting the king and the body politic: William Reynell Anson, *The Law and Custom of the Constitution*, vol 2 part 1 (A Berriedale Keith ed, 4th edn, Clarendon Press 1935) 20. See also Malcolm (n 20) 170.

[23] See Chapter 1.

[24] Malcolm (n 20) 162–63; Greenberg (n 16) 211.

[25] Roberts (n 17); Greenberg (n 16); Malcolm (n 20). Ogg also associates the maxim with ministerial responsibility and with the sovereign's 'legal irresponsibility': David Ogg, *England in the Reign of Charles II* (Clarendon Press 1934) 452–54.

[26] Roberts (n 17); Greenberg (n 16); Malcolm (n 20).

[27] Roberts (n 17) 4, 6–7.

[28] ibid 5, 59. See Greenberg's account: Greenberg (n 16) 211–12.

the king's unlawful command as a defence. These three principles, Roberts argued, render the king immune from all responsibility for his government's actions and leaves all responsibility with the king's ministers.[29] The principles Roberts attached to *the king can do no wrong* are the products of seventeenth-century political struggles. Ministerial responsibility was not yet associated with the principle that *the king can do no wrong* in the fifteenth century. In that century, use of expressions similar to the maxim that *the king can do no wrong* (discussed in Chapter 2) meant that the king was not entitled to do a wrong to a subject. Contrary to what Roberts's exposition implied, ministerial responsibility cannot be traced to *the king can do no wrong* at the end of the fifteenth century. At that time, *the king can do no wrong* had not yet appeared as a maxim and expressions similar to it still conveyed the Bractonian understanding that the king is not entitled to do wrong.[30]

Greenberg accepted the orthodox dating of *the king can do no wrong* amongst modern scholars as 1483, although she noted that it was attributed to Bracton by seventeenth-century authors.[31] She argued that the original meaning of *the king can do no wrong* was that the king was incapable of doing wrong—as God could not sin, the king could not do wrong—and that there could be no right of resistance against the king, who was not to be punished for any wrong.[32] Greenberg therefore erroneously assumed that *the king can do no wrong* was originally associated with the concept of non-resistance and obedience of the subject. She took *the king can do no wrong* to mean originally that the king was incapable of doing wrong and was therefore immune from any form of accountability. Due to her mistaken presumption, Greenberg argued that it was Parliamentarian polemicists and late seventeenth-century Whigs who perverted the meaning of *the king can do no wrong*[33] by arguing that it meant that the king was not entitled to do wrong and could be punished if he did wrong. In fact, Parliamentarians relied on the Bractonian understanding of *the king can do no wrong*—the king is not entitled to do wrong. Malcolm, commenting on Greenberg's article, correctly argued that it was not Parliamentarians—and later Whigs—who first interpreted *the king can do no wrong* as the king is under the law.[34] Malcolm's argument is that the early understanding of *the king can do no wrong* was that the king was under the law. The analysis of legal thinking in relation to *the king can do no wrong* in Chapter 2 bolsters Malcom's claim in this regard.

Malcolm accepted Anson's argument that *the king can do no wrong*—meaning that the king's ministers should be held responsible in lieu of the king—can be

[29] Roberts (n 17) 5.
[30] See Chapter 2, section 3.1.
[31] Greenberg (n 16) 209. Malcolm also noted the reference to Bracton in connection with the king being under the law in the seventeenth century: Malcolm (n 20) 161.
[32] Greenberg (n 16) 210–12, 215–16.
[33] ibid 211.
[34] Malcolm (n 20) 163–67.

traced back to the minority of Henry III.[35] To Malcolm, *the king can do no wrong* understood as ministerial responsibility contributed to tying the king's hands and limiting his exercise of power by the constraints of a growing bureaucracy.[36] The king could no longer act alone and the fact that he had to act through others meant that he was limited in his exercise of power. Malcolm's argument was that *the king can do no wrong* understood as ministerial responsibility and the consequent irresponsibility of the king contributed to ensuring that the king, although legally irresponsible in theory, was kept within the law in practice.

The practical consequences of the king's—now the crown's—status as above the law will be discussed in Chapters 4 and 5. Contrary to Malcolm's assumption, the change in the king's status in relation to law occasioned by the reinterpretation of *the king can do no wrong* in the seventeenth century did not translate in the king—now the crown—being kept under the law in practice.

Roberts, Greenberg, and Malcolm, being political scientists, focussed their analysis of *the king can do no wrong* on past political practices and political discourses. Understandably, their analysis of legal sources can often be cursory. Greenberg for instance, when relying on cases reported by Plowden, does not distinguish the majority decision from the pleadings or the dissenting opinion.[37] Their analysis of *the king can do no wrong*, although it did include a brief analysis of earlier historical periods in Malcolm's and Roberts's cases, was primarily grounded in the seventeenth century. The aim of this section is to complement the studies by political scientists in the seventeenth century by focussing on legal sources and by building on the historical study of *the king can do no wrong* from the late Middle Ages expounded in Chapter 2. I aim to demonstrate that the Bractonian understanding of *the king can do no wrong*—the king is not entitled to do wrong—and its Elizabethan application by Plowden could still be found in the seventeenth century and particularly in the work of Coke, who coined the maxim itself in legal literature.

3 Three notions underlying the king's liability

Seventeenth-century debates on *the king can do no wrong* and the evolution of its understanding in legal thinking can be traced in legal writings. This chapter follows the model elaborated in Chapter 1 and addresses how the three notions associated with *the king can do no wrong* were understood in the seventeenth century. The first notion of the model, the king's status in relation to law, was the predominant notion associated with *the king can do no wrong* in Coke's work and early seventeenth-century cases. The second notion of the model, the perfection of the king, featured

[35] ibid 170.

[36] ibid. Similar thinking can be traced to Hearn's work in the nineteenth century: William Edward Hearn, *The Government of England: Its Structure and Its Development* (1st edn, Robertson 1867) 20.

[37] Greenberg (n 16) 215.

in Finch's work in the early seventeenth century, as well as in Hale's work of the second half of the seventeenth century in the context of the Restoration. Lastly, the notion of the king's immunity from suit will be analysed in light of seventeenth-century developments in legal thinking, especially Hale's.

3.1 The king's status in relation to law

Historians of political thought[38] and legal academics[39] have studied the seventeenth century primarily from the perspective of the power struggles between Royalists, Parliamentarians, and common lawyers to determine where sovereignty understood as law-making power should reside. The king's status in relation to law was debated in the context of the issue of whether the king's prerogative was part of the law or not during the first half of the seventeenth century.[40] Few would have stated that the king was absolutely above the law. The king's prerogatives were limited by the subjects' rights, which he could not violate.[41] That the king's prerogatives could not extend to the injury of a subject or prejudice her property was common in lawyers' thinking.[42] In the mind of lawyers of the seventeenth century, the king was under the law that made him.[43] Common lawyers refused to admit, for example, that the Norman Conquest by William the Conqueror in 1066 marked a change in the laws of England, because that would have amounted to admitting that the laws of England could be changed by royal will.[44] Burgess has convincingly argued that the Stuarts' theory of divine right was not a theory of absolutism understood as the king being above the law.[45] James I elaborated his theory of divine right as a denial of the right of resistance but not as a support for the argument that the king was above the law.[46] Bacon[47] and even James I[48] recognized that the king's prerogative was part of the law and that the king was below civil laws and the common law.[49]

[38] See eg Glenn Burgess, *The Politics of the Ancient Constitution: An Introduction to English Political Thought, 1603–1642* (Macmillan 1992); Burgess, *Absolute Monarchy* (n 3); Burgess (n 1); Sommerville (n 3); Alan Cromartie, *The Constitutionalist Revolution: An Essay on the History of England, 1450–1642* (CUP 2006).

[39] Goldsworthy (n 2).

[40] Paul D Halliday, *Habeas Corpus: From England to Empire* (Belknap Press of Harvard UP 2010) 64–69.

[41] Judson (n 3) 34, 37–38; Burgess (n 1) 169.

[42] Commonplace Book, Papers of Sir W. Lee, Lincoln Inn MSS, 242 r–v; cf Judson (n 3) 38.

[43] George Garnett, '"The Ould Fields": Law and History in the Prefaces to Sir Edward Coke's Reports' (2013) 34 JLH 245, 249–50.

[44] ibid; Burgess, *Ancient Constitution* (n 38) 83.

[45] Burgess, *Absolute Monarchy* (n 3) 22–25, 49; Burgess (n 1) 146–47.

[46] Burgess (n 1) 149–50.

[47] Basil Montagu, *The Works of Francis Bacon*, vol 2 (Carey and Hart 1844) 478. See also 'The Great Case of Impositions' in TB Howell, *A Complete Collection of State Trials*, vol 2 (printed by TC Hansard 1816) 396; Burgess, *Absolute Monarchy* (n 3) 58.

[48] John P Kenyon, *The Stuart Constitution, 1603–1688: Documents and Commentary* (CUP 1969) 8.

[49] Burgess, *Absolute Monarchy* (n 3) 26–27.

In fact, English Royalists' thinking that the king was bound by the law but had no superior but God in the early Stuart Period was not different from Bracton's. This section's focus is not seventeenth-century discourse about the locus of legislative power or of 'final legal authority in government'[50] but rather this book's model's notion of the status of the king in relation to law in respect of a wrong. It is the king's status in relation to law understood as underpinning the substantive dimension of crown liability—the king's capacity to do wrong—which is analysed in this section through the understanding of *the king can do no wrong* in seventeenth-century legal thinking.

In 1611, the *Case de Commenda* summed up the king's status in relation to law by restating established principles: the king cannot dispense one from facing justice, nor can he grant a dispensation if the victim would be deprived of her action; the prerogative cannot be used to cause a tort to a subject; the king cannot change the common law by his patent.[51] With the constitutional settlement reached with the Glorious Revolution, the king's status has been said to be clearly defined as below statute.[52] The aim in this section is to demonstrate how *the king can do no wrong* was understood in the seventeenth century, as that understanding contributed in later legal thinking to the king's current status as above the law.

3.1.1 Early seventeenth-century legal understanding of *the king can do no wrong*

In this section, Coke's use of medieval sources and Plowden's reports will be analysed to show that he understood *the king can do no wrong* as the king is not entitled to do wrong. The reference to *the king can do no wrong* in early seventeenth-century cases relating to the validity of the king's grants and the application of statutes to the king will then be analysed to demonstrate that the Bractonian understanding of the concept as the king is not entitled to do wrong was prevalent in legal thinking.

3.1.1.1 Reassertion of the Bractonian understanding of the king can do no wrong

As discussed in Chapter 2, *the king can do no wrong*, although it was not yet coined as a maxim, appeared in a very similar form in Plowden's reports of *Willion v Berkley*—'the king cannot do any wrong, nor will his prerogative be any warrant to him to do an injury to another'[53]—and *Nichols Case*—'his prerogative shall never prejudice another'.[54] *The king can do no wrong* was coined as a maxim in Coke's work—'The King can do no wrong to a subject'[55]—where it featured prominently. Coke was reported to have argued as Attorney General in 1595 that 'le Roy

[50] Judson (n 3) 7.
[51] *Le Case de Commenda* (1611) Dav 68, 75 (KB—Ireland) (80 ER 552).
[52] FW Maitland, *The Constitutional History of England* (CUP 1963) 388.
[53] *Willion v Berkley* (1562) 1 Plowden 223, 246 (Brown J).
[54] *Nichols v Nichols* (1576) 2 Plowden 477, 487.
[55] Co Lit 72a. See also Co Lit 19b and Co Lit 332b.

fairoit tort [qu'] il ne poit faire',[56] while the maxim *the king can do no wrong* in its exact form, in English, was uttered in Parliament in 1601.[57] But it will be demonstrated that the association between *the king can do no wrong* as a maxim and the Bractonian understanding of *the king can do no wrong* as the king is not entitled to do wrong in legal thinking is due to Coke.

Coke attributed to Bracton 'the principle that the king by his prerogative may not do wrong' by noting a reference to Bracton's folios 368–69 in his notes.[58] No maxim can be found, however, in folios 368–69 of Bracton's treatise, nor in folio 107 ('For the king, since he is the minister and vicar of God on earth, can do nothing save what he can do de jure' and 'His power is that of jus, not injuria').[59] Moreover, there was not in Bracton's time a theorized conception of the prerogative—prerogatives were understood as privileges and still referred to the king's feudal rights.[60] Bracton could not therefore have stated that the king's 'prerogative' cannot be used to do wrong to his people. Bracton rather said that the king is capable of doing wrong, but that he then exceeds his divine mandate. As Coke noted in his *Institutes*, 'And Bracton said, *Nihil aliud potest rex, & quam quod de jure potest*'.[61] Coke, therefore, reinterpreted Bracton by referring to the evolving concept of prerogative—which was developed after the writing of Bracton's treatise—and to the ruling in *Willion v Berkley* that the king by his prerogative cannot do wrong to another. Coke then coined in Latin an expression that was very similar to *the king can do no* wrong, thereby modernizing Bracton's text by attributing to him a maxim that was not his.

Instead of using the English or Law French version of *the king can do no wrong*, Coke translated it into Latin in the case of *Magdalen College*: 'Solum Rex hoc non potest facere, quod non potest injuste agree'.[62] It was not the sole occurrence of Coke translating into Latin legal principles which could be found in Law French or in English.[63] In his *Commentary upon Littleton* on the notion of 'Discontinuance',

[56] *Welshes Case* (1595–96) Moo KB 413, 416 (72 ER 664); *Case of Alton Woods* (1600) 1 Co Rep 40b, 44b; see also 2 And 154.

[57] John Davies's submissions to the House of Commons, 20 November 1601, Debates on a Bill against Monopolies: William Cobbett (ed), *The Parliamentary History of England*, vol 1 (printed by TC Hansard for Longman et al 1806) 931.

[58] Sir John Baker, *The Reinvention of Magna Carta 1216–1616* (CUP 2017) 323 citing BL MS Harley 6687A, fo 108 (translation by Baker).

[59] 'Nihil enim aliud potest rex in terris, cum sit dei minister et vicarius, nisi id solum quod de jure potest' and 'Potestas itaque sua iuris est et non iniuriae'.

[60] At least until the middle of the sixteenth century, see JH Baker, *Oxford History of the Laws of England*, vol 6 (OUP 2003) 55–56; Margaret McGlynn, *The Royal Prerogative and the Learning of the Inns of Court* (CUP 2003) 257–58. The feudal royal rights collected in the thirteenth-century *De Prerogativa Regis* were reinterpreted and broadened at the end of the fifteenth century, and the king's fiscal rights were given new statutory footing in the sixteenth century. See also EW Ives, *The Common Lawyers of Pre-Reformation England* (CUP 1983) 247–62.

[61] 2 Co Inst 186.

[62] *Case of the Master and Fellows of Magdalen College in Cambridge* (1615) 11 Co Rep 66b, 72a (*Magdalen College*). The maxim was reported as follows in another report: 'Roy ne poet faire un tort, *non potest injuste agere*': *Warren v Smith vel Magdalen Colledge Case* (1615) 1 Rolle Rep 151, 167.

[63] Coke also used Latin to refer to the queen's two bodies: '*Rex est persona mixta*': *Magdalen College* (n 62) 69b.

Coke also translated *the king can do no wrong* into Latin. He set out that the 'The King can do no wrong to a subject. The King being tenant in tail, gives this land by patent in fee; the patent amounts to a livery; yet in the case of the King it does not make a discontinuance; for a discontinuance is a wrong. *Rex quod est injustum facere non potest*.'[64] Coke coined a new Latin maxim that is not to be found in Bracton's work, or in the Year Books.[65] The way in which the maxim is spelled out in Coke's *Commentary upon Littleton* differs from the way it is written in Coke's report of *Magdalen College* and both Coke's renditions differ from Bracton's text. However, both passages are reflective of the spirit of Bracton's treatise and mean, once translated, that the king cannot do an injustice or a wrong. Coke did not understand *the king can do no wrong* as the king is physically or mentally incapable of committing a wrong. Coke understood the concept in the Bractonian sense that the king is not entitled to do wrong.

Coke, by relying on Bracton's text, adopted the understanding that the king is under the law and is not entitled to do wrong. That Coke understood *the king can do no wrong* as the king is not entitled to do wrong is also evidenced by his reliance on Plowden and the case of *Willion v Berkley*. As in that case, Coke used the understanding that the king is not entitled to do wrong to justify applying to the king statutes which aimed to remedy a wrong. Coke also cited Plowden to support the view that the king cannot use his prerogative to wrong another. In his *Commentaries on Littleton*, in the section on fee tail,[66] Coke relied on the case of *Willion v Berkley* to support his argument that a statute aiming to prevent a wrong must apply to the king since he is not entitled to do wrong. Coke commented that the statute *De Donis Conditionalibus* prevented the king from barring the reversion when lands were given to the king and the heirs of his body, as that would have been a wrong: 'and the king's prerogative cannot alter his case, nor make it greater than the donor gave unto him; and it is a maxim in law, that the king can do no wrong'.[67] Coke correctly characterized the ruling in *Willion v Berkley*. Coke's understanding of *the king can do no wrong* was that the king is not entitled to do wrong.

Coke also relied on the Bractonian understanding of *the king can do no wrong* in the *Case of the King's Prerogative in Saltpetre*.[68] The case was about the king's prerogative to requisition land when enemies invade the land. It was found that the king could interfere with a subject's possessions and the king's agents could damage one's property and dig for saltpetre for the common good and the defence of the realm because all the king's subjects benefitted from it. However, the subject's property had to be restored after the emergency and her house could not be touched.

[64] Co Lit 72a. See also Co Lit 332b.

[65] 2 Co Inst 186. As Coke noted in the second part of his *Institutes*, 'And Bracton said, *Nihil aliud potest rex, & quam quod de jure potest*.'

[66] Co Lit 19b.

[67] ibid.

[68] (1607) 12 Co Rep 12.

The subject's possessions had to be restored to their initial state because her inheritance cannot be prejudiced by the king's prerogative: 'the King . . . cannot do any wrong'.[69] In short, even in the case of an absolute prerogative—the king's prerogative in the purveyance of saltpetre, which Coke called 'an incident inseparable to the Crown'[70]—the exercise of which was justified by the public good and the benefit of all the king's subjects, the king could not prejudice the inheritance of his subject because the king was not entitled to do wrong. The case of *Saltpetre* was reported in the twelfth part of Coke's reports, published in 1658,[71] and the accuracy of it has been put into doubt.[72] Nevertheless, the reference to the Bractonian understanding of *the king can do no wrong* in *Saltpetre* appears to be in line with other instances where Coke referred to the concept.

Although it had not been coined yet in Bracton's days, Coke ascribed to *the king can do no wrong*—a maxim he may have coined himself—the same understanding as Bracton's. The notion of the king's status in relation to law and the substantive dimension of crown liability it underpins—the king's capacity to do wrong—therefore appear to remain unchanged in Coke's work and in early seventeenth-century cases.

The king can do no wrong, understood as the king may not do a wrong, constituted a stronger statement by Coke of the understanding found in Bracton. While the king in Bracton's writings could only do what is lawful and *ought* not to do wrong, the understanding became with Coke that the king cannot—meaning may not—do a wrong. The maxim *the king can do no wrong* was coined by Coke and it is to Coke that the maxim—understood in the Bractonian sense that the king is not entitled to do wrong—is to be attributed and associated with in legal thinking.

3.1.1.2 The king can do no wrong *and the validity of the king's grants*

After having featured in Plowden's reports, *the king can do no wrong* appeared again in the early seventeenth century in cases argued and reported by Coke which involved the validity of the king's grant.[73] In *Vaughan's Case*, it had been said that the monarch could not hold land wrongfully.[74] In *Englefield's Case*, it was similarly argued by the defendant that a patent is void if it was granted by the queen and caused

[69] ibid 12.

[70] ibid 13.

[71] JH Baker, 'Coke's Note-Books and the Sources of His Reports' (1972) 30 CLJ 59, 82.

[72] Usher did not consider it to be authentic historical evidence, noting that many of Coke's contemporaries found many mistakes in it: Roland G Usher, 'James I and Sir Edward Coke' (1903) 18 Eng Hist Rev 664. See also Jenkins's preface to his reports, where he says that passages in Coke's reports published after his death that bridle the sovereign and give the reigns to the people should be expunged: David Jenkins, *Eight Centuries of Reports* (Charles Francis Morrell ed, Theodore Barlow tr, 4th edn, Sweet 1885) v.

[73] *The king can do no wrong* understood as the king is not entitled to do wrong can also be found at the end of the seventeenth century in relation to the validity of the king's grant: *Holland v Fisher* (1685) 1 Keb 395, 396 (83 ER 1015).

[74] *Vaughan's Case* (1594) Moo KB 537 (72 ER 742).

wrong to another subject.[75] Since the king was not entitled to do wrong, the king's grant would be deemed invalid when it prejudiced a subject.

Coke used the Bractonian understanding of *the king can do no wrong*—that the king was not entitled to do wrong—to justify annulling the king's grant when it was prejudicial to another. In the *Case of Alton Woods* of 1595, Coke, then Attorney General, argued that if the king is only tenant in tail, he cannot grant the reversion to another, as that would be a wrong, which the king cannot do: 'le Roy fairoit tort [qu'] il ne poit faire'.[76] Coke himself reported that his argument was 'that it was a maxim in law, that the King's patent cannot do wrong . . . and if the King's grant should make a discontinuance, it would do wrong, which the King by his grant cannot do, but his grant shall be rather void'.[77] That the king was not entitled to do wrong was the understanding of *the king can do no wrong* in *Alton Woods*. The king, if he were to pass the land in fee instead of passing it in tail, would operate a discontinuance. A discontinuance was a wrong because it deprived the king's subject of her reversion. Since the king was not entitled to do wrong, there was no discontinuance when the king granted land in fee instead of merely in tail. The king's grant was instead considered to be void. Coke reiterated that application of the Bractonian understanding of *the king can do no wrong* in his comments on discontinuance in his *Institutes*.[78]

The idea that the king cannot work a discontinuance, even by his demise, because that would be a wrong was later adopted by Jenkins in the middle of the seventeenth century.[79] Finch also cited a case dating to Edward I's reign where it was argued that the king could not grant a church which he did not possess and which belonged to another as an illustration of *the king can do no wrong*.[80]

It was found in *Darcy v Allen* that 'the queen's patents which go against the subject's usual and settled liberties are void, as well as those which tend to their grievance and their oppression'.[81] In *Darcy v Allen*, Coke argued for the queen that in the regulation and forbidding of *malum prohibitum*, the king's patent can wrong a private person if it is for the public good. Coke's arguments in that case were rejected by the court. Dodderidge, arguing for the successful defendant, quoted Bracton: 'and he [the king] ought properly to yield to the law what the law has

[75] *Englefield's Case* (1590) Moo KB 303, 331 (72 ER 595). In his report of the case, Coke noted that 'if the Queen grants *totum statum suum* (having a term, or estate for life, extent, or other particular estate) it is good enough; for the Queen doth not grant more than she may do by the law, nor doth any wrong': 7 Co Rep 11b, 12a–b.

[76] *Welshes Case* (n 56); *Case of Alton Woods* (n 56); see also 2 And 154.

[77] *Case of Alton Woods* (n 56); see also 2 And 154. Coke's argument can be traced to the defendants' arguments in *Willion v Berkley* (n 53) 233.

[78] Co Lit 72a, 332b.

[79] *Case XVIII* (1546) Jenk 204; *The King Tenant in Tail, Case LXXXIV* (1604) Jenk 307.

[80] Henry Finch, *Nomotechnia* (printed for the Societie of Stationers 1613) 21. Finch cited the case of 4 Edw I 246b, which is probably a reference to the case of 1275 of *John of Grafton v Prior of Worcester* annotated and translated in Paul Brand, *Earliest English Law Reports*, vol 1 (Selden Society 1995) 36.

[81] *Darcy v Allen* (1602) Moo KB 671, 672 (my translation).

bestowed upon him'.[82] Dodderidge also submitted that kings of England had always been content to see their patents adjudged according to the law and successfully argued for the defendant that the king by his patent cannot change the law, nor cause a wrong to a subject's inheritance or liberty.[83]

Darcy v Allen is further evidence that the king at the beginning of James I's reign was conceived of as under the law and that he could not change the law or wrong a subject by his prerogative. The Bractonian understanding of *the king can do no wrong* as the king is not entitled to do wrong was maintained in that case: the grant of a monopoly is void if the grant is made by the monarch to the prejudice of her subjects.

In summary, the Bractonian understanding that the king is not entitled to do wrong—*the king can do no wrong*—can be found in cases relating to the validity of the king's grants in the early seventeenth century.[84] Coke played an important part in using the Bractonian understanding that *the king can do no wrong* in the context of the validity of the king's grants. Coke, when he was Attorney General, resorted to the Bractonian understanding that *the king can do no wrong* to the benefit of the king—to annul grants that were too broad and that the king did not mean to concede. To some extent, *the king can do no wrong* and the annulment of the king's grant could be interpreted as feeding into the narrative of a perfect, benevolent king who was deceived when he conceded the grant. But regardless of the motives behind Coke's use of *the king can do no wrong* in this early stage of his career, his was a Bractonian understanding of *the king can do no wrong*. The king's grant which caused wrong was void.

3.1.1.3 The king can do no wrong *and application of statutes to the king*

The king can do no wrong also featured often in cases in the early seventeenth century relating to the application of statutes to the king.[85] In the *Case of Ecclesiastical Persons* in the High Court of Parliament,[86] it was found that deans and other ecclesiastical persons had made grants to the queen on the basis that the statute disabling them from making grants did not apply to her. Parliament added a clause to the Act of Confirmation to the effect that it should not extend to making any lease or grants to the queen. Coke's report of that case is to the effect that the king is bound by an act of Parliament although he was not named in it or bound by express words. It was also said that 'all statutes which are made to suppress wrong, or to take away fraud, or to prevent the decay of religion, shall bind the King although he

[82] Folios 107–07b, Henry de Bracton, *Bracton on the Laws and Customs of England*, vol 2 (George Edward Woodbine ed, Samuel E Thorne tr, Belknap Press of Harvard UP 1968) 305–06.

[83] *Darcy v Allen* (n 81) 672.

[84] It can also be traced later in the seventeenth century in the case of *Le Mannor de Wyndlesham* (1675) Jones W 277 (82 ER 146).

[85] *Warren v Smith vel Magdalen Colledge Case* (n 62) 165, 167; *Magdalen College* (n 62) 72a; *Standen & al v University D'Oxon & Whitton* (1623) Jones W 17, 21 (82 ER 11).

[86] (1601) 5 Co Rep 14a.

be not named'.[87] That statutes which suppress wrong and fraud bind the king even if he is not named was adopted by Finch in his treatise.[88] Coke also reported that 'The King being head of the commonwealth, cannot be an instrument to defeat the purview of an Act of Parliament made *pro bono publico*'.[89] Coke laid down the same reasoning in his *Institutes*, where he stated that a statute on discontinuance applied to the king even if he was not named because the statute was enacted to suppress a wrong and the king, being God's lieutenant, cannot do wrong.[90] Coke referred to the Bractonian understanding of *the king can do no wrong* to support his argument that statutes which aimed to suppress a wrong applied to the king, whether he be named in them or not.

Street has posited that the argument that statutes enacted for the public good apply to the king was not to be found elsewhere than in the losing counsel's submissions in *Willion v Berkley*.[91] Yet it appears from Coke's work that he did in fact also refer to the concept of public good. Finch also referred to the 'public good' and a similar concept of the good of the 'commonwealth' in his 1613 treatise.[92] Street did not consider Coke's *Case of Ecclesiastical Persons* to be binding because it was heard in Parliament, but the High Court of Parliament was then conceived of as a court of record.[93] Moreover, the *Case of Ecclesiastical Persons* made clear that members of the clergy could not circumvent the statutory prohibition imposed on them not to make grants. It is therefore relevant to Coke's ruling in the 1615 case of *Magdalen College* that the grant made by the master and fellows of the college to the queen on the condition that she would then pass it on to another party was fraudulent practice.[94] The notion of public good also appeared in Coke's *Note on Pardon*,[95] where he stated that the king could not pardon an offender and exempt her from her duty—such as the maintenance or repair of a bridge—when it was for the benefit of all the realm. The king's pardon in exempting the offender would have been to the damage and prejudice of the subjects and against the 'weal public'—the public good. The king could not exercise his prerogative of pardon to discharge the offender when it was to the prejudice and damage of his subjects. The concept of public good can therefore be found in more sources than Street has suggested. Although not binding in the strict sense, the sources identified here nevertheless suggest the importance of the concept of public good, and to Coke in particular.

[87] ibid 14b.

[88] Henry Finch, *A Description of the Common Laws of England* (printed for A Millar 1759) 32.

[89] *Case of Ecclesiastical Persons* (n 86) 15b.

[90] 2 Co Inst 681.

[91] Harry Street, 'The Effects of Statutes upon the Rights and Liabilities of the Crown' (1948) 7 UTLJ 357, 365.

[92] Finch, *Nomotechnia* (n 80) 21–22; Finch, *Common Laws* (n 88) 59.

[93] Coke and his contemporaries—and Thomas Smith—conceived of Parliament as a court, although not in the current sense: see Charles Howard McIlwain, *The High Court of Parliament and Its Supremacy* (Yale UP 1910) 119, 124–26, 137–39; Goldsworthy (n 2) 114–15.

[94] *Magdalen College* (n 62) 74b, 76b.

[95] *Note on Pardon* (1609) 12 Co Rep 29.

The king can do no wrong was later used by Coke as a justification for applying to the king statutes which aimed at suppressing wrongs.[96] As he had used the concept to justify the annulment of the king's grants, Coke resorted to *the king can do no wrong* to ensure that statutes applied to the king. In so doing, Coke followed in the footsteps of Brown J and Dyer CJ in *Willion v Berkley*.[97]

When discussing the application of statutes to the king in the second part of his *Institutes*, Coke explained that a statute enacted to remedy a wrong applied to the king because the king, being God's lieutenant, cannot do wrong: 'First, albeit the king is not named in the act, yet he is bound by the act, because it is made to suppresse a wrong . . . and every discontinuance worketh a wrong, and the king being God's lieutenant cannot doe wrong.'[98] In line with the ruling in *Willion v Berkley*, Coke's rationale was that if statutes suppressing wrongs were not to apply to the king, it would be tantamount to admitting that the king is entitled to do wrong. However, Coke added, because the king is God's lieutenant, he is only entitled to act lawfully. Since the king is not entitled to do wrong, statutes aiming to remedy wrongs must apply to him. Coke's reliance on the king's status as God's lieutenant is the same as can be found in Bracton's treatise and the reference therein to the king being God's vicar.[99] As Bracton, Coke used the king's status as God's anointed to mean that the king, holding his office from God, cannot act wrongly. Consequently, laws suppressing wrongs must apply to the king or he would act wrongfully, which he is not entitled to do.

Coke also correctly applied the ruling in *Willion v Berkley* and the application to the king of the statute *de Donis Conditionalibus* when commenting on the concept of 'fee tail' in his *Commentary upon Littleton*. The statute, which prevented the king from barring the reversion when lands were given to the king and the heirs of his body—as that would have been a wrong—applied to the king.[100] Coke followed Brown J and Dyer CJ's understanding that the king is not entitled to do wrong and that statutes aiming to redress a wrong must therefore also apply to the king. Bacon—who did not refer to the maxim *the king can do no wrong*—appeared nevertheless to understand, like Coke, that the king is not entitled to do wrong when granting land and that a statute preventing a wrong from being committed applies to the king.[101]

In short, Coke worked towards reinforcing the Bractonian understanding that *the king can do no wrong* in relation to the application of statutes. Coke's dictum in *Magdalen College* was followed, for instance, in the 1623 case of *Standen*, where it

[96] Baker (n 58) 328.
[97] *Willion v Berkley* (n 53) 248 (Brown J), 251–52 (Dyer CJ).
[98] 2 Co Inst, 681–82.
[99] Bracton, vol 2 (n 82) 305–06.
[100] Co Lit 19b.
[101] Francis Bacon, *The Works of Francis Bacon: Law Tracts. Maxims of the Law*, vol 4 (printed for J Johnson 1803) 242.

was decided that the 'The King is bound by the statute of 13 Eliz because the King is barred from doing wrong, but where the King is entitled to any interest in property it cannot be taken away from him without a special reference in the statute and that distinction is provided for in the said case of *Magdalen Colledge*'.[102] The statute referred to in *Standen*,[103] because it aimed to remedy a wrong, was found to apply to the king because *the king cannot do wrong*. Coke's dictum in *Magdalen College* was also followed: when the king's interests are at stake, general words in a statute do not affect them.

However, Coke's ruling in *Magdalen College* was later misconstrued. The rule of construction eventually attributed to Coke was that the king is not bound by an act except if he is expressly named.[104] The distinction between general acts and general acts aiming to suppress a wrong was omitted. Coke's dictum in *Magdalen College* that general acts do not affect the king's prerogatives was misconstrued, and the rule of construction became, with the 1947 speech of Lord du Parcq in *Province of Bombay*, that any statute, regardless of its impact on the king's prerogatives, does not apply to the king unless he is expressly named in it.[105]

In short, Coke's understanding of *the king can do no wrong* marked continuity with previous legal thinking. Coke understood that the king as God's lieutenant could do no wrong and that understanding can be traced back to Bracton: Bracton's king could only act *de jure* as God's vicar on earth. Coke's use of *the king can do no wrong* as justification for applying statutes to the king and annulling his wrongful grants also constituted continuity with earlier cases, including *Willion v Berkley*.

Coke's work and his use of the Bractonian understanding that *the king can do no wrong* can be found in other contemporaneous legal treatises. For instance, both the Law French final version of Finch's treatise, *Nomotechnia*, published in 1613,[106] and the 1627 English version of an earlier draft,[107] *Law, or a Discourse*

[102] *Standen & al* (n 85) 17 (my translation). See also *The Duke of Lenox* (1609) 2 Brownl 301 (123 ER 954), where the grant of a monopoly to the Duke of Lennox in measuring and taxing wool was at issue, and where the defendant argued that statutes for the determination of right and wrong apply to the king in a reasoning similar to Coke's in *Magdalen College* (n 62).

[103] An Act Against Frauds by Ecclesiastics 1571, 13 Eliz I c 10.

[104] Street (n 91).

[105] *Magdalen College* (n 62) 74b–75a; *Province of Bombay v Municipal Corporation of the City of Bombay* [1947] AC 58 (PC). Coke's rule of construction survived in legal thinking for centuries and could even be found in the early twentieth century: Marie-France Fortin, 'Revisiting the Application of Statutes to the Crown: A Historical Constitutional Approach' (2021) 3 J CommonwL 271. For instance, in Chancery in *De Keyser's Royal Hotel v The King* [1919] 2 Ch 197, 216–17, Swinfen Eady MR cited *Ex parte Post-Master General* [1879] 10 Ch D 595 for the proposition that 'The general rule, expressed in Bacons's Abridgment, is "that were an Act of Parliament is made for the public good, the advancement of religion and justice, and to prevent injury and wrong, the King shall be bound by such Act, though not particularly named therein"'. Similarly, the second prong of Coke's dictum—to the effect that an act of Parliament can also take away the king's prerogatives or privileges if the king is named in the statute—is reflected in Duke LJ's dissenting judgment in *De Keyser's*, 210: 'The Crown is not affected by legislation in the absence of express words to take away the prerogative.'

[106] Finch, *Nomotechnia* (n 80).

[107] Wilfrid Prest, 'The Dialectical Origins of Finch's Law' (1977) 36 CLJ 326.

Thereof, and its subsequent re-editions[108] kept the Bractonian understanding that *the king can do no wrong*. Coke's reports are cited in both versions of Finch's treatise, *Nomotechnia* and *Law*, and even early drafts of Finch's treatise contained references to Plowden's reports.[109] Finch was familiar with Plowden's and Coke's work when he wrote in 1613 that the king 'ne poet este disseisor, ne faire auscun tort' ('may not be a disseizor, nor do any wrong').[110] In both versions of Finch's treatise it is said that the king only has prerogatives 'in all things that are not injurious to the subject'[111] and that it 'stretches not to the doing of any wrong' ('ne ferra tort per son prerogative').[112] Moreover, the 1678 re-edition of *Law* read that two of the king's attributes—justice and truth—are joined because 'to do wrong, to deal untruly, is not omnipotency, but a thing of weakness and impotency: so it is with the King, he cannot be a disseisor, he can be no wrongdoer'.[113] The king can be no wrongdoer in *Law* appears to mean that the king is not entitled to do wrong. The reference in the margin to a case from 1464 discussed in Chapter 2, section 3.1, where 'the king cannot be a disseisor' meant that the king was not entitled to do wrong, supports that interpretation. In summary, both versions of Finch's treatise maintained the Bractonian understanding that the king is not entitled to do wrong.

In his mid-seventeenth-century abridgment, Jenkins, a moderate Royalist,[114] referred on multiple occasions to *the king can do no wrong* understood as the king was not entitled to do wrong. Jenkins even adopted the Latin translation of *the king can do no wrong—Rex quod injustum facere non potest*—in his comments on a case where it was decided that the king cannot delay, discharge, or stay proceedings except in his own case.[115] Coke's influence in using the Bractonian understanding that *the king can do no wrong* certainly had a role to play in Jenkins's use of *the king can do no wrong*. Jenkins in his abridgement of cases of the Exchequer Chamber mentioned the concept in his reports and comments where no mention in the original Year Books was made to it.[116] *The king can do no wrong* in its original understanding—the king is not entitled to do wrong—can also be traced in other cases of the seventeenth century that followed Coke's works.[117] The use by Coke

[108] Henry Finch, *Law, or a Discourse Thereof* (printed by Richard and Edward Atkins 1678).

[109] Prest (n 107) 344, 341.

[110] Finch, *Nomotechnia* (n 80) 21; Finch, *Common Laws* (n 88) 57.

[111] Finch, *Common Laws* (n 88) 57; Finch, *Law* (n 108) 84; Finch, *Nomotechnia* (n 80) 21.

[112] Finch, *Law* (n 108) 85; Finch, *Nomotechnia* (n 80) 12.

[113] Finch, *Law* (n 108) 83. Finch refers in the margin to (1464) YB Mich 4 Edw IV, fo 25b, pl 3, see Chapter 2, section 3.1.

[114] Burgess (n 1) 211.

[115] Jenkins (n 72) 9.

[116] '4 Hen 7 7', Jenk 177. The maxim can also be found in Latin in the first edition of Jenkins's report for *Case LXXI*, 13 E 4 8: David Jenkins, *Rerum Judicatarum Centuriæ Octo* (Thomas Neale ed, printed for Henry Seile, stationer to the Kings most excellent Majesty 1661) 133. See also *Case XL, Case of Merton College in Oxford*, Jenk 21, being a comment on (1347) YB Mich 21 Edw III, fo 46, pl 65.

[117] *Lord Sheffield v Ratcliffe* (1623) Godb 300, 305 (78 ER 1763): 'The rule *nullum tempus occurrit Regi*, is to be meant for the preserving of the King's right, but not to make the King to do wrong.' *Friend v The Duke of Richmond* (1662) Hard 460, 462 (145 ER 547): 'And the king cannot gain any thing by wrong; so that he cannot be a disseisor . . . a petition of right lies against the King in this case' (Hale CB).

of the Bractonian understanding that the king is not entitled to do wrong in the form of the maxim *the king can do no wrong*—and its Latin equivalent *rex quod est injustum facere non potest*—could therefore already be observed by the mid-1650s and was inserted in comments of cases where the maxim did not originally feature.

The Bractonian understanding of *the king can do no wrong* can be found as late as 1656. In *Attorney General v Andrew*,[118] the issue was whether the king's prerogative to be preferred in the payment of debt applied when the king's subject's title preceded that of the king. It was argued by the defendant, relying on this point in *Willion v Berkley*, that 'The King's prerogative does no wrong to the subject'. The defendant put forward the well-established rule that the prerogative did not extend to injure the subject, an application of the Bractonian understanding, given prominence by Coke, that *the king can do no wrong*.

3.1.2 The king's status in relation to law in the second half of the seventeenth century

In this section, Coke and Hale's thinking about the king's status in relation to law extends beyond the model's notion of the king's status in relation to law in the context of his liability for a wrong. The scope is extended slightly because Hale's thinking in relation to law and more specifically his theory of the three powers of the law was an important aspect of his understanding of *the king can do no wrong*. Hale's understanding of *the king can do no wrong* and its relationship with his theory of the three powers of the law is of significant importance to legal thinking and will feature again in this chapter's sections on the notions of the king's perfection and his immunity from suit.

Coke wrote in a manuscript of his report of *Magdalen College* that 'although the king is under the direction of the laws, he is not under the penalty of laws, and so no mandatory law will bind the king, for he is not subject to the command of any but God'.[119] Coke's argument was similar to Hale's understanding in the second half of the seventeenth century that the king is under the directive power of the law only, not the coercive power.[120] However, it is difficult to reconcile, on the one hand, the distinction Coke made in his manuscript of *Magdalen College* between the direction and the penalty of laws with, on the other hand, Coke's opinion in the

In *Browne v Spence* (1663) 1 Sid 163 (82 ER 1033) it was debated in relation to the presentation of parsons, whether the king could be a usurper. Wyndham J opined that the king could not do a wrong to another.

[118] *Attorney General v Andrew* (1655) Hard 23 (145 ER 360) (Exch), where the king's prerogative was found not to apply. Counsel for the defendant relied on Plowden's report of *Willion v Berkley* to argue that 'The king's prerogative does no wrong to the subject', Hard 26 (145 ER 362).

[119] *Warren v Smith* (1615) Calth MS i fo 363v, translation by Baker: Baker (n 58) 44.

[120] Matthew Hale, *The Prerogatives of the King*, vol 92 (DEC Yale ed, Selden Society 1976) 14, 176–77; Sir Matthew Hale, *On the Law of Nature, Reason, and Common Law: Selected Jurisprudential Writings* (Gerald Postema ed, OUP 2017) 197, 221, 230.

published report of *Magdalen College* that laws adopted for the remedy of a wrong and which provide a 'necessary and profitable remedy . . . to suppress wrong, shall bind the King'.[121] Coke's opinion that only the directive power of the law applies to the king in his manuscript for the case of *Magdalen College* would have constituted yet another restriction of the applicability of statutes to the monarch. It may be the reason why Coke did not include his observations on the coercive power of the law in his published report of the case.

In a similar fashion to Coke's distinction between the directive and the coercive power of the law, Hale elaborated a theory that undermined the king's status as under the law.[122] The distinction between coercive and directive laws had old roots: Thomas Aquinas thought that natural law was directive in nature and that the prince was below it, but that the prince was above positive law, which is coercive.[123] Aquinas's theory rested on the important difference between the categories of law. The prince was below natural law—the law of nature and God—but above positive law—the law of men.[124] In Hale's time, however, common law jurisprudence had lost the orderly distinction between natural law and positive law and was more result-oriented.[125] While Hale did make a distinction between divine law, natural law, and positive law, his approach was to merge them in following Coke and Selden's historical approach.[126] To Hale, positive law—human-made law, including statutes and customs—although distinct from natural law, was nevertheless grounded in it.[127] The result was that Hale did away with the distinction between natural and positive law in describing the effect of the law. In *The Prerogatives of the King*, Hale attributed the effect of the law to 'laws already made';[128] in *Reflections on Mr Hobbs his Dialogue of the Law*, to 'laws of this . . . kingdom';[129] and in a manuscript draft, he wrote of the effects of 'laws or statutes' which he described as the king's laws.[130] Instead of distinguishing between natural and positive law as medieval jurists had, Hale established a new distinction within positive law between the coercive and directive power of the law. He kept only the respective power of natural and positive law—directive and coercive. Hale attributed both the directive

[121] *Magdalen College* (n 62) 72a.

[122] Though Coke's reference to the coercive and directive power of the law can be found in an unpublished manuscript, Coke's manuscripts were in—limited—circulation and we know Hale to have had a copy of his reports: Baker (n 71) 74.

[123] Thomas Aquinas, *Summa Theologiae*, Ia IIae, qu 96, art 5. Ernst H Kantorowicz, *The King's Two Bodies: A Study in Medieval Political Theology* (first published 1957, Princeton UP 2016) 136; Burgess, *Absolute Monarchy* (n 3) 139.

[124] Kantorowicz (n 123) 136.

[125] Postema, 'Introduction' in Hale, *On the Law of Nature* (n 120) xxv.

[126] Harold J Berman, 'The Origins of Historical Jurisprudence: Coke, Selden, Hale' (1994) 103 YLJ 1651, 1703, 1709–10; Alan Cromartie, *Sir Matthew Hale, 1609–1676* (CUP 1995) 42.

[127] Postema, 'Introduction' in Hale, *On the Law of Nature* (n 120) xxxvii.

[128] ibid 221.

[129] ibid 197.

[130] Fairhurst Papers MS (Lambeth Palace) 3479, fos 69–78, 65v, ibid.

and coercive power of the law to positive law. Therefore, statutes and common law, to Hale, had a directive and a coercive power.

Following Hale's theory, because of the directive power of the law, the king was bound in conscience to God, but he was not subject to the coercive power of civil law—statutes and common law.[131] The distinction Hale developed between the directive and coercive power of the law is important for the understanding of the historical evolution of *the king can do no wrong*. In the Middle Ages, following Aquinas's theory, positive law was coercive. In Bracton's work, the king was below natural and positive law.[132] There was then no distinction within positive law between directive and coercive power. The king was under the law, meaning the whole of positive law—statutes and customs. The absence of ordinary remedies against the king was a separate issue that did not affect the king's status as under the law. Hooker, for instance, as late at the end of the sixteenth century, shared Bracton's views on the king's status as being below positive law.[133] As a result of seventeenth-century legal thought, the king's status as under the law was undermined. The effect of Hale's introduction of a distinction within positive law between its coercive and directive power was to free the king from positive law in its coercive dimension and to subject him only to the directive power of the law. Being free from the coercive power of the law justified the king's immunity from ordinary remedies and from the penalty of statutes. Regarding the directive power of the law, the king was merely bound by his conscience to subject himself to statutes and customs which extended to him.[134] The directive power of the law also included the invalidating power of the law, so that acts done contrary to law became void. The invalidating effect of the law will be further discussed in the last section of this chapter on the king's immunity from suit.

Hale's theory was to the effect that the coercive power of statutes did not apply to the king and that he was solely bound by the directive power of the law. Hale's theory was a significant caveat to the king's status as under the law. Yet to Hale, his theory that the king was under the law was a response to Hobbes's argument that the king must be above the law to be able to act in cases of emergency.[135] Hale's insistence that the king was under the law was in line with the historical approach Hale favoured, like Coke and Selden before him.[136] However, even if Hale's king was markedly under the law when compared to Hobbes's,[137] Hale's jurisprudence

[131] ibid lvi.

[132] ibid xxiv–xxv. See also Chapter 2, section 1.1.1.

[133] Richard Hooker, *Of the Laws of Ecclesiastical Polity*, vol 3 (Stephen McGrade ed, OUP 2013) 198. See Sommerville (n 3) 76; Hale, *On the Law of Nature* (n 120) xxiv, xxv.

[134] Hale, *Prerogatives* (n 120) 176–77.

[135] Berman (n 126) 1721.

[136] ibid 1732.

[137] Hobbes denied the people any residual power and joined 'the sovereign's will with the people's will in a way that creates a potential barrier against the people bringing an action against the sovereign whom they have authorised': Janet McLean, 'The Crown in the Courts' in Linda Pearson, Michael Taggart, and Carol Harlow (eds), *Administrative Law in a Changing State* (Hart Publishing 2008) 161, 176. To McLean, in order to devise a theory of political and legal responsibility in public law, one

rendered the king above a substantial part of the law—the coercive power of positive law. Hale's thinking in relation to law's three powers marked a break with previous thinking as captured in the work of Bracton.

3.2 Perfection of the king

There were elements of the notion of perfection in both the Royalists' and the Parliamentarians' theories over the course of the seventeenth century. For the Royalists, the king was God's vicar and imbued—through divine assistance—with qualities and wisdom that rendered him incapable of doing wrong.[138] For the Parliamentarians, it was Parliament that could not err and was incapable of doing wrong because of divine intervention.[139] There were elements of the notion of perfection in earlier theories about Parliament. Fortescue, Smith, and St German all believed in Parliamentary infallibility.[140] The idea that Parliament was incapable of doing wrong was grounded in the notion that the Holy Ghost guided the faithful assembled in Parliament.[141] Parliamentarians argued that the king was capable of doing wrong, but not Parliament.[142] Royalists like Henry Finch argued the opposite and emphasized that Parliament could err.[143]

Anson argued that feudal monarchs did not possess the sacredness of the seventeenth-century conception of the office of kingship.[144] Borchard argued that both Coke and Blackstone misunderstood the maxim that *the king can do no wrong* when they interpreted it to mean that the king, being characterized by an absolute perfection, could not, was incapable, was not physically or mentally able to do wrong.[145] As was demonstrated in Chapter 2, such an interpretation of a king both mentally and physically unable to do wrong, based on the notion of perfection of the king, was not to be found in Bracton's thinking in the thirteenth century, nor in

must therefore either look to specific elements of justification in Hobbes's theory or depart from it. While Martin Loughlin can be read to have chosen the latter option in *The Idea of Public Law* (OUP 2004) 158—as McLean notes in ibid—Poole appears to have chosen the former, and has noted that Hobbes allowed in *Leviathan* for a wide scope of legal challenges to the king's exercise of his sovereign power but did not conceive of these legal challenges as limits to the king's capacity to act: Thomas Poole, 'Hobbes on Law and Prerogative' in David Dyzenhaus and Thomas Poole (eds), *Hobbes and the Law* (CUP 2012) 82–83.

[138] Judson (n 3) 20–21, 180; Goldsworthy (n 2) 79–80.

[139] Goldsworthy traced in Coke's work the notion that Parliament was infallible and could not be thought to have acted wrongly: Goldsworthy (n 2) 97–99. Goldsworthy also cited to Berkeley J's speech that 'Parliament cannot err' in the *Ship-Money Case* (n 12) 1101.

[140] Goldsworthy (n 2) 72.

[141] ibid 72–73.

[142] ibid 100.

[143] Finch, *Law* (n 108) 233.

[144] William Reynell Anson, *The Law and Custom of the Constitution*, vol 1 (1st edn, Clarendon Press 1886) 19.

[145] Edwin Borchard, 'Governmental Responsibility in Tort, VI' (1926) 36 YLJ 1, 2.

late medieval or Tudor England. As was also demonstrated in Chapter 2, the king was God's vicar in Bracton's treatise but did not partake of the divine character of God: the king was just a man.[146] As was shown, Coke did not understand *the king can do no wrong* as the king is incapable of doing wrong because he is perfect.[147] Coke did not adopt the notion of a perfect king. As will be demonstrated in this section, the notion of perfection of the king progressively gained in importance in legal thought throughout the seventeenth century and figured in Hale's work in the second half of the seventeenth century. The result of seventeenth-century struggles was that both Parliament and the king came to be thought of as incapable of doing wrong.

3.2.1 Perfection of the king in seventeenth-century legal writing

That the king came to share God's perfection in legal thought in the seventeenth century is evidenced by Finch's work. Finch's treatise, *Nomotechnia*, was first published in Law French in 1613. It was the first general institute of the laws of England.[148] The English version of his work was probably written before the final Law French version but was published later, in 1627, as *Law, or a Discourse Thereof*.[149] Three other editions of *Law* followed before the end of the century.[150] A translation of Finch's treatise, closer to the 1613 edition, was made in 1759 under the title of *A Description of the Common Laws of England*. It has been argued that it was the 1613 Law French original which represents Finch's finished work.[151] It is, however, the 1627 translated edition of Finch's treatise, *Law*, and its subsequent re-editions, including that of 1678, which are more commonly used. Because it was first published in the early seventeenth century (1613) and published in English and re-edited after the Civil War and during the Restoration (1678), Finch's work and its re-editions provide an insight into the evolution of constitutional thinking in the seventeenth century. Finch's treatise and its popularity—even if overshadowed by Coke's *Institutes* and *Reports*[152]—demonstrate the increasing influence of the notion of perfection of the king in seventeenth-century legal thought.

In the 1678 edition of Finch's work, based on the 1627 English version of his treatise, the king is 'a God upon earth' and partakes of God's 'excellencies and honour'

[146] FW Maitland, 'The Crown as Corporation' (1901) 17 LQR 131, 132. See Chapter 2, section 2.2.

[147] cf David Chan Smith, *Sir Edward Coke and the Reformation of the Laws: Religion, Politics and Jurisprudence, 1578–1616* (CUP 2014) 267. Smith interprets Coke to mean that the king, being head of justice and God's lieutenant in *Magdalen College*, cannot do wrong because he is perfect. Smith sees a moral limitation that renders the king incapable of committing wrong. The idea of a self-limiting moral king has been advanced before: Cary J Nederman, 'Bracton on Kingship Revisited' (1984) 5 Hist Pol Thought 61. However, it is argued here that it is a jurisdictional issue, as could be found in Bracton: the king is not entitled to do wrong. If he does, he exceeds his powers as king. See Chapter 2, section 2.1.1.3.

[148] Finch, *Common Laws* (n 88) v; Prest (n 107) 348.

[149] Prest (n 107) 326–27.

[150] ibid 326.

[151] ibid.

[152] ibid 347.

and 'the divine perfection'.[153] In the 1759 edition of Finch's treatise—closer to the original 1613 edition—the king 'resembles the person of God' and 'the law attributes to him, in a similitudinary manner, the shadow of the excellencies peculiar to God'.[154]

In the 1613 edition of Finch's treatise—and its more accurate 1759 translation—it is the law which gives the king the shadows of the excellencies which reside in God.[155] Sovereignty, being one of those excellencies, is given to the king by the law and makes all land tenable of the king and no action possible against him because no one is above him.[156] Law also gives the king justice, which means that the king 'may not be a disseisor, nor do any wrong'.[157] In contrast, in the 1678 re-edition, it is not the law which gives the king the shadows of God's excellencies but God himself who makes the king a 'partaker' of his excellencies 'by similitude from the divine perfection'.[158] While 'perfection' was the sixth attribute of the king listed in the original 1613 edition, 'divine perfection' became the second attribute in the 1678 edition. The language of the 1678 edition also differs. The 1613 edition was more in line with the findings of the court in the *Dutchy of Lancaster* and simply read 'Perfection: for no laches, folly, infancy, or corruption of blood is presumed in the King'.[159] By comparison, the introductory sentences of the 1678 re-edition read: 'A second thing proper unto God, is the divine perfection. In the King no imperfect thing can be thought.'[160] In short, the most widely used edition of Finch's treatise, that of 1627 and its subsequent re-edition, emphasized the notion of perfection of the king.

In Finch's final version of his work, the 1613 edition, all the king's attributes—among which sovereignty, perpetuity, perfection, and justice—were grounded in the king benefitting, by analogy, of God's excellencies. Although the prerogative was given to the king by the law and did not extend to things injurious to his subjects, it was nevertheless said in the same sentence that the prerogative issued 'out of the Excellency of his person, as out of a fountain'.[161] In short, the king's similitude with God and his perfection were important aspects of Finch's discourse. Finch's work was emblematic of the increasing influence of the notion of perfection of the king as a ground for the king's incapacity to do wrong and his immunity from suit in seventeenth-century legal thought.

[153] Finch, *Law* (n 108) 81.
[154] Finch, *Common Laws* (n 88) 55; Finch, *Nomotechnia* (n 80) 20b.
[155] Finch, *Nomotechnia* (n 80) 20. The same wording is kept in the 1759 edition: Finch, *Common Laws* (n 88) 55.
[156] Finch, *Nomotechnia* (n 80) 20.
[157] ibid 21; Finch, *Common Laws* (n 88) 57.
[158] Finch, *Law* (n 108) 81.
[159] Finch, *Nomotechnia* (n 80) 21; Finch, *Common Laws* (n 88) 57. For a discussion of the notion of perfection in the *Case of the Dutchy of Lancaster* (1561) 1 Plowden 212, see Chapter 2, section 2.2.2.
[160] Finch, *Law* (n 108) 82.
[161] Finch, *Nomotechnia* (n 80) 21; Finch, *Common Laws* (n 88) 59.

In the 1637 *Ship-Money Case* on the king's prerogative right to levy a medieval tax without Parliament's consent,[162] the pleadings by counsel for Hampden, who unsuccessfully opposed the tax, and the judges who found for him show that they understood *the king can do no wrong* in the Bractonian sense that the king was not perfect, could err, and could be inclined to do wrong. Holborne, pleaded for the defendant that 'True, the law-books say, the King can do no wrong; which proves, that it is possible for a governor in his inclination to incline to wrong, and therefore the law has taken a care that he should do none; for he cannot make a disseisin nor discontinuance'.[163] Baron Denham, who found for Hampden, referred *to the king can do no wrong* in his reasons as a principle of law that the king is not entitled to do wrong.[164] But the Attorney General in his pleadings associated *the king can do no wrong* with the king's prerogative, that all the king did was lawful, and that he ought not to be questioned.[165] Finch CJ, who found for the king, reinterpreted Coke's reasons in *Magdalen College* and reasoned that because the king is '*Sponsus Regni*, as in *Magdalen College Case*', *the king can do no wrong* was to be understood as it cannot be suspected that the king would do any wrong nor anything against the public good.[166] Whereas Coke understood *the king can do no wrong* in *Magdalen College* as the king is not entitled to do wrong, Finch CJ in the *Ship-Money Case* used *the king can do no wrong* understood as the king is perfect and incapable of doing wrong.

An earlier variation in the understanding of *the king can do no wrong* could also be gleaned from Fleming CB's speech in *Bate's Case*.[167] Confirming the king's absolute prerogative to create new taxation on foreign exports, Fleming CB said 'the king cannot do wrong, and if the King seise my land without cause, I ought to sue him in humble manner, and not with such terms of opposition in the information', for the king might refuse to accede to the plaintiff's demand, 'as it was lawful for him to do'.[168] In Fleming CB's speech, *the king can do no wrong* appears to be understood as the king is immune from suit and that as a consequence, he can refuse to do right to the aggrieved party. Fleming CB could also be said to implicitly advocate for the notion of perfection of the king in *Bate's Case*. There he referred to the *Case of Mines* as authority for the 'the excellency of the king, or his person' justifying the prerogative to impose duties without Parliament's consent.[169]

162 *Ship-Money Case* (n 12).
163 ibid 972.
164 Rushworth (n 13) 219.
165 John Rushworth, 'Historical Collections: 1637', *Historical Collections of Private Passages of State*, vol 2 (1629–38) (D Browne 1721) 552–53 <https://www.british-history.ac.uk/rushworth-papers/vol2> accessed 9 October 2018.
166 Rushworth (n 13) 233.
167 *Bate's Case* (1606) 2 St Tr 371; see also the report by Lane: *An Information against Bates* (1606) Lane 22 (145 ER 267),
168 *Information against Bates* (n 167) 26.
169 ibid. *Case of Mines* (1567–68) 1 Plowden 310.

Royalists' understanding of *the king can do no wrong* eventually marked continuity in legal thinking, as Jenkins's writings illustrate. That *the king can do no wrong* was understood by Royalists as the king, assisted by divine perfection, being therefore incapable of doing wrong is evidenced by Jenkins's *Lex Terrae*, published in 1648. Jenkins, one of the later constitutional Royalists,[170] wrote that 'the law says that the king can do no wrong, that he is . . . God's lieutenant, and is not able to do an unjust thing'.[171] Jenkins cited to Coke's report of *Magdalen College* to support his claim, thereby perverting Coke's use of the Bractonian understanding of *the king can do no wrong* in that case. Jenkins reinterpreted *the king can do no wrong* in *Lex Terrae* to mean that the king is, like God, perfect and therefore incapable of doing wrong.

Jenkins also argued in *Lex Terrae* that 'it cannot be said that the king does wrong' because the king can do nothing by his grant or any other act touching his subjects' persons, properties, or liberties but according to the law.[172] Jenkins understood *the king can do no wrong* as everything the king does is lawful. Given that the king's justices are the ones responsible for adjudicating impartially between the king's subjects according to law, they must be punished if the laws are violated 'and no reflection to be made on the King'.[173]

With the death of Charles I, Jenkins adopted a conciliatory approach which was more in line with his earlier constitutional views that the king was bound by the law.[174] He correctly referred to the Bractonian understanding of *the king can do no wrong* in his abridgement of cases published in 1661. His commentaries on cases show that he understood *the king can do no wrong* as the king was not entitled to do wrong. Nevertheless, Jenkins's Royalist understanding of *the king can do no wrong* in *Lex Terrae* as the king is perfect and incapable of doing wrong, as well as the objective of shielding the king from any form of liability by reinterpreting *the king can do no wrong* as the king is perfect, incapable of doing wrong, and therefore immune from suit, was not lost to legal thought.

The case of *The King and Queen against The Bishop of London and Peter Burch*[175] exemplifies the importance of the notion of perfection of the king in the seventeenth century. It was found in that case that the dignity of the person of the king—which can be understood in the qualitative sense of perfection and in the sense of sacredness of the office of kingship—excused him from the application of the law. The case of *Burch* is evidence of the significance of the notion of perfection of the king in seventeenth-century legal thinking. The notion of perfection and

170 Burgess (n 1) 211.

171 Jenkins (n 7) 41.

172 ibid 17.

173 ibid. Jenkins's argument that the king is immune from liability because it is his justices' duty to administer the law correctly is, however, undermined by his earlier claim that the king has 'full power in all [houses] to do justice to all men': ibid 19.

174 Jenkins (n 72) xii.

175 (1694) 1 Show KB 493, 496 (89 ER 673).

the sacredness of the king were resorted to in order to withdraw the king from the application of statutes enacted by Parliament, even after the Glorious Revolution.

3.2.2 Perfection of the king in Hale's thinking and his theory of the three powers of the law

In his treatise, which he wrote in the 1660s,[176] Hale grounded the king's freedom from the coercive dimension of positive law on the 'sacredness and sublimity of his person'.[177] The king's sublimity—his perfection—justified his immunity from suit, his freedom from the coercive power of the law. Hale's thinking was not, however, fully developed. Hale's exposition of the invalidating power of the law binding the king shows that the king was, in Hale's thinking, capable of doing wrong and committing a wrongful act. The perfect king was simultaneously immune from suit because of his sublimity, but also subject to the invalidating power of the law with regard to his wrongful acts. The king was therefore not absolutely 'sublime': he was capable of thinking or doing wrong, as is evidenced by the need for Hale to elaborate on the invalidating power of the law. There was a partial flaw in Hale's theory of the three powers of the law.

As discussed in section 3.1.2, Hale's theory was that law—meaning positive law, statutes, and common law—had a threefold effect: the coercive power of the law, the directive power of the law, the latter including the invalidating power of the law, the *potestas irritans*. Hale therefore added to the directive and coercive power of the law a third one, the invalidating power of the law. Burgess has argued that Hale found the *potestas irritans* in the law in the work of Hobbes and that the phrase was not found in the early Stuart period.[178] Postema has since traced Hale's use of the concept to Suarez and canon and Roman law.[179]

In Hale's theory, the king was free from the coercive effect of the law because of his perfection—his sublimity and sacredness. The king was thereby immune from suit. The king was, however, bound by the directive power of the law, which included the invalidating power of the law. An act done contrary to the directive power of the law was rendered void by the invalidating power of the law. Hale, in creating a third, invalidating, power of the law, interpreted *the king can do no wrong* in a way that supported the Royalists' claim that the king's act done contrary to law was void and had to be answered solely by the king's ministers. By exempting the king from the coercive power of the law, Hale gave a new theoretical basis for the king's immunity from suit. The king was not immune from suit because of his feudal privilege not to be sued in his own courts; he was immune from the coercive power of the law because of his perfection and sacredness. The king was, however,

176 Cromartie (n 126) 45, 98; Hale, *On the Law of Nature* (n 120) xxvii.
177 Hale, *Prerogatives* (n 120) 15.
178 Burgess, *Absolute Monarchy* (n 3) 153.
179 Postema, 'Introduction' in Hale, *On the Law of Nature* (n 120) xxii, lvi.

under the directive power of the law. By adding the invalidating power of the law to the directive power of the law, Hale theorized the Royalists' argument that the king's acts and commands done contrary to law were void. Acts done contrary to the directive power of the law were voided by the invalidating power of the law.

Hale's theory is partly flawed from a logical point of view. On the one hand, the king's sublimity and sacredness justified the king's immunity from suit. A sublime, perfect king is incapable of doing wrong. On the other hand, Hale's theory provided for the king being capable of committing wrongful acts contrary to the directive power of the law. That the king was capable of committing acts contrary to law was the reason why Hale elaborated the invalidating power of the law, to render the king's wrongful acts void in law. How could the king be excused from ordinary actions on the basis that he was sublime and perfect but at the same time be capable of committing and ordering wrongful acts contrary to law? The perfect king was imperfect in Hale's theory.

3.3 Immunity from suit

In this section, the notion of the king's immunity from suit will be analysed in light of the status of the petition of right and of the understanding of *the king can do no wrong* in legal thinking in the seventeenth century.

3.3.1 Petition of right an equivalent remedy to an ordinary action

The petition of right remained a valid recourse against the king in legal thinking throughout the seventeenth century.[180] The last petition of right before the nineteenth century was instituted in 1605.[181] It reflected the accepted understanding that the king was bound to do right to every man. Bacon accepted that petition of 1605 and his reply read 'This is a petition of right and not of grace and out of his Majesties Justice ought to be granted'.[182] Until the nineteenth century, few petitions of right were instituted[183]—a notable exception is the political use of the petition of right in 1628.[184] However, the Bill of Rights 1688 guaranteed the right to petition the king.[185] Following the 1667 case of *Pawlett v Attorney General*, which paved the way for equitable actions against the king, it was found later that the petition of right lay to obtain equitable remedies against the king in Chancery.[186]

[180] See *Friend v The Duke of Richmond* (n 117) 462 (Hale CB).

[181] Ludwik Ehrlich, 'Petitions of Right' (1929) 45 LQR 60, 73.

[182] ibid 74.

[183] ibid 61.

[184] The petition of right was discussed in *Bankers' Case* but it was initiated not by a petition of right but by a petition to the Barons of the Exchequer: *Bankers' Case*, or *The King v Hornby* (1700) 14 St Tr 1, (1700) 5 Mod 30 (87 ER 500), Skinner 601 (90 ER 270).

[185] Bill of Rights 1688, 1 Will & Mar c 2 sess 2.

[186] *Pawlett v Attorney General* (1667) Hard 465 (145 ER 550), where Atkyns B reasoned that the king's role as fountain of justice and equity, and the presumption that he shall not be faulty in granting either

Petitions of right were not 'as of grace'. Hale made the distinction between petitions of right and as of grace: 'no suit lies against the king but by petition of grace or of right'.[187] Goldsworthy has suggested that the petition of right—which could be directed against the king himself—was entirely dependent on the king's goodwill.[188] The king could, for instance, stop the proceedings. Goldsworthy cites Holdsworth to support his argument,[189] but the latter did not in fact say that the petition of right was an appeal to the goodwill of the king. Holdsworth rather said—based on Bacon's work—that the procedure *rege inconsulto* meant that the king was consulted in matters that touched his interests and that judges were to wait for his command to proceed. The obligation for judges to consult with the king could also be found in Bracton.[190] To say that the petition of right was as of grace on the basis that the king could refuse to endorse it 'proves too much'.[191] Ever since Edward I, it was considered contrary to law for the king to refuse to endorse a petition of right or to prevent it from proceeding.[192] At the turn of the seventeenth century, Lord Somers in *Bankers' Case* opined that it is not to be supposed in law, and would be contrary to the constitution, for the king not to endorse a petition of right.[193] Acting contrary to law by refusing to endorse a petition of right was a wrongful act, and the king was not entitled to do wrong.[194]

because it would be to his dishonour, justified an equitable relief against the king. See also *Dyson v Attorney General* [1911] 1 KB 410, 415. In the eighteenth century, bills were presented to the Court of Exchequer, against the Attorney General, to obtain declaratory relief upon foreclosure or escheat, and in the nineteenth century, petitions of right were also presented to the Chancery. As to the availability of an equitable action against the king in Chancery by petition of right, see *Clayton v Attorney General* (1834) 1 Coop T Cott 97 (Courts of the Chancellor); *Taylor v Attorney General* (1837) 8 Sim 413. For proceedings instituted against the Attorney General, see *Reeve v Attorney General* (1741) 2 Atk 223 (26 ER 538) (where Lord Chancellor Hardwicke ruled that the court would not decree a foreclosure against the crown, but would allow the mortgagee to hold the premises until the crown thought proper to redeem the estate); *Penn v Lord Baltimore* (1750) 1 Ves Sen 444, 446. See also Walter Clode, *The Law and Practice of Petition of Right under the Petitions of Right Act, 1860* (Clowes 1887) 143–44; WS Holdsworth, *A History of English Law*, vol 9 (1st edn, Methuen 1926) 30–32. Whether the Chancery could only grant an equitable remedy upon a petition of right after the Exchequer's equitable jurisdiction was transferred to it in 1841 or whether it could grant equitable relief upon a bill against the Attorney General was a procedural issue that was settled only in the early twentieth century, in *Dyson v Attorney General* [1911] 1 KB 410, when the English Court of Appeal allowed both the use of the petition of right to obtain an equitable declaratory relief and an action by way of a bill against the Attorney General in Chancery.

187 Hale, *Prerogatives* (n 120) 14.
188 Goldsworthy (n 2) 84.
189 Holdsworth (n 186) 23.
190 See Chapter 2, section 2.1.1.2, where Bracton's fo 171b is discussed, and section 2.3.3.
191 Ehrlich (n 181) 74.
192 Borchard (n 145) 27; Ehrlich (n 181) 69. See also *Dyson v Attorney General* (n 186) 422 (Farewell LJ): 'It is very unusual for the responsible minister to refuse to authorize the indorsement "let right be done", and it would be unjustifiable to refuse in any case where a plausible claim is made out. As Lord Langdale says in *Ryves v Duke of Wellington* [(1846) 9 Beav 579, 600], "I am far from thinking that it is competent to the King, or rather to his responsible advisers, to refuse capriciously to put into a due course of investigation any proper question raised on a petition of right." '
193 *Bankers' Case* (n 184).
194 Ehrlich (n 181) 74.

Over the course of the sixteenth century, legal authors such as Staunford still described the petition of right as a remedy for a wide range of cases, from restitution of property and goods to the payment of damages and unpaid wages.[195] In *Sadler's Case* from the end of the sixteenth century, the petition of right was said to be a remedy at common law for the aggrieved subject.[196] The court also set out that the petition of right is a recourse 'in lieu of a real action against the King',[197] the petition of right of the subject being 'in nature of his real action'.[198] Although procedurally different, the petition of right's function was to serve as an equivalent remedy to a real action. The court also laid down the circumstances where a subject aggrieved by the king can have a *monstrans de droit* or traverse of office by the common law against the king. Where neither recourse could be had against the king, the aggrieved subject could still resort to the petition of right to see justice be done.

In the seventeenth century, the petition of right was conceived of as an equivalent remedy to an ordinary action.[199] Jenkins, in his abridgement published in the second half of the seventeenth century, believed the petition of right to be a remedy which lay at common law when other recourses such as *monstrans de droit* were not available.[200] Jenkins adopted the view that the petition of right, although made a common remedy by Edward I's proclamation, was not statutory in nature.[201]

It is possible that in practice, over the course of the fifteenth century, the petition of right lost its prevalence as other remedies filled the gap for other types of actions.[202] However, when Lord Somers turned to the scope of the petition of right at the end of the seventeenth century in *Bankers' Case*, he referred to the original, wider scope of the petition of right.[203] Lord Somers's opinion was reversed by the House of Lords, but it paved the way to a wider scope of application of the petition of right in the nineteenth century.[204] *Bankers' Case* was later considered by Lord Mansfield in the eighteenth century to support the proposition that the petition of right was available against the king in contract and was relied upon in *Thomas v The Queen* in the nineteenth century.[205]

[195] William Staunford, *An Exposicion of the Kinges Prerogative* (printed in Fleet Street by Richard Tottel 1583) 72b; Ehrlich (n 181) 83–84.

[196] *The Warden and Commonalty of Sadlers' Case* (1598) 4 Co Rep 54.

[197] ibid 54b.

[198] ibid 55b, 56a.

[199] Finch, *Nomotechnia* (n 80) 76b–77. See also Chapter 2, sections 2.3.3 and 3.1.

[200] Jenkins (n 116) 177. On *monstrans de droit*, see also Chapter 2, section 2.3.3.

[201] On the nature and origins of the petition of right, see Chapter 2, section 2.3.3.

[202] Ehrlich (n 181) 61, 80, 84.

[203] ibid 84–85.

[204] ibid; WS Holdsworth, 'The History of Remedies against the Crown II' (1922) 38 LQR 280, 283–84. The House of Lords reversed Lord Somers's decision in the Exchequer Chamber that the only available remedy was a petition of right and affirmed the Court of Exchequer's judgment that a petition lay to the Barons of the Exchequer. Unfortunately, the publication of the House of Lords' decision was strictly prohibited, as the court recounted in *Thomas v The Queen* (1874–75) Law Rep 10 QB 31, 40.

[205] *Macbeth v Haldimand* (1786) 1 TR 172, 176; *Thomas v The Queen* (n 204).

In short, although it fell into disuse for most of the seventeenth century, the petition of right was considered throughout that period to be a remedy at common law. The petition of right differed in its procedural nature from an ordinary action but its remedial aspect was thought to be equivalent to that of an ordinary action. The petition of right was also thought to be residual in nature to ensure that the subject would get justice. It was enshrined in the Bill of Rights 1688. In short, the petition of right as a direct remedy against the king remained relevant in legal thinking throughout that period.

3.3.2 Coke's understanding of the king's officials' liability

Although Coke understood *the king can do no wrong* as the king was under the law and not entitled to do wrong, he modified the understanding that the king 'is not entitled to do wrong' in its procedural dimension. While *the king can do no wrong* meant to Coke that the king was under the law and capable of doing wrong, Coke shielded the king from any liability with regard to his officials' wrongdoing by denying them the recourse to the procedure of aid prayer to the king.

While the king's officials had not always been liable for wrongful actions, their personal liability was recognized in the seventeenth century.[206] The king remained personally immune from ordinary actions. However, Coke's reinterpretation[207] of the availability to the king's officials of the procedure of aid prayer to the king also contributed to insulating the king from any form of liability. Coke wrote that the king's official shall not have aid of the king for a wrongful act committed by the official. Coke opined that because the official's wrongful act was thereby void, he could not ask aid of the king for having done wrong in his name. The king being head of justice, it stood against reason, according to Coke, that he should help his official in his wrong.[208] Coke's reasoning in relation to aid prayer was close to Hale's understanding of *the king can do no wrong* in that liability for a wrongful act was limited to the king's servant.

3.3.3 Hale's new interpretation of *the king can do no wrong*

Bracton thought that the king's wrongful act was void, because it exceeded the jurisdiction granted to the king to only act lawfully.[209] In Hale's theory, the king's wrongful act also became void by the effect of the invalidating power of the law, to which the king was subject. The punishment of the king's wrongful act or

[206] Ludwik Ehrlich, 'Proceedings against the Crown (1216–1377)' in Paul Vinogradoff (ed), *Oxford Studies in Social and Legal History*, vol 6 (Clarendon Press 1921) 28–29, 129; WS Holdsworth, 'The History of Remedies against the Crown I' (1922) 38 LQR 141; Burgess, *Absolute Monarchy* (n 3) 153.

[207] The cases cited as authority in the margins do not appear to support Coke's argument: in (1354) 28 Edw III Lib Ass 19, fo 149a, though the aid was not granted the case does not appear to involve a king's agent; in (1426) Trin 4 Hen VI, fo 30a, pl 18 the issue of aid prayer does not appear to have been adjudicated.

[208] 2 Co Inst 206.

[209] See Chapter 2, section 2.1.1.

command rested, however, with the king's minister or servant—the 'instruments' who executed the wrongful command.[210] As for the king's sacredness as a justification for the king's immunity from suit, it presented both a break and continuity with previous ideas found in Bracton. The sacredness of the king referred to the theological grounding of the office of kingship or the king's 'dignity'. To Bracton, that the king held his office from God meant that his power did not extend to do wrong. The king was immune from suit, but a wrong was still attributed to him and the petition of right was later developed to sue to the king. Hale's theory was very similar to Bracton's, but the existence of the petition of right constituted a flaw in the former's interpretation of *the king can do no wrong*.

Hale acknowledged that the king could not be a disseisor and could not gain something wrongfully.[211] He also wrote that the invalidating power of the law operated in such manner that 'the laws also in many cases bin[d] the king's acts and make them void if they are against law' and that grants made contrary to law were void.[212]

Hale added to the coercive and directive power of the law a third one, the invalidating power of the law—the *potestas irritans*. Hale gave a new interpretation of *the king can do no wrong*:

> Yet nevertheless this directive power of the law hath this effect even as to the king's actions, that it doth *irritare actus contrarios legis directioni* [invalidate acts contrary to the requirements of the law] in many cases. And therefore though the king in case of such acts done contrary to the directive power of the law is not subject to the coercive power of the law in respect of the sacredness and sublimity of his person, the instruments and ministers that are the immediate actors of such unlawful things are subject to the coercive power of the law. For the king's act in such case being void doth not justify or defend the instruments. This is one of the principal reasons of the maxim in law that the king can do no wrong, for if it be wrong and contrary to the law, it is not the act of the king but of the minister or instrument that put it in execution and consequently such minister is liable to the coercion of the law to make satisfaction.[213]

The definition of *the king can do no wrong* which Hale gave in *Prerogatives of the Crown* is similar to that found in his *History of the Pleas of the Crown*:

> [I]t is regularly true, that the law presumes, the king will do no wrong, neither indeed can do any wrong; and therefore, if the king command an unlawful act be

[210] Hale, *Prerogatives* (n 120) 15.
[211] *Duke of Richmond* (n 117) 462.
[212] *Reflections on Mr Hobbs His Dialogue of the Law* in Hale, *On the Law of Nature* (n 120) 197.
[213] *Prerogatives of the King* in ibid 221–22; Hale, *Prerogatives* (n 120) 15.

> done, the offense of the instrument is not thereby indemnified; for th[ough] the king is not under the coercive power of the law, yet in many cases his commands are under the directive power of the law, which consequently makes the act itself invalid, if unlawful, and so renders the instrument of the execution thereof obnoxious to the punishment of the law.[214]

In Hale's latter definition, that the servant's offence was not 'indemnified' meant that she was not secured against penalty and was therefore subject to it.[215] That the servant or minister—the 'instrument' who executed the king's unlawful command—was 'obnoxious' to the punishment of the law meant 'liable' to the punishment of the law in the seventeenth century.[216]

Burgess has argued that Hale's invalidating power of the law was 'crucial' in keeping the king under the law because the king's unlawful act could then be disregarded by the courts.[217] But the effect of Hale's new interpretation of *the king can do no wrong* was also to protect the king and to deny that there was any possible recourse against him by invalidating the king's wrongful act and shifting the punishment—the application of the coercive power of the law—entirely on to his officers and servants. Hale's theory of the three powers of the law shielded the king from any ordinary action. Hale rendered in legal terms the political objectives of protecting the king and the king's status in the constitutional order after the regicide.

3.3.4 Issues left unanswered in Hale's theory of the three powers of the law and *the king can do no wrong*

Hale's theory of the three powers of the law was not fully developed and issues were not all addressed in depth.[218] Hale's statement in *Prerogatives*—'for if it be wrong and contrary to the law, it is not the act of the king'[219]—was later interpreted, as will be discussed further in Chapter 4, as the legal fiction that the king's unlawful acts were not or ceased to be the king's. That the king's wrongful acts were not his or ceased to be his in the sense that they were not wrongs in law was not logically compatible with Hale's theory of the three powers of the law, as will be argued in this section. Hale also acknowledged that petitions as of right and petitions as of grace lay against the king.[220] The proposition that Hale's interpretation *of the king can do no wrong* amounted to a legal presumption that a wrongful act could not be

214 Matthew Hale, *The History of the Pleas of the Crown* (Nutt and Gosling 1736) 43–44.

215 Samuel Johnson, *A Dictionary of the English Language* (3rd edn, WG Jones 1768).

216 ibid.

217 Burgess, *Absolute Monarchy* (n 3) 139.

218 Postema explained that Hale's discussion of the three powers of the law was brief and intriguing: 'Introduction' in Hale, *On the Law of Nature* (n 120) lv–lvi.

219 Hale, *Prerogatives* (n 120) 15; Hale, *On the Law of Nature* (n 120) 222.

220 Hale, *Prerogatives* (n 120) 14; Hale, *On the Law of Nature* (n 120) 221. See also *Duke of Richmond* (n 117) 462.

the king's is negated by Hale's recognition of the existence of the petition of right.[221] However, Hale failed to address the issue of the existence of the petition of right and to theorize it in connection with his theory of the three powers of the law and the application of the coercive power of the law to the king, allowing for reinterpretations of his understanding of *the king can do no wrong* later in legal thinking.

Hale submitted that *the king can do no wrong* was to be understood as the king's act, 'if it be wrong and contrary to the law, it is not the act of the king but of the minister or instrument that put it in execution'.[222] That the invalidating power of the law rendered the king's act void so that it could not serve as an excuse for the king's servant is one aspect of Hale's statement. But Hale's statement in *Prerogatives* could also be read as the king's wrongful act or command was not only invalidated by the invalidating power of the law, it was also fictitiously neither the act nor the command of the king. The proposition that Hale understood *the king can do no wrong* as a fiction that the king's wrong was not the king's finds little support. No explanation was given by Hale as to why the wrongful act ceased to be the king's but continued to exist for the king's ministers or servant. The king was not subject to the coercive power of the law in Hale's theory, which explained why there could be no recourse against the king. But the exemption from the coercive power of the law would not of itself explain why the wrongful, invalid, act of the king could not be attributed to the king in Hale's theory. The directive and invalidating power of the law applied to the king, rendering his unlawful commands invalid. The king was therefore capable of commanding an unlawful act, contrary to the directive power of the law, and the unlawful command was invalidated by the invalidating power of the law. Hale's theory of the three powers of the law did not point to a reason as to why the unlawful command could not be attributed to the king.

The suggestion, based on Hale's statement in *Pleas of the Crown* that the law presumed that 'the king will do no wrong, neither indeed can do any wrong',[223] that Hale understood *the king can do no wrong* as whatever the king did was legal does not find support in the rest of Hale's work. Whatever the king did could not be legal in the context of Hale's theory of the three powers of the law, for the king's command issued contrary to the directive power of the law was invalidated by the invalidating power of the law, as Hale himself proceeded to explain in *Pleas of the Crown*. If *the king can do no wrong* is to be understood in Hale's thinking as the king's wrongful command not being the king's, Hale did not provide any justification or explanation to support this new interpretation. It is more likely that Hale, in his statement in *Prerogatives*, understood *the king can do no wrong* in the Bractonian sense—dominant at the time Hale wrote[224]—that the king is not

[221] The existence of the petition of right similarly negated Dicey's claim that there was no *droit administratif*—in the sense of procedures different from ordinary ones—in England: Richard Rawlings and Carol Harlow, *Law and Administration* (3rd edn, CUP 2009) 9.

[222] Hale, *Prerogatives* (n 120) 15.

[223] Hale, *Pleas of the Crown* (n 214) 43.

[224] Postema, 'Introduction' in Hale, *On the Law of Nature* (n 120) xxiv–xxv.

entitled to do wrong. As the king was not entitled to do wrong, a wrongful act was not an act of the king because the king exceeded his jurisdiction. An unlawful act could not be a kingly act because it exceeded the jurisdiction given to the king by the law to act according to law. That Bractonian understanding of *the king can do no wrong* is also compatible with Hale's theory of the three powers of the law that followed his statement that the king's wrong is not the king's.

Another aspect of Hale's theory of the three powers of the law and its relationship with *the king can do no wrong* contributes to undermining the argument that Hale understood the king's wrongful act as fictitiously ceasing to be the king's. Hale's recognition that petitions of right—and not solely petitions of grace—lay against the king[225] would negate the claim that Hale's theory on the invalidating power of the law with regard to the king's unlawful acts was that there was no wrong in the king. It could not be said that the king's wrongful act was not the king's act if there was a petition of right against the king for said wrongful act. The wrongful command was void and officials could not rely on it as an excuse. But the wrongful act was not void in the sense that it ceased to exist insofar as the king was concerned in Hale's understanding of *the king can do no wrong*. It remained the king's wrongful act because the king's subject could have a petition of right—not as of grace—and sue to the king for that act.[226]

The petition of right and the associated idea that the king was bound to act according to law in granting justice and endorsing petitions of right contradict the interpretation of Hale's statement in *Prerogatives* that the king's wrongful act ceased to be the king's. The interpretation of Hale's statement that the king's wrongful acts were not to be conceived of as the king's is also contradicted by the theoretical revival of the petition of right and the possibility to sue to the king for his wrongful act as in *Bankers' Case* at the turn of the eighteenth century.[227]

In summary, Hale's theory of the three powers of the law was to the effect that the king's wrongful act or command was void and officials could not rely on it as an excuse. But the wrongful act was not to be conceived of as void in the sense that it ceased to exist insofar as the king was concerned. It remained the king's wrongful act, as was evidenced by the fact that a king's subject could have a petition of right and sue to the king for that act. Hale himself acknowledged that the subject disposed of such a recourse by petition, as of right and as of grace. Hale's statement that the wrongful act was not the king's but that of the minister or servant who put it into execution can be interpreted as Hale attempting to ensure that the punishment for the act could only rest against the ministers and servants—who remained subject to the coercive power of the law—and not against the king himself.

[225] Hale, *Prerogatives* (n 120) 14. See also *Duke of Richmond* (n 117) 462.
[226] *Duke of Richmond* (n 117) 462, where Hale expressly referred to the petition of right lying against the king.
[227] *Bankers' Case* (n 184).

4 Conclusion: the king's capacity to do wrong and amenability to justice after the constitutional struggles of the seventeenth century

The various understandings of *the king can do no wrong* in legal thinking discussed in Chapter 1 could all be found in the seventeenth century. Sommerville, for instance, has argued that there was unanimous agreement amongst lawyers of the seventeenth century that the king could not personally be sued for his illegal actions.[228] Such agreement corresponds to *the king can do no wrong* understood as the king's immunity from suit. Omitted are the various remedies available against the king—*monstrans de droit*, traverse of office, petition of right. Sommerville adds that the agent executing the wrongful command of the king was to be sued instead.[229] Emphasis is put on the king's minister and servant's personal liability, as is often the case when *the king can do no wrong* is understood as the king is immune from suit. The *Case of the Earl of Danby*, dating to 1679, illustrates the constitutional changes that occurred over the course of the seventeenth century in that regard: the king's official cannot plead obedience to an order from the sovereign as a valid defence.[230] The liability of the king's ministers and servants—or *the king can do no wrong* understood as ministerial responsibility or as the king's wrongful commands are void and cannot serve as a defence—was a solution to what was perceived as an absolute lack of liability of the king. Sommerville further argues that *the king can do no wrong* embodied the 'basic principle' according to which the king's prerogative powers were limited. That the king's power is limited relates to the Bractonian understanding of *the king can do no wrong* that the king is not entitled to do wrong. *The king can do no wrong* understood as the king is not entitled to do wrong is distinct from the understanding of *the king can do no wrong* as the king's immunity from suit, which Sommerville first alluded to in his exposition. Different understandings of *the king can do no wrong* could indeed be found in the seventeenth century: they ranged from the Royalist denial of the king's capacity to do wrong to the new constitutional order's recognition that the king was capable of doing wrong, but was absolutely shielded from amenability to justice.

The king's immunity from suit was derived in the late Middle Ages from his feudal privilege not to be sued in his own courts. Since the seventeenth-century interpretations of *the king can do no wrong*, the king's immunity from suit is also grounded in the notion of perfection of the king—the king, because he is incapable of doing wrong, cannot therefore be sued for a wrong he is incapable of committing. *The king can do no wrong* understood as the king is perfect and incapable of doing wrong is related to the Stuart understanding that everything the king does

[228] Sommerville (n 3) 97.
[229] ibid.
[230] *Case of the Earl of Danby* (1679) 11 St Tr 599.

is legal, and the Royalist understanding that the king is perfect and incapable of doing wrong because he is divinely assisted.

The king can do no wrong understood as the king is perfect and incapable of doing wrong is distinct from *the king can do no wrong* understood as a fiction that the king's wrongful command is not a wrong in the king. That the king's wrongful command is not a wrong in the king could arguably be attributed to Hale and said to be found in seventeenth-century legal thinking. However, as was discussed in section 3.3.3, the proposition that Hale understood *the king can do no wrong* as a fiction that the king's wrong was not a wrong in law finds little support when analysed in the context of his work. That the king's wrongful command is void follows Hale's theory of the invalidating power of the law. Only the king's servant can be held liable and the king's wrongful command, being invalidated by the invalidating power of the law, does not constitute a valid justification. That the king's wrongful command is rendered void by the invalidating power of the law explains why that wrongful command cannot serve as a valid defence for the king's minister or servant executing the command. It does not, however, explain why the king himself cannot be ascribed a wrong. Resort must be had to the notion of perfection of the king and that the king is incapable of doing wrong. Although Hale justified the king's exemption from the coercive power of the law on the grounds of the notion of perfection of the king, his theory of the directive and invalidating power of the law—which both applied to the king—are not grounded on that notion of perfection. On the contrary, the king in Hale's thinking could issue wrongful commands, which were invalidated by the invalidating power of the law.

Although Hale's thinking was marked by change in justifying the king's exemption from the coercive power of the law by relying on the notion of perfection of the king, it was also in continuity with the Bractonian—and Coke's—understanding that the king is not entitled to do wrong. The Bractonian understanding that the king had an obligation to remedy his wrong and the presumption that the king—being fountain of justice—will not be faulty in administering justice contradict the interpretation of Hale's statement in relation to *the king can do no wrong* that a wrong cannot be the king's. In relation to the application of the directive and invalidating powers of the law to the king, Hale's thinking followed the Bractonian understanding that the king was not entitled to do wrong. In Hale's thinking, the king was capable of doing wrong—and of issuing wrongful commands—but as he was not entitled to do so, the commands were void.[231] In short, to interpret Hale's statement in *Prerogatives* as the king's wrongful acts were not his and were not wrongful is not supported by other elements of Hale's theory of the three powers of the law.

[231] As the king is not subject to the coercive power of the law in Hale's theory, whether the command is voidable or void *ab initio* is immaterial. The king's servant can never rely on the king's command as a defence.

During the seventeenth century, the prevalent understanding of *the king can do no wrong* in legal thinking changed from the Bractonian understanding that the king was not entitled to do wrong to become increasingly associated with the king's immunity from suit and ministerial responsibility. In political theory, the maxim *the king can do no wrong* became associated with the idea that the king's ministers are accountable before Parliament for wrongs committed in the king's name or command. That *the king can do no wrong* became strongly associated in legal thinking today with the political theory that the king is not accountable but that his ministers are can be observed in major legal treatises. Stubbs[232] and Anson,[233] for instance, traced the origins of *the king can do no wrong*—which they took to mean ministerial responsibility—to the minority of Henry III, when his ministers were to answer for the king while he was still a minor. *The king can do no wrong* as meaning ministerial responsibility also became associated in legal thinking with the king's immunity from suit.

As will be demonstrated in Chapters 4 and 5, the Bractonian understanding of *the king can do no wrong* as the king was not entitled to do wrong lost its prevalence in legal thinking, despite Coke's coining and use of *the king can do no wrong* in the early seventeenth century and despite Hale's interpretation of *the king can do no wrong* and his theory of the three powers of the law grounded in part on the Bractonian understanding that the king was not entitled to do wrong. The line between the substantive dimension of crown liability—the king's capacity to do wrong—and the procedural dimension—the king's amenability to justice—became blurred over the course of the seventeenth century. As explained in section 3.1.2, Hale's reliance on the directive and coercive power of the law, which he both applied to positive law, undermined the king's status in relation to law. Whereas the king was subject to positive law with Bracton, the king became free from the coercive power of positive law—including statute and common law—with Hale. To consider the king's immunity from suit as part of the issue of the king's status in relation to law via the king's exemption from the coercive power of the law contributed to blurring the line between the procedural and substantive dimensions of crown liability.

The Bractonian understanding of *the king can do no wrong* was that the king was not entitled to do wrong. It related to the substantive dimension of crown liability—the king was capable of doing wrong but was not entitled to. Hale's understanding of *the king can do no wrong* is reflected in the constitutional pact reached with the Glorious Revolution: the king is immune from suit but everyone else is liable instead. With the line blurred between the procedural and substantive dimensions of crown liability in the seventeenth century, *the king can do no wrong*

[232] William Stubbs, *The Constitutional History of England, in Its Origin and Development*, vol 2 (reprint of 4th edn, Clarendon Press 1906) 41.

[233] Anson (n 22) 20; Malcolm (n 20) 170.

became associated in legal thinking over time, after the seventeenth century, with the procedural dimension of crown liability and came to be understood as the king is not amenable to justice.

The king was still capable of committing a wrong and was amenable to justice through the petition of right in seventeenth-century legal thinking. However, the result of developments during that century in relation to *the king can do no wrong*, the constitutional trauma caused by the regicide, and the fact that all understandings of *the king can do no wrong* can be found during that period, allowed for *the king can do no wrong* to be eventually understood in legal thinking as the king is not capable of committing a wrong (substantive dimension of crown liability) and not amenable to justice (procedural dimension).

4
The King Can Do No Wrong in Legal Thinking in the Eighteenth and Nineteenth Centuries

1 Overview of the chapter

As was argued in Chapter 3, various understandings of *the king can do no wrong* can be found in the seventeenth century. As will be demonstrated in this chapter, they featured in legal thinking in the eighteenth and nineteenth centuries, which was marked by confusion, in particular in relation to the two dimensions of crown liability, and, from the second half of the nineteenth century, in relation to the notion of crown itself.

2 Understandings of *the king can do no wrong*: Blackstone, Bacon, Broom, Allen, Wooddeson, Anson, and Hearn

The variety of understandings of *the king can do no wrong* which could be found in the seventeenth century contributed to the confusion surrounding the concept in the eighteenth and nineteenth centuries. For instance, de Lolme denied in 1784 that *the king can do no wrong* originally meant that the king did not have the power to do wrong.[1] In 1798, the editor of Bacon's *Abridgement* criticized the previous editor's annotation to the effect that all prerogatives could only be exercised for the good of the people.[2] The criticism of the 1798 editor is evidence of the confusion surrounding *the king can do no wrong* in legal thinking of the eighteenth century. Cox thought in 1863 that the concept was originally understood as the king was incapable of doing wrong: 'the King was not capable of committing any injury which could be redressed by the ordinary process of the courts of law'.[3] To Anson, first writing in 1886, *the king can do no wrong* meant ministerial responsibility in the sense of responsible government, which was developing in the mid-nineteenth

[1] Jean Louis de Lolme, *The Constitution of England* (first published 1784, Liberty Fund 2007) 63.

[2] Matthew Bacon, *A New Abridgment of the Law*, vol 5 (Henry Gwillim ed, 5th edn, Strahan 1798) 487–89.

[3] Homersham Cox, *The Institutions of the English Government* (H Sweet 1863) 416.

The King Can Do No Wrong. Marie-France Fortin, Oxford University Press. © Marie-France Fortin 2024.
DOI: 10.1093/9780191994487.003.0005

century.[4] Anson therefore traced the origins of the concept understood as ministerial responsibility to the minority of Henry III.[5] Cox similarly identified *the king can do no wrong* with ministers' political accountability before Parliament, but argued that that understanding was only partially established before the Glorious Revolution and became a principle of the law only long after it.[6] *The king can do no wrong* understood as the king's ministers' liability for the king's wrongful command was attributed to Blackstone.[7] The fact that Blackstone named only the king's ministers as liable for the king's wrongful commands—omitting, unlike Hale, the king's other servants—also contributed to the association of *the king can do no wrong* with ministerial responsibility.

Broom's translation of *the king can do no wrong* to Latin—*Rex non potest peccare*—and its attribution to Rolle's and Jenkins's reports of cases from the seventeenth century most likely also contributed to obscuring the understanding of the concept as Bractonian.[8] However, Broom's later addition of the maxim that the king is under no man but God and the law because the law makes the king, correctly attributed to Bracton, was also referred to by Allen and Hearn in connection with *the king can do no wrong*.[9]

Despite its loss of prominence in legal thinking throughout the nineteenth century in favour of the notion of perfection of the king emphasized by Blackstone and, later, Dicey's notion of individual officers' liability, the Bractonian understanding of *the king can do no wrong* as the king is not entitled to do wrong was not completely lost, as will be demonstrated in this chapter. The Bractonian understanding of *the king can do no wrong* which underpinned Coke's and Hale's understanding was a continuing feature in legal thinking even in Blackstone's and Dicey's work.

[4] Janet McLean, *Searching for the State in British Legal Thought: Competing Conceptions of the Public Sphere* (CUP 2012) 37–38.

[5] William Reynell Anson, *The Law and Custom of the Constitution*, vol 2 part 1 (A Berriedale Keith ed, 4th edn, Clarendon Press 1935) 20. The first volume of Anson's treatise, on Parliament, was first published in 1886, and the second volume, on the crown, was first published in 1892; the second volume was further divided into part 1 and part 2 with the third edition in 1907.

[6] Cox (n 3) 247, 408, 631.

[7] Bentham adopted Blackstone's understanding of *the king can do no wrong* as the king's irresponsibility supplemented by the ministers' responsibility: Philip Schofield, *Utility and Democracy: The Political Thought of Jeremy Bentham* (OUP 2006) 95–96.

[8] That *the king can do no wrong* first appeared in Latin—and not in Law French and in English in Plowden's and Coke's reports—still appears to be the traditional view: Maurice Sunkin, 'Crown Immunity from Criminal Liability in English Law' [2003] PL 716, 720.

[9] Broom did not include Bracton's maxim in the first two editions of his work, dating to 1845 and 1848, but it features in later editions: Herbert Broom, *A Selection of Legal Maxims* (1st edn, Maxwell & Son 1845); Herbert Broom, *A Selection of Legal Maxims* (2nd ed, Maxwell & Son 1848); Herbert Broom, *A Selection of Legal Maxims* (10th edn, Sweet & Maxwell 1939) 17–18. See Cox (n 3) 408; John Allen, *Inquiry into the Rise of and Growth of Prerogative in England* (Longman, Brown, Green and Longmans 1849) 35; William Edward Hearn, *The Government of England: Its Structure and Its Development* (2nd edn, Robertson 1886) 20.

2.1 Blackstone's interpretation

The Bractonian understanding of *the king can do no wrong*, which could be found in Coke's and in Hale's work of the seventeenth century, could still be found in legal literature in the eighteenth century and early nineteenth century,[10] notably in the work of Blackstone,[11] Wood,[12] and Ferris.[13]

Blackstone, in his highly influential *Commentaries*, combined both Bracton's and Hale's understandings of *the king can do no wrong*. In his chapter on the king's duties, Blackstone cited Bracton and Fortescue for the argument that the king must rule according to law.[14] In the chapter on the king's prerogatives, Blackstone cited Finch and the principle that the king's prerogative did not extend to the doing of any wrong and Bracton's statement that the king can only act *de jure*.[15] It has recently been argued that the ideas that the king's power was limited by law and that the basis for government was the subject's consent were essential features of Blackstone's thinking.[16]

The reference to both the Bractonian *the king can do no wrong*—the king is not entitled to do wrong—and Hale's interpretation that the king's ministers are liable in lieu of the king for executing the king's wrongful orders feature in Blackstone's *Commentaries*:

> The king can do no wrong. Which ancient and fundamental maxim is not to be understood, as if every thing transacted by the government was of course just and lawful, but means only two things. First, that whatever is exceptionable in the conduct of public affairs is not to be imputed to the king, nor is he answerable for it personally to his people .... And, secondly, it means that the prerogative of the crown extends not to do any injury: it is created for the benefit of the people, and therefore cannot be exerted to their prejudice.[17]

> That the king can do no wrong, is a necessary and fundamental principle of the English constitution: meaning only, as has formerly been observed, that in the

[10] In the political realm in the eighteenth and nineteenth centuries, Whigs understood *the king can do no wrong* as the king was subject to law and as ministerial responsibility. Tories understood it as the monarch's perfection and incapacity to do wrong: see Steve Poole, *The Politics of Regicide in England, 1760–1850: Troublesome Subjects* (Manchester UP 2000) 17.

[11] William Blackstone, *Commentaries on the Laws of England*, vol 1 (facsimile of 1765–1769 1st edn, University of Chicago Press 1979) 226–28, 231–32, 239.

[12] 'The King hath a prerogative in all things that are not injurious to the subject; for the King can do no wrong: His Prerogative can never extend so far': Thomas Wood, *An Institute of the Laws of England* (W Strahan and M Woodfall 1772) 23.

[13] James Ferris, *A Standard of the English Constitution* (Printed for James Ferris 1805) 10.

[14] Blackstone (n 11) 226–28.

[15] ibid 231–32.

[16] David Lemmings, 'Editor's Introduction to Book I' in Wilfrid Prest and David Lemmings (eds), *The Oxford Edition of Blackstone—Commentaries on the Laws of England*, vol 1 (OUP 2016) xxviii.

[17] Blackstone (n 11) 238–39.

> first place, whatever may be amiss in the conduct of public affairs is not chargeable personally on the king; nor is he, but his ministers, accountable for it to the people: and, secondly, that the prerogative of the crown extends not to do any injury; for, being created for the benefit of the people, it cannot be exerted to their prejudice.[18]

The king can do no wrong to Blackstone was the Bractonian understanding that the king is not entitled to do wrong—and therefore that the prerogative cannot be used to do wrong[19]—and Hale's interpretation that the king's official was liable for the king's wrongful command. However, Hale had included all the servants—the 'instruments'—executing the king's command as liable, not only the king's ministers. Blackstone, as appears from these excerpts, only referred to the king's ministers' responsibility to the people for the king's wrongful commands. Blackstone's reference to the ministers' political accountability is an early example of the enduring understanding of *the king can do no wrong* as ministerial responsibility.[20]

Not only did Blackstone adopt the Bractonian—and Coke's and Hale's—understanding of *the king can do no wrong*, but he added to his attempted synthesis of previous literature the Tudor doctrine of the two bodies of the king. Blackstone specified that the king is not 'personally' accountable[21] and emphasized the notion of perfection which attached to the king's body politic in the doctrine of the king's two bodies:

> The law also attributes to the king, in his political capacity, absolute perfection. The king can do no wrong. . . . The king, moreover, is not only incapable of *doing* wrong, but even of *thinking* wrong: he can never mean to do an improper thing: in him is no folly or weakness.[22]

The notion of perfection of the king is referred to again by Blackstone in his *Commentaries* in Book IV on *Public Wrongs*, where deficiencies in understanding negating one's criminal liability are discussed in relation to the king:

[18] William Blackstone, *Commentaries on the Laws of England*, vol 3 (facsimile of 1765–1769 1st edn, University of Chicago Press 1979) 254–55.

[19] See Chapter 2, section 2.1.

[20] See eg Clayton Roberts, *The Growth of Responsible Government in Stuart England* (CUP 1966); Janelle Greenberg, 'Our Grand Maxim of State: "The King Can Do No Wrong"' (1991) 12 Hist Pol Thought 209; Joyce Lee Malcolm, 'Doing No Wrong: Law, Liberty, and the Constraint of Kings' (1999) 38 J Brit Stud 161; Grégoire Webber, 'Loyal Opposition and the Political Constitution' (2017) 37 OJLS 357. Bentham may have disapproved of Blackstone's use of fictions in connection with the state, but he enthusiastically approved of the latter's understanding of *the king can do no wrong* as the king's irresponsibility supplemented by the ministers' responsibility: Schofield (n 7) 95–96; McLean (n 4) 4. For associations between *the king can do no wrong* and ministerial responsibility, see Cox (n 3) 408, 415; Anson (n 5) 20.

[21] Blackstone (n 11) 238–39.

[22] ibid.

> To these we may add one more, in which the law supposes an incapacity of doing wrong from the excellence and perfection of the person; which extend as well to the will as to other qualities of his mind. I mean the case of the king: who, by virtue of his royal prerogative, is not under the coercive power of the law; which will not suppose him capable of committing a folly, much less a crime. We are therefore, out of reverence and decency, to forbear any idle enquiries, of what would be the consequence if the king were to act thus and thus: since the law deems so highly of his wisdom and virtue, as not even to presume it possible for him to any thing inconsistent with his station and dignity; and therefore has made no provision to remedy such a grievance.[23]

Blackstone defined public wrongs as crimes, an innovation at a time when criminal offences were not yet part of the legal technical vocabulary, the theoretical boundaries between civil and criminal law were not well defined, and the distinction between a criminal and civil action was not easy to make.[24] His application of his interpretation of *the king can do no wrong* to the king in the realm of criminal liability was thus innovative and he appears to have been one of the first legal authors to discuss the king's immunity from criminal liability in connection with the concept. Hale had discussed *the king can do no wrong* in the context of criminal liability of the king's subjects in his *History of the Pleas of the Crown* but not the criminal liability of the king himself.[25]

Hale, like Blackstone in the excerpted passage, also relied on the notion of the king's perfection—his sublimity—to ground the king's immunity from suit. That aspect of Hale's interpretation was the weakest because it exposed a contradiction in his theory on the directive, invalidating, and coercive powers of the law.[26] In Hale's interpretation of *the king can do no wrong*, the king was capable of doing wrong and his wrongful orders were voided by the invalidating force of the law. Hale relied on the king's perfection and sacredness to justify the king's exemption from the coercive power of the law. Hale's interpretation was contradictory: the king's perfection justified his exemption from the coercive power of the law, yet the same perfect king was capable of doing wrong and his wrongful commands were invalidated by the invalidating power of the law. Blackstone nevertheless relied on the notion of perfection of the king (per Hale's interpretation) in his own exposition of *the king can do no wrong*. Blackstone added the idea that the king was incapable of doing wrong and the consequent absence of legal recourses against the

[23] William Blackstone, *Commentaries on the Laws of England*, vol 4 (facsimile of 1765–1769 1st edn, University of Chicago Press 1979) 32–33.

[24] Ruth Paley, 'Editor's Introduction to Book IV' in Wilfrid Prest and Ruth Paley (eds), *The Oxford Edition of Blackstone: Commentaries on the Laws of England*, vol 4 (OUP 2016) vii–viii.

[25] Matthew Hale, *The History of the Pleas of the Crown* (Nutt and Gosling 1736) 43–44.

[26] See Chapter 3, section 3.3.4.

king. Blackstone's interpretation was even more deferential and protective of the king than Hale's.

Blackstone's reliance on the notion of perfection, which he associated with the notion of perfection of the king's body politic, influenced later understandings of *the king can do no wrong*. Anson, for example, writing in the twentieth century, still relied on the attribute of perfection of judgement of the king as the ground for ministerial responsibility,[27] the notion of perfection of the king was referred to even in the last edition of Broom's *Legal Maxims* in 1939[28] and the king's incapacity to do wrong, derived from the king's perfection, can be found in Bell's 1948 treatise on crown proceedings.[29]

Blackstone's reliance on the perfection of the king to interpret *the king can do no wrong* eclipsed Hale's nuanced theory of the directive, invalidating, and coercive powers of the law in legal literature. Broom, in his immensely successful and long-lived[30] collection of English maxims, copied Blackstone's definition, including its Bractonian, Coke, and Hale elements, as well as the notion of perfection and of the king's two bodies. Broom also added a reference to Hale's distinction between the directive and coercive powers of the law but he was the only one to do so in discussing *the king can do no wrong*.[31]

In adopting Blackstone's interpretation of *the king can do no wrong*, Broom also adopted its flaws. Broom and Blackstone's understanding was that the king was under the law and that *the king can do no wrong* did not mean that everything the king did was lawful. Their understanding implied that the king was in fact capable of doing things which were unlawful, but it was contradicted by their subsequent claim that the king was incapable of thinking or doing wrong. That the perfect king was nevertheless capable of committing a wrongful act such as dispensing with something or granting something to the injury of another was antinomic. Blackstone and Broom reconciled that contradiction by adding that the king was deceived into misusing his power by evil counsellors.[32] That a perfect king can be deceived is, however, illogical. It should not be possible to deceive a perfect king. Broom's reliance on Hale's explanation that the king was subject to the directive

[27] William Reynell Anson, *The Law and Custom of the Constitution* vol 2 part 1 (3rd edn, Clarendon Press 1907) 5; Anson (n 5) 19–20.

[28] Broom, 10th edn (n 9) 22.

[29] Ronald McMillan Bell, *Crown Proceedings, Being a Full Statement of the Law Relating to Actions by and against the Crown as Affected by the Crown Proceedings Act, 1947* (Sweet and Maxwell 1948) 19.

[30] AWB Simpson, 'The Rise and Fall of the Legal Treatise: Legal Principles and the Forms of Legal Literature' (1981) 48 U Chi LR 632, 647. See n 9.

[31] The distinction already featured in the first edition: Broom, 1st edn (n 9) 13; see also Broom, 2nd edn (n 9) 40–41.

[32] Blackstone (n 11) 237–39; the fiction was a constant feature of Broom's treatise: Broom, 1st edn (n 9) 13; Broom, 2nd edn (n 9) 41; Broom, 10th edn (n 9) 22. They reinterpreted the fiction that the king was deceived in his grant and changed it from the Bractonian understanding Coke had adopted in annulling the king's injurious grants, see Chapter 3, section 3.1.1.2, and see Chapter 2, section 2.1.1.2, for Bracton.

force of the law and that his unlawful acts were invalidated by it[33] also demonstrates that the notion of a perfect king fitted uneasily with the rest of Hale's interpretation of *the king can do no wrong* that the king's wrongful commands were void and could not serve as a valid defence.

Broom relied—as had Blackstone—on the doctrine of the king's two bodies to attempt to reconcile the logical flaw in the interpretation of *the king can do no wrong* caused by the notion of a perfect king incapable of doing wrong. Broom's explanation that the king was 'in a personal sense' incapable of doing wrong but that 'his acts may in themselves be contrary to law, and, on that account, be set aside by the law' did not provide any more assistance in solving the conundrum and added to the confusion.[34]

Blackstone himself attempted to resolve the difficulty posed by the notion of a perfect king issuing wrongful commands by stating that 'that the king himself can do no wrong; since it would be a great weakness and absurdity in any system of positive law, to define any possible wrong, without any possible redress'.[35] Blackstone gave a new conceptual basis for the king's immunity from suit: since there was no remedy, there was no wrong. Blackstone's explanation was strongly criticized by Allen, who pointed out that to say that there can be no wrong because there is no remedy is akin to saying that there is no disease if there is no cure for it.[36]

In short, Blackstone's understanding had Bractonian, Coke, and Hale elements in it. However, Blackstone's influential emphasis on the notion of perfection of the king in his exposition effected a change in the understanding of *the king can do no wrong*, as is further explored in section 3.2. The impact of Blackstone's writings on American and Irish legal thinking is discussed in Chapter 6, sections 2.1.2 and 3.1.2.

2.2 Alternative interpretations

Wooddeson (delivering his lectures from 1777), Allen (1849), and Hearn (1867) tried to provide new interpretations of *the king can do no wrong*.[37]

Wooddeson's original interpretation of *the king can do no wrong* married the Bractonian understanding that the king is not entitled to do wrong and Hale's

[33] Broom, 1st edn (n 9) 13; Broom, 2nd edn (n 9) 40–41; Broom, 10th edn (n 9) 22.
[34] Broom, 10th edn (n 9) 23.
[35] Blackstone (n 11) 237.
[36] Allen (n 9) 32.
[37] Richard Wooddeson, *A Systematical View of the Laws of England: As Treated of in a Course of Vinerian Lectures, Read at Oxford, During a Series of Years, Commencing in Michaelmas Term, 1777*, vol 1 (T Payne 1792); Allen (n 9); Hearn (n 9). The first edition of Hearn's treatise of 1867 was out of print and already difficult to procure as of 1888: DG Ritchie, 'Review of *The Government of England, Its Structure and Its Development*' (1888) 3 Eng Hist Rev 556, 557. The 1886 second edition of Hearn's work is referred to herein.

emphasis on the liability of the king's ministers and advisers by drawing a distinction between past and future acts. To Wooddeson, with regard to acts done in the past, the king's wrong could not be imputed to him and his advisers had to be sued instead. With respect to the future, however, *the king can do no wrong* had to be understood as the king cannot exercise his prerogative to do wrong.[38]

Allen created a duality of the two kings: the real and the ideal king.[39] The ideal king was the king of theory and the real king was constrained in practice. The ideal king was above the law but the real king was subject to law in Allen's thinking.[40] Allen's duality was not clearly associated with the doctrine of the king's two bodies in his work because the association was not consistently maintained. He ultimately failed to provide an original understanding of *the king can do no wrong*. Allen posited that the king was immune from suit because he was fountain of justice in his ideal capacity and because of his sovereignty, supremacy, and his ideal attributes—including perfection and the incapacity of thinking or doing wrong.[41] Allen argued that lawyers transferred the ideal attributes of the ideal king to the real king and that the transfer ensured his immunity from suit in his natural capacity.[42] Yet he later argued that the notion of perfection of the king was not easily transferred to the real king.[43] Moreover, Allen's reliance on the king's sovereignty and pre-eminence to ground his immunity from suit was undermined by Allen's own criticism of Blackstone's reliance on the same concepts: sovereignty and pre-eminence could not vest in the king while also recognizing that absolute authority rested with Parliament.[44] To Allen, *the king can do no wrong* was to be understood as the king's immunity from suit in his personal capacity but the grounds of the king's immunity were the same as those Blackstone had posited. Allen simply added the gloss that the causes of the king's immunity from suit—his status as fountain of justice, his sovereignty and perfection—were passed on from the ideal king to the real king. Allen's attempt at reinterpreting Blackstone's exposition of *the king can do no wrong* based on a distinction between the real and the ideal king ultimately failed.

Hearn—like Blackstone and Allen before him—also relied on the doctrine of the king's two bodies to theorize *the king can do no wrong*. Hearn, in contradistinction to Blackstone, understood this to mean all acts the king did are lawful—when done in his political capacity. Hearn's thinking was that all the acts of the king were to be made according to defined procedures and were therefore lawful.[45] The

[38] Wooddeson (n 37) 81–82.
[39] Allen (n 9) 79.
[40] ibid 34–35.
[41] ibid 31, 32, 94.
[42] ibid 31, 89, 94.
[43] ibid 35–36.
[44] ibid 34.
[45] Hearn's thinking is not dissimilar to Hobbes's, where the king's acts, before they receive the seal of England, are private wishes but become public commands once they receive it: see Thomas Poole, 'Hobbes on Law and Prerogative' in David Dyzenhaus and Thomas Poole (eds), *Hobbes and the Law* (CUP 2012) 84.

association of *the king can do no wrong* with the idea that the acts of the king acquired legal force only after they were authenticated by high officers could also be found in the work of Paley.[46] If acts were not made in the manner prescribed by law, they were not official acts of the crown.[47] 'Thus no injury, no legal wrong, can be done by the King, because all his official acts are done in accordance with law.'[48] As no unlawful command could be a command of the crown, they were made under colour of royal authority only and could not excuse the king's servants executing them.[49] Not only was the servant liable, she could also face the king's displeasure at not having followed his true, lawful command—implying that the king was perfect and benevolent.

Hearn cited Bracton's statement that the king only has the power to act according to law to support his exposition of *the king can do no wrong*. In fact, Hearn offered a new interpretation of Bracton's statement. While Bracton said that the king's wrongful acts were not those of a king because the king was not entitled to do wrong, he did not also imply that the king was incapable of doing wrong and that the wrongful act was not the king's.[50] The Bractonian king was capable of doing wrong and had to answer for his wrongful actions. Hearn, although citing Bracton to support his interpretation, in fact changed the latter's meaning that the king's wrongful acts were not the acts of a king. Bracton did not mean to say that all the king's acts were lawful because the king was not entitled to do wrong. Bracton's statement was not a fiction that the king did not commit the wrongful act either. It laid down the scope of the king's jurisdiction—which extended only to acting lawfully. When exceeding his authority, the king committed a wrong. Bracton did not state that the king was incapable of committing a wrong and that all the king's acts were lawful.

Hearn explained that the second understanding of *the king can do no wrong* was that the king in his personal capacity was capable of doing wrong but was immune from suit. No grounds for that immunity were given, but Hearn observed that other persons such as ambassadors also benefitted from similar immunities from suit. *The king can do no wrong*, in relation to the king in his personal capacity, was essentially associated by Hearn with the procedural dimension of crown liability and the notion of immunity from suit.

Dicey admired Hearn's work.[51] Hearn's insistence that every servant of the crown is personally liable for the legality of her acts before ordinary tribunals and

[46] William Paley, *The Principles of Moral and Political Philosophy* (first published 1785, CUP 2013) 478–79.

[47] Hearn (n 9) 20.

[48] ibid. For a similar interpretation, see Sir John Baker, *An Introduction to English Legal History* (5th edn, OUP 2019) 177.

[49] Hearn (n 9) 21–22.

[50] See Chapter 2, section 2.1.1.3.

[51] AV Dicey, *Lectures Introductory to the Study of the Law of the Constitution: The Oxford Edition of Dicey*, vol 1 (JWF Allison ed, OUP 2013) 5.

his mistrust of the French system[52] are reflected in Dicey's work.[53] Dicey also borrowed from Hearn's interpretation of *the king can do no wrong* that all the crown's acts are lawful because they must go through procedural requirements to be acts of the crown.[54]

Ultimately, Allen's, Wooddeson's, and Hearn's new interpretations were eclipsed, as will be discussed in section 3.3.3, by Dicey's interpretation of *the king can do no wrong* as the king's immunity from suit and the liability of individual officers.

3 Three notions underlying crown liability

The rise and fall of the three notions associated with *the king can do no wrong*—the king's status in relation to law, his perfection, and his immunity from suit—in legal thinking since the eighteenth century is analysed in this section.

3.1 The king's status as under the law

The king can do no wrong and the interpretation of statutes and their application to the king have an interrelated history. Coke understood *the king can do no wrong* as the king is not entitled to do wrong and referred to that Bractonian understanding to justify his conclusion that statutes aiming to suppress a wrong applied to the king.[55] In Hale's interpretation, the directive and invalidating forces of the law—including statutes—applied to the king while all ministers, officials, and servants were subject to the full force of the law, including its coercive power.[56] That the king was under the law featured in Blackstone's *Commentaries*, where *the king can do no wrong* was said not to be understood as everything the government did was just and lawful and where it was argued that the king can only act *de jure* and that statutes enacted by Parliament bound the king himself.[57] Broom also stated that *the king can do no wrong* 'must not be understood to mean, that the king is above the laws'.[58]

Coke's rule of interpretation of statutes, grounded in the Bractonian understanding that *the king can do no wrong*, was that statutes for the public good or which provided remedies to the subject bound the king—the king was bound by general words in a statute except if they affected his titles, estates, rights, and

52 Hearn (n 9) 101, 102, 107, 109.
53 Dicey (n 51) 100–04, 233.
54 Hearn (n 9) 20; Dicey (n 51) 21.
55 See Chapter 3, section 3.1.1.3.
56 See ibid.
57 Blackstone (n 11) 178, 226–28, 232, 238–39.
58 Broom, 1st edn (n 9) 12; Broom, 2nd edn (n 9) 40.

privileges.[59] Jenkins's report of Coke's advisory opinion in the *Case of the King, Tenant in Tail*, where Jenkins coined the expression that the king is not bound by a statute unless he is named in it,[60] perverted Coke's ruling in *Magdalen College*.[61] The express mention of the king in a statute for him to be bound became the accepted norm. Nevertheless, the essence of Coke's rule of statutory interpretation, although only infrequently attributed to Coke, can be found in the work of Blackstone, Wood, Bacon, Chitty, Comyns, Dwarris, and Broom, and a variation of it in Maxwell's *Interpretation of Statutes* as late as the eighth edition of 1937.[62] Coke's rule of statutory construction can be found in cases up until the twentieth century,[63] including the seminal case of *Province of Bombay*, where Lord du Parcq modified the rule of interpretation by requiring that the beneficent intent of a statute must be wholly frustrated by the crown's exemption from it for the crown to be bound by the statute.[64] Williams, in his important work on crown proceedings, also believed that provisions of a general character enacted for the public safety bound the crown by necessary implication.[65]

The confusion surrounding *the king can do no wrong* in legal thinking obscured the Bractonian understanding underpinning Coke's rule of interpretation of statutes as it was adopted by legal authors after him. The nineteenth-century

[59] See Chapter 3, section 3.1.1.3.

[60] See Chapter 3, sections 3.1.1.2 and 3.2.1; (1604) Jenk 307; Adam Tomkins, 'Crown Privileges' in Sebastian Payne and Maurice Sunkin (eds), *The Nature of the Crown: A Legal and Political Analysis* (OUP 1999) 174.

[61] *The Case of the Master and Fellows of Magdalen College in Cambridge* (1615) 11 Co Rep 66.

[62] See Marie-France Fortin, 'Revisiting the Application of Statutes to the Crown: A Historical Constitutional Approach' (2021) 3 J CommonwL 271; Blackstone (n 11) 254; Wood (n 12) 21; Bacon (n 2) 559; Joseph Chitty, *A Treatise on the Law of the Prerogatives of the Crown* (Butterworth & Son 1820) 382–84; John Comyns, *A Digest of the Laws of England* (Anthony Hammond and Thomas Day eds, Collins & Hannay 1825) 324; Sir Fortunatus Dwarris, *A General Treatise on Statutes* (W Benning 1848) 523–24; Broom, 1st edn (n 9) 16–17; Broom, 2nd edn (n 9) 50–51; Broom, 10th edn (n 9) 39–40; Peter Benson Maxwell, *The Interpretation of Statutes* (Gilbert HB Jackson ed, 8th edn, Sweet & Maxwell 1937) 120.

[63] *The Queen v Tutchin* (1704) 6 Mod 268, 280 where the Attorney General pleaded that 'the known and true rule in law' is that 'general words of an Act of Parliament for furtherance of justice, or suppressing of wrong, shall bind the king'; *Archbishop of Armagh et al v Attorney General* (1722) 1 Str 516, 517–18, where the losing counsel argued Coke's rule and Eyre CJ approved of it before giving a final judgment to the contrary; *R v Eaststaff* (1818) Gow 138, 153–54; *The King v Wright* (1834) 1 Ad & E 434, where Tindal CJ found that the act was passed expressly for the advancement of justice and was general so as to encompass the king as prosecutor although he was not expressly named in the statute; *The Mayor, Aldermen and Burgesses of Weymouth et al v Nugent* (1865) 6 B&S 22 and *In re Bonham* [1879] 10 Ch D 595, where it was found that the crown could not be divested of its ancient prerogative because it was not expressly named in the statute; *Somerville v Lord Advocate* (1893) 20 R 1050, 1057, 1061 (Lord Trayner), 1063–64 (Lord Wellwood, to whom the statute, because it suppressed a wrong and was enacted for the public good, would have bound the crown were it not for the fact that it also created judicial functions for the Dean of Guild and that the crown's privilege not to be sued in inferior courts could not be displaced by a general statute), 1065 (Lord Killachy, who stated that the established rule was that the crown was bound by a general statute unless its prerogatives were affected), 1071, 1073–74 (Lord Kincairney); *Attorney General v Hancock* [1939] 1 KB 427, 435–39.

[64] *Province of Bombay v Municipal Corporation of the City of Bombay* [1947] AC 58 (PC) 62–63.

[65] Glanville Llewelyn Williams, *Crown Proceedings: An Account of Civil Proceedings by and against the Crown as Affected by the Crown Proceedings Act, 1947* (Stevens 1948) 49–50.

understanding that *the king can do no wrong* was synonymous with the king's immunity from suit, a development discussed in section 3.3, contributed to pervert Coke's rule of statutory construction. The rule became that the king is not bound by a statute unless expressly named or by necessary implication.[66]

Coke's rule of interpretation of statutes, grounded in the Bractonian understanding of *the king can do no wrong*, subsisted in legal literature and cases until the late twentieth century. A close reading of Lord du Parcq's speech in *Province of Bombay* shows that the fact that a statute's intent is to promote the public good—its beneficent purpose—can lead to the conclusion that the king is bound by the statute. Although Lord du Parcq rejected the proposition that the crown is bound by a statute for the sole reason that it was enacted for the public good on the ground that all statutes must be presumed to be intended to be made for the public good,[67] he did not cast aside Coke's rule of interpretation and said that, should the beneficent purpose of the act be wholly frustrated were it not apply to the crown, the court may conclude that the crown is bound.[68] It was only in *Dumbarton* that Coke's rule of statutory interpretation grounded in *the king can do on wrong* was formally abandoned.[69] Until the end of the twentieth century, elements of Coke's rule of statutory construction were an instantiation of the surviving Bractonian understanding of *the king can do no wrong.*

3.2 Perfection

In recent legal literature, it is said that by 1750 the king's perfection was the basis for the king's immunity from suit.[70] The notion of perfection of the king could already be found, notably, in Hale's interpretation of *the king can do no wrong*, where the king's sublimity justified the king's exemption from the coercive power of the law.[71] Hale had not, however, resorted to the notion of perfection of the king to also posit that the king was incapable of doing wrong. Hale's interpretation was that the king was subject to the directive power of the law and therefore implied that the king

[66] The concept of the necessary implication exception, which was first elaborated in the United States in *US v Hoar* (1821) 2 Mason 311, was applied for the first time in England in *Attorney General v Edmunds* (1870) 22 LTR 667: Harry Street, 'The Effects of Statutes upon the Rights and Liabilities of the Crown' (1948) 7 UTLJ 357, 367–68.

[67] *Province of Bombay* (n 64) 63.

[68] ibid.

[69] *Lord Advocate v Dumbarton District Council* [1990] 2 AC 580, 598 (Lord Keith). The wholly frustrated test was extended to other purposes of a statute in *R(Black) v Secretary of State for Justice* (2017) UKSC 81, [2018] AC 215 [36] (Lady Hale).

[70] Bradley Selway, 'Of Kings and Officers: The Judicial Development of Public Law' (2005) 33 FL Rev 187, 205.

[71] Matthew Hale, *The Prerogatives of the King*, vol 92 (DEC Yale ed, Selden Society 1976) 15; Sir Matthew Hale, *On the Law of Nature, Reason, and Common Law: Selected Jurisprudential Writings* (Gerald Postema ed, OUP 2017) 221–22. See Chapter 3, section 3.2.2.

was capable of doing a wrong, contrary to the directive force of the law. To Hale, the king was also subject to the invalidating power of the law, rendering his wrongful act or command void. According to Hale's interpretation, the king was not subject to the coercive force of the law and there could be no action against him. But an important aspect of Hale's interpretation was that the king's wrongful command was voided by the invalidating power of the law, making it impossible for the king's servant to rely on the king's command as a defence. The king originally issued a wrongful command, which was subsequently invalidated by the directive force of the law. The king was in fact capable of committing a wrong and the petition of right was available.

Both Matthew Bacon[72] and Blackstone adopted Hale's interpretation of *the king can do no wrong* that the king was under the directive power of the law but not the coercive power. They did not, however, add Hale's nuance that the king's wrongful command was void because of the invalidating power of the law. As will be shown, Bacon and Blackstone instead chose to emphasize the other interpretation that Hale's exposition lent itself to—that the king was perfect and therefore not only immune from suit, but also incapable of committing or commanding a wrong.[73]

Bacon adopted Hale's interpretation but emphasized more than Hale had the king's perfection due to the dignity of his office and person. Bacon stated that the king was incapable of doing wrong because of the dignity of his office and person—implying that the incapacity to do wrong attached to the king's political and personal capacities, in line with Bacon's statement that the king had two capacities.[74] Even if Bacon correctly explained Hale's interpretation that the blame was to be put on the servant who executed the king's command, the emphasis on the king's perfection laid bare the weakness in Hale's interpretation that the king is immune because of his perfection. The fact that the king was capable of commanding a wrong—a command which was void because it was unlawful—was a negation of the king's perfection. Shifting the focus to the king's servants' liability for executing the wrongful command did not solve the logical flaw posed by Bacon's reliance on the king's perfection and his incapacity to do any wrong. In fact, the king being capable of doing wrong was implicit in Bacon's work, as the phrase 'if the king command an unlawful act' suggests.[75] The attempt to obscure, first, the fact that the king must logically be capable of doing wrong for there to be unlawful commands and, second, that such capacity to do wrong cannot be reconciled with the notion of perfection of the king failed with Bacon as it did with Hale.

The notion of perfection was given prominence by Blackstone, who attributed to the royal dignity the attribute of absolute perfection and associated it with *the*

[72] Bacon (n 2) 550.
[73] See Chapter 3, section 3.3.4.
[74] Bacon (n 2) 550–51.
[75] ibid 550.

king can do no wrong.[76] As had Bacon, Blackstone adopted Hale's interpretation, and added that 'Incapacity to err is the mark of the Deity'.[77] The king being God-like, he was perfect and incapable of doing wrong. Blackstone added the doctrine of the king's two bodies to his treatment of *the king can do no wrong*. Where Hale had not referred to the king's two bodies—possibly because of the danger of separating them[78]—Blackstone did not only associate the notion of perfection with the dignity and the king's 'political capacity'[79] but also with the king personally.[80] Borrowing from Finch, Blackstone's king 'is not only incapable of doing wrong, but even of thinking wrong: he can never mean to do an improper thing: in him is no folly or weakness'.[81]

The notion of perfection in Blackstone's work was highly influential and can be traced through cases and legal literature to this day. It manifests itself not only as the king's absolute perfection and his consequent incapacity to do wrong, but also as the fiction that the benevolent king was deceived by ill-intentioned advisers. Its impact was such that it is sometimes thought, even now, that *the king can do no wrong* originated in an era where the king was ascribed absolute perfection.[82]

References to the notion of the king's perfection show the prevalence of the notion in the eighteenth and nineteenth centuries. Wood, writing in 1772, referred to the case of the first year of Henry VII's reign, discussed in Chapter 2, to support the claim that ascending to the throne cured the king of all defects and that there could not be imperfection, negligence, folly, or laches in the king.[83] In eighteenth-century editions of Bacon's *Abridgement*, annotations emphasized the notion of perfection of the king associated with *the king can do no wrong* by pointing to Finch's work on the king partaking of God's excellencies and to the notion of perfection in Hale's work.[84] The editor of the fifth edition of Bacon's *Abridgement* of 1798, in a note to Bacon's discussion of the prerogative in the fourth volume, added a reference to Finch's treatise. In Finch's treatise, as the editor notes, the king's divine character was a dominant theme and the king's incapacity to do wrong was explained by the fact that the king partakes of God's 'excellencies'. In short,

[76] Blackstone (n 11) 238–39.

[77] William Blackstone, *Commentaries on the Laws of England*, vol 2 (facsimile of 1765–1769 1st edn, University of Chicago Press 1979) 253.

[78] On the—fatal—consequences of having separated the king's two bodies during the reign of Charles I, allowing Parliament to proceed without the king, see Greenberg (n 20) 217–22; Martin Loughlin, 'The State, the Crown and the Law' in Maurice Sunkin and Sebastian Payne (eds), *The Nature of the Crown: A Legal and Political Analysis* (OUP 1999) 33.

[79] Blackstone (n 11) 238.

[80] ibid 239.

[81] ibid.

[82] *Halsbury's Laws of England*, vol 29 (5th edn, LexisNexis 2014) [52]; see Chapter 2, section .2.2.2. See also *Trudel Thibault v R* (2012) QCCA 2212 [9], where the Lieutenant Governor of a province was prosecuted for fraud while in office and claimed—unsuccessfully—*the king can do no wrong* as an immunity.

[83] Wood (n 12) 19.

[84] Bacon (n 2) 486.

the editor to Bacon's *Abridgement* appears to have adopted Blackstone's emphasis on the notion of perfection of the king and consequently increased the importance of the notion of perfection of the king in Bacon's *Abridgement* by resorting to Finch's understanding—a Royalist—of *the king can do no wrong*. Chitty adopted Blackstone's treatment of the notion of perfection of the king in his influential work on the king's prerogatives.[85]

Anson also adopted Blackstone's notion of perfection of the king and wrote of the 'perfection of judgement of the king' which he identified as one of the sources of the king's prerogative and the basis for ministerial responsibility.[86]

That *the king can do no wrong* meant total immunity from suit because the king was ascribed the quality of perfection was also held in *In Re His Late Majesty George III* in 1822, where the court decided it did not have jurisdiction to hear the claim instituted by an alleged child of the Duke of Cumberland, brother of George III, to receive money which was allegedly to be given to her according to an unauthenticated will of George III. The court adopted in full Blackstone's definition of *the king can do no wrong*, his emphasis on the king being perfect and incapable of doing wrong and, like Blackstone, ascribed perfection to the king constitutionally but also in his personal capacity.[87] The court also emphasized the benevolence of the king:

> It would be to some degree presumptuous, and almost disrespectful, for the Court to express its full conviction of the impossibility of his Majesty, personally, entertaining the slightest disposition to exercise any such power of defeasance. The Sovereign can have no personal wish on this subject but that of doing justice.[88]

That the king is perfect was also surmised in *Feather*, where *the king can do no wrong* was said to apply also to personal wrongs of the king, 'if such a thing can be supposed to be possible'.[89]

The application of the notion of perfection also led Bacon and Blackstone to reinterpret the fiction that the king was deceived in his grant. The fiction that the king was deceived in his grant was used by Coke to annul the king's grant.[90] Coke's rationale for the annulment was grounded in the Bractonian understanding that the king was not entitled to do wrong and that the king's grant being wrongful, it

[85] Chitty (n 62) 5.

[86] Anson (n 5) 19–20. That the prerogatives of the king partake of his excellency also figures in the 1927 annotation of the editor of the English Reports on *R v Eaststaff* (1818) 171 ER 864, 870.

[87] *In Re His Late Majesty George III* (1822) 1 Add 255, 270, 273. The court's reasoning marks a departure from Tudor courts' nuanced interpretation of the king's two bodies so as not to undermine the Bractonian understanding of *the king can do no wrong*: see Chapter 2, section 2.2.3.

[88] ibid 273. The concept of a perfect, benevolent king also featured in *King v Layer* (1722) 8 Mod 82, 94, where the judge in passing his sentence on the accused for high treason encapsulated the notion that the king is perfect, benevolent, incapable of causing wrong to his subjects, and wishes only their good.

[89] *Feather v The Queen* (1865) 6 B&S 257, 295.

[90] See Chapter 3, section 2.1.1.2.

was void. In order to save the king's honour, Coke added to the application of the Bractonian *king can do no wrong* the fiction that the king was deceived and did not, in fact, want to do wrong.

To Bacon and Blackstone however, the fiction that the king was deceived in his grant was not grounded in the Bractonian understanding that the king was not entitled to do wrong. Rather, Bacon and Blackstone reinterpreted Coke's rule that the king was deceived in his grant when it was wrongful by grounding in the notion of perfection of the king the fiction that the king was deceived. *The king can do no wrong* was not understood by Bacon as the king is not entitled to do wrong. On the contrary, the fiction that the king was incapable of doing wrong was adopted: 'it cannot be presumed the king would do wrong to any person'.[91] The king being incapable of doing wrong, he was deceived in his grant and it ought to be annulled. The perfect, benevolent king was the focus of Bacon's reinterpretation of the rule of construction that the king's wrongful grant was void. Likewise, Blackstone's interpretation of the legal fiction that the king was deceived was that the law presumed, if there was a wrongful grant, that the king was deceived by false representations and would not impute a wrong to him.[92]

Bacon and Blackstone's legal fiction that the king was deceived was grounded in the notion of perfection of the king and his incapacity to do wrong and resulted in the impossibility of imputing a wrong to the king. It was the opposite of the Bractonian understanding, where a wrong was attributed to the king who was not entitled to do wrong and consequently came under an obligation to make reparations, albeit an obligation which was not enforceable in a court of law by ordinary action. It also differed from Coke's reasoning, which was that the king, because he was not entitled to do wrong, could not make a wrongful grant and that it had to be annulled on that basis. The Bacon-Blackstone legal fiction that the king was deceived amounted to a change in understanding.

From *the king can do no wrong* understood as the king not being entitled to do wrong as the cause of the invalidation of a wrongful grant with Coke, legal thinking with Bacon and Blackstone turned to the fiction that the king was perfect and that the wrongful grant must be annulled because he was deceived by his agents. The reason for the change in understanding is laid out by Blackstone: 'not to lessen him [the king] in the eyes of his subjects'.[93] But in this new paradigm of the king's perfection and of ill-intentioned counsellors laid down by Blackstone, the starting point was the fiction that the king was perfect. The fiction that the king was perfect and ill-advised was diametrically opposed to Bracton and Coke's premise that the king was not entitled to do wrong and that a wrong could be attributed to the king.

[91] Matthew Bacon, *A New Abridgment of the Law*, vol 4 (Henry Gwillim ed, 5th edn, Strahan 1798) 190–91.

[92] Blackstone (n 11) 239.

[93] ibid.

The premises were radically different. In the Bractonian, Coke's, and even Hale's mind, the king was not entitled to do wrong and it was that limitation imposed on the king that justified the annulment of the wrongful possession or grant. In contrast, with Blackstone, the king was perfect and was incapable of doing or thinking wrong, so a wrongful grant by the king could not possibly have been intended by him—'the law will not suppose the king to have meant either an unwise or an injurious action'[94]—and had to be annulled.

Chambers, in a course of lectures from 1767–1773, argued that the 'fiction of legal indefectibility' associated with *the king can do no wrong* was often true because the king was ill-advised by 'evil ministers'.[95] Chambers accepted the idea of a benevolent king whose purity of intention was never to be questioned and who was deceived by evil advisers. Hearn's thinking also showed elements of the concept of a perfect, benevolent king, offended by the wrong done by his servant.[96] To Hearn, a wrongful command was not the crown's and was only issued under the colour of royal authority. Therefore, the servant's act done pursuant to that wrongful command offended the king. Hearn's conception of *the king can do no wrong* implied that the perfect king was deceived by evil advisers and that wrongful commands, issued without respecting lawful requirements, were not his. Wrongful acts committed pursuant to wrongful commands offended the perfect, benevolent king in Hearn's thinking.

In short, despite the logical flaw caused by the notion of perfection of the king in conjunction with Hale's theory on the coercive, directive, and invalidating powers of the law, the notion of perfection of the king was given prominence in legal literature by Bacon and especially by Blackstone. They both added to the notion of perfection the concept of the king's incapacity to do wrong, which Blackstone clearly associated with *the king can do no wrong*.

There was an increase of the importance of the notion of perfection from the eighteenth century until the mid-nineteenth century. Various prominent legal authors of the nineteenth century—with the exception of Dicey—relied on the notion of perfection, either explicitly or implicitly by referring to the king's incapacity to do wrong. Blackstone's notion of perfection of the king grounding the king's incapacity to do wrong resulted in the courts and late nineteenth- and twentieth-century legal authors adopting the view that the king was incapable of doing wrong and that it was how *the king can do no wrong* was to be understood.[97] Although they said that little practical consequences flow from it, Keir and Lawson argued that

[94] ibid.

[95] Sir Robert Chambers, *A Course of Lectures on the English Law*, vol 1 (Thomas Curley ed, OUP 1987) 163.

[96] Hearn (n 9) 20–22.

[97] Walter Clode, *The Law and Practice of Petition of Right under the Petitions of Right Act, 1860* (Clowes 1887) 53; Bell (n 29) 19.

the notion of perfection still attaches to the crown.[98] It is said in *Halsbury's* that the notion of the king's absolute perfection still clothes the person of the monarch and that it is how *the king can do no wrong* should be understood. [99] The king is therefore still regarded in law as incapable of thinking or meaning to do an improper act, in large part as a result of Blackstone's influential *Commentaries*.[100]

3.3 Immunity from suit

The objective over the course of the latter part of the seventeenth century had been to protect the king—both personally and constitutionally—which motivated Hale's interpretation that the king is not subject to the coercive power of the law.[101] The objective of protecting the king, both personally and constitutionally, also frequently resurfaced in Blackstone's *Commentaries*.[102]

The issues left unaddressed following Hale's theory of the three powers of the law caused by his reliance on the notion of the king's perfection to justify the king's exemption from the coercive power of the law were exacerbated by Bacon and Blackstone's conception of the perfect king as incapable of doing wrong. The emphasis on the notion of the king's perfection led to the issue of determining who issued the wrongful command, if the perfect king was incapable of doing wrong. Moreover, the continued existence of the petition of right—which Hale admitted was available against the king—contradicted the proposition that Hale understood *the king can do no wrong* as the king's wrong is not his. The continued recognition of the petition of right as an available remedy also raised the issue of the extent of the king's exemption from the coercive power of the law.

Blackstone's attempt at providing a theoretical solution to the gap in the understanding of *the king can do no wrong* since the latter part of the seventeenth century was to rebrand—in a counterfactual and ahistorical manner[103]—the petition of

[98] David L Keir and FH Lawson, *Cases in Constitutional Law* (FH Lawson and DJ Bentley eds, 6th edn, Clarendon Press 1979) 95.

[99] *Halsbury's Laws of England* (n 82) [52].

[100] ibid. See also Tom Cornford, 'Legal Remedies against the Crown before and after M' in Maurice Sunkin and Sebastian Payne (eds), *The Nature of the Crown: A Legal and Political Analysis* (OUP 1999) 235; Rodney Brazier, 'Royal Incapacity and Constitutional Continuity: The Regent and Counsellors of State' (2005) 65 CLJ 352, 353; Joshua Getzler, 'Personality and Capacity: Lessons from Legal History' in Tim Bonyhady (ed), *Finn's Law: An Australian Justice* (The Federation Press 2016) 152, 170.

[101] See Chapter 3, section 3.3.3.

[102] Blackstone (n 11) 233–34, 236, 239, 240, 255.

[103] Ludwik Ehrlich, 'Proceedings against the Crown (1216–1377)' in Paul Vinogradoff (ed), *Oxford Studies in Social and Legal History*, vol 6 (Clarendon Press 1921) 187; WS Holdsworth, 'The History of Remedies against the Crown I' (1922) 38 LQR 141, 147–49; Edwin Borchard, 'Governmental Responsibility in Tort, VI' (1926) 36 YLJ 1, 25, 27–28; Ludwik Ehrlich, 'Petitions of Right' (1929) 45 LQR 60, 69; David E Engdahl, 'Immunity and Accountability for Positive Governmental Wrongs' (1972) 44 U Colo L Rev 1, 5.

right as a petition of grace.[104] The petition of right could not logically be available in Blackstone's interpretation of *the king can do no wrong*, because the king was perfect and incapable of thinking or doing wrong. The emphasis on the king's incapacity to do wrong—because he was sublime and therefore perfect—led the petition of right to be considered as a remedy as of grace and no longer as of right. Even Clode, in his late nineteenth-century influential treatise on the petition of right,[105] was said to have been erroneously influenced by Blackstone's claim that the petition of right was a remedy as of grace.[106] The king being perfect was incapable of doing wrong. If a wrong was committed, it was to be attributed to the king's minister or servant. When the king's agent could not remedy the wrong that had been done, the king 'graciously' accepted petitions of right to be submitted to him.[107] The petition of right was rebranded as a remedy as of grace, out of the magnanimity of a perfect king who was incapable of doing wrong.

However, the traditional view that the petition of right was 'to all essential purposes a right',[108] 'akin to a writ',[109] and 'is in the nature of an action against the king, or of a writ of right for the party'[110] because the king could not refuse to give justice was made clear by other authors, who also kept its qualification as a common law remedy.[111] The court in *Feather* also made the distinction between a petition of right and a petition as of grace.[112] The king had to let the petition of right proceed as of right.[113] Moreover, after the theoretical revival of the petition of right and the possibility to sue to the king for his wrongful act in *Bankers' Case* at the turn of the seventeenth century,[114] the proposition that the petition of right was to be conceived of as a remedy as of grace was also disproved by cases which allowed the petition of right in contract. The issue of the availability of the petition of right

[104] Blackstone (n 11) 236.

[105] Clode (n 97) 16–17.

[106] Ehrlich, 'Petitions of Right' (n 103) 69. Clode's recounting of the evolution of the petition of right was in fact more nuanced, but the emphasis he put on the lack of an ordinary action against the king as justification for negating the existence of a right was certainly Blackstonian: Clode (n 97) 24.

[107] Jeffrey Goldsworthy, *The Sovereignty of Parliament: History and Philosophy* (first published 1999, OUP 2004) 82. Goldsworthy explains that the king remained bound by his judges' decision on the merit of the petition because of his oath to do justice.

[108] Allen (n 9) 94.

[109] Richard Wooddeson, *Lectures on the Law of England*, vol 1 (2nd edn, Richards and Co 1834) 55.

[110] James Manning, *The Practice of the Court of Exchequer* (2nd edn, Printed by A Strahan 1827) 84.

[111] Chitty (n 62) 340, 345; WS Holdsworth, *A History of English Law*, vol 9 (1st edn, Methuen 1926) 15–16; Ehrlich, 'Petitions of Right' (n 103) 69. Clode also explained that depending on the matter raised by the suppliant in the petition, after investigation by a commission, it was sent either to the Exchequer, the ordinary tribunals, the local courts, the justice of the forest, or even to specially created tribunals: Clode (n 97) 9, 18.

[112] *Feather* (n 89) 295.

[113] *Thomas v The Queen* (1874–75) Law Rep 10 QB 31, 35–36 where Coke was cited to support the proposition (2 Co Inst 269). See also *Ryves v Duke of Wellington* (1846) 9 Beav 579, 601 (Lord Langdale); *Dyson v Attorney General* [1911] 1 KB 410, 422 (Lord Farwell). Anson also cites to *In Re Nathan* (1884) 12 QBD 479 for the proposition: William Reynell Anson, *The Law and Custom of the Constitution*, vol 2 part 2 (A Berriedale Keith ed, 4th edn, Clarendon Press 1935) 334.

[114] *Bankers' Case* (1696, 1698, 1701) 14 St Tr 1, 105.

in contract, raised in *Macbeth v Haldimand*, was resolved in *Thomas v The Queen*, where the petition of right was found to be available for damages in breach of contract.[115] Having to proceed by petition of right instead of an ordinary action was said to be a 'mere matter of judicial machinery' and 'the petition presupposes a "right" in the subject, which, according to English procedure, falls to be vindicated in that way'.[116]

It will be shown that Blackstone's solution—to consider the petition of right to be merely as of grace—was not adopted by the courts. Another approach was devised, however, that of developing further the concept of the king's incapacity to do wrong. Not only was the perfect king incapable of doing wrong, but the law was further said to presume that no wrong can be imputed to the king.

The courts also narrowly defined what 'wrong' gave rise to a petition of right and excluded torts from that category. The distinction made by the court in *Thomas* between claims in contract and in tort—relying on that point on the trilogy of *Viscount Canterbury*, *Tobin*, and *Feather*[117]—to justify allowing the petition of right for the former but not the latter is not convincing.[118] It is not clear why a 'wrong' for which the petition of right lay should have been translated into 'tort'. A breach of contract was as much a legal wrong as any tort[119] and torts against property could be the subject of the petition of right. It was as 'indecent' and as inconsistent with the notion of the king's perfection to admit of the king's contractual breach as it was of his commission of a tort.[120] It was not clear, therefore, why pure torts could not also be included.[121] In *Monckton v Attorney General*, a broader conception of the scope of the petition of right was adopted: it was said to extend to injuries arising from the acts of the crown.[122] Under that understanding, there was no limitation so as to exclude torts.[123]

[115] *Macbeth v Haldimand* (1786) 1 TR 172; *Thomas v The Queen* (n 113) 35–36. See also *Windsor and Annapolis Railway Co v The Queen* (1886) 11 App Cas 607 (PC), 613–14.

[116] *Macgregor v Lord Advocate* 1921 SC 847, 848 (Lord Anderson).

[117] *Viscount Canterbury v Attorney General* (1843) 1 Ph 306; *Tobin v The Queen* (1864) 16 CB NS 310; *Feather* (n 89).

[118] *Thomas* (n 113). For similar criticism on the issue of the discrepancy of crown liability in contract and in tort, see Janet McLean, 'Personality and Public Law Doctrine' (1999) 49 UTLJ 123, 144: 'If the crown has sufficient legal personality to enter a lease, why can't it commit a tort?'.

[119] William Wade, Christopher Forsyth, and Julian Ghosh, *Administrative Law* (12th edn, OUP 2022) 654.

[120] Robert Dorsey Watkins, *The State as a Party Litigant* (Johns Hopkins Press 1927) 29–30.

[121] Borchard (n 103) 36; Paul Craig, *Administrative Law* (9th edn, Sweet & Maxwell 2021) 907.

[122] (1850) 2 Mac&G 402, 412 (Lord Cottenham). The claim of the petitioner was ultimately rejected on a procedural basis. See also *Baron de Bode's Case* (1845) 8 QB 208, 273–74 where the petition of right was found to lay for wrongs in respect of money.

[123] See Chapter 6, section 4: in colonial Australia, particularly in New South Wales, legislation was passed to give the petition of right statutory footing; the scope of the colonial statute was extended to actions resounding in tort by the Privy Council in *Farnell v Bowman* [1887] 12 AC 643. In Canada, the petition of right was available in contract and its scope was eventually extended to include certain actions grounded in tort for damages caused by the undertaking of public works under the Canadian Petition of Right Act 1876, 39 Vict c 27 (SC 1876).

The petition of right in the nineteenth century was said to lie only for contractual claims. This narrowing down of the availability of the petition of right was effectuated by relying on *the king can do no wrong* and further developing the notion of the perfect king incapable of doing wrong.

It was also the courts of the latter part of the nineteenth century which developed the formal notion of 'crown', moving from *the king can do no wrong* to *the crown can do no wrong*. In contrast, Dicey did not rely on the notion of perfection. As will be demonstrated, his approach to *the king can do no wrong* nevertheless marked continuity with the courts' approach to the formal notion of the crown.

The first focus of this section of the chapter is the courts' approach to *the king can do no wrong*, which was developed in cases on the petition of right and the notion of the crown. The notion of the crown itself was also important to Dicey's interpretation of *the king can do no wrong* and is the second focus of this section. The third focus of this section is Dicey's interpretation of *the king can do no wrong* itself.

3.3.1 Nineteenth-century cases on the petition of right

The revival of the petition of right in the nineteenth century, especially with *Viscount Canterbury*, *Tobin*, and *Feather*,[124] occurred at a time when the notion of the king's perfection and his consequent incapacity to commit a wrong were dominating legal thinking on *the king can do no wrong*. While Blackstone's interpretation of the concept was partly based on the Bractonian and Hale's understanding, such that the king was said to be under the law and not entitled to do wrong, it will be shown that the courts used the other elements of Blackstone's interpretation of *the king can do no wrong*—the notion of perfection of the king, the notion of his incapacity to do wrong, and Blackstone's argument that if there is no remedy there is no wrong.

In *Viscount Canterbury*, the servants of the Commissioners of Woods and Forests burned the tallies of the Royal Exchequer in the stoves of the House of Lords but the stoves overheated and fire spread to the palace of Westminster, including the house of the Speaker of the House of Commons, who petitioned the king for the damage the fire caused to his belongings. Lord Lyndhurst found that no negligence or misconduct can be imputed to the king and that 'if they occur in fact, the law affords no remedy',[125] a proposition similar to Blackstone's that there is no wrong if there is no remedy. But *Viscount Canterbury* went further than Blackstone had gone. Blackstone had said—as had Hale—that the petition of right was available against the king.[126] In contrast, Lord Lyndhurst stated that 'It is admitted that, for the personal negligence of the Sovereign, neither this [the petition of right] nor any other proceedings can be maintained'.[127] The king's personal wrong as an

[124] *Viscount Canterbury* (n 117); *Tobin* (n 117); *Feather* (n 89).
[125] *Viscount Canterbury* (n 117) 321.
[126] Blackstone (n 11) 235; Blackstone (n 18) 254–55.
[127] *Viscount Canterbury* (n 117) 321.

employer in choosing his employees or misdirecting them could not be imputed to the king.[128] That the king 'cannot be required to answer for his own personal acts',[129] including via the petition of right, is a step further than Blackstone's interpretation of *the king can do no wrong*. Yet it does not appear that Lord Lyndhurst referred to the notion of perfection of the king which grounded the king's incapacity to do wrong, for he admitted that if the king's wrongs were to occur, there would be no remedy. With *Viscount Canterbury*, the king was in fact capable of doing wrong, but that wrong could not be imputed to the king and there was no remedy against him—not even the petition of right.

The understanding of *the king can do no wrong* in *Tobin* is different from Lord Lyndhurst's in *Viscount Canterbury*. Mr Tobin, survived by his son, the petitioner, was the owner of a ship that was confiscated by a Captain Douglas who was commanding Her Majesty's vessel in the performance of his duties in eradicating the slave trade pursuant to various acts of Parliament. The ship was destroyed on the ground that it was involved in the slave trade, an allegation which proved to be unfounded. Erle CJ denied the petition, reasoning that Captain Douglas was not acting on a command from Her Majesty, but was performing his duty imposed by Parliament; that even if he were an agent employed by the queen to seize vessels engaged in the slave trade, he was not acting within the scope of his authority in seizing a ship which was not in fact engaged in the slave trade and therefore his principal, Her Majesty, could not be held liable; and that a petition of right could not be maintained to recover unliquidated damages for a trespass.[130]

Erle CJ then relied on *the king can do no wrong* to support his conclusion and cited Coke, Hale, and Blackstone but without noticing that they had different understandings of the concept. Not only did Erle CJ fail to notice the distinctions between the various authors' understanding, he opined to the contrary that '[t]his maxim has been constantly recognized'.[131] Erle CJ appears to have understood *the king can do no wrong* both as the king was not entitled to do wrong,[132] and as the king's immunity from suit. That Erle CJ associated *the king can do no wrong* with immunity from suit in *Tobin* is supported by his statement that the concept 'is true in the sense that he is not liable to be sued civilly or criminally for a supposed wrong'.[133] But Erle CJ in *Tobin* also appeared to have understood that the king was not entitled to do wrong: 'if the command is unlawful, it is in law no command'.[134] The Bractonian understanding that could still be found in Blackstone's work was still present in Erle CJ's speech in *Tobin*.

128 ibid.
129 ibid.
130 *Tobin* (n 117) 347–53.
131 ibid 355.
132 Watkins (n 120) 40.
133 *Tobin* (n 117) 353–54.
134 ibid 354.

In defining *the king can do no wrong* in *Tobin*, Erle CJ relied on a Haleian interpretation and made clearer the distinction between the king's personal wrongs and those committed by his commands. As for the acts done by the king personally, 'the law presumes [they] will not be wrong', wrote Erle CJ. For the king's wrongs done personally, Erle CJ appears to have relied on Hale's interpretation of *the king can do no wrong* laid out in *Pleas of the Crown*, where Hale wrote that 'it is regularly true, that the law presumes, the king will do no wrong, neither indeed can do any wrong'.[135] As for the acts done by command of the king, Erle CJ wrote: 'that which the sovereign does by command to his servants, cannot be a wrong in the sovereign, because, if the command is unlawful, it is in law no command, and the servant is responsible for the unlawful act, the same as if there had been no command'.[136]

Erle CJ adopted Hale's theory of the invalidating power of the law in relation to the unlawful acts done by command of the king. Hale's interpretation of *the king can do no wrong* that the king's unlawful command did not constitute a valid defence for the king's servant, which was adopted in *Tobin*, had also been adopted in many other cases, including Mansfield's speech in *Leach*.[137] Clode, writing in 1887, appears to have adopted Erle CJ's interpretation of *the king can do no wrong*—based on Hale's—as applied not only to the king's personal acts, but also to those which were done by his servant by his command.[138] There were still, therefore, Bractonian and Haleain elements in legal thinking on *the king can do no wrong* in the eighteenth and nineteenth centuries. Moreover, that the wrongful command was annulled if it was unlawful in Erle CJ's speech pointed to the king being capable of issuing the wrongful command to begin with. As had Hale, Erle CJ opined that the servant was to be sued for the wrongful act. However, it appears that Erle CJ further reinterpreted *the king can do no wrong* and relied on an interpretation of Hale's statement in relation to *the king can do no wrong* in *Prerogatives of the King* that the wrongful act 'for if it be wrong and contrary to the law, it is not the act of the king'.[139] Erle CJ in *Tobin* interpreted Hale's concept of the invalidating power of the law as having two effects: first, annulling the unlawful command of the king so that it could not be relied upon as a defence by the king's servants and, second, making the unlawful command cease to be the king's. To Erle CJ in *Tobin*, the wrong was not to be conceived of as the king's because the king's unlawful command was invalid. In other words, in Erle CJ's thinking, as the king was not entitled to do wrong, his wrongful acts and orders are consequently invalid and therefore there was no wrong in the king.

[135] Hale (n 25) 43.
[136] *Tobin* (n 117) 353–54.
[137] ibid; *Money v Leach* (1765) 3 Burr 1742; see also *Wilkes v Wood* (1769) 19 St Tr 1406; *Mostyn v Fabrigas* (1774) 1 Cowp 161; *Glynn v Houston* (1841) 2 Man&G 337; *Cobbett v Grey* [1849] 4 Ex 729.
[138] Clode (n 97) 53.
[139] Hale, *Prerogatives* (n 71) 15.

In adopting an interpretation of Hale's statement on *the king can do no wrong* found in *Prerogatives of the Crown* as a fiction that the king's wrong was not a wrong in the king, Erle CJ also adopted its flaws. The interpretation of Hale's statement in *Prerogatives* as a fiction that the king's wrong was not the king's implied that the invalidating power of the law had two effects—invalidating the command and fictitiously making the king's wrong not the king's. However, to adopt the view that the invalidating power of the law had two effects did not comprehensively address the issue of the directive force of the law. Following Hale's thinking, the king was subject to the directive force of the law, which made the king's command unlawful to begin with. But in *Tobin*, the directive power of the law which rendered the command unlawful was undermined by the implication that the invalidating power of the law had two effects—invalidating the command and negating that it was the king's. The invalidating power of the law not only rendered the unlawful command invalid, it also negated that it was a wrong to be imputed to the king. Yet the command had first to be unlawful according to the directive power of the law to then be invalidated by the invalidating power of the law. The reasoning in *Tobin* shows the flaws associated with adopting the view that Hale's passage in relation to *the king can do no wrong* in *Prerogatives* was meant to convey the fiction that the king's wrong was not his. Ascribing to the invalidating power of the law the effect not only of invalidating the wrongful command, but also of making the king's wrongful command cease to be the command of the king created a logical problem. The issue became that of the wrongful command having to originate from somewhere. The wrongful command must initially be issued to then be declared unlawful by the directive power of the law. Once unlawful, it could then be invalidated by the invalidating power of the law. But the unlawful command could not be declared unlawful or invalidated if it was not issued to begin with as Erle CJ's approach implied.

Although Cockburn CJ in *Feather* also drew a distinction between the king's personal acts and the acts committed by the king's commands,[140] he offered a different approach to Erle CJ's in *Tobin* in relation to Hale's *the king can do no wrong*. Feather was the inventor of a process to build ships and received a patent for it from the crown. The crown subsequently used Feather's process, in breach of his patent. The issue arose as to whether the patent's exclusion applied to the crown and whether a petition of right laid in this case against the crown for the infringement of Feather's patent rights. Cockburn CJ found that, in the absence of express words, the crown was not contemplated by the patent's exclusion.[141] In *obiter*, he added that the only remedy available to the patentee was by way of ordinary action against the individual officers who used his invention, relying on *the king can do no wrong* to justify his conclusion.[142]

140 *Feather* (n 89) 295.
141 ibid 283–86.
142 ibid 293–97.

Instead of distinguishing between the king's personal wrongs and those committed pursuant to his unlawful commands, Cockburn CJ argued logically that if the king could not do wrong, he could not authorize wrong either.[143] To Cockburn CJ, Hale's statement that the law presumed that the king would do no wrong or could do no wrong—also adopted by Blackstone[144]—or that a wrongful act was not an act of the king must apply to his personal acts as well as to his commands. As Cockburn CJ reasoned, neither the king's acts nor his commands could be wrongs in the eyes of the law.[145] Cockburn CJ also reversed Blackstone's interpretation of *the king can do no wrong* and argued that there can be no remedy if there is no wrong in the eyes of the law. The result of Cockburn CJ's interpretation of *the king can do no wrong* in *Feather* was a fiction that no wrong existed insofar as the king was concerned. Yet the fiction adopted by Cockburn CJ was imperfect. Cockburn CJ himself lifted the veil by adding that 'the authority of the Crown would afford no defence' for the crown servant who executed the wrongful command.[146] The authority of the king not being a sufficient defence implied that the wrongful command did originate with the king to begin with.

Recall that Blackstone admitted that the petition of right was available to sue to the king. To be consistent with his interpretation of *the king can do no wrong* as a perfect king incapable of doing wrong, Blackstone argued that the petition of right was a petition as of grace. The court did not follow suit in *Feather* and, given the statutory footing given to the petition of right by Parliament in the Petitions of Right Act 1860, posited instead that the petition of right was not a petition of grace.[147] The court could also have chosen to go further than Blackstone in the application of the notion of perfection of the king and the fiction flowing from it that he was incapable of doing wrong. Cockburn CJ could simply have said that there could not be a petition of right against the king because the king was incapable of doing wrong. But instead, to Cockburn CJ, the wrongful command ceased to exist insofar as the king was concerned but continued to exist and fell on the servant's head for having executed it.[148]

As Erle CJ before him, Cockburn CJ's interpretation of *the king can do no wrong* was not devoid of Bractonian, Coke's, and Hale's—and even Blackstone's—understandings of *the king can do no wrong* as the king was not entitled to do wrong. The king in Hale's interpretation was capable of doing a wrong but he was subject to the directive force of the law, which rendered his act or command wrongful because contrary to law. Being wrongful, the king's command was rendered void by the invalidating force of the law—as was the case in Cockburn CJ's interpretations.

143 ibid 295.
144 Blackstone (n 23) 32–33.
145 *Feather* (n 89) 295–96.
146 ibid 296.
147 ibid 295; Petitions of Right Act 1860, 23 & 24 Vict c 34.
148 *Feather* (n 89) 295–96.

However, Cockburn CJ's reasons in *Feather*—as Erle CJ's reasons in *Tobin*—created the 'conundrum' of the crown ordering wrongful acts which are not wrongful insofar as the crown is concerned—a 'special kind of damnum sine injuria'.[149] The issue of whence the command came was obscured as a result of the courts in *Tobin* and *Feather* elaborating the fiction that there is no wrong in the king.

In short, the reasons in *Tobin* and *Feather* can be seen as based on the passage in Hale's *Prerogatives* that a wrongful command of the king rendered void by the invalidating force of the law is not the act of the king but of the minister or instrument that put it into execution.[150] That passage was relied on in *Tobin*.[151] That passage in Hale's *Prerogatives*, which, as was argued in Chapter 3, should be read as a restatement of the Bractonian understanding of *the king can do no wrong*,[152] was reinterpreted in *Tobin* and *Feather*. To Erle CJ, a wrong cannot be the king's—'That which the sovereign does personally, the law presumes will not be wrong; that which the sovereign does by command to his servants cannot be a wrong in the sovereign.'[153] To Cockburn CJ, 'As in the eye of the law no such wrong can be done, so, in law, no right to redress can arise.'[154] To the court in *Tobin* and *Feather*, the king was not entitled to do wrong or to authorize a wrong, therefore there was no wrong in the king—even if a wrong was committed by the king or commanded by him. Following *Tobin* and *Feather*, because the king was not entitled to do wrong, when a wrong was committed it disappeared insofar as the king was concerned.

The courts in *Viscount Canterbury*, but more importantly in *Tobin* and *Feather*—based on their adoption of a fiction that no royal wrong exists in the eyes of the law because the king was not entitled to do wrong—concluded that the petition of right could not lie against the king. In adopting the fiction that the king's wrongs are not wrongs in the king, however, nineteenth-century courts undermined the cohesiveness of Hale's theory on law's three powers (directive, invalidating, and coercive). The application of the directive power of the law to the king—which rendered the king's unlawful command invalid—was undermined. The result was an understanding of *the king can do no wrong* which was both in line and divorced from its historical evolution in legal thinking and its Bractonian and Haleian understanding. The king was still not entitled to do wrong, but his wrongful acts and commands were fictitiously no longer the king's in the eyes of the law. The fiction elaborated in *Tobin* and *Feather* that the king's wrong is not a wrong in the king left unresolved the issue of from whence did wrongful commands originate and obscured the issue of the king's capacity to do wrong.

149 Getzler (n 100) 172.
150 Hale, *Prerogatives* (n 71) 15.
151 *Tobin* (n 117) 353–54.
152 See Chapter 3, section 3.3.4.
153 *Tobin* (n 117) 354.
154 *Feather* (n 89) 296.

3.3.2 Nineteenth-century cases on the formal notion of the crown

The crown went from being perceived as the person of the king in the first half of the nineteenth century to change progressively to an abstract notion in the later part of the nineteenth century. The 'crown' was a formal concept developed by the courts to distinguish between public bodies which benefitted from various immunities and those which did not. 'By the crown was meant all departments of the Central Government.'[155]

3.3.2.1 From the king personally to the crown as central government

In *Viscount Canterbury*, the crown was still perceived to be Queen Victoria herself, and the palace of Westminster where the damage had occurred as a result of the negligence of the servants of the Commissioners of Woods, Forests and Buildings was still associated with the monarch personally.[156] Lord Lyndhurst opined in that case that there could not be a remedy for the 'personal negligence of the Sovereign' and that the 'Crown cannot be guilty of negligence or personal misconduct', a demonstration that the king personally was still referred to as the crown.[157] In *Baron de Bode's Case*, the suppliant's petition of right was similarly rejected because Queen Victoria did not personally benefit from the money taken.[158] One of the reasons why the petition of right failed in *Tobin* was that the queen personally had not issued commands to the crown servant in *Tobin*.[159] The monarch personally was still a person to be deferred to and powers were not granted to the sovereign for fear that the grant would be taken literally and that it would have been undignified for the courts to discuss the queen's duties.[160]

Until the middle of the nineteenth century, the civil service structure was still essentially personalized—there were few public officials and civil servants and their relationship with individuals was close.[161] It was not a bureaucratic state apparatus—central government counted only approximately 21,000 civil servants[162]—but one relying on commissioners and local officials.[163] The civil service was constituted by officeholders who were liable for their own wrong or

[155] ECS Wade, 'Liability in Tort of the Central Government of the United Kingdom Governmental' (1954) 29 NYUL Rev 1416, 1416.

[156] Stuart Anderson, 'Public Law' in WR Cornish and others (eds), *The Oxford History of the Laws of England*, vol XI (OUP 2010) 370; McLean (n 4) 138–39.

[157] *Viscount Canterbury* (n 117) 321, 325

[158] *Baron de Bode's Case* (n 122) 284–85 (Lord Denman CJ). The case was rejected by the barons of the Exchequer Chamber on the ground that Parliament had, by statute, granted discretion to the Treasury in dealing with the funds: *Baron de Bode v The Queen* (1848) 13 QB 364, 381ff. See Michael Lobban, 'The Commissioners for Claims on France and the Case of the Baron de Bode, 1815–1861' in Mark Godfrey (ed), *Law and Authority in British Legal History, 1200–1900* (CUP 2016) 238–44.

[159] *Tobin* (n 117) 348, 352.

[160] Anderson (n 156) 345.

[161] Selway (n 70) 189, 211.

[162] David Roberts, *Victorian Origins of the British Welfare State* (Yale UP 1960) 14; Craig (n 121) 55.

[163] Paul Craig, *UK, EU and Global Administrative Law: Foundations and Challenges* (CUP 2015) 65–95.

negligence in discharging their duties and criminally liable for maladministration.[164] They were not vicariously liable for the torts of crown servants.[165] It has been shown that in England in the nineteenth century, governmental institutions were a patchwork of public bodies and agencies created by the prerogative, by order in council, or were mere agglomerations of crown servants, only some of whom had corporate status or statutory provisions providing that they could sue or be sued.[166] From 1830 to 1850, the functions of central government expanded and regulatory reforms were accomplished.[167] In the 1860s and afterwards, agencies, with the centralization of powers, became controlled by ministries and not by Parliament.[168] From a few, proprietary-based offices bought and held personally by officials, the governmental apparatus changed from the middle of the nineteenth century to a bureaucratic—although highly aristocratic[169]—civil service.[170]

From the courts' normative reasons to confer immunities to public bodies in the first part of the nineteenth century, such as their public purpose and benefit to the public—a 'public purpose immunity'—courts conferred immunities only to the 'crown' in the latter part of the nineteenth century.[171] Crown immunity has been said to have become 'a hollow formalistic concept' applied without reference to principle and restricted to the crown by reference to *the king can do no wrong* 'understood in a formalistic sense that did not do any normative work'.[172] McLean and Anderson call 'formalistic' the courts' approach to crown liability in that period because it was a binary approach to define the crown as central government departments which would benefit from immunities and non-crown entities who would not.[173] The crown benefitted from immunities because of the 'dogma that the Crown could do no wrong'.[174]

While the effect of the courts' formalistic approach was indeed binary—a public body could benefit from the immunities or it could not[175]—two criteria were

[164] Selway (n 70) 195–205; McLean (n 4) 26–28.

[165] *Lane v Cotton* (1701) 1 LD Raym 646 (91 ER 1332) (KB); *Whitfield v Lord Le Despencer* (1778) 2 Cowp 754 (Lord Mansfield); *Bainbridge v Post-Master General* [1906] 1 KB 178; McLean (n 4) 25. Note, however, that in *Lane v Cotton*, Holt CJ would have allowed the plaintiff to sue, based on medieval precedents, an illustration of how Bractonian understandings were still relevant to legal thinking; see also Louis L Jaffe, 'Suits Against Governments and Officers: Sovereign Immunity' (1963) 77 Harv L Rev 1, 13–14.

[166] George Stuart Robertson, *The Law and Practice of Civil Proceedings by and against the Crown and Departments of Government* (Stevens 1908) 21–108; Anderson (n 156) 342–66.

[167] Craig (n 121) 56–57. See also Roberts (n 162); Derek Fraser, *The Evolution of the British Welfare State: A History of Social Policy since the Industrial Revolution* (4th edn, Palgrave Macmillan 2009).

[168] Anderson (n 156) 360.

[169] McLean (n 4) 140.

[170] Paul D Finn, *Law and Government in Colonial Australia* (OUP 1987) 8–33; Selway (n 70) 208–15; McLean (n 4) 21–36.

[171] JAG Griffith, 'Public Corporations as Crown Servants' (1952) 9 UTLJ 169, 178; Anderson (n 156) 366–84; McLean (n 4) 141–42, 159.

[172] McLean (n 4) 142.

[173] ibid 141–42, 152, 216; Anderson (n 156) 374, 376.

[174] Anderson (n 156) 376.

[175] A public body could not be 'private' for certain functions and the 'crown' for others: *Gilbert v Corporation of Trinity House* (1886) 17 QBD 795, 803 (Wills J).

developed to determine if a given public body was part of the crown: the public or governmental purpose of the public body and its historical association with the king. Three different categories of public entities having a public purpose were developed in the *Mersey Docks* cases: those bodies part of central government; bodies which fall within the province of 'government' and are in *consimili casu* with servants of the crown; and remaining public bodies having public purposes (among which local bodies).[176] Only the public bodies falling within the first category and participating in the royal authority were crown servants and were therefore the 'crown' for the purposes of benefitting from its immunities, including immunity from suit.[177] Lord Cranworth described the process as the 'extension of the shield of the Crown to what might more fitly be described as the public government of the country'.[178] As Moore observed, English lawyers at the beginning of the twentieth century were 'still engaged in the task of fitting to the State and the Government the prerogatives and immunities of the monarch, and of reaching the State through the person of the King', and the formal distinction between the crown and non-crown public bodies following *Mersey Docks* led to defining the crown as 'either "the State" or an organ of the government'.[179] With the development of an organized governmental bureaucracy, the 'crown' understood as central government became a repository for immunities in the second half of the century, in contrast with non-crown public bodies and local bodies, because, it has been argued, of the 'dogma' that *the crown can do no wrong*.[180]

Anson's explanation of the law of crown liability following the *Feather* case is evidence of the confusion between the king and government departments, and the ensuing uncertainty as to their respective liability:

> And there are injuries for which the subject can obtain no redress from the Crown, or, what is the same thing, from a department of government, because a master is only liable for the acts of his servants on the principle that their wrongdoing is his

[176] *Mersey Docks Trustees v Cameron* (1864) 11 HLC 443 (on the issue of the applicability to the trustees of the rates payable under the statutes providing for relief of the poor); *Mersey Docks Trustees v Gibbs* (1866) 1 LR 93 (HL) (on the issue of damages caused to Gibbs's ship because of the trustees' negligence in maintaining the docks under their statutory powers): Griffith (n 171) 172.

[177] *Gilbert v Corporation of Trinity House* (n 175) 801 (Day J). Griffith and Moore argued that the two criteria were outdated and that the concept of 'governmental purpose' did not provide significant guidance. They advocated the criterion of 'control' by the crown over the public body: Griffith (n 171) 185–87; Harrison Moore, 'Liability for Acts of Public Servants' (1907) 23 LQR 12, 20. See also, in Australia: Geoffrey Sawer, 'Shield of the Crown Revisited' (1958) 1 Melb ULR 137; and in Canada: Robert Flannigan, 'Crown Agent Status' (1988) 67 Can Bar Rev 229.

[178] *Mersey Docks Trustees v Cameron* (n 176) 508.

[179] Moore (n 177) 13–14, 18.

[180] Wade (n 155) 1416; Anderson (n 156) 374–76; McLean (n 4) 8, 36, 50. See *Graham v Public Work Commissioners* [1901] 2 KB 781, 789–90, where Philimore J, said that 'The Crown cannot be sued' by ordinary action, including in contract, but ultimately opined that the Commissioners were liable to be sued in contract because they were incorporated for the purpose of conducting business engagements and to sue and be sued speedily, like ordinary parties.

> wrongdoing; so if the master 'can do no wrong', he cannot be made liable for the wrongful acts of the persons in his employment.[181]

Anson, writing at the end of the nineteenth and in the early twentieth centuries, adopted the court's fiction in *Feather* that there can be no wrong resting with the king in law, and therefore the wrongs of others cannot be attributed to him. But Anson also conceived of government departments as the crown—and therefore as masters of the crown servants—because of the ambiguous use of the word crown, which referred to both king and government departments. Government departments, in effect, became the king and their liability for a wrong was consequently denied.

3.3.2.2 Critical assessment

That the courts' thinking in relation to the notion of the crown was formalistic and not fully developed transpires from the nineteenth-century trilogy of cases on the petition of right. The crown was to be understood as the king personally in *Viscount Canterbury* and *Tobin*.[182] The crown was also clearly said to be a corporation sole of perpetual continuance in the 1861 case of *Attorney General v Köhler*.[183] But the 'crown', in the context of using a patent, was in *Feather*—and *Dixon v London Small Arms Co*[184]—to be understood as the whole central government, a corporation aggregate to which the patent did not apply.[185] As a result, departments and civil servants could use Feather's patented invention 'in the public service'.[186] Cockburn CJ equated 'crown' and 'department of government'. Cockburn CJ again adopted the notion of the crown as a corporation aggregate in *R v Lords Commissioners of the Treasury*, where he opined in relation to mandamus that: 'Over the Sovereign we can have no power. In like manner where the parties are acting as servants of the Crown, and are amenable to the Crown, whose servants they are, they are not amenable to us in the exercise of our prerogative jurisdiction.'[187] As Williams noted, the crown meant not only the king but also the administrative officers in Cockburn CJ's dictum.[188] But the crown was again conceived of as a corporation

[181] Anson (n 5) 20. See also Anson, 3rd edn (n 27) 5. Anson's original explanation was the same, albeit phrased slightly differently: William Reynell Anson, *The Law and Custom of the Constitution* vol 2 (1st edn, Clarendon Press 1892) 4–5.

[182] *Viscount Canterbury* (n 117); *Tobin* (n 117).

[183] *Attorney General v Köhler* (1861) 9 HLC 654, 671 (Lord Cranworth). See also *Re Mason* [1928] Ch 385, 401–03 (Romer J).

[184] *Feather* (n 89); *Dixon v London Small Arms Co* [1876] 1 AC 632.

[185] Selway (n 70) 217–18. See *Kirk v The Queen* (1872) LR 14 Eq 558 a petition of right in Chancery where the Solicitor General spoke of the Queen personally (567–68) while Vice Chancellor Wickens used the term crown to refer to the government department (571).

[186] *Feather* (n 89) 297.

[187] *R v Lords Commissioners of the Treasury* (1872) LR 7 QB 387, 394.

[188] Williams (n 65) 149.

sole when the court addressed the issue of its liability in tort, as was the case in *Feather*. Only the crown servants individually were to be sued.

Evidence of the nineteenth-century courts' inconsistent approach to the concept of the crown is also manifest in the contradiction between the status of the crown as a corporation sole in the realm of tort liability and its status as a corporation aggregate in connection with the application of statutes. The crown was a corporation sole in the context of the master–servant relationship with civil servants—the 'crown' as the master of civil servants was the king only. Public officials and government departments were not the masters of the civil servants; they were fellow crown servants.[189] The fact that central government departments were not the masters of crown servants was one of the reasons why government departments were not vicariously liable for the wrongs of crown servants.

In contrast, the notion of the crown in relation to the application of statutes was broader and encompassed the central government.[190] The 'crown' and 'its servants and agents' could claim the crown's immunity from the application of a statute and a minister, 'as agent of the Crown, cannot be bound by a statute that does not bind the Crown'.[191] The justification given for treating the crown as a corporation aggregate in the context of application of statutes was that for the exemption to be effective, it had to extend to officers and servants of the crown.[192] The crown understood as government departments—the crown's officers, servants, and agents including the ministries—could claim not to be subject to statutes.

In short, the crown since the nineteenth century and early twentieth century has been understood as a corporation aggregate when determining if a statute binds the 'crown' or not. Yet the crown reverted to the king only—a corporation sole—in the context of liability for the wrongs of crown servants. As a result, only the crown servant individually could be sued. The same individual crown servant who could claim that a statute did not bind her in accomplishing her duties because she was part of the crown conceived of as a corporation aggregate, found herself alone to

[189] ibid 32–35; Griffith (n 171) 192; Cornford (n 100) 239–40. *Raleigh v Goschen* [1898] 1 Ch 73; *Bainbridge* (n 165); *Adams v Naylor* [1946] AC 543, 2 All ER 241 (HL).

[190] Before *Mersey Docks v Cameron* put an end to the use of the public purpose criterion in exempting property from the statutes providing for the relief of the poor, the crown's exemption extended to all property 'occupied for the purposes of the government of the country': *Mersey Docks v Cameron* (n 176) 464 (Blackburn J); the exemption was restricted to cases 'in which the interests of the Crown, or the Crown through its servants were directly concerned': ibid 509 (Lord Cranworth). The scope of the central government that benefits from the rule of construction that the crown is not bound by a statute unless named in it remains significant. For a recent example, see *R(Black) v Secretary of State for Justice* (n 69) [1], where Lady Hale pointed out that the conclusion that the crown was not bound by Part 1 of the Health Act 2006 resulted in all crown premises being exempted from the smoking ban enacted in that Act—including 'the myriad of premises which are occupied by central government departments'; see Fortin (n 62) 281.

[191] *The Brabo* [1949] AC 326, 346–47 (Lord Simons), 355 (Lord du Parcq).

[192] Moore (n 177) 14–16; *Cooper v Hawkins* [1904] 2 KB 164, 173–74 (Mills J).

face an action as the crown shrank back to being a corporation sole in the context of liability for torts.

It has been said that no reasoning was offered as to why the king's personal privileges should be passed on to the formal 'crown'—central government departments.[193] One motivation for narrowing the immunities of the crown to central government departments in *Mersey Docks* was to limit the range of public bodies which could benefit from an exemption to pay the poor rates.[194] The other cause of the courts' reluctance to find government bodies liable was their interpretation of Parliament's intent in allocating funds to those departments and the courts' understanding of their own constitutional role *vis-à-vis* the role of Parliament. The courts reasoned that the funds allocated by Parliament to fulfil a department's statutory purposes did not include the payment of damages for the wrongs of the crown servants working for the departments.[195] Judges used the façade of immunities of the crown for central departments because they were reluctant to order them to pay for damages out of funds which came out of the consolidated revenue controlled by Parliament when Parliament had not expressly provided for the liability of government departments.[196] The courts used the immunities of the king and passed them on to government departments because of their conception of the delimitation between their jurisdiction and that of Parliament and because they wanted to circumscribe narrowly the scope of public bodies which were to be exempted from taxation.[197] There was no discussion of the concepts underlying the notion of the crown itself.

In short, in relation to the formal notion of the crown and the passing to it of the king's immunities, courts in the second half of the nineteenth century did not provide a developed concept of the public sphere. The courts' approach in defining the formal notion of the crown as central government departments was said to be both simplistic and binary—a given public authority was the crown or not. The court's approach to the notion of the crown was also inconsistent—the crown was a corporation sole in the context of suing a crown servant but a corporation aggregate when determining the application of a statute or exemption. However, the courts' passing of the king's immunities to the formal notion of the crown was motivated by the desire to respect what the courts conceived of as an application of the separation of powers between them and Parliament.[198] The courts' approach in defining the formal notion of the crown as central government departments was also motivated by the objective of narrowing down the range of public entities that could

[193] Watkins (n 120) 12; Selway (n 70) 237; McLean (n 4) 142, 159.

[194] Griffith (n 171) 172, 178; Anderson (n 156) 368–69.

[195] Anderson (n 156) 370; Getzler (n 100) 171.

[196] Williams (n 65) 21; Anderson (n 156) 380, 384. See *Whitfield v Lord Le Despencer* (n 165) 764–65 (Lord Mansfield).

[197] Gleeson E Robinson, *Public Authorities and Legal Liability* (University of London Press 1925) 21.

[198] See eg *Baron de Bode* (n 158) and Lobban (n 158) 243, 249.

benefit from the king's immunities. Despite the passing of the king's immunities to the formal notion of the crown understood as central government departments, the objective of narrowing down the entities who benefitted from the immunities to the formal notion of the crown only can be interpreted as having served a principled objective of ensuring greater equality before the law. Despite their binary and inconsistent approach in defining the formal notion of the crown, the courts' objective in narrowing down the scope of application of immunities was not completely divorced from Hale's understanding of *the king can do no wrong*, which was to limit the immunity from suit to the king only.

3.3.3 Dicey's interpretation of *the king can do no wrong*

Dicey's interpretation of *the king can do no wrong* followed Hale's. Dicey understood *the king can do no wrong* as the king is immune from suit—not subject to the coercive power of the law in Hale's terms—and as the king's orders are not a valid defence for his ministers and servants. However, as Erle CJ and Cockburn CJ before him, Dicey did not address the issue of the king's capacity to do wrong. Dicey also adopted the formal notion of the crown which was being developed by the courts in the later part of the nineteenth century but avoided providing any conceptual construct to underpin it. Dicey instead emphasized the individual liability of the king's officers.

3.3.3.1 Obfuscation of the king's capacity to do wrong

The first, substantive dimension of crown liability—the king's capacity to do wrong—is obfuscated in Dicey's understanding of *the king can do no wrong* by the emphasis he put on the king's immunity from suit. To Dicey, *the king can do no wrong* was to be understood, first, as 'by no proceeding known to the law can the King be made personally responsible for any act done by him'.[199] To Dicey, the king was absolutely immune and could not be criminally responsible even for murdering the Prime Minister by shooting him in the head.[200] Dicey also stated that there can be no petition of right to the king for the tort of a crown servant, accepting the result of the nineteenth-century trilogy of *Viscount Canterbury*, *Tobin*, and *Feather*.[201] Having emphasized the king's immunity from suit, Dicey did not then proceed—as had Hale—to describe how the king's unlawful command was voided by the invalidating power of the law in his exposition of *the king can do no wrong*. Dicey instead immediately added that *the king can do no wrong* was to be understood, second, as the command of the king not serving as a justification: 'no one can plead the orders of the Crown or indeed of any superior officer in defence of any act not otherwise justifiable by law'.[202] By neglecting to discuss bases for

199 Dicey (n 51) 21.
200 ibid.
201 ibid 412.
202 ibid 21.

the invalidation of the king's wrongful command, Dicey excluded the element of Hale's interpretation of *the king can do no wrong* which pointed to the king's capacity to issue a wrongful command to begin with. As discussed in Chapter 3, Hale's theory that the king was subject to the directive and invalidating powers of the law—which rendered the king's wrongful orders invalid—and his admission that the petition of right was available against the king pointed to the recognition of the king's capacity to do wrong. By contrast, Dicey's exposition of *the king can do no wrong* as a 'law of the constitution'[203] obfuscated the substantive dimension of crown liability—the king's capacity to do wrong. He emphasized instead the king's immunity from suit and the amenability to justice of the king's servants—the procedural dimension of crown liability.

3.3.3.2 The notion of government and individual officers' liability

The formal concept of the crown which was elaborated in nineteenth-century cases was adopted by Dicey:[204] 'no one can plead the orders of the Crown' and 'Some person is legally responsible for every act done by the Crown';[205] 'the Crown, or in other words, . . . the Government';[206] 'the Crown, i.e. the Government'.[207] To Dicey, the 'crown', 'government', and, for example, 'Admiralty' who paid for the servant's wrong were the same entity.[208] But the concept of the crown or government was not discussed or theorized by Dicey.[209]

Dicey drew a distinction between the naval officer at the service of the Admiralty and the Admiralty itself as part of the government, the crown. Only the officer, said Dicey, can be sued by aggrieved individuals. Dicey's terminology indicates that the 'government', or 'crown', was the government departments, to the exception of the individual officers. There was no discussion of the rationale for passing on the king's immunity from suit to the government departments. Nor was there any discussion as to why, as in *Feather*, the whole crown understood as a corporation aggregate including the government departments *and* the crown servants could use a patent or could claim not to be bound by a statute but that the same crown servants were not to be conceived of as part of the crown when sued for a tort.

There was also a lack of rationalization in Dicey's work as to how it was appropriate for the crown to pay in lieu of its servant if it could not be sued to begin with. There was equally an absence of anticipation that the crown might refuse to pay, deny that the tortfeasor was its servant or that she was acting in the course of

[203] ibid.
[204] cf McLean (n 4) 44–50.
[205] Dicey (n 51) 21.
[206] ibid Note XII to the 7th edn, 412.
[207] ibid.
[208] ibid 412–13.
[209] Dicey also overlooked the older common law concept of the body politic manifested in Parliament which could have acted as the basis for a theory of the state distinct from the Hobbesian tradition: Mark Walters, *A. V. Dicey and the Common Law Constitutional Tradition* (CUP 2020) 169–74.

her employment, or that an injustice might arise—as it eventually did in *Adams v Naylor*[210] and *Royster v Cavey*[211]—when the wrong could not be ascribed to a servant in particular,[212] contrary to Dicey's assertion that 'the technical immunity of the Crown in respect of such torts is not a subject of public complaint, and in practice works very little, if any, injustice'.[213]

From *the king can do no wrong* understood as the king's personal immunity from suit, there was an—unexplained—enlargement of the immunity to the government, as evidenced by Dicey's '*the Crown can do no wrong*'.[214] Dicey equated crown with government, as was later done in *Town Investments*.[215] The equation between crown and government in *Town Investments* was found to be problematic because it logically implied—it was argued, most famously by Wade—that the ministers and civil servants (the 'government') were the crown and therefore were immune from suit.[216] Wade did not point out that Dicey had drawn the same terminological equivalence between crown and government. Dicey did use the word 'Crown'[217] and specified that it meant the 'government' but when it came to tortious liability, the servants of the crown were not to be conceived of as part of the crown, a similar outcome to Cockburn CJ's in *Feather*. In *Feather*, however, the crown in the realm of tortious liability was to be conceived of as a corporation sole—the king. To Dicey, the crown in the realm of tortious liability was understood as the—much larger—formal notion of the crown meaning central government departments. The result was that the corporation aggregate that was central government—to the exclusion of individual servants—was now immune from suit.

In summary, although Dicey wrote 'Crown' to mean 'government', he did not discuss the rationale for its 'technical immunity' from suit in tort. Instead, he famously emphasized the individual officer's suability by ordinary action before ordinary courts when he discussed his notion of the equality before the law as part of the rule of law and his interpretation of *the king can do no wrong*.[218] Dicey emphasized that all officers, high and low, could be sued for unlawful acts before ordinary tribunals according to the law of the land. Dicey gave examples of high officials like secretaries of state and governors having been sued for their wrongs.[219] That

[210] *Adams v Naylor* (n 189).
[211] *Royster v Cavey* [1947] KB 204 (CA).
[212] Williams (n 65) 17–18.
[213] Dicey (n 51) 413.
[214] ibid 412.
[215] *Town Investments Ltd v Department of the Environment* [1978] AC 359 (Lords Diplock and Simon).
[216] William Wade, 'Injunctive Relief against the Crown and Ministers' (1991) 107 LQR 4; William Wade, 'The Crown: Old Platitudes and New Heresies' (1992) 142 NLJ 1275; William Wade, 'The Crown, Ministers and Officials: Legal Status and Liability' in Maurice Sunkin and Sebastian Payne (eds), *The Nature of the Crown* (OUP 1999).
[217] cf McLean (n 4) 50.
[218] Dicey (n 51) 21, 100.
[219] ibid 123.

statement is accurate and can be traced back to *Entick v Carrington*.[220] What Dicey omitted, however, was that high public officials were only liable for their own wrongs.[221] They were not vicariously liable for the wrongs of the crown servants they directed. If Dicey resorted to the concept of crown in explaining *the king can do no wrong*, he ignored the problematic body of law that was being developed in the nineteenth and twentieth centuries on the absence of liability of public officials and government departments for the wrongs of the crown servants they instructed.

Dicey did not outline, for instance, that public officials were liable only for personal wrongs because they are fellow crown servants and are not the employers of the crown servants and inferior officers.[222] Nor did Dicey point out that government departments were not liable because they were also crown servants. When it was said that the 'crown' was the master of crown servants, the crown meant the king, as in *Viscount Canterbury* and *Tobin*. Only the king was the master of the crown servants.[223] In *Viscount Canterbury* especially, Lord Lyndhurst's reasons were in part to the effect that the monarch did not himself appoint nor direct the servants working for the Commissioners and could not therefore be held vicariously liable for their wrongs.[224] The fiction that the king was the master of the crown servants was exposed in that same case, as it was the Commissioners in *Viscount Canterbury* who appointed the servants. The king could not be held liable for the wrongs of the Commissioners themselves, reasoned Lord Lyndhurst, because even if they were called crown servants, they were in fact creatures of the legislature and the fact that the monarch appointed them was not enough to create a master–servant relationship. The Commissioners were crown servants in theory only, not in practice. Since the king could not be liable for the wrongs of the Commissioners themselves, he could not be liable, opined Lord Lyndhurst, for the wrongs of the servants under the direction of the Commissioners. It was the Commissioners who selected and appointed the servants, 'the selection or control of whom the Crown has no concern'.[225] The vacuity of the idea that the king was the master of the crown servants was exposed by Lord Lyndhurst. The objective of shielding the monarch from petitions of right by reasoning that he did not appoint or issue commands to the crown servants in *Viscount Canterbury* lifted the veil of the term 'crown servant' which covered the Commissioners. It also lifted the veil of the king as master of the servants working for the Commissioners. The effect was that no one was the

[220] *Entick v Carrington* (1765) EWHC KB J98, (1765) 2 Wilson KB 275, (1765) 19 St Tr 1030.

[221] To McLean, Dicey denied a 'unified will to do wrong': McLean (n 4) 44–50.

[222] *Lane v Cotton* (n 165); *Raleigh v Goschen* (n 189). See also *Dibley v Lord Palmerston* (1822) 3 Brod & Bing 275, 285–86 (Dallas CJ) (129 ER 1290): there was no relationship of employment between the Secretary of war and the plaintiff or 'any undertaking in any way to be personally responsible to him' and 'an action will not lie against a public agent for any thing done by him in his public character or employment'.

[223] Griffith (n 171) 191.

[224] *Viscount Canterbury* (n 117) 323–25.

[225] ibid 325.

master of the crown servants. It showed that the idea that the king was the master of crown servants did not correspond to reality.

The higher officials and departments directed the crown servants, but they were not their masters and therefore could not be sued for the crown servants' wrongs. The irresponsibility of the public officials and government departments was also later buttressed by the courts' interpretation that Parliament did not allocate funds for the purpose of compensating aggrieved individual for the wrongs caused by the crown servants fulfilling the orders of the public officials and government departments.[226] Various government departments' lack of corporate status or the insufficiency of statutory provisions granting them the capacity to sue or be sued was also raised as a shield from vicarious liability for the wrongs of the crown servants working for the departments.[227] Moreover, provisions granting corporate status or the capacity to sue government departments were considered sufficient for given departments to be sued in contract, but not in tort.[228] Legal thinking was unsatisfactory as the servants had two heads: the king as their master in theory and the public officials and government departments as their master in practice. But neither the king nor the public officials or government departments were to be ascribed liability for the servants' wrongs. Dicey ignored this gap in the law of crown liability and proceeded instead to emphasize that individual servants were liable.

3.3.4 Consequences for legal thinking

The effect of Dicey's interpretation of *the king can do no wrong* and the emphasis he placed on the personal liability of crown servants according to ordinary law before ordinary tribunals can be perceived in cases mentioning *the king can do no wrong* from the late nineteenth century to the first half of the twentieth century. The courts' interpretation of *the king can do no wrong* in that period was also affected by the nineteenth-century formal notion of the crown. The ambivalence between the crown as the king, a corporation sole—as in *Viscount Canterbury* and *Tobin*—and the crown as a corporation aggregate regrouping king, central government departments, public officials, and crown servants—as in *Feather*—was still observable in cases in that period. The formal notion of the crown meaning central government departments, and not other public bodies such as local public bodies following *Mersey Docks*, also had an impact on the evolution of *the king can do no*

[226] Some ministries did have corporate status: Anderson (n 156) 380. See Robertson, who provided a list of central governmental bodies and their capacity to sue or be sued: Robertson (n 166).

[227] Anderson (n 156) 378.

[228] *Graham v Commissioners of Works* (1901) 2 KB 781; *Mackenzie-Kennedy v Air Council* [1927] 2 KB 517; Williams (n 65) 4–5, 20–21; Robertson (n 166) 21–108. cf *Gilleghan v Minister of Health* [1932] 1 Ch 86, where the Minister, although incorporated and the object of a provision providing that he could sue and be sued, was found not subject to an action for breach of contract, the proper remedy being to sue the crown by petition of right.

wrong. The facts that central government was called the crown and that the king was also referred to as the crown led *the king can do no wrong* to be equated with *the crown can do no wrong*. The 'crown' understood as 'government' was said to represent the 'crown' understood as the king. For instance, in Robertson's work of 1908 on proceedings against the crown, the section entitled 'The Crown' focusses on the liability of the monarch and of central government departments, referred to as departments of the 'Crown or Government'.[229] The crown was both the king and central government departments. As a result of the ambiguous use of the term 'crown', the king's immunities were passed on to central government because both were called the 'crown'.

The emphasis that Dicey—following the courts' lead in *Tobin* and *Feather*—placed on *the king can do no wrong* meaning the king's immunity from suit manifested itself in *King v Speyer*.[230] In that case, a writ of *quo warranto* was sought against two members of the Privy Council on the basis that they were not born in Great Britain and were not qualified as naturalized citizens to sit as privy councillors. The Attorney General argued that it was against the maxim that *the king can do no wrong* to grant a *quo warranto* against the king's choice of a privy councillor. Lord Reading CJ found that the court had no power over the sovereign, but that the judgment against the respondents would have an effect against them only.[231] To Avery J, *the king can do no wrong* was sometimes misunderstood, and meant only 'that His Majesty individually and personally and in his natural capacity is independent of, and not amenable to, any other earthly power or jurisdiction'.[232] *The king can do no wrong* meant only the king's personal immunity from suit. It could not shield others from judicial recourse. That understanding of *the king can do no wrong* was in fact not only attributable to Dicey but had roots in Hale's interpretation of *the king can do no wrong*, where only the king was exempted from the application of the coercive power of the law. But the court's modification in *Tobin* and *Feather* of Hale's interpretation of *the king can do no wrong* which resulted in the petition of right not being available against the king was by then well established, as is evidenced by Avery J's reasoning that the king is not amenable to any other 'earthly power or jurisdiction'.

Hale's interpretation of *the king can do no wrong*, which could still be found in part in Dicey's understanding of the concept that while the king is immune his orders do not constitute a defence was, however, altered in other cases from the late nineteenth century onwards. The alteration of Hale's *the king can do no wrong*

[229] Robertson (n 166) 2.

[230] *King v Speyer* [1916] 1 KB 595. The court's reasoning in the *King v Speyer* in relation to prerogative writs is perhaps foreshadowing the House of Lords' ruling in *M v Home Office* [1994] AC 377 (HL), at the end of the twentieth century, that ministers cannot hide behind the cover of *the crown can do no wrong* in judicial review proceedings; see Chapter 5, section 2.4.1. See also Chapter 1, section 2.3.

[231] *King v* Speyer (n 230) 610.

[232] ibid 619.

was caused by the formal notion of the crown which was developed in nineteenth-century cases and adopted by Dicey.

The formal nineteenth-century notion of the crown as embraced by Dicey was apparent from the case of *Raleigh v Goschen*, where Romer J found that if a crown servant commits a wrong, 'the order of the executive Government, or of any officer of State'[233] cannot act as a justification and the person remained personally liable. Hale's interpretation of *the king can do no wrong* that the wrongful command of the king did not constitute a defence, because if it was unlawful it was invalid, was transposed by Romer J—as it was by Dicey[234]—to government departments' and officers' commands. It was no longer the king's unlawful commands which were invalidated by the invalidating power of the law, it was now the commands of the 'executive Government' and 'officers of State'. The transfer of the king's immunity from the coercive power of the law in Hale's interpretation of *the king can do no wrong* to the government highlighted a flaw in legal thinking about crown liability. The 'crown' was the master of the crown servants executing the unlawful commands. The master of the crown servants was not the government departments nor public officials, who were rather also crown servants. The principle that the crown understood as a corporation sole (the king) was the master of crown servants was maintained, but it was no longer the king who was said to issue wrongful commands to his servants. *Raleigh v Goschen* highlighted the reality that government departments and public officials were *de facto* the masters of crown servants and issued commands to them. In *Raleigh v Goschen*, as in Dicey's work, the unlawful commands of *de facto* masters—public officials and government departments—were invalid if unlawful. Yet government departments or public officials were not to be liable for the wrongs committed by the crown servants executing their commands. The court found in *Raleigh v Goschen* that public officials issuing commands to the crown servants could not be sued merely in their official capacity as representatives of the government departments. A given public official had to be personally and directly involved in commanding the wrong or committing it to be liable. The court in *Raleigh v Goschen* transferred the king's immunity from the coercive power of the law to the government departments and public officials for issuing wrongful commands. Hale's interpretation of *the king can do no wrong* on both the invalidating and the coercive powers of the law was applied to government departments and public officials. Their wrongful orders, like the king's, were rendered void by the invalidating power of the law and could not serve as a defence to individual crown servants. The king's immunity from the coercive power of the law was also passed on to government departments and public officials for issuing the unlawful commands. The public officials could not be sued in their representative capacity merely for having issued commands to the crown servants of the

233 *Raleigh v Goschen* (n 189) 77.
234 Dicey (n 51) 21.

government departments—a degree of personal involvement was necessary for an action in tort to lie against them.

In *Johnstone v Peddlar*, a case on the doctrine of act of state for the wrongful acts of crown servants committed abroad dating to 1921, Viscount Finlay's, Viscount Cave's, and Lord Phillimore's expositions of *the king can do no wrong* in the domestic context were in line with Hale's interpretation and Dicey's understanding that a wrongful command of the king could not constitute a valid defence for the crown servant.[235] But Dicey's interpretation of *the king can do no wrong* and the formal nineteenth-century notion of the crown as meaning central government are apparent in Viscount Finlay's reasoning. In *Johnstone*, Viscount Finlay spoke of the 'British Government' in the context of acts of state committed abroad.[236] Instead of using the word 'king', Viscount Findlay said that the crown's unlawful command did not constitute a defence in the domestic context. The crown did not mean the king to Viscount Finlay. He also drew a distinction between the king personally and the crown understood as government when he discussed the domestic application of *the king can do no wrong*. The distinction between crown and king personally is apparent from Viscount Finlay's statement that:

> It is the settled law of this country . . . that if a wrongful act has been committed against the person or the property of any person the wrongdoer cannot set up as a defence that the act was done by the command of the Crown. The Crown can do no wrong, and the Sovereign cannot be sued in tort, but the person who did the act is liable in damages, as any private person would be.[237]

Viscount Finlay's emphasis on the individual officer's liability according to ordinary law at the end of the sentence is Diceyan. As for the distinction in his speech between 'Crown' and 'Sovereign', it suggests that 'the Crown can do no wrong' meant the 'British Government' can do no wrong, not only the king personally. Like Dicey and courts from the second half of the nineteenth century, Viscount Finlay used 'Crown' to mean 'Government'. Viscount Finlay's choice of words—'the Crown can do no wrong'—is also revealing when contrasted with Lord Phillimore and Viscount Cave's use of *the king can do no wrong* in its traditional form in their respective speeches, where they spoke of the king personally issuing commands. The logical conclusion to be drawn from Viscount Finlay's reasons and the difference in syntax between *the king can do no wrong* and *the crown can do no wrong* is that even in the domestic context, the British government's wrongful orders could not be imputed to it and it was immune from

[235] *Johnstone v Peddlar* [1921] 2 AC 262, 271 (Viscount Finlay), 275 (Viscount Cave), 295 (Lord Phillimore).

[236] ibid 271 (Viscount Finlay).

[237] *Johnstone v Peddlar* (n 235) 271.

suit for them, as in *Raleigh v Goschen*. Only the individual crown servant could be sued, as Dicey prescribed.

By the first half of the twentieth century, the crown was not referring to the king personally as was the case in *Viscount Canterbury* and *Tobin*. The court in *Feather* had implicitly accepted that the concept of corporation aggregate meant the crown, indicating an early confusion about to whom the immunity from suit attached. The confusion led to Lord Cranworth explicitly extending the king's personal privileges to government departments: 'by extension of the shield of the Crown to what might more fitly be described as the public government of the country'.[238] The result can be seen in *Macgregor* and *Adams v Naylor*, where the crown was found to be immune.

In *Macgregor*, the argument of the War Department, which was being sued for the wrongful conduct of a civil servant in the course of his duty, was that 'Each Department of State . . . is a branch of the Government; the Government, constitutionally, is the Sovereign; and the Sovereign can do no wrong, personally or by any of his Ministers, cognisable in a Court of Law.'[239] The plaintiff conceded that point and Anderson, Lord Ordinary, considered the Department's argument to be a settled point of law.[240] All misconstrued the court's ruling in *Feather*. It was Queen Victoria herself who was sued to in that case, via the petition of right, not a government department. In *Macgregor*, the Department itself was sued, and by ordinary action, not by petition of right. There was a fundamental misunderstanding of the seventeenth-century constitutional settlement of *the king can do no wrong* as reflected in Hale's interpretation that the king was immune from suit, but his wrongful commands were void and his ministers and servants were to be punished for executing them.

Lord Justice-Clerk Scott Dickson's speech in the Second Division in *Macgregor* highlighted similar flaws in legal understanding of *the king can do no wrong*. He cited precedents for the proposition that while a subject can sue an individual servant he cannot sue the government, or any public department of His Majesty's government, because they represent the king.[241] Lord Justice-Clerk Scott Dickson relied on the interpretation of *the king can do no wrong* found in *Glegg on Reparation* that the 'protection' of the maxim 'extends to public departments, to officers of public departments when their action has been instructed by the State'.[242] Extending the immunity from suit to government departments and officers of public departments when they were following commands of the 'State' was a reversal of *the king can do no wrong* as understood since Hale and the seventeenth-century constitutional settlement that the king's wrongful command was not an excuse to a servant

[238] *Mersey Docks Trustees v Cameron* (n 176) 508.
[239] *Macgregor* (n 116) 847 (Lord Anderson).
[240] ibid 847–48.
[241] ibid 851.
[242] ibid 852.

of the king. Government departments and public officials were conceived of as crown servants. For that reason, the reasoning went, they cannot be liable for other crown servants' wrongs. A fundamental element of the seventeenth-century constitutional settlement understanding of *the king can do no wrong* was that the king was immune from suit but that as a counterpart, his advisers and servants were liable. Were the court in *Macgregor* to have applied *the king can do no wrong* as it stood since the seventeenth century, it would have reached the conclusion that government departments and public officials, being crown servants, were liable for executing the king's commands. Instead, the impact of the confusion surrounding the notion of the crown and the resulting impossibility of distinguishing between the king and the formal notion of the crown understood as central government allowed the court in *Macgregor* to alter the seventeenth-century constitutional settlement understanding of *the king can do no wrong*.

Lord Dundas and Lord Salvesen agreed with Lord Scott Dickson's understanding of *the king can do no wrong* in *Macgregor*. Lord Salvesen, however, added that the law was unsatisfactory—to his mind, it should not have been left to departments to choose to accept liability for the wrongful conduct of civil servants when it pleased them.[243] In summary, in *Macgregor*, government departments were confused with the king and partook of the immunity from suit which was the king's alone—instead of being liable like other crown servants such as ministers as the seventeenth-century constitutional settlement required.

The seventeenth-century constitutional settlement understanding of *the king can do no wrong* was again not applied in *Adams v Naylor* due to the formal notion of the crown which had been devised in the nineteenth century.[244] The House of Lords in that case took the crown to mean government departments. The government departments were called 'Crown authorities' by Viscount Simon, who also referred to 'Crown ships' and 'Crown vehicles', implying that the crown meant the government.[245] Similarly, Lord Thankerton used the concept of 'crown' and not that of 'king' as the latter was used in *Viscount Canterbury* and *Tobin*.[246] The court rather followed Cockburn CJ's use of the crown as a corporation aggregate in *Feather* and as a formal notion referring to central government in *Mersey Docks*. In the same vein, Lord Uthwatt adopted Maitland's concept of the crown as the head of a highly organized corporation aggregate of many and argued that 'it embraces the state'.[247] Calling central government departments the 'crown' was a result of the formalistic test elaborated in the nineteenth century in *Mersey Docks* to differentiate between the crown and non-crown public bodies. However, that the crown understood as government departments—which were crown servants—could

[243] ibid 852–53.
[244] *Adams v Naylor* (n 189).
[245] ibid 244.
[246] ibid.
[247] ibid 247. FW Maitland, 'The Crown as Corporation' (1901) 17 LQR 131, 138.

not be sued was not the understanding of *the king can do no wrong* which resulted from the constitutional struggles of the seventeenth century. The confusion surrounding the notion of the crown and the absence of a distinction between the king and the government—both referred to as the crown—appears to have allowed the seventeenth-century constitutional understanding of *the king can do no wrong* to be altered by extending the king's immunity from suit to government departments.

The assimilation of the formal notion of the crown—government departments—to the king is also apparent from the case of *Anglo-Saxon Petroleum*, where the officials and servants who salvaged a ship were referred to as the king exercising his duty as *parens patriae* himself.[248] *The king can do no wrong* was perceived as a shield from any liability for ministers and government departments, when the concept was understood since the later part of the seventeenth century, after the constitutional struggles, as ensuring that the king's ministers and servants were to be liable precisely because the king was not.

The result of equating the concept of crown with that of central government also led to other theoretical flaws. The court in *The Brabo* found that the crown and its servants and agents—including the ministry—could claim immunity from statutes.[249] The minister was liable for the king's wrongful commands under Hale's seventeenth-century understanding of *the king can do no wrong* and that of Dicey, but her ministry was found not to be subject to the application of statutes in *The Brabo*. The minister was distinct from the king in the realm of tortious liability, but both the minister and the ministry partook of the king's immunity from the application of statutes as part of the crown.

Evidence of the confusion surrounding *the king can do no wrong* caused by the formal notion of the crown of the nineteenth century can also be found in Lord Morris's dissent in *Town Investments*. Lord Morris said that when a minister acts in her official capacity, the crown's immunities extend to her. However, the minister does not become absolved from liability for a personal tortious act.[250] Lord Morris's speech highlighted the problem caused by the formal notion of the crown of the nineteenth century. Lord Morris said that the crown's immunities sometimes extend to ministers. He was in fact acknowledging that the crown understood as a corporation aggregate—including the ministers—benefits from immunities, as *Feather* opened the door to and was evidenced in *The Brabo*. But to Lord Morris, a minister could be sued in his personal capacity for personal wrongs: 'he does not become absolved from liability for a personal tortious act even though "the Queen can do no wrong" '.[251] The seventeenth-century constitutional settlement understanding of *the king can do no wrong*—that the minister is responsible for

[248] *Anglo-Saxon Petroleum Co Ltd v Damant*; *Anglo-Saxon Petroleum Co Ltd v R* [1947] KB 794.
[249] *The Brabo* (n 191) 346–47 (Lord Simons), 355 (Lord du Parcq).
[250] *Town Investments* (n 215) 393.
[251] ibid.

the king's wrongful orders—was not acknowledged. The crown in the context of tortious liability was a corporation sole—the king only—and only the king was immune. Attempts by Lord Morris and others[252] at solving the conundrum caused by the formal notion of the crown and the inconsistent approach of the nineteenth-century courts, resulting in the minister being sometimes part of the crown but not part of it at other times, were to distinguish between the minister's official and personal capacity. This distinction was misguided. It was perhaps prompted in part by the reference in the Crown Proceedings Act 1947 (CPA) to 'an officer of the Crown as such'.[253] Yet the distinction is not to be drawn, based on a historical analysis, between the minister acting officially or personally, but between the king and government departments. The distinction between the king and government departments was rendered difficult to make because the crown was used to refer to both the king (a corporation sole) and to central government (a corporation aggregate including ministers, government departments, and civil servants). The confusion was compounded by the misconceived equation between *the king can do no wrong* and *the crown can do no wrong.*

More recent cases encapsulate the result of the evolution in legal thinking of *the king can do no wrong*. It is now associated with the procedural dimension of crown liability—the king's non-amenability to justice—and now extends to the formal notion of the crown, namely central government.

For instance, in *Mulcahy v Minister of Defence*, Neill LJ recounted that, until the CPA, 'two principles of ancient though doubtful origin' inhibited actions against the crown.[254] The first principle was that the king could not be sued in his own courts, the effect of which was that other proceedings had to be resorted to, such as the petition of right. The second principle, 'the King could do no wrong', prevented proceedings in tort from being brought against the crown. Neill LJ said:

> It may that at one time the maxim 'The King can do no wrong' meant that the king was not privileged to commit illegal acts, but it came to be understood to be a rule barring actions in tort against the Crown.[255]

Neill LJ alluded to the Bractonian understanding of *the king can do no wrong*—the king is not entitled to do wrong—but emphasized that it is now understood as immunity from suit for the crown understood as central government—not only the king.

Similarly, Lord Bingham in *Matthews v Ministry of Defence* understood the 'doctrine' that '*the king could do no wrong*' as the crown was under no liability in tort at

[252] *M v Home Office* (n 230) 395 (Lord Templeman), 409–10 (Lord Woolf).
[253] Crown Proceedings Act 1947, 10 & 11 Geo VI c 44, s 2(3).
[254] *Mulcahy v Ministry of Defence* [1996] QB 732 (CA) 740.
[255] ibid 740.

common law.[256] In *Rahmatullah*, a case on the scope of the doctrine of crown act of state, Lady Hale adopted the common mistaken equation of *the king can do no wrong* with the feudal privilege that the king cannot be sued in his own courts.[257] Her assertion that, prior to the adoption of the CPA in 1947, the courts had to address the possibility that the king's prior command or subsequent approval could act as a defence with respect to the servant's liability also reflects the confusion surrounding the concept. Post seventeenth-century constitutional struggles, *the king can do no wrong* did not mean that the king's command or subsequent approval was a defence. Properly understood in its historical context and evolution in legal thinking, *the king can do no wrong* does not mean that the king, being incapable of doing wrong, can only issue rightful orders or that the king's immunity from suit extends to the official conducting the wrongful command. *The king can do no wrong* does not mean that the king's immunity from suit and his incapacity to do wrong can serve as a defence, or that his command or subsequent approval of the officials' actions can.

4 Conclusion: the king's capacity to do wrong and amenability to justice since the eighteenth century

The use of the expression *the 'crown' can do no* wrong since the end of the nineteenth century is revealing. The slippage from *the king can do no wrong* to *the crown can do no wrong* illustrates the relatively recent extension of immunities to central government since the nineteenth century. Not only has *the king can do no wrong* been synonymous with immunity from suit since that period, but the confusion surrounding the notion of 'crown' deprived *the king can do no wrong* of its seventeenth-century constitutional settlement meaning that only the king is immune and that all the king's ministers, servants, and, therefore, government departments, are liable. The assimilation of the king with the formal notion of the crown understood as central government since the *Mersey Docks* cases led to the alteration of the seventeenth-century constitutional settlement understanding of *the king can do no wrong* which had subsisted even in Dicey's work.

The confusion surrounding *the king can do no wrong* and, therefore, the law of crown liability, was caused in part by Hale's interpretation. Hale had not fully addressed the issue posed by the existence of the petition of right or how it could be reconciled with his interpretation of *the king can do no wrong*. Hale's interpretation implied that the king was capable of issuing wrongful orders—wrongful because

[256] *Matthews v Ministry of Defence* (2003) UKHL 4, [2003] 1 AC 1163 [4] (Lord Bingham).

[257] *Rahmatullah (No 2) v Ministry of Defence and another* (2017) UKSC 1, [2017] AC 649 [16] (Lady Hale). One of the issues the Supreme Court had to decide was whether the doctrine included a defence to an action in tort brought by a foreigner against the UK government for a tort committed abroad pursuant to its foreign affairs policy.

contrary to the directive power of the law which applied to the king. The king's wrongful orders were voided by the invalidating force of the law. Hale acknowledged the existence of the petition of right, which confirmed that the king was capable of doing wrong and raised the issue of the extent of the king's amenability to justice. The seventeenth-century constitutional settlement understanding of *the king can do no wrong* was that the king was thought unable to be sued but the petition of right's existence indicated that the king was amenable to justice for a wrong. The courts in the cases on the petition of right in the nineteenth century—especially *Tobin* and *Feather*—had elements of the Bractonian understanding of *the king can do no wrong*—also found in Coke and Hale's thinking—that the king was not entitled to do wrong. However, the courts also reinterpreted *the king can do no wrong* as no wrong could be imputed to the king, in order to deny the king's amenability to justice for a wrong. Decisions of the nineteenth-century courts marked a departure from Hale's theory of the three powers of the law, which was grounded in the recognition that the king was capable of doing wrong. The result of the nineteenth-century cases on the petition of right was to render the remedy devoid of all usefulness in tort.

The ambiguity of the word 'crown' also had an impact on the understanding of *the king can do no wrong* in the nineteenth and twentieth centuries. The king was referred to as the crown in the first half of the nineteenth century and the crown was then understood as a corporation sole. In the second half of the nineteenth century, the formal notion of the crown was developed to refer to central government departments, a corporation aggregate. Both the king and central government departments were called the crown although the word 'crown' referred to two different concepts. As a result, the king and central government departments were not distinguished. The king's immunity from suit was extended to government departments in the early twentieth century because they were considered to be representatives of the king. The seventeenth-century constitutional understanding of *the king can do no wrong* was thereby emptied of its meaning. *The king can do no wrong* became *the crown can do no wrong*. The immunity from suit which was meant to attach to the king only was extended to the 'crown' understood as the whole government apparatus. The result was an inconsistency in the law of crown liability. On one hand, government departments were said not to be the masters of crown servants but rather fellow crown servants and therefore could not be liable for the wrong of other crown servants. On the other hand, the same government departments were said to be the crown and partook of the king's immunity from suit. Government departments were at the same time crown servants and the crown itself. Because they were not masters of crown servants but rather crown servants themselves, public officials and government departments were not recognized as capable of doing wrong because they did not issue wrongful commands as masters. They were not amenable to justice either, both because they were not vicariously liable for the wrongs of fellow crown servants but also, paradoxically, because they fell under the formal notion of the crown.

5
Revisiting and Understanding Crown Liability from a Historical Constitutional Perspective

1 Overview of the chapter

In this chapter, the evolution of the understanding of *the king can do no wrong* in light of this book's model is outlined. A discussion of current legal thinking in relation to crown liability is presented, informed by the historical constitutional approach adopted in this book. An analysis of *the king can do no wrong* as an ahistorical basis for crown immunity is conducted. The Diceyan influence on the current understanding of crown liability and on the Crown Proceedings Act 1947 (CPA)[1] is discussed. A possible reorientation of our understanding of crown liability is suggested, based on a historically informed understanding of *the king can do no wrong*.

2 Two dimensions of crown liability and three notions of *the king can do no wrong*—outline of their evolution

The king can do no wrong is now widely believed to be an 'ancient procedural maxim' which meant immunity from suit and was grounded in the king's feudal privilege.[2] Despite the fact that it has been noted in legal literature that *the king can do no wrong* did not originally mean that the king is immune from suit,[3] the orthodox view is that from a procedural maxim conveying immunity from

[1] Crown Proceedings Act 1947, 10 & 11 Geo VI c 44.

[2] FW Maitland, *The Constitutional History of England* (CUP 1963) 100; Carol Harlow, *Compensation and Government Torts* (Sweet & Maxwell 1982) 17–18. *M v Home Office* [1994] 1 AC 377 (HL) 407 (Lord Woolf); *Rahmatullah (No 2) v Ministry of Defence and another* (2017) UKSC 1, [2017] AC 649 [16] (Lady Hale).

[3] See eg Ludwik Ehrlich, 'Proceedings against the Crown (1216–1377)' in Paul Vinogradoff (ed), *Oxford Studies in Social and Legal History*, vol 6 (Clarendon Press 1921); Edwin Borchard, 'Governmental Responsibility in Tort, VI' (1926) 36 YLJ 1; Maurice Sunkin, 'Crown Immunity from Criminal Liability in English Law' [2003] PL 716; Greg Weeks, *Soft Law and Public Authorities: Remedies and Reform* (Hart Publishing 2016) 182–83; Sir John Baker, *The Reinvention of Magna Carta 1216–1616* (CUP 2017) 45.

The King Can Do No Wrong. Marie-France Fortin, Oxford University Press. © Marie-France Fortin 2024.
DOI: 10.1093/9780191994487.003.0006

suit, *the king can do no wrong* became the principle that the king cannot be held liable, whether in tort or for criminal offences. It is thought that, from a procedural maxim, *the king can do no wrong* changed meaning in the seventeenth century and came to mean that the king cannot be guilty of torts or crimes[4] and that the 'modern doctrine' was developed that the king's ministers and servants are liable in his stead.[5] The understanding of the evolution of *the king can do no wrong* which underpins the orthodox view is partly flawed. *The king can do no wrong* was not, in medieval times, a 'procedural maxim' conveying the king's feudal privilege not to be sued in his courts.[6] In medieval times, the concept—the phrase *the king can do no wrong* was not yet coined in the late Middle Ages—was understood as the king is capable of doing a wrong but not entitled to commit a wrong.[7] *The king can do no wrong* was not a procedural maxim conveying immunity from suit but a substantive legal idea. The understanding of the concept evolved in the seventeenth century as constitutional changes occurred: the emphasis was placed on the king's immunity from suit and the liability of his ministers and servants—but the king remained capable of doing and ordering a wrong in legal thinking. The king could be 'sued to' by petition of right, which was a substitute for an ordinary action. Over the course of the eighteenth and nineteenth centuries, the king became conceived of as perfect, incapable of doing or thinking wrong, and ultimately as one to whom a wrong could not be attributed. The petition of right became unavailable to a wronged subject in tort. The term 'crown' replaced the king at the turn of the twentieth century. Crown liability—understood as the crown's capacity to do wrong (the first, substantive, dimension of the model) and as the crown's amenability to justice for a wrong (the second, procedural, dimension of the model)—was marked by confusion in legal thinking.

In this first section of the chapter, the outline of the evolution of *the king can do no wrong* in legal thinking in light of the model is analysed. The impact in legal thinking of the evolution of the understanding of the three notions associated with *the king can do no wrong* on the two dimensions of crown liability is then scrutinized.

2.1 Late medieval and Tudor eras

According to Bracton and under the Tudors, the king was under the law, not perfect—or had a body politic which was perfect but which did not entitle the

[4] Harlow (n 2) 17–18.

[5] Maitland (n 2) 102–03; Harlow (n 2) 17–18.

[6] Baker (n 3) 45.

[7] See Chapter 2.

king to do wrong[8]—and immune from suit. To Bracton, although the king was appointed by God, he could commit a wrong and if he did, he exceeded his jurisdiction. His wrongful acts were not those of a king, because they exceeded the king's jurisdiction. Nevertheless, the king had to answer for them and correct them—or face God's punishment—because the wrong remained that of the king, not his agents'.[9]

The king could be sued to by petition of right and remedies such as *monstrans de droit* were available against him. The king was also conceived of as not entitled to do wrong. The result was that the king was capable of doing wrong and amenable to justice.

2.2 Seventeenth-century constitutional settlement

Since the seventeenth-century constitutional settlement, the focus of crown liability has been on the absence of the king's amenability to justice—the second, procedural, dimension of *the king can do no wrong*.

To Matthew Hale, the king was subject to the directive and invalidating powers of the law.[10] The king, therefore, was capable of doing wrong but his unlawful orders were invalidated. The king, however, was immune from the coercive power of the law because of his sacredness and sublimity. Only the king's ministers and servants—the instruments executing the king's commands—were subject to the coercive power of the law in relation to the king's wrongful acts and commands in Hale's thinking.

Hale's interpretation of *the king can do no wrong* based on the three powers of the law was nuanced. The king was under the law, as he was subject to the directive and invalidating powers of the law, but not under the coercive power of the law. The king's perfection—the king's sacredness and sublimity—justified his exemption from the coercive power of the law. The king was immune from suit and the availability of the petition of right was acknowledged but not addressed in depth.

2.3 Nineteenth-century developments

The king can do no wrong understood in the Bractonian sense that the king is not entitled to do wrong implies that the king is under the law, not perfect, and therefore capable of doing wrong under the first, substantive, dimension of the model.

[8] Case of the *Dutchy of Lancaster* (1561) 1 Plowden 212; *Willion v Berkley* (1562) 1 Plowden 223; see Chapter 2, sections 2.2.2 and 2.2.3.

[9] See Chapter 2, sections 2.1 and 2.3.

[10] See Chapter 3, section 3.3.3.

Since the Middle Ages, the king has been immune from suit, either because of his feudal privilege not to be sued in his courts or because of his sacred character as God's chosen one. But he was otherwise amenable to justice under the second, procedural, dimension of the model as he could be sued to with the petition of right and was subject to other remedies such as *monstrans de droit* and traverse of office.

The premise that only the king's servants can be sued was developed as a result of *the king can do no wrong* being associated with the notion of immunity from suit or with the notion of perfection of the king. Hale's interpretation of *the king can do no wrong* emphasized the king's immunity from suit, while acknowledging that the king was capable of doing wrong. As for the association between *the king can do no wrong* and the notion of perfection, the king conceived of as perfect was incapable of doing wrong and could not therefore be sued for a wrong which he was incapable of committing. The king's incapacity to do wrong—the first, substantive, dimension of the model—logically indicated his non-amenability to justice—the second, procedural, dimension of the model. That description of the two dimensions corresponds generally to Blackstone's interpretation of *the king can do no wrong*. The king was conceived of as perfect and incapable of doing wrong following Blackstone's influence. As a result, he was immune from suit and not subject to the petition of right. The petition of right has been conceived, following Blackstone, as a remedy as of grace,[11] divorced from its essence as an alternative remedy to an ordinary action.

In Bracton and Hale's thinking with regard to *the king can do no wrong*, the king's capacity to do wrong—the first, substantive, dimension of the model—impacted the understanding of the king's amenability to justice—the second, procedural, dimension of the model. Following the Bractonian understanding of *the king can do no wrong*, which underpinned Hale's thinking, the king was capable of doing wrong. The second dimension of the model—the king's amenability to justice—was dependent on the status of the first dimension. As the king was capable of doing wrong, a wrong was attributable to the king and he, although immune from suit, could be sued to by the petition of right and other remedies which became available against him over time.

Blackstone's interpretation of *the king can do no wrong* was also based on the understanding of the first, substantive, dimension—the king's capacity to do wrong—as impacting the interpretation of the second, procedural, dimension of the model—the king's amenability to justice. To Blackstone, *the king can do no wrong* was to be understood as the king was perfect and incapable of doing wrong. The king's incapacity to do wrong dictated the understanding of the second, procedural, dimension—the king's non-amenability to justice. As the king was incapable of doing or even of thinking wrong in Blackstone's interpretation of *the king*

[11] See Chapter 4, section 3.3; see also William Wade, 'The Crown, Ministers and Officials: Legal Status and Liability' in Maurice Sunkin and Sebastian Payne (eds), *The Nature of the Crown* (OUP 1999) 25.

can do no wrong, the king's amenability to justice was denied and the petition of right was reinterpreted as a remedy as of grace. The Blackstonian understanding of *the king can do no wrong* can therefore, in part, be interpreted as following the same analytical sequencing as previous legal thinkers and authors—the king's (in) capacity to do wrong was determined and his (non)amenability to justice followed. However, a reverse analytical ordering of the two dimensions of crown liability is also apparent in Blackstone's thinking. Blackstone's understanding of the procedural dimension—the king's amenability to justice—also dictated the understanding of the substantive dimension—the king's capacity to do wrong. As Blackstone argued, if the law provided no remedy, there could be no wrong.[12] Blackstone thus also analysed first the procedural dimension to then determine that there was no wrong. Blackstone's treatment of *the king can do no wrong* can therefore be interpreted as an analysis of, first, the substantive dimension of the model and, second, the procedural dimension, and vice versa.

In *Tobin* and *Feather*—and in Dicey's interpretation of *the king can do no wrong*—the emphasis was on the notion of the king's immunity from suit.[13] The emphasis put on the notion of the king's immunity from suit without the king being also perfect—as was the case in *Tobin*, *Feather*, and Dicey's work—shifted the focus to the second dimension of the model—the king's non-amenability to justice. The understanding of *the king can do no wrong* in *Tobin* and *Feather* was that the king's wrongful act or command did not constitute a wrong in the eyes of the law insofar as the king was concerned.

The interpretation of *the king can do no wrong* in cases on the petition of right in the nineteenth century can be seen as a confirmation of the reversal of the order of the two dimensions in understanding crown liability. The courts in *Tobin* and *Feather*, in particular, primarily understood *the king can do no wrong* as the king is not amenable to justice. In *Tobin*, Erle CJ began his interpretation of *the king can do no wrong* by stating that it is to be understood as the king 'is not liable to be sued civilly or criminally for a supposed wrong'.[14] In *Feather*, Cockburn CJ's speech was also procedurally oriented: he reasoned that to determine if the petition of right was available, the plaintiff had to demonstrate that, but for the king's immunity from suit, her claim could be the subject of an ordinary action in law or equity.[15] His statement that 'As in the eyes of the law no such wrong can be done, so, in law no right to redress can arise'[16] can appear to address first the issue of the king's capacity to do wrong so as to deny that he was amenable to justice. However, the crux of Cockburn CJ's reasoning was to render impossible the attribution of a wrong

[12] William Blackstone, *Commentaries on the Laws of England*, vol 1 (facsimile of 1765–1769 1st edn, University of Chicago Press 1979) 237.

[13] See Chapter 4, section 3.3.

[14] *Tobin v The Queen* (1864) 16 CB NS 310, 354.

[15] *Feather v The Queen* (1865) 6 B&S 257, 295.

[16] ibid 296.

to the king—'no wrongful act can be alleged against the Crown'[17]—and resulted in the king's non-amenability to justice as the primary feature of crown liability, to the detriment of the substantive dimension. In Cockburn CJ's speech, the issue of the king's capacity to do wrong was obfuscated. He did not discuss whether the king was subject to law—or the directive and invalidating powers of the law—or whether the king was perfect and consequently incapable of doing wrong. The fiction elaborated in *Tobin* and *Feather* that a wrong was not the king's in the eyes of the law circumvented the analysis of the king's capacity to do wrong—the first, substantive, dimension of the model. *The king can do no wrong* in *Tobin* and *Feather* was interpreted primarily in relation to the second dimension of the model—the king's amenability to justice—to deny that the petition of right was available against the king personally in tort.

The king can do no wrong understood as it was in *Tobin*, *Feather*, and Dicey's work can be described according to the model as being associated primarily with the notion of the king's immunity from suit and the second, procedural, dimension of crown liability—the king's non-amenability to justice. The king being immune from suit as the primary notion associated with *the king can do no wrong* pointed to the king's non-amenability to justice. Because the king was conceived as not amenable to justice, the petition of right could not be allowed against the king in *Tobin* and *Feather*. The second dimension of crown liability—the king's non-amenability to justice—was prominent in the new interpretation of *the king can do no wrong* in *Tobin* and *Feather*. The king's wrong was not a wrong in the eyes of the law and negated the king's capacity to do wrong—the first dimension of the model. A wrongful command of the king ceased to be a wrong in the king and could not be ascribed to the king. As the use of the word crown came to replace that of the word king, *the crown can do no wrong* subsequently resulted in a lack of conceptualization of the central government's capacity to issue wrongful commands and the attribution of a wrong to it.

The king can do no wrong understood as the king's wrongful command being void follows Hale's interpretation of the invalidating power of the law. Only the king's agent can be held liable. In *Tobin* and *Feather*, however, the king's wrongful command could not be a wrong attributed to the king in the eyes of the law. The legal fiction in *Tobin* and *Feather* that the king's wrong was not a wrong in the eyes of the law, because its effect was to make the king's wrongful act disappear insofar as the king was concerned, obscured the principle found in Bracton that the king had an obligation to remedy his wrong. The king's obligation to remedy his wrong was the rationale that underlay the creation of direct remedies against the king—including the petition of right—which were conceived of as common law remedies. Similarly, it was the king's role as fountain of justice and equity and the

[17] ibid 297.

presumption that he shall not be faulty in granting either that grounded equitable relief against the king.[18] The king's obligation to remedy his wrong and the presumption that the king—being fountain of justice—would not be faulty in administering justice were in contradiction with the court's interpretation of *the king can do no wrong* in *Tobin* and *Feather* that a wrong cannot be the king's.

The rationale behind the direct remedies against the king was obscured over time due to the development in legal thinking that the king's wrongful acts are void and that his agents must be sued instead. Bracton and Hale had held that the king could not commit a wrongful act and had argued that his wrongful acts were not those of a king. However, Bracton and Hale did not mean that the king's wrongful acts were not to be attributed to the king because of their wrongful character. On the contrary, the Bractonian understanding was that the wrong remained that of the king and he had to remedy it—or else have his judges remedy it—precisely because it was a wrong, and he was not entitled to do wrong. The petition of right—a remedy which Hale acknowledged was available against the king—was elaborated to address the lack of an ordinary remedy against the king when he committed a wrong.

Since *Viscount Canterbury*, *Tobin*, and *Feather*, a wrong understood as a tort cannot be imputed to the king. The effect of the courts' interpretation of *the king can do no wrong* was to obfuscate the king's capacity to do wrong—the substantive dimension of crown liability. There can be no remedies against the king as a result because a wrong is not a wrong in the king and cannot, therefore, be imputed to him. The king's capacity to do wrong has been obfuscated and he is no longer amenable to justice. To Blackstone, if there was no remedy there was no wrong; to Cockburn CJ in *Feather*, there was no remedy because there was no wrong. There has been a conflation of the king's capacity to do wrong with the king's amenability to justice. Legal thinking in relation to crown liability has been either that a wrong cannot be imputed to the king because the law offers no remedy or, as a result of a wrong not being imputable to the king due to a legal fiction that there is no wrong in the king, there can be no remedy.

In short, legal thinking in relation to the king's capacity to do wrong—the substantive dimension of the model—changed from the Bractonian and Haleian understanding that the king was capable of doing wrong to the Blackstonian eighteenth-century legal thinking that the king was incapable of doing wrong.[19] In the nineteenth century, the revival of the petition of right led the courts to depart from Hale and Blackstone's view on the availability of the petition of right against the king and to rely on an interpretation of Hale's statement in *Prerogatives* as the

[18] See *Taylor v Attorney General* (1837) 8 Sim 424, where the court found against the king on a petition of right brought in equity.

[19] As was discussed in Chapter 4, section 2.1, Blackstone's thinking was inconsistent as he also adopted the Bractonian understanding of *the king can do no wrong* as the king was not entitled to do wrong.

fiction that the king's wrongful order was not a wrong in the king.[20] The result of the nineteenth-century courts' reinterpretation of *the king can do no wrong* was that no wrong could be imputed to the king. No wrong being imputable to the king, the petition of right was not available. As no wrong could be imputed to the king, the first dimension of crown liability became irrelevant. *The king can do no wrong* has been increasingly associated with the procedural dimension of crown liability and as a result has often been assimilated in current legal thinking to the feudal privilege that the king could not be sued in his own courts.[21]

In conclusion, an analysis of the interpretations of *the king can do no wrong* in legal thinking shows that the Bractonian understanding of the concept underpinned legal thinkers' understanding of it until the nineteenth century. As a result, the first dimension of crown liability—the king's capacity to do wrong—indicated that the king was amenable to justice—the second dimension of crown liability. A first indication of the shift in the analysis of the two dimensions can be found in Blackstone's work, where he argued that if there is no remedy, there is no wrong. The reversal of the analytical sequencing of the two dimensions of crown liability was confirmed in *Tobin* and *Feather*. As emphasis was placed on the procedural dimension, the king's—and soon thereafter the crown's—capacity to do wrong was obfuscated and the possibility of ascribing a wrong to them was negated, resulting in an underdeveloped theory of the substantive dimension of the central government's liability.

2.4 Current legal thinking

Of the three notions associated with *the king can do no wrong* and which underpin crown liability, the notions of perfection of the king and of the king's immunity from suit have come to dominate legal thinking on *the king can do no wrong*. The king's status as below the law was modified throughout the nineteenth and twentieth centuries. The king is now above the law in the sense that he cannot commit a wrong—even when he does commit a wrong or issue a wrongful command, it is fictitiously not a wrong in the eyes of the law. While the notion of perfection is contested as applied to the formal notion of the crown understood as government departments, the notion of perfection of the king is conceived of as a constitutional tenet.[22] After the nineteenth-century cases on the petition of right—especially *Viscount Canterbury*, *Tobin*, and *Feather*—*the king can do no wrong* also became

[20] See Chapter 4, section 3.3.1.

[21] See eg Harlow (n 2) 17; Wade (n 11) 24–25; Sunkin (n 3) 720. *M v Home Office* (n 2) 407 (Lord Woolf).

[22] David L Keir and FH Lawson, *Cases in Constitutional Law* (FH Lawson and DJ Bentley eds, 6th edn, Clarendon Press 1979) 72; *Halsbury's Laws of England*, vol 29 (5th edn, LexisNexis 2014) [52]. See Chapter 1.

synonymous with immunity from suit.[23] In this subsection, the current status of the three notions associated with *the king can do no wrong* is discussed. The impact of the three notions' status on the conception in legal thinking of the two dimensions of crown liability—substantive and procedural—is then analysed.

2.4.1 A crown above the law, immune from suit, and perhaps perfect?

Generally, in current legal thinking, the king and government bodies are thought of not as having been created by the law but as existing independently of it.[24] As a result of nineteenth- and twentieth-century case law, the king is above statute law and only subject to it if expressly named or by necessary implication.[25] Elements of Coke's rule of interpretation of statutes as to their application to the king—a rule which was grounded in the Bractonian understanding of *the king can do no wrong*—subsisted until the end of the twentieth century.[26] However, the rule of construction which became accepted over the course of the twentieth century is that the formal notion of the crown—understood as central government departments—is above statute law unless expressly named in it or by necessary implication. As section 40(2)(f) CPA maintains the rule of construction that statutes do not apply to the crown—unless expressly named or by necessary implication—the formal notion of the crown is not automatically bound by statutes which provide for liability.[27]

Since the eighteenth century, *the king can do no wrong* has been understood in legal thinking as either the king being incapable of doing wrong—due to Blackstone's notion of perfection—or as the king being capable of doing wrong but not being accountable due to the king's wrong being non-existent in the eyes of the law following the fiction developed in *Tobin* and *Feather*.[28] To Hale, the invalidating effect of the law was such that the wrongful act or command of the king was invalidated because the king did not have the authority to do or command a wrong. In *Tobin* and *Feather*, not only was the king's wrongful command invalid,

[23] See eg William Reynell Anson, *The Law and Custom of the Constitution*, vol 2 part 2 (A Berriedale Keith ed, 4th edn, Clarendon Press 1935) 336; William Edward Hearn, *The Government of England: Its Structure and Its Development* (2nd edn, Robertson 1886) 20–21; AV Dicey, *Lectures Introductory to the Study of the Law of the Constitution: The Oxford Edition of Dicey*, vol 1 (JWF Allison ed, OUP 2013) 21.

[24] David Howarth, 'The Politics of Public Law' in Mark Elliott and David Feldman (eds), *The Cambridge Companion to Public Law* (CUP 2015) 44, 46. cf Wade, to whom 'the Crown, i.e. the Executive, is under the law': ECS Wade, 'Introduction' in AV Dicey, *Introduction to the Study of the Constitution* (10th edn, Macmillan 1959) c.

[25] *Province of Bombay v Municipal Corporation of the City of Bombay* [1947] AC 58 (PC).

[26] See Chapter 4, section 3.1; Marie-France Fortin, 'Revisiting the Application of Statutes to the Crown: A Historical Constitutional Approach' (2021) 3 J CommonwL 271.

[27] s 40(2) CPA: 'Except as therein otherwise expressly provided, nothing in this Act shall: — . . . (f) affect any rules of evidence or any presumption relating to the extent to which the Crown is bound by any Act of Parliament; . . . '. See Harry Street, 'The Effects of Statutes upon the Rights and Liabilities of the Crown' (1948) 7 UTLJ 357, 382–83; Sue Arrowsmith, *Civil Liability and Public Authorities* (Earlsgate 1992) 158–60; Paul Craig, *Administrative Law* (9th edn, Sweet & Maxwell 2021) 900–01. See also *R(Black) v Secretary of State for Justice* (2017) UKSC 81, [2018] AC 215.

[28] *Tobin* (n 14); *Feather* (n 15). See Chapter 4, section 3.3.

it also ceased to be a wrong in law as far as the king was concerned. Hale's theory that the king was subject to the directive and invalidating powers of the law was undermined as a result.

As to the notion of the king's perfection, since the end of the nineteenth century, it is either expressly accepted, implied, or denied any current relevance without being formally rejected.[29]

The notion of the king's immunity from suit has been extended to the crown understood as government departments, an immunity lifted as late as 1947 in the United Kingdom with the adoption of the CPA—although not completely.[30] The crown's immunity from suit is lifted only to the extent that the cause of action falls within the ambit of section 2 CPA—there is otherwise no residual liability,[31] for instance when systemic failures occur. The petition of right was deprived of its essence as a direct remedy in tort against the king in legal thinking in the nineteenth century before it was abolished by the CPA in 1947. There can be no injunction against the crown in civil proceedings in tort.[32] As Lord Woolf asserted in *M v Home Office*, the immunity extends to government departments and high public officers, including the Attorney General, when they act in their representative capacity.[33] As was made clear in *Raleigh v Goschen*, a public official cannot be sued in tort at common law in her representative capacity only.[34] She can only be sued for the wrong of a subordinate if she was directly involved in committing the wrong or in ordering or authorizing it. The understanding of crown liability at common law evidenced in *Raleigh v Goschen* is that the crown cannot be sued and as a result, officials cannot be sued in their official capacity of agents 'representing the Crown, or the Government'.[35] A similar conclusion was reached in *Trawnik*, where a German homeowner sued the Ministry of Defence in the United Kingdom for nuisance caused by a firing range on an airfield occupied by the crown in Berlin. A certificate had been issued under section 40(2)(b) to certify that the matter did not relate to Her Majesty's government in the United Kingdom and effectively barred Trawnik from suing the crown under the CPA. Trawnik therefore sued the crown at common law and framed his recourse as a declaration of rights. In finding in favour of the crown on the basis that it could not be sued in tort at common law, the Court of Appeal reasoned that the Attorney General as representative of the crown could not be added as a party to a declaration that the crown cannot commit a wrong.[36] To the Court of Appeal, the nuisance that was complained of 'cannot be

[29] See *Halsbury's Laws of England* (n 22) [52].

[30] See section 4.2.1.

[31] See eg *Trawnik v Gordon* (1985) 1 WLR 532 (CA); *Morgan v Ministry of Justice* (2010) EWHC 2248 (QB), (2010) All ER (D) 117 (Sep); Peter Cane, *Controlling Administrative Power: An Historical Comparison* (CUP 2016) 373–74.

[32] ss 21 and 23(2)(c) CPA.

[33] s 21(2) CPA. See also *M v Home Office* (n 2) 412–13 (Lord Woolf).

[34] *Raleigh v Goschen* [1898] 1 Ch 73, 79.

[35] ibid.

[36] *Trawnik* (n 31) 548 (Lawton LJ).

a legal wrong *by the Crown* since, apart from the Crown Proceedings Act 1947, the Crown could not commit a tort'.[37]

Lord Woolf's speech in the case of *M v Home Office* offers an excellent illustration of, first, the confusion surrounding *the king can do no wrong* and, second, that the crown's liability at common law results in an inconsistency between judicial review and civil proceedings. First, that Lord Woolf understood *the king can do no wrong* in different ways is apparent from his speech in that seminal case. To him, 'that the Sovereign could do no wrong did not mean that a servant of the Crown could do no wrong'.[38] In his mind, therefore, *the king can do no wrong* appears to refer to both the king's immunity from suit and to the idea that the king was incapable of doing wrong whereas his servant was. That Lord Woolf understood *the king can do no wrong* as the king's immunity from suit is also apparent from his discussion that there was nonetheless the possibility of having recourse to the petition of right against the crown.[39] But Lord Woolf also understood *the king can do no wrong* as 'the immunity of the Crown' extending to the governmental apparatus under the guise of the 'historic maxim' that 'the Crown can do no wrong'.[40] To Lord Woolf, the fact that officials could be sued personally for a wrong committed as they were acting in their official capacity could be reconciled with the maxim that 'the Crown can do no wrong' on the basis that 'as the Crown could no wrong, the Crown could not be considered to have authorised the doing of wrong, so the tortfeasor was not acting with the authority of the Crown'.[41] As is apparent from this statement, Lord Woolf also understood *the king can do no wrong* as the king's and the crown's incapacity to do wrong and, consequently, as the absence of royal authority which could serve as a defence to officers sued personally for acts performed in the exercise of their official functions. But the need to reconcile *the crown can do no wrong* with the possibility of suing crown officials personally for acts performed in the exercise of their functions can only arise if 'the Crown can do no wrong' is understood as an immunity from suit that extended to the officials and to the government. Were *the king can do no wrong* understood in Lord Woolf's speech as conferring an immunity from suit on the person of the king only, no need would arise to reconcile the 'Crown's immunity' with individual officers' liability in tort. The confusion as to the identity and contours of the 'crown' that issued the wrongful orders to the officers, but that is also incapable of issuing wrongful orders because it cannot be considered to have authorised the doing of wrong, becomes apparent. *The crown can do no wrong* is understood primarily as immunity from suit for the king and the government in Lord Woolf's speech. It is also understood as incapacity to do wrong, but who is incapable of doing wrong besides the king remains unclear.

[37] ibid 552 (Browne-Wilkinson LJ).
[38] *M v Home Office* (n 2) 408.
[39] ibid.
[40] ibid 409–10.
[41] ibid 410.

Second, since *M v Home Office*, the crown is a corporation sole in judicial review proceedings: an injunction and a finding of contempt can be made against a government department or a minister in her representative capacity precisely because they are not the crown. In the realm of judicial review proceedings, the crown is a corporation sole of one person—the king—leaving government departments and ministers subject to injunctions and findings of contempt of court. On the other hand, it is the nineteenth-century formal notion of the crown (as a corporation aggregate) which is referred to in civil proceedings. In civil proceedings, as Lord Woolf makes plain in *M v Home Office*, ministers and government departments cannot be subject to injunctions in their representative capacity and, as was decided in *Raleigh v Goschen*, they cannot be sued in tort at common law on the sole basis that they are representatives of the crown.[42]

In short, ministers and government departments are the crown in civil proceedings, while they are not part of the crown and are merely its servants in judicial review proceedings. The seventeenth-century constitutional understanding of *the king can do no wrong* prevails in the realm of judicial review while the confusion surrounding the concept, caused by the ignorance of its evolution in legal thinking, is still present in civil proceedings.

2.4.2 Status of the two dimensions

The result of the evolution of legal thinking in relation to *the king can do no wrong* throughout the nineteenth century is that the king has been not only immune from suit, but also that as no wrong could be imputed to the king, his capacity to do wrong has been obscured.

Moreover, due to the late nineteenth-century formal notion of the crown understood as central government—high public officers in their representative capacity and government departments—central government came to be equated with the 'king' in *the king can do no wrong* and to partake of the king's immunities, including immunity from suit. The result of the confusion surrounding the notion of the crown and its simultaneous association with both the king and high public officers and government departments has been a modified understanding of *the king can do no wrong*, different from the understanding developed in the context of the seventeenth-century constitutional settlement. The association of the king with central government under the umbrella of the term 'crown' led to the opacity surrounding the king's capacity to do wrong being extended to the formal notion of the crown understood as high public officers in their representative capacity and government departments. While Bracton and Hale conceived of the king as capable of doing wrong, no wrong is now to be imputed to the king or to high public officers as representing the king or to government departments at common law.[43]

42 ibid 412–13; *Raleigh v Goschen* (n 34).
43 *Trawnik* (n 31).

While the petition of right and other remedies were created to fill the gap left by the king's immunity from suit when the king was conceived of as capable to do wrong in legal thinking, the eighteenth- and nineteenth-century understandings that the king was incapable of doing wrong and therefore not amenable to justice—and later that a wrong was not a wrong in the king in the eyes of the law—rendered the petition of right meaningless in the realm of tort liability.

The current state of legal thinking is apparent from *Matthews v Ministry of Defence*, a case on the crown's immunity from suit in negligence claims brought forward by ex-servicemen on the basis of section 10 CPA—a provision repealed in 1987 but which was still in force when Mr Matthews, then an electrical mechanic, was in service and exposed to asbestos. In discussing the crown's immunity, Lord Millett said that the principle that *the king can do no wrong* was long established in constitutional law and resulted in the crown not being liable in tort at common law.[44] Lord Bingham also opined that 'Few common law rules were better-established or more unqualified than that which precluded any claim in tort against the Crown, and since there was no wrong of which a claimant could complain (because the King could do no wrong) relief by petition of right was not available'.[45] It appears from Lord Bingham's speech that *the king can do no wrong* does not merely convey immunity from suit. There can be no liability because there is absence of a wrong in law: a wrong is fictitiously not a wrong in the king and cannot be attributed to him (*Tobin* and *Feather*); hence the impossibility even of having recourse to the petition of right. Lord Bingham's speech highlights how *the king can do no wrong* is now associated in legal thought with the king's non-amenability to justice, the second dimension of the model. His use of both the words king and crown also illustrates how the fiction that there is no wrong in the king was passed on to the central government as if the two were interchangeable.

That the king is immune from suit figured in the seventeenth-century constitutional settlement understanding of *the king can do no wrong* as reflected in Hale's interpretation. However, that a wrong was not to be imputed to the king because he was perfect and incapable of doing wrong (Blackstone), or as the result of the fiction elaborated by the courts in *Tobin* and *Feather* that there is no wrong in the king, is a relatively recent construct. Lord Bingham's claim that *the king can do no wrong* is understood as the crown cannot be sued in tort—at common law—and is well-established should be contrasted with Neill LJ's speech in *Mulcahy*, where the two principles referred to—the king cannot be sued in his own courts and *the king can do no wrong*—were said to be of 'doubtful origin'.[46] To Lord Bingham, there was historically no right to claim in tort against the crown: 'It was clear that such claim

[44] *Matthews v Ministry of Defence* (2003) UKHL 4, [2003] 1 AC 1163 [81].
[45] ibid [4].
[46] *Mulcahy v Ministry of Defence* [1996] QB 732 (CA) 740.

was absolutely barred.'[47] While it has been 'clear' since Bracton's days that there can be no ordinary action against the king, it was as late as the mid-nineteenth century, in *Tobin* and *Feather*, that *the king can do no wrong* was interpreted as a fiction that there was no wrong in the king, that no wrong was to be attributed to the king as a result, and that the petition of right could no longer, therefore, be resorted to against the king personally for a wrong committed by his servant. The omission of the history of the petition of right and of the king's capacity to do wrong in legal thinking prior and pursuant to the constitutional struggles of the seventeenth century is characteristic of current legal thinking in relation to *the king can do no wrong*. The fact that *the king can do no wrong* was reinterpreted in *Tobin* and *Feather* in the context of a petition of right against the king personally is also omitted from the analysis. The passing of *the king can do no wrong* understood—following *Tobin* and *Feather*—as the absence of a wrong in the king personally to the formal notion of the crown is overlooked. For instance, Lawton LJ in *Trawnik* said that 'it is trite law that the Crown cannot be sued in tort' and proceeded to cite *Viscount Canterbury* and *Adams v Naylor*.[48] Lawton LJ did not note that the former case related to a petition of right against the monarch personally while in the latter, a civil servant was sued by way of ordinary action, having been selected as a nominated defendant by a government department.

To conclude, *the king can do no wrong* understood as conveying the crown's ancient immunity from suit is an ahistorical basis for the crown's absolute immunity from suit at common law. *The king can do no wrong* was first interpreted as a fiction that there is no wrong in the king and that, therefore, the king is not amenable to justice even by way of the petition of right in the nineteenth century only. Even then, *the king can do no wrong* was interpreted in the context of petitions of right against the monarch. The effect of the nineteenth-century courts' interpretation of *the king can do no wrong* was to protect the king personally from suit, but it was not to allow the king to do wrong either personally or indirectly through his servants. With the confusion surrounding the notion of the crown from the second half of the nineteenth century, the crown understood as the king personally became the formal notion of the crown understood as central government—high public officers in their representative capacity and government departments. *The king can do no wrong* became *the crown can do no wrong*, with the result that ministers and other instruments which would have been held liable under the seventeenth-century constitutional settlement understanding of *the king can do no wrong* for executing the king's commands are no longer so liable at common law, because they are associated with the crown.

[47] *Matthews* (n 44) [15]. See also Lord Browne-Wilkinson's speech in *Trawnik* (n 31) 550, where he said that the CPA rendered the crown liable in tort for the first time.

[48] *Trawnik* (n 31) 548. See Chapter 4, section 3.3.

3 *The king can do no wrong* as an ahistorical basis for the crown's absolute immunity from suit

The analysis of the evolution of *the king can do no wrong* in legal thinking demonstrates that the claim that it always conveyed the king's incapacity to do wrong and non-amenability to justice is unfounded. As will be further demonstrated in this section, the immunity from suit at common law of high public officers in their representative capacity and government departments is not supported by a historically informed understanding of *the king can do no wrong*.

Until the *Mersey Docks* cases,[49] the reason why public institutions were immune in the nineteenth century was not related to *the king can do no wrong* but to their lack of corporate status or capacity, the absence of separate funds, and the fact that they were not the employers of crown servants but merely fellow crown servants.[50] In *Trawnik*, for example, an action under the CPA was not available and an action at common law against the Ministry of Defence was found to be impossible because the Ministry was not a person or corporate entity known to the common law.[51] Having no corporate existence, the Ministry could not be sued.

The immunity from vicarious liability which had been granted to public officers who bought their proprietary charges in the eighteenth century and were not to be held liable for the wrongs of the lower officials and servants under their supervision[52] was also transposed, in the nineteenth and twentieth centuries, to government departments conceived of as crown servants. As was mentioned in Chapter 4, public officers since the eighteenth century enjoyed an immunity from suit for the wrongs of inferior officers.[53] As Lord Mansfield noted, the Postmaster General was, like all other public officials such as the Lords Commissioners of the Treasury, the Commissioners of the Customs and Excise, and the Auditors of the Exchequer, not liable for any negligence or misconduct of the inferior officers in their department.[54] As public officials were crown servants, they could not be sued for the wrongs of fellow crown servants.[55] As crown servants are not liable for the wrong of other crown servants,[56] government departments—being themselves conceived of as crown servants—were not liable for the wrongs of other crown servants.[57]

[49] *Mersey Docks Trustees v Cameron* (1864) 11 HLC 443; *Mersey Docks Trustees v Gibbs* (1866) 1 LR 93 (HL).

[50] See Chapter 4, section 3.3.2.

[51] *Trawnik* (n 31) 547 (Lawton LJ).

[52] Sheriffs and local officers remained vicariously liable and subject to special liabilities in damages: Stuart Anderson, 'Public Law' in WR Cornish and others (eds), *The Oxford History of the Laws of England*, vol XI (OUP 2010) 370; Bradley Selway, 'Of Kings and Officers: The Judicial Development of Public Law' (2005) 33 FL Rev 187, 197, 215. See Chapter 2, section 2.3.4.

[53] See Chapter 4, sections 3.3.2 and 3.3.3.

[54] *Whitfield v Lord Le Despencer* (1778) 2 Cowp 754, 765–66; see Selway (n 52) 215.

[55] See Chapter 4, sections 3.3.2 and 3.3.3.

[56] See *Bainbridge v Postmaster-General* [1906] 1 KB 178.

[57] Glanville Llewelyn Williams, *Crown Proceedings: An Account of Civil Proceedings by and against the Crown as Affected by the Crown Proceedings Act, 1947* (Stevens 1948) 32, 35; JAG Griffith, 'Public

There was a conceptual slippage as the immunity of individual public officials was transposed to government departments on the basis that they were also crown servants, although they were not individuals but institutions.

The reasons for government departments' immunity from suit were not related to *the king can do no wrong* until the later part of the nineteenth century. After the rejection in *Mersey Docks* of the broad 'public purpose immunity' which had spanned the crown and other public institutions,[58] another basis for the immunity of the crown—understood as central government departments—was grounded in *the king can do no wrong*. There was a change in the understanding of the phrase. For most of the nineteenth century, courts understood *the king can do no wrong* as conveying the king's absolute immunity from suit. In *Feather*, a case on the application of the petition of right, only the king was sued to and Cockburn CJ opined that the law granted immunity from suit to 'the person of the Sovereign'.[59] The liability of government departments was not at issue. It was only at the turn of the twentieth century that government departments were said to be immune from suit at common law because they represented the crown. That central government was conceived of as immune from suit because it represented the crown was perhaps a result of the 'novel sense of sanctity' which surrounded ministers and government departments in the latter part of the nineteenth century.[60] In 1898, in *Raleigh v Goschen*, high public officers in their official capacity were said not to be liable for the wrong committed by lower officials, on the basis that the former represented the crown.[61] In the 1921 case of *Macgregor*, *the king can do no wrong* was taken to mean that public departments and officers were not to be liable because they represented the king.[62] Similarly, in the 1946 case of *Adams v Naylor* the government department involved was called crown and was said not to be liable.[63] In 1984, in *Trawnik*, the Attorney General was conceived of as a representative of the crown. As a result, he could not be joined as a party to declaration proceedings to the effect that the crown could not use or permit its servants to use land so as to cause a nuisance because the crown could not commit a legal wrong.[64] While the seventeenth-century constitutional settlement understanding of *the king can do no wrong* was that a minister or servant of the king such as the Attorney General was to be held liable for a wrong ordered by the king and could not invoke the king's command

Corporations as Crown Servants' (1952) 9 UTLJ 169, 176, 191; Tom Cornford, 'Legal Remedies against the Crown before and after M' in Maurice Sunkin and Sebastian Payne (eds), *The Nature of the Crown: A Legal and Political Analysis* (OUP 1999) 239–40.

[58] Anderson (n 52) 372–76. See Chapter 4, section 3.3.2.
[59] *Feather* (n 15) 295.
[60] Stephen Sedley, 'The Crown in Its Own Courts' in Christopher F Forsyth and Ivan Hare (eds), *The Golden Metwand and the Crooked Cord: Essays in Honour of Sir William Wade QC* (OUP 1999) 258.
[61] *Raleigh v Goschen* (n 34).
[62] *Macgregor v Lord Advocate* (1921) SC 847.
[63] *Adams v Naylor* (1946) AC 543, 2 All ER 241 (HL).
[64] *Trawnik* (n 31) 552 (Lord Browne-Wilkinson).

as a defence, the opposite result was reached in *Trawnik*. The Court of Appeal's reasoning that, as the crown could do no wrong, the Attorney General could not be sued in his representative capacity of the crown was diametrically opposed to the seventeenth-century constitutional settlement understanding that the king's minister is to be sued in lieu of the king precisely because she acts for the king and that the king himself cannot be sued. The court's reasoning in *Trawnik* that as the crown could do no wrong, the Attorney General could not be sued in his representative capacity of the crown can be contrasted with Lord Templeman's speech in *M v Home Office* to the effect that 'The judges cannot enforce the law against the Crown as monarch because the Crown as monarch can do no wrong but judges enforce the law against the Crown as executive and against the individuals who from time to time represent the Crown'.[65] Lord Templeman's understanding of *the king can do no wrong* as the monarch is immune from the coercion of the law but not the crown understood as central government—including ministers—contradicts the understanding of *the king can do no wrong* in *Trawnik*.

Nineteenth- and twentieth-century developments fundamentally altered the seventeenth-century constitutional understanding of *the king can do no wrong* that the king's instruments are liable while the king is immune from suit. Under the seventeenth-century constitutional settlement understanding of *the king can do no wrong*, the king's instruments—his ministers and crown servants, including government departments—must be liable because the king is immune. The seventeenth-century constitutional settlement understanding of *the king can do no wrong* was altered by conceiving of government departments—and even public officers, including ministers—not as instruments of the king, but rather as the crown.

In defining the formal notion of the crown as central government, the courts also created an inconsistency. High public officers in their representative capacity and government departments were found not to be liable because they represented the crown. Yet high public officers and government departments were also said not to be vicariously liable for the wrongs of other crown servants because high public officers and government departments were themselves crown servants. The reasoning for granting immunity from suit to central government was flawed—high public officers in their representative capacity and government departments were immune because they were both the crown and crown servants.

In short, there were historically distinct rationales for why central government was not found to be liable at common law. The first rationale for the absence of liability dates to the nineteenth century and was technical. It was grounded first in the lack of corporate status of certain government departments or entities. Second, high public officers and government departments were not conceived of as the master of the crown servants as they were simply their fellow crown servants. They

[65] *M v Home Office* (n 2) 395.

could not, therefore, be sued for a wrong committed by a fellow servant. Lastly, funds were not allocated to government departments and the payment of compensatory damages would have to have come out of the consolidated fund, a result the courts thought improper for them to reach without Parliament's assent.[66] The second rationale for the lack of liability of central government was developed in the latter part of the nineteenth century and was caused by the *Mersey Docks* cases and the confusion the use of the word 'crown' entailed. The crown was the king. The government was also referred to as the crown. The use of the middle term 'crown' to refer to both the king and government led the government to partake of the king's immunities. The syllogism was flawed, however, as the 'crown' as a middle term did not have the same meaning in the two premises. The king is the crown in the medieval sense that he is the head of the body politic[67] or the crown as a corporation sole in Coke's understanding in *Sutton's Hospital*.[68] In contrast, the formal notion of the crown first elaborated in the nineteenth century referred to central government. The crown could refer to the king himself or to central government—high public officers and departments—executing the king's commands. The formal notion of the crown—central government—was confused with the king—also referred to as the 'crown'. As a result, central government became immune on the basis that the 'crown' can do no wrong.

The twentieth-century courts' extension of the king's immunity from suit to government departments—from *the king can do no wrong* to *the crown can do no wrong*—could be conceived of as a policy decision. It was argued at the beginning of the twentieth century, for example, that for the king's exemption from the application of statutes to have any effect, it had to extend to the crown in the formal sense of government departments and high public officers in their representative capacity.[69] A similar argument that the crown's immunity from suit had to extend to government departments to have any effect could be taken to have been made by the courts at the beginning of the twentieth century. Legal authors contemporary to the period, however, blamed the confusion entailed by the term 'crown' instead of 'king'.[70]

Current understanding of *the king can do no wrong* in legal thinking is based on the belief that that understanding is historically grounded, as is evidenced by Lord

[66] See Chapter 4, section 3.3.2.2.

[67] Ernst H Kantorowicz, *The King's Two Bodies, A Study in Medieval Political Theology* (first published 1957, Princeton UP 2016) 225; JWF Allison, *The English Historical Constitution: Continuity, Change and European Effects* (CUP 2007) 55–56.

[68] *Sutton's Hospital Case* (1612) 10 Co Rep 23a, 29b. Coke's understanding of the notion of the crown is not clear, as he also accepted the legal doctrine of the two bodies of the king and the notion of the crown as the king's body politic encompassing the kingdom in *Calvin's Case* (1608) 7 Co Rep 1a, 10a; see Marie-France Fortin, 'The King's Two Bodies and the Crown a Corporation Sole: Historical Dualities in English Legal Thinking' (2021) HEI 1, doi: 10.1080/01916599.2021.1914934 5-10.

[69] Harrison Moore, 'Liability for Acts of Public Servants' (1907) 23 LQR 12, 15–16.

[70] Pitt Cobbett, '"The Crown" as Representing "The State"' (1903) 1 CL Rev 23, 27; Robert Dorsey Watkins, *The State as a Party Litigant* (Johns Hopkins Press 1927) 12.

Bingham and Lord Millet's speeches in *Matthews*,[71] discussed earlier, and by the fact that the king cannot be sued in his own courts and *the king can do no wrong* are referred to indiscriminately as immemorial principles.[72] As has been demonstrated in this book, the understanding of *the king can do no wrong* evolved historically in English legal thinking. The king conceived of as not amenable to justice, and whose capacity to do wrong is consequently denied in law, is an idea which dates only to the second half of the nineteenth century. That the formal notion of the crown understood as central government is immune from suit because the king's immunities were extended to it is a product of late nineteenth-century conceptual confusion. The evolution of *the king can do no wrong* in legal thinking does not provide support for the claim that central government's immunity from suit is dictated by centuries of legal thinking.

To claim, on the one hand, that high public officers in their representative capacity and government departments are immune from suit at common law because that immunity is historically rooted is to base one's argument on an erroneous understanding of the evolution in legal thought of *the king can do no wrong*.

In light of the evolution of *the king can do no wrong* and its continuity in legal thinking, it cannot support the proposition that the formal notion of the crown's immunity from suit at common law is grounded in historically entrenched notions. *The king can do no wrong* being invoked as a medieval maxim to justify the crown's blanket immunity is a misuse of history.

4 Revisiting crown liability

In this section, an analysis of the current understanding of crown liability is conducted. Based on a historically informed understanding of *the king can do no wrong*, Dicey's influence on our current understanding of crown liability and the consequences it entails for the UK Parliament's Crown Proceedings Act 1947 (CPA) are scrutinized. There are other possible case studies of the consequences of adopting a historically informed approach to *the king can do no wrong* and of revisiting our understanding of crown liability but consequences for the CPA were chosen due to the prevalent association in current legal thinking between *the king can do no wrong* and crown immunity from suit.

Canadian law reflects English law in the realm of crown liability. The Canadian federal statute governing crown liability, the Crown Liability and Proceedings Act[73]—first adopted in 1953 as the Crown Liability Act[74]—is modelled on the

[71] *Matthews* (n 44) [4], [81].

[72] *M v Home Office* (n 2) 407 (Lord Woolf); *Rahmatullah* (n 2) [16] (Lady Hale). See eg Watkins (n 70) 192; Wade (n 11) 24.

[73] RSC 1985, c C-50.

[74] SC 1952-53, c 30. See Peter W Hogg, Patrick Monahan, and Wade K Wright, *Liability of the Crown* (4th edn, Carswell 2011) 8–10.

UK Parliament's CPA. The Canadian Crown Liability and Proceedings Act's predecessor, the Petition of Right Act 1875,[75] subsequently re-enacted the following year,[76] was itself very similar to the UK Parliament's Petitions of Right Act 1860.[77] Nineteenth-century English courts' understanding of *the king can do no wrong* has also been adopted and cited to by Canadian courts.[78] The Privy Council, on appeal from Canadian courts, relied on the English nineteenth-century understanding of *the king can do no wrong* to interpret Canadian legislation on crown proceedings,[79] instead of adopting a different approach as it did for Australian colonies only a year later.[80] Observations and analysis pertaining to the CPA in this chapter will therefore apply, mutatis mutandis, to Canadian federal law on crown liability.

4.1 Diceyan understanding of crown liability in legal thinking

The current understanding of crown liability has for its cornerstone the notion of equality before the law elaborated by Dicey, according to which individual crown servants are suable according to ordinary law before ordinary courts. The result of Dicey's influential notion of equality before the law in our current understanding of crown liability is that the fault is attributed to individual civil servants, not the government itself.

4.1.1 Dicey's emphasis on individual officers' liability

The king's status as below the law was modified throughout the nineteenth and twentieth centuries. The king is now above the law. He cannot commit a wrong in the sense that even when he does commit a wrong or issue a wrongful command, it is fictitiously not a wrong in the eyes of the law. He is not bound by a statute unless expressly named in it or by necessary implication.[81] With Dicey's rule of law and the emphasis on the notion of equality before the law, another change occurred. The idea that an individual officer is personally liable for her wrongdoing could be traced back to *Lane v Cotton* and was declared to be one 'of the most vital doctrines of our constitutional law'.[82] However, it was Dicey's notion of equality between the

[75] 38 Vict c 12 (SC 1875).

[76] Petition of Right Act 1876, 39 Vict c 27 (SC 1876).

[77] 23 & 24 Vict c 34.

[78] See eg *Halifax City Railway v R* (1877) 2 Ex CR 433; *R v McFarlane* (1882) 7 SCR 216; *R v McLeod* (1883) 8 SCR 1 (cf Fournier J, dissenting); *R v Eldorado Nuclear Ltd; R v Uranium Canada Ltd* [1983] 2 SCR 551; *Arishenkoff v British Columbia* 2005 BCCA 481.

[79] *Windsor and Annapolis Railway Company v The Queen and the Western Counties Railway Company* (1886) 11 App Cas 607 (PC).

[80] *Farnell v Bowman* (1887) 12 App Cas 643 (PC); see Chapter 6, section 4.1.1.

[81] *Province of Bombay v Municipal Corporation of the City of Bombay* (n 25). See Chapter 4, section 3.1.

[82] *Lane v Cotton* (1701) 1 LD Raym 646 (KB) (91 ER 1332); Moore (n 69) 15–16.

king's officers and ordinary citizens which became the reference point in conceptualizing crown liability.[83]

Dicey's notion of equality before the law as part of his interpretation of the rule of law was criticized. Dicey's emphasis on individual officers' liability according to ordinary law before ordinary tribunals was disapproved of on the ground that he ignored the numerous immunities the crown enjoys, that public officials and public authorities dispose of prerogative and statutory powers which a private individual does not possess, and that the very nature of government implies a relationship of unequals.[84] Criticism of Dicey's treatment of equality before the law is in part due to the confusion surrounding the term 'crown' and the development in the nineteenth century of the formal notion of the crown understood as central government.[85]

Equality between officers of the king and ordinary individuals was not the relationship which grounded the conceptualization of the king's liability prior to the nineteenth century. Historically in legal thought, prior to current forms of modern government, the king was above the people.[86] It was the king's superiority, the fact that he was not an equal to his subjects, which led to the absence of ordinary actions against the king as there were between subjects.[87] The king was the ultimate feudal lord and God's chosen. The king was above all others and the law granted him special privileges. Yet the king was—like all his subjects—under God and the law. He had to remedy a wrong and wronged individuals could sue to the king with the petition of right and other remedies.[88]

The king was above his subjects, but he was also—like all his subjects—equally under the law and not entitled to do wrong. The privileges which the law granted to the king put him in a more favourable position but that special status of the king *vis-à-vis* his subjects was conceptually different from the king's status in relation to law itself in the realm of liability. The king's privileges did not alter the fact that he was under the law and capable of doing a wrong—the first, substantive, dimension of crown liability. Although privileges exempted the king from being sued by ordinary action in his own courts, they could not negate entirely the king's amenability to justice—the second, procedural, dimension of crown liability. Privileges and liability raised two distinct issues. Privileges were the result of the unequal status of the king *vis-à-vis* his subjects, but the king's liability—his capacity to do

[83] Hogg, Monahan, and Wright (n 74) 2–4; Mark Elliott and Jason Varuhas, *Administrative Law: Text and Materials* (5th edn, OUP 2017) 586–87.

[84] Ivor Jennings, *The Law and the Constitution* (5th edn, University of London Press 1959) 312; Wade (n 24) cxvi; Martin Loughlin, 'The State, the Crown and the Law' in Maurice Sunkin and Sebastian Payne (eds), *The Nature of the Crown: A Legal and Political Analysis* (OUP 1999) 64; Richard Rawlings and Carol Harlow, *Law and Administration* (3rd edn, CUP 2009) 16–18; Hogg, Monahan, and Wright (n 74) 4–5.

[85] See Chapter 4, sections 3.3.2 and 3.3.3.

[86] Martin Loughlin, 'The Constitutional Imagination' (2015) 78 MLR 1, 4.

[87] See Chapter 2, section 2.3.

[88] Hogg, Monahan, and Wright (n 74) 4–5. See Chapter 2, sections 2.1 and 2.3.

wrong and his amenability to justice, the substantive and procedural dimensions of crown liability[89]—did not depend on the equality of his status in relation to his subjects. The king's liability was underpinned by a different rationale, that of the king under the law and not entitled to do wrong. Even his prerogatives could not be used to do wrong.[90] As Broom explained, 'although . . . the king is greatly favoured by the law, being exempted from the operation of various rules applicable to the subject, he is on the whole, and essentially, beneath not superior to it' and 'he is under, and not above the laws, and is bound by them equally with his subjects'.[91]

Under the Bractonian understanding of crown liability, the king—although he was above all others—was, like all others, subject to law, capable of doing wrong, and answerable for his wrongs although not through ordinary action. The king in Hale's interpretation of *the king can do no wrong* was under the directive and invalidating force of the law, although not the coercive force. With the nineteenth-century cases of *Tobin* and *Feather*, the king's wrong became not a wrong in the eyes of the law. The king's status as under the directive power of the law was undermined because his wrongful acts and commands were no longer wrongs in law. The king—who was already above the coercive power of the law following Hale's theory—became above the directive power of the law. With the Diceyan understanding of crown liability, the notion of equality before the law of the king's individual officials was emphasized but the king himself, and the formal notion of the crown understood as central government, were not subjected to law.

Dicey highlighted the king's immunity from suit when he discussed *the king can do no wrong*.[92] Dicey pointed out that an action lies for a wrong done to a subject 'against governors of colonies, against secretaries of state, against officers who have tried by Court-martial persons not subject to military law, against every kind of official high or low'.[93] As is clear from Dicey's account of the officers liable before ordinary courts according to the law of the land, the king and government departments were excluded from the list. Dicey's notion of equality before the law applied only to the king's agents' individual liability.[94] The issue of government departments' liability was put into focus in Dicey's Note XII to the seventh edition of his lectures.[95] In that note, the absence of equality before the law in relation to the 'Crown, or in other words, against the Government',[96] was not raised by Dicey. Dicey stated that no action nor petition of right could lie against the government. In practice, Dicey added, little injustice flew from the unavailability of the petition of right because the crown agreed most of the time to pay for its agent's

89 See Chapter 1.
90 *Willion v Berkley* (n 8); cf *The King v John Cotton, Esquire* (1751) Park 112 (Exch).
91 Herbert Broom, *A Selection of Legal Maxims* (10th edn, Sweet & Maxwell 1939) 18, 22.
92 Dicey (n 23) 21.
93 ibid 123.
94 ibid 412.
95 ibid.
96 ibid.

actions.[97] Dicey did not attempt to reconcile the government's unequal position with his concept of the rule of law, other than to minimize that inequality's practical importance.

Dicey's change of focus from the king's liability to his officers' was influential. The king's agents' liability became the focus of crown liability because it involved being suable according to ordinary law before ordinary tribunals and was congruent with Dicey's notion of equality before the law. Dicey's emphasis on the individual liability of crown servants was, however, a gloss on history. His omission of the government in discussing his notion of equality before the law overlooked an important aspect of constitutional history: prior to the development of the common law with regard to individual public officers' liability in the eighteenth century, individual officers' wrongs were to be righted by the king. Such was Dicey's influence, however, that even Maitland's understanding of *the king can do no wrong* has Diceyan traits:

> [F]rom Henry III's reign we get both from Bracton and from the Plea Rolls the most positive statements that the king cannot be sued or punished. In this meaning, the maxim that the king can do no wrong is fully admitted. If the king breaks the law then the only remedy is a petition addressed to him that he will give redress.
>
> . . .
>
> The law was left as it was, as it is at this very moment that against the king law has no coercive power, it has no punishment for the king, it cannot compel him to make redress—or, as we say, the king can do no wrong. It was left to later ages to work out consistently the other side of our modern doctrine, namely, that though the king can neither be punished nor sued, no other person, no servant of the king, is protected against the ordinary consequences of an unlawful act by the king's command.[98]

To Maitland, like Dicey, *the king can do no wrong* related to procedural immunity from the law, and not to the king's status as above or below the law. Maitland also implied a 'modern' Diceyan meaning of *the king can do no wrong* when he explained that the king's immunity from suit conveyed by the maxim is complemented by the absence of such an immunity for the king's officers. Maitland, like Dicey, omits to say that officers could be sued in the Middle Ages, but he is right to suggest that it is Dicey who later gave this individual officer's liability component of crown liability a theoretical underpinning, by elaborating the equality aspect of the notion of rule of law.

[97] ibid 412–13.
[98] Maitland (n 2) 100, 102–03.

4.1.2 The king's officials' individual liability from a historical perspective

In addition to the king's status as above the law since the nineteenth century, only the king's officials were to be liable in tort following the nineteenth-century trilogy of cases on the petition of right. The emphasis Dicey put on individual officers' liability can also be traced to nineteenth-century cases other than *Viscount Canterbury*, *Tobin*, and *Feather*. In *The Queen v Lords Comm'rs of the Treasury*, for instance, Cockburn CJ referred to the Lords of the Treasury as 'servants of the Crown' against whom mandamus could not be ordered.[99] In his exposition of his theory of the rule of the law, Dicey argued that the equality before the law component was already an essential characteristic of English institutions in the seventeenth century. Yet Dicey's statement—also found in Hearn's work—glossed over the evolution of individual officers' liability, as is argued in this section.

The responsibility of the king's agent was not yet individual in the late Middle Ages. Wrongful acts committed by agents of the king were attributed to the king, and the latter could decide to assume liability himself.[100] In the late Middle Ages, there were no common law remedies against the king's officers until the writ of action on the case was created and statutes enacted to provide the king's subjects with remedies against his sheriffs (but not all his officers).[101] The privilege not to be sued at common law belonged only to the king. If his lower agent was sued before the Court of the Exchequer on the basis of that privilege, the king could decide to waive the privilege and see his agent answerable before an ordinary court, which Edward I came gradually to do.[102] Only lower servants were amenable to suit before the Court of the Exchequer under Edward I, but all agents could be complained of to the king himself.[103] The rule under Edward II and III became more general: although agents were still not to be sued before ordinary courts, they were to be brought to suit either before an *ad hoc* court or the Court of the Exchequer.[104] But the king's officials were not yet answerable before ordinary courts as Dicey's myth propounds.

As for the king's order, when agents were to answer for their acts before the Court of the Exchequer, the fact that the unlawful act was due to an order of the king was considered to be a good justification, at least as late as the reign of Edward III.[105] Plea rolls in the king's courts for the fourteenth century show that the issue

[99] *The Queen v Lords Comm'rs of the Treasury* (1872) LR 7, QB 387.
[100] Ehrlich (n 3) 28–29, 129. See Chapter 1.
[101] Statute of Westminster II 1285 ('Execution of Process Act'), 13 Edw I St 1 c 39. It provided the king's subjects with a remedy against a wrongdoing sheriff, including damages (ss 8, 18) and for the sheriff's punishment by judges and the king himself (s 20). See Chapter 2, section 2.3.4.
[102] Ehrlich (n 3) 111.
[103] ibid.
[104] ibid 153.
[105] ibid 129, 200.

of a superior's command as a valid defence became a controversial issue.[106] There was not an established and generalized immunity from suit for officials[107] but there was not full liability either: in two cases involving the Statute of Malborough, for instance, there was a discussion of the king's[108] and the queen's[109] agents' special status as differing from that of common persons. Although the king's command, when only given orally, was not a valid defence, individual officers could claim the king's order as a valid defence if it was in written form at the end of the fifteenth century,[110] contrary to Hearn's general statement that individual officers' liability for the king's unlawful command is 'a principle, which is one of the highest importance in Constitutional law, has long been thoroughly established'.[111] Nor was it a 'steady and consistent application of a wider and more elementary principle of general law'.[112] The rewriting of history by Hearn to the effect that the king's officer could not invoke the king's command as a defence was taken up by Dicey and fed into the myth of equality before the law as a long-standing principle in the time of the Stuarts.[113] Dicey stated that 'the legal dogma, as old at least as the time of Edward the Fourth, that if any man arrest another without lawful warrant even by the King's command he shall not be excused but shall be liable to an action for false imprisonment'.[114] But Dicey's statement is a misinterpretation of Huse CJ's dictum early in the reign of Henry VII, discussed in Chapter 2.[115] The purpose of Huse CJ's dictum was rather to reaffirm the principle that the king was not entitled to do wrong while taking into account his immunity from suit. Huse CJ opined that since the king is immune from suit, the king could not therefore arrest a subject, as the subject would otherwise be deprived of a remedy against her unlawful detention.

That the king's unlawful command, even when written, does not constitute a defence and that an individual officer can be sued for it, understood as a constitutional principle, dates back only to the seventeenth century. The House of Lords in *M v Home Office*, not unlike Dicey, equally omitted to mention the first stage in the evolution of legal thinking in relation to individual officers' liability and the possibility to invoke the king's command as a defence. The Lords' statement that, from the thirteenth to the fifteenth centuries, 'The corollary was that the King's

[106] Morris S Arnold, *Select Cases of Trespass from the King's Courts, 1307–1399*, vol 1 (Selden Society 1985) xxxvi–xxxvii. See also (1333) YB Trin 7 Edw III, fo 23b, pl 1.

[107] Arnold (n 106) xxxvii. Nightwatchmen were especially at risk of being sued: ibid xxxviii–xxxix.

[108] *Strode v Ergleys et al* (1311) Hil 5 Edw II, pl 26 in William Craddock Bolland, *Year Book of Edward II (1311–1312)* (Selden Society 1915) 119.

[109] (1356) YB Hil 30 Edw III, fo 5, unnumbered plea.

[110] (1438) YB Trin 16 Hen VI, fo 83r, pl 182 (see Anthony Fitzherbert, *Fitzherbert's Abridgement* (Richart Tottel 1577) 'Monstrauns' 182); (1485) YB Mich 1 Hen VII, fo 4b, pl 5.

[111] William Edward Hearn, *The Government of England: Its Structure and Its Development* (2nd edn, Robertson 1886) 102.

[112] ibid 102–03.

[113] ibid 107; Dicey (n 23) 249.

[114] Dicey (n 23) 160.

[115] See Chapter 2, section 2.2.2.

servants could not rely on royal orders as a defence, even where they in fact acted on royal authority',[116] was not, therefore, historically accurate. The fact that, before the seventeenth century, officials could invoke as a valid defence the unlawful order of the king qualifies Dicey's claim that it is a long-standing feature of the common law that all officials must be brought to justice before ordinary courts and judged according to the common law.[117]

Dicey's account of the common law on crown servant's individual liability has nevertheless had an enduring impact on public law thinking. Such is Dicey's influence and gravitational pull that even authors who cite Ehrlich to highlight that *the king can do no wrong* meant hundreds of years ago that '[i]n fact, the Crown was generally considered to be subject to the law, as consonant with principles of justice'[118] then shift their focus to Dicey's notion of equality before the law in the next paragraph. Dicey's omissions allowed him to entrench the individual liability of public officials in legal thinking on crown liability.

4.1.3 The king, the crown, and the servant

Dicey's notion of equality before the law and his defining of the rule of law as a constitutional pillar still ground leading authors' conception of crown liability. Hogg, like Dicey before him, rejected in his seminal work on crown liability the French model of state liability where different law applies before dedicated tribunals.[119] Hogg argued that the state cannot be subject to ordinary law because it 'governs'—an act that ordinary citizens cannot perform. Hogg's acceptance of Dicey's rule of law results in a limitation of the notion of equality before the law. It is of the essence of the state to govern. The act of governing as the justification to withdraw the state from the application of ordinary law results in ordinary law not applying to the state. Unless the difficult distinction between the state's governmental—or public—and commercial—or private—endeavours can be drawn,[120] resorting to the argument that the state cannot be subject to ordinary law because it governs risks amounting to a negation of the notion of equality before the law.

Dicey's aim to emphasize the role of equality before the law in English constitutional law led him to give prominence to the king's agents' individual liability before ordinary courts according to ordinary law because it acted as a proxy for the notion of equality before the law—an integral component of his theory of the rule of law. However, the prominence given by Dicey to the king's agents' individual liability in his objective to promote equality before the law does not accord with the fundamental historical constitutional principle that the king has never been

[116] *M v Home Office* (n 2) 389–90.

[117] Dicey (n 23) 100–01.

[118] Mads Andenas and Duncan Fairgrieve, 'Reforming Crown Immunity: The Comparative Law Perspective' [2003] PL 730.

[119] Hogg, Monahan, and Wright (n 74) 8.

[120] Carol Harlow, 'The Crown: Wrong Once Again?' (1977) 40 MLR 728.

equal. By redefining English constitutional law based on the rule of law and particularly the notion of equality before the law, Dicey ignored the historical development in relation to the king's liability and his unequal constitutional status. It was the inequality underpinning the king's constitutional status—he is under the law but above all others—which led to the king's personal immunity from suit after the Glorious Revolution and the concept of ministerial responsibility as a counterweight. What is now termed 'crown' liability revolves in fact around the king's servants' liability. The king's servants' liability became the focus of crown liability because they were suable according to ordinary law before ordinary tribunals—ant that was congruent with Dicey's notion of equality before the law. Omitting the crown and the government in discussing equality before the law ironed out the wrinkles caused by the king's immunity from suit and the confusion surrounding the notion of crown.

The proposition that immunities were extended to government departments because of the confusion the term 'crown' occasioned appears to be accurate. The policy decision in the nineteenth-century trilogy of cases on the petition of right was to shield the king personally from recourses by petition of right.[121] The policy decision in *Mersey Docks* was to reduce the scope of public bodies which could claim various exemptions and immunities because of their 'public' character.[122] The two policies—shielding the king personally and reducing the scope of public bodies which could benefit from immunities—do not indicate a clear policy choice to pass on the king's personal immunities to government departments. The confusion the term 'crown' occasioned may, however, have served as a convenient justification to grant immunities to central government departments.

Another difficulty created by Dicey's work and his interpretation of *the king can do no wrong* is a result of his gloss over the medieval period, when individual officers could invoke the king's command as a valid defence and when the king could assume the blame for his servant's wrongdoing. Omitting that historical development deprives us of a reflection on the legitimacy of ascribing liability solely on one individual servant who was following commands, without also considering the commander's liability. Perhaps Dicey's emphasis on individual servants' liability was apt in the nineteenth century, when the postmaster, the sheriff, and the tax collector and their employees were still individuals known personally by the public. When they committed a wrong, they could easily be identified by their victims. The wrong that could be inflicted by an individual postmaster or tax collector, however, is nothing compared to the wrong that can be caused by governmental entities manned by thousands of civil servants through dozens of departments administering multiple services under a panoply of statutory schemes. Asking of a wronged member of the public to identify the wrongdoing civil servant may be

[121] See Chapter 4, section 3.3.

[122] See Chapter 4, sections 3.3.2 and 3.3.4.

tantamount to finding a needle in a haystack and is hardly commensurate with the machinery of the modern-day governmental apparatus: often it is not a needle in the haystack that is the issue, but the fact that the haystack itself is part of various processes in a vast, complex, multi-tiered and technologically advanced organization that is the governmental apparatus.

The emphasis on individual liability as a result of Dicey's notion of equality before the law and the resulting focus on it in the CPA is explored in more detail in section 4.2. The historical insight into officers' liability and into the possibility or not of invoking the king's command as a defence allows us to shine a new light on the courts' reluctance to ascribe blame on public officials who were fulfilling their functions. Even in *M v Home Office*, albeit a case grounded in the realm of judicial review and not in tortious liability, the Lords stopped short of finding the minister personally guilty of contempt, and ascribed the blame to the department instead.[123] In denying the existence of systemic wrongs in the realm of governmental liability on the basis that crown liability is solely vicarious and must be grounded in an identifiable individual crown servant's wrong,[124] the courts have failed to grapple with their reluctance to ascribe blame to a public officer in cases where their conduct was not so egregious as to amount to misfeasance in public office. Holt J's reliance on medieval precedents to ground the liability of high public officers for the wrongs of their subordinate in his dissent in *Lane v Cotton* is an example of the fertile reflections that can be brought about by a longer perspective on the evolution of crown liability.[125]

The issue with the crown in the realm of crown liability is not the failure to distinguish the king from the state, it is the failure to distinguish the king from government departments. The state is not solely the governmental apparatus, as that would result in an 'impoverished' notion of state.[126] Maitland's notion of corporation aggregate of the Commonwealth[127] and the medieval notion of the crown as the body of the realm with its democratic potential[128] would be a better starting point for the state.[129] The fact that the state is not the governmental apparatus means that the distinction between, on one hand, king and state and, on the other

[123] *M v Home Office* (n 2).

[124] *Hinse v Canada (Attorney General)* [2015] 2 SCR 621; *Canada (Attorney General) v Thouin* [2017] 2 SCR 184. Hinse was wrongly convicted and his repeated applications for mercy were denied or ignored by successive ministers over a lengthy period of time. The Supreme Court of Canada ruled that he could not obtain compensation from the crown because he could not claim that there was 'one continuous fault that subsumed the individual actions of the successive Ministers'; he had instead to point to the wrongful conduct of each individual minister and crown servant: *Hinse* [92].

[125] *Lane v Cotton* (n 82); Holt J's dissent is discussed with much insight in Louis L Jaffe, 'Suits against Governments and Officers: Sovereign Immunity' (1963) 77 Harv L Rev 1, 13–14.

[126] Loughlin (n 84) 40; Quentin Skinner, 'A Genealogy of the Modern State' (2009) 162 Proceedings of the British Academy 325, 326, 363–64.

[127] FW Maitland, 'The Crown as Corporation' (1901) 17 LQR 131.

[128] Allison (n 67) 56. See also Fortin (n 68).

[129] Loughlin (n 84).

hand, the distinction between king and governmental apparatus are different. The distinction between the king and the state is an issue that relates to the broader concept of the public sphere and statehood. It is the distinction between the king and the governmental apparatus which is at issue in the realm of tortious liability. In the realm of crown liability for a wrong, the issue of to whom the 'unified will to do wrong'[130] should be ascribed does not pertain to the distinction between the king and the state; it relates to the distinction between the king and the government understood as the formal notion of the crown which was first developed in the nineteenth century.

4.2 The Crown Proceedings Act

In this section, it will be shown that the confusion surrounding the term 'crown'—caused by the development of the formal notion of the crown understood as central government—and Dicey's influential notion of equality before the law in legal thinking on crown liability are both evidenced in the CPA.

4.2.1 Diceyan influence

The CPA creates distinct liabilities under section 2 CPA. The crown is directly liable in relation to its duties as an occupier but is vicariously liable only for the torts of its servants.[131] Outside these areas, immunity from liability remains.[132]

Prior to the adoption of the CPA, not all government departments had corporate status or the capacity to sue or be sued. The fact that government departments and ministerial offices did not have legal capacity has been found to constitute a bar to actions in tort against them at common law.[133] While the CPA remedies the lack of legal standing of government departments and renders them vicariously liable for

[130] Janet McLean, *Searching for the State in British Legal Thought: Competing Conceptions of the Public Sphere* (CUP 2012) 50.

[131] s 2(1)(a), (b), (c) CPA:

> 2 (1) Subject to the provisions of this Act, the Crown shall be subject to all those liabilities in tort to which, if it were a private person of full age and capacity, it would be subject:—
>
> (a) in respect of torts committed by its servants or agents;
>
> (b) in respect of any breach of those duties which a person owes to his servants or agents at common law by reason of being their employer; and
>
> (c) in respect of any breach of the duties attaching at common law to the ownership, occupation, possession or control of property:
>
> Provided that no proceedings shall lie against the Crown by virtue of paragraph (a) of this subsection in respect of any act or omission of a servant or agent of the Crown unless the act or omission would apart from the provisions of this Act have given rise to a cause of action in tort against that servant or agent or his estate.

See eg Cane (n 31) 373.

[132] See eg *Morgan* (n 31).

[133] *Trawnik* (n 31). Sedley (n 60) 261, 264–65.

the wrongs of individual crown servants, it does not create direct liability for government departments except for defined situations, such as occupiers' liability.[134] Section 2(1) CPA renders the crown liable, as if it were 'a private person of full age and capacity', for a tort committed by its servant only—torts committed by the crown itself do not give rise to an action under the CPA.[135]

Authorized high public officers and government departments referred to as parties in proceedings against the crown under section 17 CPA are liable only for a tort committed by other servants, not for a tort committed by government departments themselves. The crown—understood as the formal notion of the crown referring to central government—is only vicariously liable in tort. The absence of direct liability of the formal notion of the crown—high public officers in their representative capacity and government departments—in tort is problematic in cases of systemic or institutional failures where the wrong cannot be ascribed to a particular individual or group of individual servants, for instance where it occurred over an extensive period of time where the hierarchical and departmentalized structure of government does not allow one to identify a specific wrongdoer.[136] As a result of Dicey's influential notion of equality before the law and the emphasis on individual servant's wrongful conduct and suability, what is now termed 'crown' liability revolves in fact around the king's agents' liability. The 'state' is understood as incapable of doing wrong and not liable at common law.[137] There is no 'public institutional wrong-doing by government as a whole', only individual civil servants' wrongful conduct.[138] The crown is not only incapable of doing wrong at common law, but also no wrongful command can originate in the crown and no wrong can be ascribed to it under the CPA either.[139] The king and the formal notion of the crown's capacity to commit or command a wrong has been obfuscated.[140]

4.2.2 The crown in the CPA

The CPA does not expressly specify who is the 'crown'—the king, the formal crown understood as government departments, or the medieval notion of the crown[141] as a body politic. Evidence that the CPA refers to these various notions of the crown is found in numerous provisions. In section 40(1), the king in his private capacity is ensured immunity from suit: 'Nothing in this Act shall apply to proceedings by

134 s 2(1)(a), (c). Williams (n 57) 28.

135 *Chagos Islanders v Attorney General* (2004) EWCA Civ 997, (2004) All ER (D) 85 (Aug) [20] (Sedley LJ).

136 See eg *Morgan* (n 31); *Hinse* (n 124). See also Sunkin (n 3) 724; Hogg, Monahan, and Wright (n 74) 182–87.

137 McLean (n 130) 204–05.

138 ibid 205.

139 ibid 229–30.

140 See *Trawnik* (n 31).

141 Maitland (n 127) 132–35; Kantorowicz (n 67) 225, 363; Allison (n 67) 55–56.

or against, or authorise proceedings in tort to be brought against, His Majesty in His private capacity.' Section 32 relates to the 'demise' of the 'crown', a reinterpretation of the late medieval understanding that there is demise of the king's body natural but that the king's body politic never dies and the crown passes on to the next king: 'No claim by or against the Crown, and no proceedings for the enforcement of any such claim, shall abate or be affected by the demise of the Crown.'[142] As there can be no proceedings against the king in his private capacity, a 'claim by or against the Crown' in section 32 refers to another entity, perhaps the king in his politic capacity or the formal notion of the crown understood as governmental departments. The 'demise of the Crown' in section 32 refers, however, to the king's passing. While the orthodox understanding has been that the crown never dies, although the king's body natural demises, the CPA provides that the crown demises. That there is demise of the crown in the CPA would point to the conclusion that the 'Crown' that demises in section 32 *in fine* means the king personally, in his private capacity. The crown understood as the office of kingship is immortal and has perpetual continuity.[143] The word 'crown' is therefore used twice in section 32 but conveys different meanings. As for section 31(1), it provides that the 'Crown' can take advantage of statutes even if not named in them, and refers therefore to the formal notion of the crown understood as central government—government departments, agencies, and the civil servants working therein.[144] The 'Crown' in section 31(1) refers to the notion of the corporation aggregate of all crown officers, government departments, and crown servants who can take advantage of statutes—a concept similar to the crown as corporation aggregate being excluded from the ambit of a patent in *Feather*.[145] On the other hand, the crown appears to be conceived of as another power or entity distinct from both the king personally and the government—ministers, departments, crown servants—in sections 25(4) and 35(2)(g)(iii) and (iv) CPA.[146] In those provisions, the 'Crown' is treated separately or is represented by authorized government departments, crown officers, or the Attorney General—implying that the 'Crown' is distinct from them, as was the

[142] *Hill v Grange* (1556–1557) 1 Plowden 163, 177–77a.

[143] Kantorowicz (n 67) 344–45, 382–85.

[144] s 31(1): 'This Act shall not prejudice the right of the Crown to take advantage of the provisions of an Act of Parliament although not named therein; and it is hereby declared that in any civil proceedings against the Crown the provisions of any Act of Parliament which could, if the proceedings were between subjects, be relied upon by the defendant as a defence to the proceedings, whether in whole or in part, or otherwise, may, subject to any express provision to the contrary, be so relied upon by the Crown.' See *R(Black) v Secretary of State for Justice* (n 27) [1].

[145] *Feather* (n 15). See Chapter 4, sections 3.3.2.2, 3.3.3.2, and 3.3.4.

[146] s 25(4): 'Save as aforesaid no execution or attachment or process in the nature thereof shall be issued out of any court for enforcing payment by the Crown of any such money or costs as aforesaid, and no person shall be individually liable under any order for the payment by the Crown, or any Government department, or any officer of the Crown as such, of any such money or costs'; s 35(2)(g)(iii): 'that the Crown, when sued in the name of a Government department'; and s 35(2)(g)(iv): 'that the Crown, when sued in the name of the Attorney General.'

case in *Trawnik*.[147] In short, while certain provisions of the CPA could be read as implying that the crown is an entity distinct from the government departments, the Attorney General, and the king in his private capacity, other provisions point to government departments and the Attorney General as instantiations of the crown as a corporation aggregate and to the king as an instantiation of the crown as a corporation sole. In summary, the crown in the CPA does not have a defined or consistent meaning and refers to the king, the medieval notion of the crown as a body politic, government departments, and perhaps as another separate entity—the king's body politic or the office of the crown.

One explanation of the inconsistency of the notion of the crown in the CPA is the fact that the act covers both contractual recourses and tortious recourses against the crown. The two types of recourse were underpinned by different understandings of crown liability before they were merged in the CPA. In contract, a remedy could be had against the king directly, by petition of right.[148] Since *Haldimand*, an officer acting in his official capacity and contracting in the king's name was not to be held personally liable for entering into a contract for the crown.[149] It was confirmed in *Thomas* that the petition of right lay against the king in contract.[150] Even following the adoption of the CPA, it remains possible to sue to the king in contract by petition of right at common law, the Petitions of Right Act 1860 having been abolished by the CPA.[151] On the other hand, since the nineteenth-century cases on the petition of right, the king could not be sued to in tort via the petition of right and a remedy could only be had by ordinary action against an individual crown servant or against a high public official if the latter was directly involved in commanding or committing the wrong complained of.[152] The different understandings which underpinned crown liability in contract and in tort prior to the adoption of the CPA are apparent from the wording of the act. Section 1 covers only actions that were covered by the petition of right (contractual claims and real actions) and statutory actions. Section 1 is titled 'Right to sue the Crown', reflecting the right to sue to the king directly by

[147] In *Trawnik*, an action at common law against the Ministry of Defence was found to be impossible because the Ministry was not a person or corporate entity known to the common law: *Trawnik* (n 31) 547 (Lawton J). It could only be sued pursuant to s 17 CPA, which was inapplicable following a certificate issued by the Secretary of State under s 40(3) CPA to the effect that the proceedings did not pertain to Her Majesty's government in the United Kingdom (s 40(2)(b) CPA). The Attorney General in *Trawnik* was therefore representing the crown understood not as the Ministry of Defence, but as either the king or another, abstract entity, referred to in *Adams v Naylor* as the head of a highly organized corporation aggregate of many which embraces the state: *Adams v Naylor* (n 63) 247 (Lord Uthwatt).

[148] Government departments could also be sued in contract, in their names, prior to the adoption of the CPA: Harry Street, *Governmental Liability: A Comparative Study* (CUP 1953) 93–94.

[149] *Macbeth v Haldimand* (1786) 1 TR 172; Cornford (n 57) 236.

[150] *Thomas v The Queen* (1874–75) Law Rep 10 QB 31. Harrison Moore, 'The Crown as Corporation' (1904) 20 LQR 351, 352–54.

[151] *Franklin v Attorney General* [1974] QB 185; Harry Street, 'Crown Proceedings Act, 1947' (1948) 11 MLR 129, 132–33; Williams (n 57) 8; Joseph Chitty, *Chitty on Contracts* (Sweet & Maxwell 2012) 853; William Wade, Christopher Forsyth, and Julian Ghosh, *Administrative Law* (12th edn, OUP 2022) 664.

[152] *Raleigh v Goschen* (n 34).

petition of right in contract 'subject to the grant of His Majesty's fiat'. By contrast, section 2 is not titled 'Right to sue the Crown in tort' but rather 'Liability of the Crown in tort' because one does not sue the crown directly under the CPA, but rather sues a government department or the Attorney General. By being included in the CPA, contractual actions became conceptually separated from the king and became actions against the crown understood not as the king but as the formal notion of the crown understood as central government. As is evidenced in section 1 CPA, while it was 'His Majesty' who was sued to by petition of right in contract prior to the commencement of the Act, it is now the 'Crown' against whom proceedings are instituted. Under the CPA, the Attorney General, government departments, and crown officers 'as such' are the crown for the purposes of 'proceedings against the Crown' (s 23). The bringing together of contractual and tortious remedies in the CPA required the drafter to treat the different strands of legal thinking in the same statute: the crown understood as the king in contract and the crown understood as the formal notion of government departments in tort. Implicit in the discrepancy between the titles of sections 1 and 2 CPA is the history of crown liability where the crown—the king, a corporation sole—could be sued to by petition of right in contract but not in tort since the nineteenth century.

4.3 A historically informed understanding of crown liability

In this section, a possible reinterpretation of the notion of the crown is proposed in light of a historically informed understanding of the evolution of *the king can do no wrong* in legal thinking and the two dimensions of crown liability. The consequences of that possible interpretation on the CPA are also discussed.

The argument defended in this section is that the crown should be called the king, in whose name ministers and government departments conduct government. While the crown—as the king only—is immune from suit, the formal notion of the crown first developed in the nineteenth century—ministers, government departments, and servants to the exclusion of the king—is not, even at common law.

In light of an analysis of relevant provisions of the CPA and recent debates in legal literature on the status of the crown as a corporation sole or aggregate, a historically informed understanding of *the king can do no wrong*, including the seventeenth-century constitutional settlement understanding and nineteenth-century developments, can allow us to conceive of the king—a corporation sole—separately from the formal notion of the crown understood as government departments, ministers, and servants—a corporation aggregate.

4.3.1 The crown as a corporation sole and aggregate

The concept of the crown as corporation sole (the king), as advocated by Wade, and the formal notion of the crown understood as central government (ministers and other crown officers, government departments, and servants to the exclusion of the king), as was laid down by Lord Diplock in *Town Investments*,[153] can be useful guideposts.

The use of the term 'crown' occasioned confusion in the realm of crown liability between the king and the formal notion of the crown understood as central government. As Lord Templeman pointed out in *M v Home Office*, 'The expression "the Crown" has two meanings; namely the monarch and the executive'.[154] Adopting a seventeenth-century understanding of *the king can do no wrong* and thereby addressing the issue of whence do wrongful commands come—from the king or the high public officers and government departments—can lead to a clearer conception of the crown as both a corporation sole and aggregate.

A better understanding of the historical evolution of the understandings of *the king can do no wrong* and the notions underpinning it can shed new light on the law of crown liability and possibly lead to legal reform by revisiting the elusive notion of the crown.

The confusion surrounding *the king can do no wrong* has been compounded by the confusion surrounding the crown itself. Such confusion surrounding the crown has contributed to the obscurity covering principles which are justified on the basis that *the king can do no wrong*, most prominent among them crown immunities.[155]

Inconsistency in relation to the notion of the crown relates in part to its status as a corporation: sometimes the crown is said to be a corporation sole—a corporation of one—while on other occasions it shares the attributes of a corporation aggregate—a corporation of many. The ambivalence in relation to the crown's status as a corporation sole is discernible even from Wade and Forsyth's *Administrative Law* treatise,[156] where the authors, having first been adamant that the crown is a corporation sole, then explain that in relation to immunity from statute:

> An Act of Parliament is presumed no to bind the Crown in the absence of express provision or necessary implication. This is a long-standing rule of interpretation, which has nothing to do with the royal prerogative. 'The Crown' in this case includes the Crown's ministers and servants, since it is necessarily by their agency that the Crown's immunity is enjoyed.

The inclusion of ministers and servants within the notion of the crown is the definition of the crown as a corporation aggregate, a 'corporation of many'. But the conclusion that the crown is a corporation aggregate in the case of immunity from

[153] *Town Investments Ltd and others v Department of the Environment* [1978] AC 359, 381.

[154] *M v Home Office* (n 2) 395. Hogg similarly ascribes to the crown two meanings—the king in his political capacity and the executive branch of government: Hogg, Monahan, and Wright (n 74) 11–13.

[155] JWF Allison, *A Continental Distinction in the Common Law: A Historical and Comparative Perspective on English Public Law* (revised edn, OUP 2000) 81.

[156] Wade and Forsyth (n 151) 667.

statute is directly opposed to the implication of the House of Lords' decision in *M v Home Office*, drawn by Wade and Forsyth, that the crown is a corporation sole. In that seminal case, the minister was excluded from the notion of the crown in order that the crown's immunity from injunction would not extend to him. The implied conclusion of that decision of the House of Lords was that the crown is a corporation sole, separate from its ministers and departments.[157]

There are, therefore, two different rationales at play, and two different notions of the crown: the crown is a corporation sole in relation to tort actions, but a corporation aggregate in relation to the application of statutes. The notion of the crown is expanded to include ministers so as to cover them under the umbrella of the crown's immunity from statute under section 40(2) CPA,[158] whereas the crown is restricted to a corporation sole so that its immunity from tort does not extend to the ministers under section 21(2) of the same act.

The interplay between the confusion surrounding the *king can do no wrong* and that surrounding the crown can be found even in *Halsbury's Laws of England*, where there is no clear demarcation as to *the king can do no wrong* being a personal attribute of the sovereign or that of the crown. There is an imperceptible shift from the use of the word sovereign to that of crown and that slippage avoids the discussion of why this personal attribute of the monarch that *the king can do no wrong* should extend to the crown:

> The monarch can do no wrong.
>
> *The law clothes the monarch's person* with absolute perfection; hence the common law maxim that 'the King can do no wrong', and no remedy lies against the monarch in person either in civil or criminal matters, for the prerogative is created for the benefit of the people and cannot be exerted to their prejudice.
>
> *The monarch* is regarded in law as being incapable of thinking wrong or meaning to do an improper act. . . .
>
> In pursuance of the same principle of perfection, no laches or negligence can be attributed *to the monarch* at common law, and no delay will bar her right, the maxim of law being that 'time does not run against the King'. In certain cases, however, *the Crown* is limited by statute as to the time within which proceedings may be begun.[159] [Emphasis added]

Similarly, in a footnote accompanying the notion that the law clothes the monarch with absolute perfection, a transfer of privileges from the person of the

[157] *M v Home Office* (n 2). The conclusion that the crown is a corporation sole is wholly supported by Wade and Forsyth, who argued that attempts by Lord Diplock and Lord Simon in *Town Investments* (n 144) to redefine the crown as including its ministers were 'radically misconceived' and should be 'confined to property transactions': Wade and Forsyth (n 151) 40, fn 32.

[158] See *R(Black) v Secretary of State for Justice* (n 27).

[159] *Halsbury's Laws of England* (n 22) [52].

monarch to the crown taken as government occurs without there being a discussion of the justification for such a transfer:

> This generalisation [the absolute perfection of the monarch] no longer carries conviction and can now serve only as a historical basis for the various privileges described. They now stand on their own feet, and it is probable that *the Crown* now has to invoke a specific privilege rather than the general characterisation of the monarch.[160] [Emphasis added]

No justification is given either as to the continued existence of those privileges that were originally the monarch's, or as to how they now 'stand on their own feet'. Other passages illustrate the confusion surrounding *the king can do no wrong* and its current status in law. For instance, a similar slippage from the monarch to the crown is noticeable in relation to crown proceedings:

> Under the general rule at common law no proceeding, civil or criminal, was maintainable *against the monarch in person*, for, it was said, the courts, being *the King's* own, could have no jurisdiction over him. . . . *The Crown enjoyed numerous immunities and privileges*, in particular immunity from liability for damages for torts committed by Crown servants. Similarly, there were available to the Crown special methods of enforcing its own claims in the courts, and proceedings by the Crown followed special forms of procedure.[161] [Emphasis added]

A historical perspective on *the king can do no wrong* can enlighten the notion of the crown itself.

As has been discussed,[162] the absence of a clear identity of the head of the government departments and crown servants was revealed in *Viscount Canterbury*.[163] The king—who was in law the master of the negligent crown servants—was said by Lord Lyndhurst not to be liable for the negligent commissioners who supervised the servants who had set fire to the Palace of Westminster. The fact that the king had appointed the commissioners was insufficient to impose liability on the king for the commissioners' wrong. *A fortiori*, it was found, the king could not be liable for the wrongs of the servants who had been appointed by the commissioners and who were working under their direction. The commissioners themselves were not to be held vicariously liable for the servants' negligence because they were, in law, fellow crown servants. The commissioners—crown servants—were not the masters of the lower crown servants. There was, effectively, no master.

[160] ibid fn 1.
[161] ibid.
[162] See Chapter 4, section 3.3.1.
[163] *Viscount Canterbury v Attorney General* (1843) 1 Ph 306, 324–25.

In *Tobin*, the court made a distinction between acts of the king and commands of the king—thereby indicating that the king issued commands.[164] In *Feather*, Cockburn CJ treated the whole governmental apparatus as the crown—a corporation aggregate—to justify the use of the patent by government departments and crown servants.[165] However, as was discussed in Chapter 4, the crown reverted back to being a corporation sole—the king only—in Cockburn CJ's reasons in *Feather* on the issue of the application of the king's immunity from suit. Cockburn CJ emphasized that the king is immune from suit both for personal wrongs—acts done by the king—and for 'political wrongs'—wrongful commands of the king or the king's authorization to commit wrongful acts.[166] The wrongful command originated with the 'crown' understood as the king in Cockburn CJ's reasons.

Wade's view that the crown is a corporation sole and that its separation from its servants is a fundamental principle[167] supports the position previously adopted by the courts that government departments—which are not part of the crown because it is a corporation sole—are crown servants.[168] Being crown servants, government departments cannot be sued for the wrongs of other crown servants, an issue the CPA aimed to rectify. Government departments cannot be crown servants and be the crown itself. Government departments are as much 'instruments' of the king—to borrow from Hale—as are his ministers. The word 'instrument' was in fact used to describe government departments in the early twentieth century.[169] The king is the crown—a corporation sole—and all others are his servants and are liable for the king's wrongful commands. It would follow that government departments are no more entitled to do wrong than the ministers heading them.

On the other hand, ECS Wade held the view that the crown is a corporation aggregate—'By the Crown was meant all the departments of the Central Government.'[170] The notion of the crown as a corporation aggregate of government departments is often associated with Lord Diplock and Lord Simon's respective speeches in *Town Investments*.[171] Lord Simon described the government as a corporation aggregate of ministers, departments, civil servants, and the king.[172] Lord Simon's definition of the crown as a corporation aggregate is similar to the recent argument that we should conceive of the government as a corporation aggregate which includes corporations sole such as the office of the crown and the

164 *Tobin* (n 14) 353–54.
165 See Chapter 4, sections 3.3.1 and 3.3.2.2.
166 *Feather* (n 15) 295.
167 William Wade, 'The Crown: Old Platitudes and New Heresies' 142 NLJ 1275.
168 See Chapter 4, section 3.3.2.2.
169 Moore (n 69) 20.
170 ECS Wade, 'Liability in Tort of the Central Government of the United Kingdom Governmental' (1954) 29 NYUL Rev 1416, 1416.
171 *Town Investments* (n 153) 381 (Lord Diplock), 400 (Lord Simon).
172 ibid 397–400.

king himself.[173] Lord Diplock, however—and this particular point has often been misunderstood[174]—did not include the king in his definition of the crown as a corporation aggregate. Lord Diplock's notion of the crown is similar to the formal notion of the crown elaborated in *Mersey Docks* to refer to central government.[175] On a close reading of Lord Diplock's speech, he distinguished the monarch, who is privileged in that liability cannot be imposed on him, from the government. Lord Diplock in fact considered the government to be the corporation established for the providing of services advanced by Harlow.[176] Lord Diplock wrote twice that the crown is a corporation sole.[177] When he wrote that the vocabulary currently used is ancient and not appropriate for the twentieth century, and that instead of 'Crown' we should say 'government', Lord Diplock meant that ministers, departments, servants, and statutory bodies are the 'government', a corporation aggregate. But the crown, a corporation sole, should be understood as the king. In Lord Diplock's speech, the crown as a corporation sole is the king only and the crown as a corporation aggregate of many—but to the exclusion of the king—is the government.

The notion of the crown as a corporation sole was attributed to Coke.[178] Lord Diplock's notion of the government—to the exclusion of the king—as a corporation aggregate is similar to the formal notion of the crown elaborated in the nineteenth century by Cockburn CJ in *Feather* and Blackburn J in *Mersey Docks*. As Lord Templeman ascribing two meanings to the crown in *M v Home Office* demonstrates, and as Lord Woolf astutely remarked in that seminal case, the two notions survive to this day.[179] The crown is a corporation sole (the king) and a corporation aggregate (central government, to the exclusion of the king).

Adopting a historically informed understanding of *the king can do no wrong*, the CPA could receive a different interpretation. Bearing in mind the seventeenth-century constitutional settlement understanding of *the king can do no wrong*, while taking into account the formal notion of the crown first elaborated in the nineteenth century, can contribute to a different understanding of the notion of the crown. The seventeenth-century constitutional settlement understanding of *the king can do no wrong* was that the king issued the wrongful command and ministers and servants—and now also government departments—executed it. A clearer notion of the crown could thereby be attained: the king, a corporation sole, would

[173] Jason Grant Allen, 'The Office of the Crown' (2018) 77 CLJ 298, 313; Sebastian Howard Hartford Davis, 'The Legal Personality of the Commonwealth of Australia' (2019) 47 Fed L Rev 3, 10–11, 17–20; Jason Grant Allen, *Non-Statutory Executive Powers and Judicial Review* (CUP 2022) 79–113. On the crown as an office, see also Cobbett (n 70) 26.

[174] Harlow (n 120) 729–30; Wade (n 11) 24.

[175] Allison (n 67) 61–63.

[176] Harlow (n 120) 730.

[177] *Town Investments* (n 153) 384.

[178] Maitland (n 127) 131; Cobbett (n 70) 26.

[179] *M v Home Office* (n 2) 395 (Lord Templeman), 424 (Lord Woolf).

remain conceptually separate from the formal notion of the crown—a corporation aggregate including ministers, government departments, and crown servants. That corporation aggregate executes the fictitious commands of the king, a corporation sole.

The understandings of the crown as a corporation sole (the king) and the crown as a corporation aggregate (central government, to the exclusion of the king) can be interpreted as being not in contradiction, but as complementary. In light of the developments recounted in section 2 in relation to the formal notion of the crown—which culminated in Lord Diplock's definition in *Town Investments*—our current understanding of the notion of the crown can be revisited in light of the historical evolution of *the king can do no wrong* in legal thinking. If the term 'crown' were to be avoided except to refer to the notion of the undying office of kingship—the 'dignity' of the king[180]—it may allow clarity in defining a notion separate from the person of the king and which would not be confused with the king's body politic. The crown understood as the office of kingship would not then be part of the government.[181] The 'government' would refer to the corporation aggregate Lord Diplock defined in *Town Investments* and which was first elaborated in the second half of the nineteenth century. The notion of government understood as a corporation aggregate has roots in the nineteenth-century formal notion of the crown and includes ministers, government departments, and crown servants, but not the king.

The king in *the king can do no wrong* of the seventeenth-century constitutional settlement did not refer to the ministers, servants, and public bodies exercising the executive powers of the king for him. The king alone was not subject to the coercive force of the law. It was precisely because the king was not liable that his ministers and servants were liable in his stead. The shift from the 'king' can do no wrong to the 'crown' can do no wrong in the twentieth century can be explained by the use of the formal notion of crown which was developed by the courts from the mid-nineteenth century to determine the scope of public bodies covered by the king's immunity from suit. But the substitution of the 'king' for the 'crown' in *the king can do no wrong* was not historically informed and constituted a change in constitutional thinking. The formal notion of the crown understood as central government said to be the 'crown' was not the king from a seventeenth-century constitutional settlement understanding of *the king can do no wrong*. Ministers, the government departments they are heading, and the civil servants manning them are not immune from suit because they are liable in lieu of the king who, alone, is immune from suit because *the king can do no wrong*. If a historically informed understanding of *the king can do no wrong* were to be adopted, central government understood as a corporation aggregate—ministers, government departments, servants—would

[180] Kantorowicz (n 67) 448–49; Allison (n 67) 51.
[181] cf Allen (n 173).

be kept conceptually separate from the king. Central government's liability at common law would also be more readily obvious.

The king is immune from suit. That immunity can be conceived as grounded in the king's feudal privilege not to be sued in his courts or as grounded in the fact that the king is not subject—following Hale's theory—to the coercive force of the law. The king's immunity from the coercive power of the law was grounded in the notion of the king's perfection. However, current legal thinking is to the effect that the notion of perfection cannot be relied on by the formal notion of the crown understood as ministers, government departments, and servants.[182] Ministers, government departments, and servants—unlike the king—are not perfect. Following Hale's theory of the three powers of the law, they are not, therefore, exempt from the application of the coercive power of the law. The king's immunity from the coercive power of the law subsisted because his 'instruments' were liable in his stead. If a historically informed understanding of *the king can do no wrong* were adopted, the 'instruments' of the king who are liable in his stead would be understood as a corporation aggregate including ministers, government departments, and servants—the formal notion of 'crown' understood as central government since the second half of the nineteenth century and which was referred to by Lord Diplock in *Town Investments*.[183]

4.3.2 Two dimensions of crown liability

In legal thinking in relation to *the king can do no wrong* prior to the second half of the nineteenth century, the two dimensions of crown liability were distinct. The king could not be sued by ordinary action, but *the king can do no wrong* was not limited to the notion of the king's immunity from suit. *The king can do no wrong* in legal thinking raised issues as to the king's capacity to do wrong and his amenability to justice—the two dimensions of crown liability elaborated in this book. Adopting a historically informed approach to crown liability by revisiting *the king can do no wrong* could allow us to develop a new understanding of crown liability by asking the question whether the crown is capable of doing wrong and whether it is amenable to justice.

The suggestion that the crown—understood as the king—can issue wrongful commands and ministers and government departments and servants execute them, in line with the seventeenth-century constitutional settlement understanding of *the king can do no wrong*, finds support in the CPA. In addressing the issues of the crown's capacity to do wrong and amenability to justice, the identity of the entity issuing the wrongful command—whether the king or central government (high

[182] *Halsbury's Laws of England* (n 22).

[183] *Town Investments* (n 153) 381. To avoid confusion, the term 'crown' could be reserved exclusively to refer to the king's dignity—the office of kingship—a corporation sole vesting in the king only: see Kantorowicz (n 67) 344–45, 383, 443–45, 448–49. cf Fortin (n 68) 11–14.

public officers and government departments)—would have to be addressed. As will be shown, the CPA can support the view that the crown, understood as the king, fictitiously issues the command and his servants, including government departments, execute it.

Under the CPA, government departments and listed public officials are not directly liable for their wrongful commands; they are only liable for the crown servants' wrong in executing the commands. There are two degrees of remoteness in the CPA: the crown itself is not sued; it is represented by authorized government departments or high public officers like the Attorney General—who are the parties to the action under section 17(3) CPA—and who are themselves sued for a tort committed by an individual servant.

That the crown is distinct from crown officers and government departments is evidenced in the CPA. Section 2(4)[184] provides that when a crown officer or government department commits a tort, proceedings against the crown in relation to that tort—committed not by the crown, but by that crown officer or government department—shall nevertheless allow the crown to rely on limitations of liability which the law grants that wrongdoing crown officer or government department as if the proceedings were instituted against that crown officer or government department itself.[185] It appears from section 2(4) that torts committed by government departments or officers are not the crown's torts. Section 2(4) CPA can therefore be read as supporting the view that the wrongdoing government department is separate from the crown and akin to an officer of the crown. As is clear from section 2(4), the government department is not the crown. It is a crown servant—an 'instrument' of the crown, to borrow from Hale's terminology. The CPA states, in section 2(3), that when an officer of the crown commits a tort pursuant to a function conferred on her by the common law or by statute, the liabilities that ensue for the crown are the same as if only the crown had itself issued lawful instructions:

> Where any functions are conferred or imposed upon an officer of the Crown as such either by any rule of the common law or by statute, and that officer commits a tort while performing or purporting to perform those functions, the liabilities of the Crown in respect of the tort shall be such as they would have been if those functions had been conferred or imposed solely by virtue of instructions lawfully given by the Crown.

[184] s 2(4): 'Any enactment which negatives or limits the amount of the liability of any Government department . . . or officer of the Crown in respect of any tort committed by that department or officer shall, in the case of proceedings against the Crown under this section in respect of a tort committed by that department . . . or officer, apply in relation to the Crown as it would have applied in relation to that department . . . or officer if the proceedings against the Crown had been proceedings against that department . . . or officer.'

[185] For examples of such statutory limitations of liability, see Wade and Forsyth (n 151) 657.

As section 2(3) illustrates, the crown also issues lawful (or unlawful) commands and government departments and crown officers execute them. The liability that ensues is the same regardless of the source—statutory or not—of the crown officer's powers. The interpretation that the king understood as the crown—an entity distinct from government departments, as section 2(4) indicates—issues lawful and unlawful commands and that his instruments—crown officers, including ministers, and government departments—are liable for executing them can be supported by section 2(3) read together with section 2(4) CPA.

Section 17(3) CPA provides that proceedings against the crown must be instituted against authorized government departments or the Attorney General, not the crown:

> Civil proceedings against the Crown shall be instituted against the appropriate authorised Government department, or, if none of the authorised Government departments is appropriate or the person instituting the proceedings has any reasonable doubt whether any and if so which of those departments is appropriate, against the Attorney General.

Government departments and the Attorney General are themselves not directly liable; they are only vicariously liable for a given individual crown servant's wrong pursuant to section 2(1)(a): 'in respect of torts committed by its servants or agents'. Under the CPA, both the crown and government departments are immune from suit for issuing wrongful, invalid commands. The CPA shows how *the king can do no wrong* has been understood as *the crown can do no wrong* and therefore as the formal notion of the crown—central government—benefitting from the legal fiction that the crown's wrong is not a wrong in the eyes of the law. Both the crown and government departments are only vicariously liable for a wrong committed by individual crown servants in executing the command. The crown, however, is twice removed from liability: the crown is not sued in its own name, only in the name of an authorized officer, government department, or the Attorney General, who in turn are only vicariously liable for the wrong of individual servants. The crown can therefore be understood as separate from government departments in the CPA. Government departments, ministers, and high public officials, to the exclusion of the king, are the corporation aggregate that executes the fictitious commands of the king, a corporation sole. Only the crown as a corporation sole is immune from suit and is constitutionally sheltered from suit since the seventeenth-century constitutional pact. The CPA can be read according to this historical constitutional understanding of *the king can do no wrong*, failing a recognition of institutional wrongdoing according to which central governmental departments would not only be conceived of as capable of issuing wrongful orders but could also be ascribed a wrong and be held liable before the courts at common law.

4.3.3 Remaining issues following the adoption of the CPA

A historically informed approach to revisiting our understanding of crown liability would render moot the need for the CPA to establish liability of the formal notion of the crown—central government. A historically informed approach to *the king can do no wrong* could also have the potential to resolve some of the remaining 'gaps'[186] in the CPA, as is discussed in this section. Rethinking our understanding of crown liability based on a historically informed understanding of *the king can do no wrong* could lead to broader liability of the government understood as the corporation aggregate of ministers, government departments, and servants than that allowed for in the CPA.

The CPA creates distinct liabilities—direct liability of the crown as an occupier and employer in addition to the vicarious liability of the crown for the tort of its servants.[187] However, outside these areas, immunity from liability remains.[188] There can be no injunction against the crown in civil proceedings.[189] Moreover, as was pointed out by the House of Lords in *M v Home Office*, there can be no injunction or order against the crown when the power is conferred on it directly, not in the name of a minister, to preserve its immunity.[190] Although these instances are now rare,[191] a residual immunity remains. In addition, the CPA covers only what the petition of right used to cover, leaving open the possibility for the government to contest a claim on the basis that it exceeds the area that was covered by the petition of right.[192] There is also a risk that a plaintiff's action against the crown may fail because it is impossible to identify the wrongdoing crown servant,[193] making it impossible to prove that she was acting in the course of employment[194] or was paid out of public money as section 2(6) CPA mandates.[195] If the crown agent's servants—who are therefore crown servants—are paid not out of the Treasury fund but out of the fund of the agent, then the CPA does not apply either.[196] The statement by Viscount Simon in *Adams v Naylor* that there can be no direct claim against the crown still stands[197]—to the exception, notably, of liability in relation to occupier's duties[198]—even after the adoption of the CPA. The crown is not sued; the authorized crown officer or government department referred to under section 17

[186] Cane (n 31) 373.
[187] s 2(1)(a), (b), (c) CPA.
[188] See eg *Morgan* (n 31).
[189] s 21(1)(a), (b) CPA.
[190] *M v Home Office* (n 2) 413.
[191] William Wade, 'Injunctive Relief against the Crown and Ministers' (1991) 107 LQR 4, 5.
[192] Wade and Forsyth (n 151) 660.
[193] Williams (n 57) 17–18.
[194] ibid.
[195] Hogg, Monahan, and Wright (n 74) 163. See eg *Alexander v The Queen* (1960) 23 DLR (2d) 369 (SCC); *Morgan* (n 31) [43]–[52]; *Hinse* (n 124) [92].
[196] Williams (n 57) 40; Arrowsmith (n 27) 151.
[197] *Adams v Naylor* (n 63) 244.
[198] s 2(1)(c) CPA.

CPA is. Authorized crown officers and government departments are not sued for their own wrong, they are sued for a wrong committed by another individual servant, if she was appointed by the crown and paid out of the Consolidated Fund.[199]

Conceiving of the government as under the law and not immune from suit at common law following a seventeenth-century constitutional settlement understanding of *the king can do no wrong* could fill in the gaps left by the CPA. The suggestion that we conceive of government departments' liability as twofold—direct liability for the government department's own wrong and vicarious liability for the wrong of the servant—finds support in legal literature for the past century.[200] Subjecting government departments to direct liability for a wrong would address the issue of the absence of recourses for institutional failures as well as where a specific wrongdoer cannot be identified.[201] Conceiving of central government as liable at common law would also address the risk of a lack of discipline encouraged by what is perceived to be the crown's immunity, as well as addressing the cause for public outrage at the impossibility of suing the government for the wrongful death of a crown servant.[202] It would also solve the uncertainty surrounding the application to the crown of statutes—other than the CPA—that create liability in tort.[203] Direct liability of the crown would also address the issue of the crown currently being immune from suit if the wrongdoing servant herself is not liable in tort because she can rely on a defence or exemption.[204]

Even if central government were to be considered directly liable at common law in addition to being liable for the wrong of other individual crown servants based on a historically informed approach to *the king can do no wrong*, procedural issues would likely remain in relation to government departments lacking corporate status in the absence of the CPA, as they did in *Trawnik*.[205]

Nevertheless, if a historically informed approach to rethinking crown liability by relying on a historically informed understanding of *the king can do no wrong* were to be adopted, it could have an important impact on the interpretation of the CPA. It could support a teleological interpretation of the CPA and the assumption that it simply facilitates proceedings[206] against a government which is liable at common law.

[199] s 2(6) CPA.

[200] Williams (n 57) 41; Street (n 148) 36–37; Hogg, Monahan, and Wright (n 74) 159–87.

[201] See eg *Hinse* (n 124). Hogg, Monahan, and Wright (n 74) 182–87. See also David Cohen, 'Thinking about the State: Law Reform and the Crown in Canada' (1986) 24 Osgoode Hall LJ 379, 383.

[202] Sunkin (n 3) 716–17.

[203] Street (n 148) 152–54; Arrowsmith (n 27) 158–60; Craig (n 27) 900–01. See s 40(2) CPA.

[204] The crown's direct liability would curtail the crown as a master benefitting from an exemption which benefits the servant, see Street (n 148) 38.

[205] *Trawnik* (n 31). See Williams (n 57) 4–6, 20–21. The belief that the lack of corporate status entails an impossibility to sue was decried by Wade (n 167).

[206] That the essence of the CPA was to facilitate recourses against the crown was the view held by ECS and William Wade: ECS Wade, 'Crown Proceedings: Extent of Protection Given by Crown Proceedings Act, 1947, To Individual Minister' (1955) 13 CLJ 133, 135; Wade (n 11) 27.

5 Conclusion: constitutional coherence in public law and the crown's liability at common law

The fact that the king was above all others did not impact the conceptualization of the king's capacity to do wrong or his amenability to justice in Bracton, Coke, and Hale's thinking. Even Blackstone, who claimed that the king was perfect and incapable of doing wrong, thought like Bracton and Plowden that the king could only act *de jure* and that his prerogative did not stretch to the doing of any wrong.[207] The unequal status of the king—his superiority over ordinary subjects—was not the rationale underlying the king's liability—his capacity to do wrong and his amenability to justice. The king was liable not because he was equal to his subjects, but because he was also under the law. Under Bracton, Coke, Hale, and even Blackstone's understanding of crown liability, there could not be the same remedies against the king as there were between ordinary individuals because the king was not equal to his subjects, but there could be other remedies against the king because he was equally under the law. Under the current, Diceyan understanding of crown liability, individual civil servants and public authorities are liable at common law according to ordinary law before ordinary tribunals, but the king and the formal notion of the crown—central government comprising high public officers in their representative capacity and government departments—are not.

Seminal cases of the twentieth century on issues of statutory interpretation and judicial review—including the case of *M v Home Office* discussed in this chapter—made abundantly clear that seventeenth-century constitutional fundamentals cannot be reversed.[208] More recently, in the context of the United Kingdom's departure from the European Union (EU), the United Kingdom Supreme Court also grounded its decisions in *Miller 1* and *Miller 2* in core features of the constitutional arrangement reached in the seventeenth century—the consecration of parliamentary sovereignty and ministerial responsibility.[209] Although *the king can do no wrong* does not feature expressly in *Miller 2*, the court's implicit refusal to ascribe a wrong to the late Queen Elizabeth II in acceding to the Prime Minister's request to prorogue Parliament and exercise her prerogative accordingly is in line with the seventeenth-century understanding that the king cannot be sued, but that his ministers must be held accountable instead.[210] In the same vein of seventeenth-century constitutional continuity, revisiting our understanding of crown liability

[207] Blackstone (n 12) 231–32.

[208] *British Broadcasting Corporation v Johns* [1965] 1 Ch 32, 79 (Lord Diplock): 'it is 350 years and a civil war too late for the Queen's courts to broaden the prerogative'; *M v Home Office* (n 2) 395 (Lord Templeman); see section 2.4.1.

[209] *R(Miller) v Secretary of State for Exiting the European Union* (2017) UKSC 5 (*Miller 1*); *R(Miller) v Prime Minister* (2019) UKSC 41 (*Miller 2*).

[210] *Miller 2* (n 209) [15]; Marie-France Fortin, 'Rule of Law, Parliamentary Sovereignty and Executive Accountability in English Legal Thinking: The Recent Revival of The King Can Do No Wrong' (2022) 44 J Const Hist 43.

based on a historically informed understanding of *the king can do no wrong* can support the conclusion that the formal notion of the crown elaborated in the nineteenth century—central government—is liable at common law. There would, consequently, be no need to separate government departments from ministers and they together, along with individual servants, could be conceived of as a corporation aggregate—the government—as was advocated by Lord Diplock in *Town Investments*.[211] The government conceived of as a corporation aggregate that does not include the king, as Lord Diplock suggested, is a result of nineteenth-century developments in relation to the formal notion of the crown, and the government's liability at common law is also in line with seventeenth-century constitutional fundamentals. Such an understanding of crown liability, grounded in a historical constitutional approach, would ensure both continuity with fundamental constitutional principles as well as an adaptation to the changes that occurred with the development of government and parliamentary democracy since the seventeenth century.

Conceiving of crown liability in light of the seventeenth-century constitutional arrangement—and adopting thereby a Bractonian understanding of *the king can do no wrong*—would also bring it in line with the law governing the liability of public authorities and local governments. In *Robinson*, for instance, where the police were held liable in negligence for the physical injury caused to an elderly passer-by during an arrest, Lord Reed, citing to *Entick v Carrington* and *Mersey Docks v Gibbs* to support the proposition that all are equal before the law,[212] also quoted Dicey's famous statement that all officers and public servants, high or low, are equally liable to be sued before ordinary tribunals for their unlawful acts.[213] Lord Reed could invoke, in relation to public authorities, the prevailing Diceyan view that 'if conduct would be tortious if committed by a private person or body, it is generally equally tortious if committed by a public authority'.[214] His Lordship recognized that there was an important exception at common law in relation to the crown, but considered, as is also the dominant view in current legal thinking, that all difficulties in that regard were resolved with the adoption of section 2 CPA.[215] Yet we have seen in this chapter that despite the adoption of the CPA—and perhaps in part because of it—issues remain in the realm of civil proceedings against the crown, as the stories of Messrs Trawnik, Matthews, and Hinse illustrate.[216] The Diceyan notion of equality before the law and its corollary emphasis on the individual liability of crown servants reflected in the CPA and the crown's vicarious

[211] *Town Investments* (n 153) 381.

[212] *Entick v Carrington* (1765) EWHC KB J98, (1765) 2 Wilson KB 275, (1765) 19 St Tr 1030; *Mersey Docks Trustees v Gibbs* (n 49); see Chapter 4, sections 3.3.2.1 and 3.3.3.2.

[213] *Robinson v Chief Constable of West Yorkshire Police* [2018] UKSC 4, [32]; see Chapter 4, section 3.3.3.2, and this chapter's section 4.1.

[214] *Robinson v Chief Constable of West Yorkshire Police* [2018] UKSC 4, [33].

[215] ibid.

[216] *Trawnik* (n 31); *Matthews* (n 44); *Hinse* (n 124) (see sections 2.4.1, 2.4.2, 4.2.1, and 4.3.3).

liability it enacts have left unaddressed the issue of direct institutional liability of the government.

A historical constitutional approach to *the king can do no wrong* can inform our understanding of the law of crown liability. Its evolution is enlightened and the historical constitutional fundamentals which attach to it—the king's immunity from suit, ministerial responsibility, and liability of all ministers, servants, and instruments—become clearer. The central government conceived of as liable at common law, on an equal footing with individuals and public authorities, is consonant with the seventeenth-century constitutional arrangement that shielded the king personally from suit but held his ministers and servants liable. The central government's liability at common law would also resolve the difficulty in justifying the difference between public authorities' liability at common law and the formal notion of crown's immunity at common law. Conceiving of the central government as liable at common law based on seventeenth-century constitutional principles would also bring the law of crown liability in line with that of judicial review and of the prerogative.

6

The King Can Do No Wrong's Travels and Travails Across the Common Law World

1 Overview of the chapter

This chapter examines first the death, survival, and mutations of *the king can do no wrong* in two former parts of the British empire—the American and Irish republics. The analysis then turns to understandings of *the king can do no wrong* in Australia, where the crown's liability—its capacity to do wrong—at common law differs from English and American understandings.

While the Americans cut ties with the crown as early as 1776, the Irish Constitution is more recent, and dates to 1937. As will be explained, American law retained the feudal element of the king's immunity from suit while rejecting other understandings of *the king can do no wrong*, such as imputed ministerial responsibility and the fiction that there is no wrong in the king. The American doctrine of sovereign immunity also rests on a premise that is most un-English—the sovereign's status as above the law.

In defining Irish constitutional law in relation to state liability, twentieth-century Irish courts faced challenges of modernity in a republican context. As is the case in the text of the American Constitution—'We the People' in the preamble—sovereignty under the Irish Constitution also resides with the people—'We, the people of Éire'—in the preamble of the 1937 Constitution. Irish courts turned to their American republican counterparts for inspiration shortly after the creation of the Irish Free State (*Saorstát Éireann*) in 1922. Irish courts also drew from Blackstone's guidance but differed in their approach from their American brethren in that they used the prerogative as their main focal point. In a turn of events which marked a further departure from the American approach to sovereign immunity, seminal Irish cases, post 1937 and the current Constitution of the Republic of Ireland, have rejected altogether *the king can do no wrong* understood as the relic of a feudal monarchical past, conceived of as incompatible with the idea of a modern republic. *The king can do no wrong* understood as an immunity from suit inextricably attached to the English king as feudal overlord was found not to have survived even the birth of the Irish Free State in 1922.

Australia, when compared to the rest of the common law world, has a longer history of adopting statutes to subject the crown to suits brought forth by individuals.

The King Can Do No Wrong. Marie-France Fortin, Oxford University Press.
DOI: 10.1093/9780191994487.003.0007

While American constitutional law has played a significant role in influencing the scope of the courts' jurisdiction in the Australian constitutional order, Irish cases on state liability feature in seminal Australian cases on crown immunity. Australian legal thinking also offers an interesting perspective on the Commonwealth's capacity to do wrong and its liability for a tort at common law.

Throughout the chapter, relationships between English, American, Irish, and Australian legal thinking on *the king can do no wrong* and the law governing state—or crown—liability will be highlighted.[1]

Apart from throwing light on understandings of *the king can do no wrong* in jurisdictions closely related to English legal thinking, the purpose of the comparison in this chapter is to test the possible relevance of the heuristic model developed in Chapter 1 when applied to the historical evolution of *the king can do no wrong* in a historical comparison of jurisdictions. The objective in this chapter is in part to determine the extent to which—and, in the affirmative, the reasons why—the model is, or is not, useful in a historical comparison.[2] Comparative history, even in English-influenced jurisdictions, can imply significant divergences due to external considerations, and substantially increases contingency on other past factors external to the model alluded to in Chapter 1. For instance, as will be shown in this chapter, although strongly influenced in their constitutional interpretation by American constitutional law, with which they share a federal structure and similar written constitutions, Australian courts instead looked to Irish cases in interpreting the Commonwealth Constitution in the realm of governmental liability, despite obvious differences in relation to the monarch within their respective constitutional order.

2 United States: *the king can do no wrong* and sovereign immunity

In 1963, the renowned American scholar Louis L Jaffe identified two 'distinct and independent concepts' in relation to the liability of the state: the sovereign's immunity from suit—which Jaffe called 'sovereign immunity'—and the sovereign's

[1] Canadian legal thinking on *the king can do no wrong* mimics English legal thinking. The Canadian Petition of Right Act 1875 was modelled on the UK Parliament's Petitions of Right Act 1860, and Canadian courts of the late nineteenth and early twentieth centuries adopted nineteenth-century English courts' understanding of *the king can do no wrong* found in petition of right cases (for a discussion of these cases, see Chapter 4, section 3.3). The Privy Council, on appeal from Canadian courts, also relied on the English nineteenth-century understanding of *the king can do no wrong* to interpret Canadian legislation on crown proceedings. When Canada's federal legislation on crown immunity was adopted in 1953, it was modelled on the United Kingdom's Crown Proceedings Act 1947 (CPA). References to Canadian law and legal thinking on crown liability can be found in Chapter 5, section 4.

[2] I am thankful to JWF Allison for his typically insightful comments on the historical comparative use of the model; see his enlightening discussion of 'An historical-comparative jurisprudence' in JWF Allison, *A Continental Distinction in the Common Law: A Historical and Comparative Perspective on English Public Law* (revised edn, OUP 2000) 27–33.

capacity to violate or not violate the law—which Jaffe associated with the 'the King can do no wrong'.[3] The two components of sovereign liability identified by Jaffe are easily transposed to this book's heuristic model and correspond to the two dimensions of crown liability in English legal thinking: the crown's amenability to justice and the crown's capacity to do wrong.

In the American context, more specifically, the notions of immunity from suit and that of the status of the sovereign in relation to law—understood as sovereignty—capture essential aspects of American legal thinking on the issue of governmental liability. The dissenters in the seminal case of *Seminole Tribe of Florida*, for instance, illustrated very clearly this dual dimension of the doctrine of sovereign immunity when they wrote:

> The doctrine of sovereign immunity comprises two distinct rules, which are not always separately recognized. The one rule holds that the King or the Crown, as the font of law, is not bound by the law's provisions; the other provides that the King or Crown, as the font of justice, is not subject to suit in its own courts. . . . The one rule limits the reach of substantive law; the other, the jurisdiction of the courts.[4]

The king as font of law is above it, and therefore incapable of doing wrong, and the king as the font of justice is not amenable to suit before his own courts. The two dimensions of governmental liability in American legal thinking on sovereign immunity differ from the two dimensions of crown liability derived from the understandings of *the king can do no wrong* in English legal thinking taken historically. The idea that the king is not bound by the law flies in the face of deeply entrenched constitutional principles: since the days of Bracton, the English king has been subject to law.[5] The consecration of parliamentary sovereignty in the seventeenth century also negated the king's role as the font of law. Even in Matthew Hale's theory of the powers of the law in the seventeenth century, the king—although free from the coercive power of the law—was nevertheless subject to its invalidating power.[6]

The dissenters' use of the words 'the King or the Crown' in *Seminole Tribe* as if the terms were interchangeable demonstrates, however, the dissenting justices' contemporary stance. In this regard, although it is true that ever since *Province of Bombay* the crown is not bound by a statute unless its provisions expressly say

[3] Louis L Jaffe, 'Suits against Governments and Officers: Sovereign Immunity' (1963) 77 Harv L Rev 1, 4. Borchard also associated *the king can do no wrong* with the sovereign's incapacity to do wrong: 'The maxim, "The king can do no wrong" was perverted from its historical meaning that he was not privileged to do wrong into the modern meaning that he was incapable of doing wrong.' Edwin Borchard, 'Governmental Responsibility in Tort, VI' (1926) 36 YLJ 1, 35.

[4] *Seminole Tribe of Fla v Florida* (1996) 517 US 44, 102–03 (Souter J, dissenting).

[5] See Chapter 2.

[6] See Chapter 3, sections 3.1.2 and 3.3.3.

so or by necessary implication,[7] this recent mid-twentieth-century development runs afoul of a long-held understanding in English legal thinking that the king was bound even by a general statute.[8]

Trends in American legal thinking reflect conceptions of the sovereign as above the law and immune from suit, and are pulled in opposing directions by two different conceptions: that of the 'People' as the sovereign and that of the states as enjoying a constitutional protection of their sovereignty in a power-sharing federal structure where powers are allocated between the states and the United States. The people are the sovereign, yet the states also retain a residual sovereignty, which must be protected against encroachment by Congress and in the context of judicial proceedings before the courts, including their own.

In addition to the text of the Constitution itself—which begins with the very words 'We The People'[9]—the people have been identified as the sovereign on numerous occasions: to Jay CJ in the seminal case of *Chisholm v Georgia*, sovereignty remains with the people;[10] in *Yick Wo v Hopkins*, it was said that 'sovereignty itself remains with the people by whom and for whom all government exists and acts';[11] and in *US v Lee*, it was found that 'Under our system the people . . . are the sovereign'.[12] Legal scholarship has also advocated for the recognition that sovereignty resides with the people.[13] But the states themselves were also conceived of as the sovereigns who consented to contract a federal union: '[the Constitution] is the authoritative language of the American people, and . . . of the American States'.[14] In The Federalist Papers No 81, Hamilton argued that this attribute of sovereignty inhered in the states:

[7] *Province of Bombay v Municipal Corporation of the City of Bombay* [1947] AC 58.

[8] Harry Street, 'The Effects of Statutes upon the Rights and Liabilities of the Crown' (1948) 7 UTLJ 357; Paul Craig, *Administrative Law* (9th edn, Sweet & Maxwell 2021) 899–900; Marie-France Fortin, 'Revisiting the Application of Statutes to the Crown: A Historical Constitutional Approach' (2021) 3 J CommonwL 271.

[9] The Preamble to the United States Constitution reads in full: 'We the People of the United States, in Order to form a more perfect Union, establish Justice, insure domestic Tranquility, provide for the common defence, promote the general Welfare, and secure the Blessings of Liberty to ourselves and our Posterity, do ordain and establish this Constitution for the United States of America.' The people also feature, in provisions other than those relating to rights, in s 2 of Art I (the people are entrusted with choosing members of the House) and the Tenth Amendment (powers not ascribed to the federal government are reserved to the states and to the people).

[10] *Chisholm v Georgia* (1793) 2 US (2 Dall) 419, 470. According to Amar, although Iredell J, dissenting in *Chisholm*, spoke of authority rather than sovereignty, he also accepted that ultimate sovereignty lay in the people: ibid 448, Akhil Reed Amar, 'Of Sovereignty and Federalism' (1987) 96 YLJ 1425, 1471.

[11] *Yick Wo v Hopkins* (1886) 118 US 356, 370 (Matthews J).

[12] *US v Lee* (1886) 106 US 196, 208 (Miller J).

[13] 'True sovereignty lies with the people': Amar (n 10) 1435.

[14] *Cohens v Virginia* (1821) 19 US 264, 381 (Marshall CJ) (opinion on the motion for dismissing the writ of error for want of jurisdiction in the Court). Marshall CJ also wrote, in the same vein: 'The American States, as well as the American people, have believed a close and firm Union to be essential to their liberty and to their happiness', ibid 380, although he subsequently conferred 'supreme' sovereignty on the people: 'The people made the Constitution, and the people can unmake it. It is the creature of their will, and lives only by their will', ibid 389.

> It is inherent in the nature of sovereignty, not to be amenable to the suit of an individual without its consent. This is the general sense and the general practice of mankind; and the exemption, as one of the attributes of sovereignty, is now enjoyed by the government of every state in the Union.[15]

The locus of sovereignty in the American Constitution is impacted by the federal dimension of the constitutional order and the allocation of power between the states and the United States it created. As Marshall CJ explained in *Cohens v Virginia*: 'if a State has surrendered any portion of its sovereignty, the question whether a liability to suit be a part of this portion depends on the instrument by which the surrender is made'.[16] The issue of the subjection of the states to Congress's legislative powers—enumerated under Article I, section 8 but also found in the Enforcement clause of the Fourteenth Amendment[17]—is a matter of constitutional interpretation which must also take into account the Tenth and the Eleventh Amendments.[18]

As a result of both the political context surrounding the creation of a federal republic in the eighteenth century and the influence of Blackstone's *Commentaries* and his flawed theorization of the relationship between the prerogative, the king's perfection, and *the king can do no wrong*, the 'sovereign' in American legal and political circles was conceived in the Hobbesian[19]—and later Austinian[20]—school of

[15] Alexander Hamilton, James Madison, and John Jay, *The Federalist* (Jacob E Cooke ed, 1st edn, Wesleyan UP 1961) 548–49. cf Souter J, dissenting in *Alden v Maine*, according to whom: 'Some Framers thought sovereign immunity was an obsolete royal prerogative inapplicable in a republic; some thought sovereign immunity was a common law power defeasible, like other common law rights, by statute; and perhaps a few thought, in keeping with a natural law view distinct from the common law conception, that immunity was inherent in a sovereign because the body that made a law could not logically be bound by it. Natural law thinking on the part of a doubtful few will not, however, support the Court's position': *Alden v Maine* (1999) 527 US 706, 764.

[16] *Cohens v Virginia* (n 14) 381 (Marshall CJ) (opinion on the motion for dismissing the writ of error for want of jurisdiction in the Court).

[17] Fourteenth Amendment, Section 5 (Enforcement clause): 'The Congress shall have the power to enforce, by appropriate legislation, the provisions of this article.' As for the Fourteenth Amendment's Due Process clause, it provides: 'Section 1. All persons born or naturalized in the United States, and subject to the jurisdiction thereof, are citizens of the United States and of the State wherein they reside. No State shall make or enforce any law which shall abridge the privileges or immunities of citizens of the United States; nor shall any State deprive any person of life, liberty, or property, without due process of law; nor deny to any person within its jurisdiction the equal protection of the laws.'

[18] The Tenth Amendment of the United States Constitution states: 'The powers not delegated to the United States by the Constitution, nor prohibited by it to the States, are reserved to the States respectively, or to the people'; and the Eleventh Amendment provides that: 'The Judicial power of the United States shall not be construed to extend to any suit in law or equity, commenced or prosecuted against one of the United States by Citizens of another State, or by Citizens or Subjects of any Foreign State.'

[19] Famously, to Hobbes, in Chapter 26, 2, 'The Sovereign of a Commonwealth, be it an Assembly, or one Man, is not Subject to the Civil Laws', see Thomas Hobbes, *Leviathan* (Richard Tuck ed, CUP 1991); David Schraub, 'Finding the "Sovereign" in "Sovereign Immunity": Lessons from Bodin, Hobbes, and Rousseau' (2017) 29 Critical Review 388.

[20] To Austin, a positivist, the crucial characteristic of law is that it rests on the command of the sovereign: 'Every positive law or every law simply and strictly so called, is set by a sovereign person, or a sovereign body of persons, to a member or members of the independent political society wherein that

thought. The American concept of sovereign immunity is tied to the federal structure of the American constitution and is based on the idea that the sovereign as law-maker is above the law. The theoretical underpinnings of sovereign immunity in the American legal context are, therefore, diametrically opposed to the long-held view in English legal thinking, stretching back to the Middle Ages, that the king is subject to law. The creation of the American republic marked a very deep severance from English constitutional fundamentals, and liability of the executive was no exception.

The analysis begins in the first section with an overview of the American scholarly inclination to studying the past, including English sources. An overview of Blackstone's writings and their influence over the development of the doctrine of sovereign immunity then follows, with particular emphasis on its impact in the judges' reasoning in the seminal case of *Chisholm v Georgia*. The second section focusses on how the justices' speeches in *Chisholm* have found echo ever since in discussions of sovereign immunity.

2.1 Birth of the American republic: rejection (and retention) of English constitutional principles

American colonists were well-read in English constitutional law and literature: Coke and Blackstone were widely relied upon.[21] Colonies—regardless of their status as provinces, governmental or by charter—were originally governed by the English common law,[22] and the Founders were very knowledgeable of English constitutional principles, particularly as they related to government.[23]

After the American War of Independence of 1775–1783, the United States of America became a republic and cut ties with the British crown and empire. The Declaration of Independence of the thirteen British colonies dates to 1776, and delegates met at the Constitutional Convention in 1787 to draft the Constitution of

person or body is sovereign or supreme' and the 'sovereign or supreme power is incapable of legal limitation': John Austin, *The Province of Jurisprudence Determined* (Wilfrid E Rumble ed (written 1832), CUP 1995) 16, 188. See John Hudson, 'Maitland and Austin, Legal History and Legal Thought in the Late Nineteenth Century' in *Law and Authority in British Legal History, 1200–1900* (CUP 2016) 295–96. On the relationship between the work of Hobbes and Austin, see eg John Dewey, 'Austin's Theory of Sovereignty' (1894) 9 Pol Sci Q 31, 31; David Runciman, *Pluralism and the Personality of the State* (CUP 1997) 73–74; Janet McLean, 'Personality and Public Law Doctrine' (1999) 49 UTLJ 123, 136–38.

[21] George H Pugh, 'Historical Approach to the Doctrine of Sovereign Immunity' (1952) 13 La L Rev 476, 481.

[22] Joseph Story, *Commentaries on the Constitution of the United States*, vol 1 (Melville Madison Bigelow ed, 5th edn, William S Hein & Co 1994) 116; Bradley Raboin, 'Punish the Crown, but Protect the Government: A Comparative Analysis of State Tort Liability for Exemplary Damages in England and Punitive Damages in the United States' (2016) 14 Cardozo J Int'l & Comp L 261, 268.

[23] Guy I Seidman, 'The Origins of Accountability: Everything I Know About the Sovereign's Immunity, I Learned from King Henry III' (2005) 49 St Louis ULJ 393, 480.

the United States of America, which, after rounds of negotiations, came into force in March 1789.

The same year that the Constitution came into force, the Bill of Rights 1688 was a hundred years old. Parliamentary sovereignty was, by then, an English constitutional tenet that had not escaped colonists in New England—as is evidenced by Benjamin Franklin's writings[24] and the popularity of the rallying cry 'no taxation without representation'.[25]

Many features of the English Constitution were rejected under the American Constitution. Liability of the executive by way of ministerial responsibility was one of them. In Britain, the king's personal immunity from suit as part of the constitutional arrangement reached after the upheavals of the seventeenth century and the Glorious Revolution was not contested and was reflected in the understanding of *the king can do no wrong*. The king still played an important part in selecting ministers until responsible government became a fixture of political life in Britain in the middle of the nineteenth century.[26] Nevertheless, the liability of the king's ministers as a counterweight to the king's personal immunity was also an integral part of the English constitutional pact, and ministerial responsibility in lieu of the king's liability was also associated with *the king can do no wrong*.

Delegates from the colonies at the Convention rejected the British model of ministerial responsibility when they met in Philadelphia in 1787, opting instead to maximize liability of the executive by creating a unitary model: the presidency.[27] The delegates hoped that the concentration of executive powers in the president as the sole organ of the executive branch would avoid the dilution of the attribution of blame onto ministers.[28] *The king can do no wrong* understood as the king's immunity from suit for the acts of his subordinates was not to benefit the president, a fundamental feature of constitutional design which was subsequently confirmed by the courts.[29] As a result, sovereign immunity in the American

[24] Letter from Benjamin Franklin to William Shirley, dated 4 December 1754 in *The Papers of Benjamin Franklin*, vol 5 (Leonard W Labaree ed, Yale UP 1962) 443–47.

[25] Taxation imposed on the American colonists by their imperial masters included that provided for in the Sugar Act 1764, 4 Geo III c 15; the Stamp Act 1765, 5 Geo III c 12; and the Tea Act 1773, 13 Geo III c 44.

[26] Janet McLean, *Searching for the State in British Legal Thought: Competing Conceptions of the Public Sphere* (CUP 2012) 36–37.

[27] Michael W McConnell, *The President Who Would Not Be King: Executive Power under the Constitution* (Princeton UP 2020) 34, 57, 82.

[28] ibid.

[29] Although the Court ultimately decided on other grounds, see the plaintiff in error's pleadings in *Kendall v US ex rel Stokes* (1838) 37 US 524, 543–44:

> The President appoints these officers, and can remove them at pleasure. . . . He administers the affairs of government through them. Now, who does not see that if he can have his will this done by his subordinates, and escape all censure and responsibility for what is dcoile wrong, by saying it was done by them. . . .
>
> The framers of our constitution were wise enough to see this, and they have left him no ground for such an excuse; and the people have always held him to this responsibility. . . . And as long as the

context is conceptually distinct from the president's liability and limited executive immunity.[30]

Debates in the realm of governmental liability in American legal thinking as to the legitimacy of sovereign immunity are still topical today. Sovereign immunity is often perceived as a relic of a rejected monarchical past. But as will be explained in this chapter, what is perceived in American legal thinking as a monarchical relic is in fact grounded in a Hobbesian or Austinian understanding of sovereignty: the sovereign is the absolute law-making authority who issues commands and is therefore above the law.[31] Moreover, the notion of sovereignty in American legal thinking was developed in the context of creating and implementing the American federal constitutional structure. Federalism was indeed a novelty when, following the Articles of Confederation,[32] it was devised as a constitutional form of government by the Committee of Detail of the Convention in the summer of 1787.[33] From a historical constitutional approach, it is a mistake to see in *the king*

government shall last, this is the true constitutional ground . . . and was it not so, we should have the English maxim, that the king can do no wrong, made applicable to the President.

[30] The president's liability was at issue in the following cases: *Mississippi v Johnson* (1867) 4 Wall 475, 501: 'this court has no jurisdiction of a bill to enjoin the President in the performance of his official duties' (Chase CJ); *US v Nixon* (1974) 418 US 683: the president may be subject to a subpoena to provide information relevant to an ongoing criminal prosecution; *Nixon v Fitzgerald* (1982) 457 US 731, 749: '[the president] is entitled to absolute immunity from damages liability predicated on his official acts' and 756: 'absolute Presidential immunity from damages liability for acts within the "outer perimeter" of his official responsibility' (Powell J); *Franklin v Massachusetts* (1992) 505 US 788, 802: the president's actions in relation to the census conducted under Art I, s 2, cl 3 of the Constitution, and the distribution of Representatives in Congress were not challengeable under the Administrative Procedure Act for reasons grounded in the separation of powers (O'Connor J for the plurality); *Clinton v Jones* (1997) 520 US 681, 694: the president's immunity from suit for his actions within his official capacity does not extend to unofficial acts—the immunity attaches to the nature of the function and not to the person (Stevens J). The president's liability is also distinct from the king's immunity: the president is subject to impeachment and 'elected from the mass of the people [to which he then] returns': *US v Burr*, 25 F Cas 30, 34 (CCD Va 1807) (No 14,692d), cited in Daphna Renan, 'The President's Two Bodies' (2020) 120 Colum L Rev 1119, 1162.

[31] The sovereign, in Hobbes's thinking, is the representative of the state: Quentin Skinner, 'Hobbes and the Purely Artificial Person of the State' (1999) 7 J Pol Phil 1, 20. The identity of that sovereign, however, is not clearly defined in Hobbesian and Austinian thinking: Hobbes's theory 'is not an explicitly legal or even a descriptive account of the state', while Austin 'glosses the question of where sovereignty resides': McLean (n 20) 128, 137. 'Austin did not strictly speaking produce a theory of the state at all': Runciman (n 20) 74. Austin's theory of sovereignty as applied to the United States was criticized: see Dewey (n 20) 38–39. Given Austin's posthumous influence on American legal thinking in the nineteenth and twentieth centuries, his shortcomings in relation to the identity of the sovereign are consequential for the development of the doctrine of sovereign immunity for that period. On Austin's influence in America, see eg William Loutit Morison, *John Austin* (Stanford UP 1982); Wilfrid E Rumble, 'Legal Positivism of John Austin and the Realist Movement in American Jurisprudence' (1981) 66 Cornell L Rev 986.

[32] The Articles of Confederation were drafted in 1777 and were the basis for the political organization and government of the colonies during the War of Independence. They were superseded by the United States Constitution when it came into force: see McConnell (n 27) 19.

[33] Federalism and the enumeration of powers assigned to Congress were constitutional innovations: ibid 64, 74.

can do no wrong the origins of the American sovereign immunity doctrine. The American concept of sovereign immunity is as much a product of federalism and the allocation of power in the Constitution between two levels of government—federal and states—as it is grounded in the idea that the sovereign is above the law. The theoretical underpinnings of the American doctrine of sovereign immunity are diametrically opposed to the king's status as below the law that makes him in the English legal tradition. The American republican sovereign is more a Leviathan than the English monarch ever was.

2.1.1 A long tradition of American scholarly inclination

In the realm of sovereign immunity more specifically, American legal scholars have long demonstrated a keen interest in historical analysis.[34] Borchard and Jaffe, perhaps the most prominent among them, knew that there is 'adequate evidence that the expression "the King can do no wrong" originally meant precisely the contrary to what it later came to mean'.[35] Twentieth-century legal scholars on the western side of the Atlantic knew of English legal historians' work—including Erhlich's.[36] They knew, therefore, of Bracton's understanding that the king was not allowed to do wrong, and was subject to law.[37]

Many, however, nevertheless referred to th*e king can do no wrong* as meaning that the king was absolutely above the law and immune from suit. Borchard, for example, in analysing the UK Parliament's Crown Proceedings Act 1947 (CPA) and the American Congress's Federal Tort Claims Act (FTCA), wrote that the two statutes mark a rejection of the concept that *the king can do no wrong* and allow the 'state' to be sued:

> The United States and Great Britain have recently undertaken what may justly be called a revolution in legal principles. Instead of adhering to the old maxim that

[34] Borchard, Pugh, Jaffe, and Massey are but a few examples of legal scholars whose interest in the history of sovereign immunity has shed light on the American doctrine: Edwin Borchard, 'Government Liability in Tort' (1924) 34 YLJ 1; Edwin Borchard, 'Government Liability in Tort' (1924) 34 YLJ 129; Edwin Borchard, 'Government Liability in Tort' (1925) 34 YLJ 229; Borchard, 'Governmental Responsibility in Tort, VI' (n 3); Edwin Borchard, 'Governmental Responsibility in Tort, V' (1926) 36 YLJ 757; Edwin M Borchard, 'Government Liability in Tort' (1948) 26 Can Bar Rev 399; Herbert Barry, *The King Can Do No Wrong, and Other Papers Contributed to the Virginia Law Review* (Michie Co 1931); Pugh (n 21); Jaffe (n 3); Louis L Jaffe, 'Suits against Governments and Officers: Damage Actions' (1963) 77 Harv L Rev 209; Calvin R Massey, 'State Sovereignty and the Tenth and Eleventh Amendments' (1989) 56 U Chi L Rev 61; Seidman (n 23). See also Stanwood R Duval, 'Sovereign Immunity, Anachronistic or Inherent: A Sword or a Shield?' (2010) Tul L Rev 1471.

[35] Jaffe (n 3) 3–4.

[36] Ludwik Ehrlich, 'Proceedings against the Crown (1216–1377)' in Paul Vinogradoff (ed), *Oxford Studies in Social and Legal History*, vol 6 (Clarendon Press 1921).

[37] Borchard, 'Governmental Responsibility in Tort, VI' (n 3) 21–23; Borchard, 'Governmental Responsibility in Tort, V' (n 34) 798–99; Jaffe (n 3) 3–4. See *Owen v City of Independence, Mo* (1980) 445 US 622, 645 (Brennan J), citing to Borchard for the view that 'the meaning traditionally ascribed to this phrase [the king can do no wrong] is an ironic perversion of its original intent'.

'the King can do no wrong', inadvertently adopted in the case of the United States, each has enacted a statute by which the country is subject to suit in tort.[38]

The excerpt shows that in the American legal mind, *the king can do no wrong* means immunity from suit. The—ahistorical—understanding of *the king can do no wrong* as an ancient doctrine of the common law tied to the king's status as feudal overlord is deeply engrained in American legal thinking. More recently, the dissenters in *Seminole Tribe* also conceived of sovereign immunity as 'an ancient doctrine'.[39] Borchard himself wondered how *the king can do no wrong* had survived in the American republic: 'How it came to be applied in the United States where the prerogative is unknown, is one of the mysteries of legal evolution.'[40]

As the previous chapters have demonstrated, conceiving of the sovereign as above the law is not characteristic of English legal thinking, taken historically. While divine right and the prerogative may be conceptually associated with the king's immunity from suit, the king's status as above the law was not resorted to as a justification for his immunity from suit—except for the short period in the early seventeenth century when the most convinced Royalists supported the Stuarts' claim to divine status.[41] Even Blackstone did not unequivocally invoke the king's status as above the law in defining the prerogative: he defined the prerogative as the pre-eminence the king holds in preference to other persons, but that privileged status, although 'out of the course of the common law', did not entail that the king was to be conceived of as supralegal—Blackstone was also firmly of the Bractonian view that the law made the king and that it limited his prerogative.[42]

Nevertheless, Blackstone's influence over the early American legal foundations was such that it merits yet another analysis in attempting to uncover the theoretical and historical foundations of sovereign immunity in American law. Other

[38] Borchard, 'Government Liability in Tort' (1948) (n 34) 399. As we have seen in Chapter 5, section 4, conceiving of the 'country' as subject to suit in tort as Borchard implies in this excerpt is an erroneous statement of the law in England if what is meant is that the state or crown is directly liable. Under the CPA, the crown is only vicariously liable for the acts of its officers and servants. The crown itself is not conceived as capable of having committed a tort.

[39] *Seminole Tribe of Florida v Florida* (n 4) 96 (Souter J, dissenting).

[40] Borchard, 'Governmental Responsibility in Tort, VI' (n 3) 4. See also James Fleming, 'Tort Liability of Governmental Units and Their Officers' (1954–55) 22 U Chi L Rev 610, 612: 'Just how an immunity which had its roots in feudalism and in a political philosophy associated with the divine rights of kings was transplanted to the new republic in America remains something of a mystery'; Bernard Schwartz and William Wade, *Legal Control of Government: Administrative Law in Britain and the United States* (OUP 1972) 185: 'It is a source of wonder to an English lawyer that American law should cling so tenaciously to the doctrine of sovereign immunity, battered tough it is by statutory inroads, by judicial hostility, and by almost universal disapproval. It seems quite incapable of justification, yet it casts a kind of spell which can produce quite irrational arguments from the greatest American judges.' See also *Owen v City of Independence, Mo* (n 37) 645 (Brennan J): 'it has never been understood how the doctrine of sovereign immunity came to be adopted in the American democracy'.

[41] See Chapter 3, sections 3.1 and 3.2.

[42] William Blackstone, *Commentaries on the Laws of England*, vol 1 (facsimile of 1765–1769 1st edn, University of Chicago Press 1979) 230–33. See Chapter 4, section 2.1.

understandings of *the king can do no wrong* in the eighteenth and nineteenth centuries and their inadequacy in the American constitutional context are also outlined.

2.1.2 Blackstone and his influential flaws: a Trojan horse in the republic

A significant contextual element to understanding the historical foundations of American sovereign immunity is that Blackstone had written his influential *Commentaries on the Laws of England* when the American colonists put themselves to the task of writing their Constitution. We know that the Founders read and relied on the *Commentaries* in devising the constitutional text.[43] United States Supreme Court justices Iredell, Marshall, and Story's admiration for and reliance on Blackstone's work is also well known.[44] Such heavy reliance on the *Commentaries*, it will be argued below, contributed to the confusion surrounding the historical and theoretical groundings of *the king can do no wrong* and sovereign immunity in American legal thinking.

Blackstone's understanding of *the king can do no wrong* in his *Commentaries on the Laws of England* encapsulated both the king's personal immunity from suit and his ministers' liability. Blackstone also inherited, however, the logical flaws caused by the continued existence of the petition of right, to which he added the notion of perfection of the king. As we have seen in Chapter 4 and as will be further explained below, Blackstone's work was an attempt to bring together the thoughts of many past thinkers. His analysis was, as a result, lacking in consistency in certain respects. Hobbesian elements of sovereignty ascribed to the king in Blackstone's *Commentaries* are hardly reconcilable with the Bractonian understanding that the king is under the law—which Blackstone also espoused.

Blackstone's work, although appealing to the reader in its clear organization of subject matters, was essentially a formidable achievement in terms of collecting prior authors' thoughts. The debate as to the merit of Blackstone's *Commentaries* has opposed historically illustrious scholars and thinkers admirative of the *Commentaries*—among which Burke, Lord Mansfield, and Maitland—and others, highly critical of it—such as Bentham, Maine, and Austin.[45] Blackstone's

[43] C Ellis Stevens, *Sources of the Constitution of the United States, Considered in Relation to Colonial and English History* (2nd edn, Macmillan 1894) 48; Pugh (n 21) 481; Alan Watson, *Legal Transplants: An Approach to Comparative Law* (University Press of Virginia 1974) 93–94; Dennis R Nolan, 'Sir William Blackstone and the New American Republic: A Study of Intellectual Impact' (1976) 51 NYU L Rev 731; Duncan Kennedy, 'The Structure of Blackstone's Commentaries' (1979) 28 Buffo L Rev 205, 209; John W Cairns, 'Blackstone, an English Institutist: Legal Literature and the Rise of the Nation State' (1984) 4 OJLS 318, 318; John V Orth, 'Blackstone' in Markus Dirk Dubber and Christopher L Tomlins (eds), *The Oxford Handbook of Legal History* (OUP 2018) 375–76. The Supreme Court itself found that 'two of the greatest English jurists, Lord Chief Justice Hale and Sir William Blackstone ... exerted considerable influence on the Founders': *Reid v Covert* (1957) 354 US 1, 26.

[44] Nolan (n 43) 757–58 (Black J).

[45] AV Dicey, 'Blackstone's Commentaries' (1932) 4 CLJ 286, 287–88. On Bentham's criticism of Blackstone: William Renwick Riddell, 'Bentham on Blackstone: A Review' (1929) 15 ABAJ 676; Richard

Commentaries resemble more an adept compendium of past legal literature arranged in a romanist, Justinian fashion than a product of his own thinking about the law. Blackstone set out to use a deductive method, as Finch had done before him, but failed to think it through and instead borrowed from others' theories—namely Matthew Hale's.[46] The result is closer to a well-presented collage than a legal treatise reflecting the author's own analysis: there are gaps and flaws in Blackstone's otherwise well-organized exposition of the law. It has rightly been lamented, for example, that Blackstone creates an absolute sovereign but does not reconcile this with parliamentary sovereignty, and that his definition of the social contract borrows rather surprisingly from both Locke and Hobbes.[47] Blackstone's contradictions in defining *the king can do no wrong*, exposed in Chapter 4, follow from his incompatible conception of the king as both under the law and simultaneously absolute sovereign in a constitution anchored in parliamentary sovereignty.

Of importance to our understanding of *the king can do no wrong* and its meaning in American legal thinking is that Blackstone's *Commentaries* are also lacking in the realm of public officers' liability. The seminal cases of *Ashby v White* and *Entick v Carrington* and the liability of public officers they set out were already fundamental elements of constitutional law by the time the drafters of the American Constitution met to discuss its contents.[48] Yet, although the first volume of his *Commentaries* appeared the same year as *Entick v Carrington* was

A Posner, 'Blackstone and Bentham' (1976) 19 JL & Econ 569. The debate was more recently mirrored in the second half of the twentieth century as scholars offered opposite views on the merits of Blackstone's magnum opus: Kennedy (n 43); Alan Watson, 'The Structure of Blackstone's Commentaries' (1988) 97 YLJ 795.

[46] Michael Lobban, 'Blackstone and the Science of Law' (1987) 30 Historical J 311, 318–19, 328; Michael Lobban, 'Rationalising the Common Law: Blackstone and His Predecessors' in Anthony Page and Wilfrid Prest (eds), *Blackstone and His Critics* (Hart Publishing 2018). As one would expect, excellent and sometimes very critical scholarship has been written on Blackstone's work: Jeremy Bentham, *A Comment on the Commentaries and a Fragment on Government* (HLA Hart and JH Burns eds, Athlone Press 1977); Kennedy (n 43); Cairns (n 43); Watson (n 45); Wilfrid Prest (ed), *Blackstone and His Commentaries: Biography, Law, History* (Hart Publishing 2009); Wilfrid Prest (ed), *Re-Interpreting Blackstone's Commentaries: A Seminal Text in National and International Contexts* (Hart Publishing 2014); Anthony Page and Wilfrid Prest (eds), *Blackstone and His Critics* (Hart Publishing 2018). On Finch, see Henry Finch, *A Description of the Common Laws of England* (printed for A Millar 1759); Henry Finch, *Nomotechnia* (Printed for the Societie of Stationers 1613); Wilfrid Prest, 'The Dialectical Origins of Finch's Law' (1977) 36 CLJ 326.

[47] Lobban, 'Blackstone and the Science of Law' (n 46) 327; Mark Walters, *A.V. Dicey and the Common Law Constitutional Tradition* (CUP 2020) 214: Walters notes that Blackstone's reliance on early seventeenth-century Royalist thinking led him to espouse a 'Romanist or civilian absolutism'. On Blackstone's awkwardness in the face of 1688, see Robert Willman, 'Blackstone and the "Theoretical Perfection" of English Law in the Reign of Charles II' (1983) 26 Historical J 39. On his unjustifiable repetition of Montesquieu's flawed depiction of the separation of powers in the British Constitution, see Martin Loughlin, *The Idea of Public Law* (OUP 2003) 24; and on his contradictory depictions of royal power and sovereignty, see Josh Chafetz, 'Beating a Dead Corpse' (2022) 120 Mich L Rev 1187, 1190–91 (reviewing Don Herzog, *Sovereignty, RIP* (Yale UP 2020)).

[48] *Ashby v White* (1703) 92 ER 126; *Entick v Carrington* (1765) EWHC KB J98, (1765) 2 Wilson KB 275, (1765) 19 St Tr 1030.

decided (1765), Blackstone mentions only impeachment and indictment as instances where the king's agents had no defence against the victim of governmental wrongdoing.[49] American delegates at the Convention were well cognizant of the parliamentary procedure of impeachment of elected ministers, but equally that it had fallen into desuetude ever since the beginning of the eighteenth century.[50] It was that lesson that prompted them to create a unitary executive—the president—subject to impeachment under Article II, section 4. Had Blackstone taken into account recent judicial developments relating to the personal, legal, liability of public officers and ministers instead of emphasizing impeachment as the sole—political—mode of redress, perhaps the delegates would have charted a different constitutional path.

In his *Commentaries*, Blackstone adopted a sovereigntist account of the king's immunity from suit, which he grounded in the king's status as above all others:

> [Our king] owes no kind of subjection to any other potentate on earth. Hence it is, that no suit or action can be brought against the king, even in civil matters, because no court can have jurisdiction over him. For all jurisdiction implies superiority of power: authority to try would be vain and idle, without an authority to redress; and the sentence of a Court would be contemptible, unless the Court had power to command the execution of it: but who, says Finch, shall command the king?[51]

Blackstone's theorization of the prerogative powers as limited by the law and of the king's status as below the law, although he was superior to other persons, was inconsistent with his understanding of the king's immunity from suit as grounded in the king's sovereignty. Blackstone knew of the petition of right, for instance, and describing it as he did as a petition as of grace allowed him to conceptualize the king's immunity from suit as grounded in the king's status as sovereign, omitting the petition of right's nature as recourse founded in a subject's right. To Blackstone's rhetorical question 'who shall command the king?', however, one would not need to be Edward Coke to answer 'Parliament'. Parliament as legislative sovereign—even if conceived of as King-in-Parliament—negated the idea of an independent sovereign king sitting atop Parliament since the Glorious Revolution. The notion of sovereignty entails that no one is above the sovereign, and that sovereign was already Parliament in English constitutional thinking by time the Founders of the Constitution met in Philadelphia in 1787.

In short, Blackstone's account of the king's immunity from suit as grounded in sovereignty faced a major theoretical difficulty: the consecration of parliamentary

[49] SFC Milsom, 'The Nature of Blackstone's Achievement' (1981) 1 OJLS 1, 4.
[50] McConnell (n 27) 57.
[51] Blackstone (n 42) 235.

sovereignty in 1688. Blackstone's *Commentaries* were therefore analytically flawed. But they were also inconsistent: he acknowledged elsewhere in his *Commentaries* that the king is subject to law, and is not allowed by the law to do wrong.

Blackstone's *Commentaries*' unparalleled influence over the development of American law most certainly contributed to the American understanding of *the king can do no wrong* as the king's immunity from suit derived from the king's perceived status as above the law in English constitutional thinking. Borchard, for instance, pointed to Blackstone as the guilty party, one of the king's 'faithful servitors' who perverted the meaning of *the king can do no wrong* and turned it into a synonym for sovereign immunity.[52]

The overall anachronistic picture of the king depicted by Blackstone was perhaps more consonant with early Americans' views of their former king: the king acting in his imperial role was indeed more powerful than he was when acting domestically, where the English Constitution's limitations on his prerogatives were far more significant. While the king still exercised his prerogative over foreign affairs and war in matters relating to his colonies and the empire—including his power to legislate by royal proclamation over conquered territories[53]—he had lost the prerogative to legislate and to administer justice personally as king of England (and later Scotland and Ireland) since before the Glorious Revolution of 1688. Constitutional constraints which limited the king's prerogatives in England did not apply to the same extent in relation to imperial matters, and while early Americans knew of the English parliamentary form of constitutional government, it is with an imperial king they had interacted before they declared war on him. Perhaps this familiar rendering of their former imperial sovereign contributed to the success of Blacktone's *Commentaries* among American legal thinkers and judges. Of Blackstone's inconsistent depiction of the king in the English constitutional order, American legal thinking has retained one dimension: the portrayal of the king as a perfect being granted pre-eminence. In the republican American constitutional order, that king became an abstract sovereign of Leviathan proportions—but its identity as between the states, the United States, and the people is still debated.

2.2 Sovereignty, republicanism, and federalism

To Blackstone's influence over the development of the American understanding of *the king can do no wrong* must be added another significant variable: the federal structure of the American constitution. As Jaffe observed, in the American context, 'By a magnificent irony, this [English] body of doctrine and practice, at least

[52] Borchard, 'Governmental Responsibility in Tort, VI' (n 34) 799.

[53] See eg Proclamation of 7th Oct, 1763, issued by George III, in Adam Shortt and Arthur G Doughty, *Documents Relating to the Constitutional History of Canada, 1759–1791* (SE Dawson 1907) 119.

in form so favorable to the subject, lost one-half of its efficacy when translated into our state and federal systems.'[54]

Federalism is a fundamental component of American case law and literature on sovereign immunity. If immunity is conceived of as flowing from sovereignty, then identifying the sovereign is of paramount importance. Although *the king can do no wrong* is understood differently in American and English legal thinking, the two legal traditions nevertheless share a common conceptual conundrum. The locus of sovereignty in English legal thinking is still subject to debate—although the King-in-Parliament was recognized as the legislative sovereign with the monarchs consenting to the Bill of Rights, 1688. In English legal thinking it is the contours of the crown which are hazy, leading to much confusion as to which governmental entities—if any—could benefit from the king's feudal privilege not to be sued in his own courts. In American legal thinking, it is the identity of the sovereign that has led to much debate, in part because the issue was first raised judicially in *Chisholm v Georgia*, a case involving states' immunity before federal courts and the scope of the latter's jurisdiction under Article III, section 2. The debate surrounding sovereignty was also most certainly due to the innovative federal structure of the union, where sovereignty was divided for the first time between a federal and federated entities. Indeed, cases involving sovereign immunity arose in the context of the interpretation of Article III and the jurisdiction it confers on federal courts,[55] on the Eleventh Amendment, and on the extent of Congress's power—or not—to abolish state sovereign immunity, notably under Article I or under the Fourteenth Amendment.[56] Sovereign immunity also arose in the context of an action based in a federal right of action or on the ground that a federal constitutional right was violated,[57] on a given state's amenability to justice before the courts of another,[58] or on the applicability of state law to the federal government.[59]

[54] Jaffe (n 3) 2.

[55] See eg *Chisholm v Georgia* (n 10); *Cohens v Virginia* (n 14).

[56] On the impact of the Eleventh Amendment on Art III, see *Hans v Louisiana* (1890) 134 US 1; on Congress's powers to abolish state immunity, see eg *Alden v Maine* (n 15) 754, where the Supreme Court held that states 'retain immunity from private suit in their own courts, an immunity beyond the congressional power to abrogate by Article I legislation'; see also *Seminole Tribe* (n 4) 73, where the Court found that 'Article I cannot be used to circumvent the constitutional limitations placed upon federal jurisdiction'. Note that the issue of sovereign immunity and its scope was not clearly set out when the Constitution was drafted: John F Manning, 'The Eleventh Amendment and The Reading Of Precise Constitutional Texts' (2004) 113 Yale LJ 1663, 1674–76.

[57] See eg *Bivens v Six Unknown Named Agents of Federal Bureau of Narcotics* (1971) 403 US 388; *Fitzpatrick v Bitzer* (1976) 427 US 445; *Will v Michigan Dept of State Police* (1989) 491 US 58; see also, in the case of municipalities, *Owen v City of Independence, Mo* (n 37); *Employees v Missouri Pub Health Dept* (1973) 411 US 279; *Florida Prepaid Postsecondary Education Expense Board v College Savings Bank* (1999) 527 US 627; *Alden v Maine* (n 15); *Seminole Tribe of Florida v Florida* (n 4); *Board of Trustees of University of Alabama v Garrett* (2001) 531 US 356; *Central Va Community College v Katz* (2006) 546 US 356; *US v Georgia* (2006) 546 US 151.

[58] *Nevada v Hall* (1979) 440 US 410, 414 (Stevens J): 'The doctrine of sovereign immunity is an amalgam of two quite different concepts, one applicable to suits in the sovereign's own courts and the other to suits in the courts of another sovereign.'

[59] See eg *US v Hoar* (1821) 26 Fed Cas 329, 330, where Story J, who was a Supreme Court justice acting in this case as a circuit court judge for the state of Massachusetts, held that the federal government was

In addition to the debate about the locus of sovereignty in the American Constitution, American legal thinking must also address the impediment caused by the erroneous belief that sovereign immunity is inherited from the English legal tradition. For example, to Amar—to whom we owe an incisive critique of sovereign immunity in American law—the idea of a sovereign above the law is British:

> [A]bsolute government immunity from all suits . . . is simply not part of our Constitution's structure. Its sole basis is the British idea that the sovereign government, as the source of all law, cannot itself be bound by any law absent its consent.[60]

American sovereign immunity is grounded in part in the Austinian positivist idea of a lawmaker above the law and thus incapable of doing wrong because of his position in relation to law.[61] Holmes J's reasons in *Kawananakoa v Polyblank* illustrate the premise well: 'A sovereign is exempt from suit, not because of any formal conception or obsolete theory, but on the logical and practical ground that there can be no legal right as against the authority that makes the law on which the right depends.'[62]

Holmes J's thinking on sovereign immunity can also find distant historical roots as far back as the very early days of the American republic. The seminal case of *Chisholm v Georgia*, dating to 1793, laid down the theoretical groundings of sovereign immunity in American legal thinking. The speeches of the justices in *Chisholm* find echo in other, more recent cases on sovereign immunity—including in Holmes J's speech in *Kawananakoa v Polyblank*, but also in the dissenters' speech in *Seminole Tribe*. The concept of 'sovereignty' as entailing a superior position and consequent immunity from suit is a common thread that finds its source in *Chisholm* and Blackstone's *Commentaries*, upon which the justices relied in support of their majority and dissenting views. The blame for the existence of sovereign immunity in American constitutional law does not lay at the feet of an

privileged not to be bound by the state's statute with regard to limitations, unless a federal statute waived the privilege. Compare, however, with *US v Lee* (n 12), where the cause of action was based on a state's statute and the violation of the Fifth Amendment, and where the action was directed against federal officials. On that latter point, see the parallel with *Ex parte Young* (1908) 209 US 123, where it was found that a state officer could be sued in lieu of the state to enforce a federal right.

[60] Amar (n 10) 1490. cf Bradley Raboin, 'Punish The Crown, But Protect The Government: A Comparative Analysis Of State Tort Liability For Exemplary Damages In England And Punitive Damages In The United States' (2016) 24 Cardozo J Int'l & Comp L 261, 277: 'Rather, American jurisprudence has consistently indicated that U.S. government sovereignty is a purely American creation, based instead on the structure of democracy, the United States Constitution, and the essential belief that ultimate sovereignty remains with the American populace comprising that government.'

[61] See David E Engdahl, 'Immunity and Accountability for Positive Governmental Wrongs' (1972) 44 U Colo L Rev 1, 3; Harold J Laski, 'The Responsibility of the State in England' (1919) 32 Harv L Rev 447, 464.

[62] *Kawananakoa v Polyblank* (1907) 205 US 349, 353.

English feudal king: the king was long subject to law when the Founders met at the Convention. The blame is instead attributable to the irreconcilable ideas in the work of Blackstone. The influence his *Commentaries* had over the course of the foundational period of the American polity has resulted in a debate in American legal thinking on the relationship between the concepts of republic, sovereignty, and federalism. The difficulty of that conceptual challenge was compounded by the fact that the novel form of government the Founders devised in drafting the Constitution in 1787—a federal union where sovereignty was divided between the states and United States—'presented a prospect unknown to the common law prior to the American experience'.[63]

2.2.1 *Chisholm v Georgia*, Blackstone, and the origins of sovereign immunity

The issue of the locus of sovereignty in the Constitution first arose judicially in *Chisholm v Georgia*,[64] a seminal case where the state of Georgia was sued before the Supreme Court by the citizen of another state for payment due for the merchandise that was supplied to Georgia during the War of Independence. The issue before the Supreme Court was whether Article III, section 2 granted the Court original jurisdiction over a dispute between a state and the citizen of another state.

To Cushing J, who wrote with the majority of justices in *Chisholm v Georgia*, 'the point before the court' in that seminal case 'turned not upon the law and practice of England or indeed upon that of any other country, but solely upon the Constitution of the United States as established by the people'.[65] Yet the justices relied heavily on English law and practice in delivering their speeches, and Blackstone's *Commentaries* took pride of place.

Iredell J—a fervent admirer of Blackstone's *Commentaries*—relied on them in favouring Georgia's claim for immunity in his dissenting opinion.[66] To Iredell J, the states were 'solely and completely sovereign' in their own courts, and therefore immune from suit.[67] The states' existence, in his opinion, predated that of the federal government of the United States, and was owed to the sacred will of the people.[68] The states were immune because they were sovereigns, and their existence as such was not impacted by the creation of the federal union unless the Constitution provided otherwise.

[63] *Seminole Tribe of Florida v Florida* (n 4) 104 (Souter J, dissenting).

[64] As Iredell J notes in his dissenting opinion, the matter was not raised in the previous case of *Maryland*, where the Attorney General of that state, unlike Georgia's, had appeared voluntarily before the Court: *Chisholm v Georgia* (n 10) 429–30 (Iredell J); see *Van Staphorst v Maryland* (1791) 2 US (2 Dall) 401.

[65] *Chisholm v Georgia* (n 10) 466 (Cushing J).

[66] ibid 437, 442–43 (Iredell J, dissenting); see Nolan (n 43) 757–58.

[67] *Chisholm v Georgia* (n 10) 437 (Iredell J).

[68] ibid 448 (Iredell J): 'A State does not owe its origin to the Government of the United States, in the highest or in any of its branches. It was in existence before it. It derives its authority from the same pure and sacred source as itself: the voluntary and deliberate choice of the people.'

Iredell J reached his conclusion after an analysis focussed on the procedural dimension of crown liability in England[69]—essentially, the petition of right—and relied in particular on Blackstone's claim that the petition of right was a remedy as of grace, subject to the king's pleasure in granting fiat to allow the claim to proceed.[70] Focussing as he did on the availability of remedies against the king at common law—the procedural dimension of crown liability—Iredell J did not take into account the king's status in relation to law or that the king was not conceived of as being perfect and was therefore capable of doing wrong—the substantive dimension of crown liability.

To Wilson J in *Chisholm*, the 'Sovereign' under the United States Constitution was the people. But Wilson J, like Iredell J in his dissenting opinion, also relied on Blackstone's *Commentaries* to define sovereignty. Blackstone ascribed sovereignty to the king, who was, as a result, subject to the jurisdiction of no other: 'Hence it is that no suit or action can be brought against the King, even in civil matters, because no court can have jurisdiction over him, for all jurisdiction implies superiority of power.'[71] Wilson J, in *Chisholm*, rejected Blackstone's notion of sovereignty defined as belonging to a superior other than the people, but he built on Blackstone's work to define sovereignty as '[t]he principle . . . that all human law must be prescribed by a superior'.[72] To Wilson J, the consent of the people in subjecting themselves to the law made them the true sovereign.

Likewise, to Jay CJ, 'From the Crown of Great Britain, the sovereignty of their country passed to the people of it',[73] and in America, 'the sovereignty of the nation is in the people of the nation, and the residuary sovereignty of each State in the people of each State'.[74] Even Jay CJ's speech, although he did not cite Blackstone in it, is infused with the *Commentaries*' skewed views of the status of the king. For instance, to Jay CJ, 'the sovereignties in Europe, and particularly in England, exist on feudal principles', where the king is the sovereign and is conceived of as 'the fountain of honor and authority', from whose 'grace and grant derives all franchises, immunities and privileges', and endowed with 'personal powers, dignities, and preeminences'.[75] Jay CJ's feudal view of the English Constitution is remarkably similar to Blackstone's discussion of the king in his *Commentaries* and his omission of the fundamental constitutional changes that were brought about over the course of the seventeenth century—notably parliamentary sovereignty. The dissenting justices in *Dalm* and in *Seminole Tribe* were right to point out that Americans' understanding of sovereign immunity was derived from Blackstone's.[76]

69 ibid 435–45 (Iredell J).
70 ibid 442 (Iredell J).
71 Blackstone (n 42) 235.
72 *Chisholm v Georgia* (n 10) 458 (Wilson J).
73 ibid 470 (Jay CJ).
74 ibid 471 (Jay CJ).
75 ibid 471–72 (Jay CJ).
76 *US v Dalm* (1990) 494 US 596, 622 (Stevens J, dissenting); *Seminole Tribe of Florida v Florida* (n 4) 131 (Souter J, dissenting).

2.2.2 Sovereign's status as above the law and feudal privileges

It was subsequently Iredell J's dissenting opinion in *Chisholm v Georgia* that led the way to the adoption of the Eleventh Amendment consecrating the states' sovereign immunity from suit before the federal courts. But if Iredell J's views in *Chisholm* led to the adoption of the Eleventh Amendment, Wilson J's understanding of sovereignty as entailing a superiority of status also forms part of the origins of sovereign immunity in American law. So does Jay CJ's view that 'Sovereignty is the right to govern; a nation or State sovereign is the person or persons in whom that resides'.[77]

Holmes J, in *Kawananakoa*, rejected the view that the American understanding of sovereign immunity was to be found in bygone eras or the divine rights of kings. But like Wilson J in *Chisholm*, he adopted the view of a sovereign above the law in tracing to Hobbes, Bodin, and thinkers who preceded him the American understanding of sovereign immunity:

> Some doubts have been expressed as to the source of the immunity of a sovereign power from suit without its own permission, but the answer has been public property since before the days of Hobbes. (*Leviathan*, c. 26, 2.). A sovereign is exempt from suit not because of any formal conception or obsolete theory, but on the logical and practical ground that there can be no legal right as against the authority that makes the law on which the right depends. 'Car on peut bien recevoir loy d'autruy, mais il est impossible par nature de se donner loy.' Bodin, *Republique*, 1, c. 8, ed. 1629, p. 132; Sir John Eliot, *De Jure Maiestatis*, c. 3. *Nemo suo statuto ligatur necessitative*. Baldus, *De Leg. et Const. Digna Vox*, (2d ed. 1496, fol. 51b, ed. 1539, fol. 61).[78]

Holmes's reasoning in *Kawananakoa* is not dissimilar to Maitland's argument that it was not possible, in feudal times, to obtain a writ against the king for the reason that the king could not issue a writ against himself.[79] It is on the basis of the argument first expounded by Maitland—that the sovereign cannot command himself—that Holmes J buttressed the foundations laid in *Chisholm* of the theoretical justification for the doctrine of sovereign immunity in the twentieth-century United States.

The American rationale underlying sovereign immunity is different from that underlying *the king can do no wrong* in England, where the king's immunity from liability is the result of feudal privileges, theories about perfection of the monarch, and a legal fiction that there can be no wrong in the king. The king's immunity from

[77] *Chisholm v Georgia* (n 10) 472 (Jay CJ).

[78] *Kawananakoa v Polyblank* (n 62) 353.

[79] FW Maitland, *The Constitutional History of England* (CUP 1963) 100; Frederick Pollock and FW Maitland, *The History of English Law Before the Time of Edward I*, vol 1 (2nd, reissued edn, CUP 1968) 516; Ehrlich (n 36) 24–25; Robert Dorsey Watkins, *The State as a Party Litigant* (Johns Hopkins Press 1927) 6–7.

suit in English legal thinking has characteristically not been a consequence of the king being above the law. As Figgis has noted in his *Divine Rights of Kings*, Austin's theory that the sovereign is above the law because he makes the law is a modern concept entailing supremacy of an authority; such supremacy was not to be found in Bracton's thinking, for whom the king was under the law that made him.[80] The Royalists' claim that the Stuart king was supreme and above the law[81] met with opposition in England in the seventeenth century because it was contrary to accepted and deeply rooted constitutional thinking.

In short, in English legal thinking, *the king can do no wrong* understood as conveying an immunity from suit to the king has had to be reconciled with the king's long-standing status as under the law, a concept first expressed in Bracton and reiterated in Blackstone's *Commentaries*. It would therefore be misguided to consider the American concept of 'sovereign immunity'—based on an Austinian view of the supremacy of the sovereign over the law—to be equivalent or synonymous with *the king can do no wrong* in English legal thinking. The American sovereign makes the law above which he stands because he makes it, whilst the English king is below the law that makes him.

The sovereign's status as above the law is not the only component of the doctrine of sovereign immunity which can be traced to *Chisholm*. Jay CJ's view that sovereignty is defined as the right to govern has also had a profound impact on the doctrine. Sovereignty understood as the right to govern resides not only in the states, but also in the federal government, and the courts subsequently found that the latter also benefits from sovereign immunity and cannot be sued without its consent before federal courts.[82]

This latter dimension of the doctrine of sovereign immunity—that the right to govern entails sovereign immunity—is not tied, however, to the federal structure of the Constitution and is the most open to criticism if it is conceived of as founded in the common law. It is in this dimension of sovereign immunity—the revival in the republican American context of the king's personal feudal prerogatives and privileges—that the view that 'the doctrine is an anomalous import within our own'[83] is the most pertinent.

[80] John Neville Figgis, *The Divine Right of Kings* (2nd edn, CUP 1914) 13–14.

[81] See King James I's 'The Trew Law of Free Monarchies' in Charles H McIlwain (ed), *Political Works of James I* (Harvard UP 1918).

[82] *Larson v Domestic & Foreign Commerce Corp* (1949) 337 US 682, 688 (Vinson J); *US v Mitchell* (1980) 445 US 535, 538 (Marshall J): 'It is elementary that "[t]he United States, as sovereign, is immune from suit save as it consents to be sued . . . and the terms of its consent to be sued in any court define that court's jurisdiction to entertain the suit"', citing *US v Sherwood* (1941) 312 US 584, 586. Moreover, a waiver of sovereign immunity 'cannot be implied, but must be unequivocally expressed': *US v King* (1969) 395 US 1, 4 (Black J). 'In the absence of clear congressional consent, then, "there is no jurisdiction in the Court of Claims more than in any other court to entertain suits against the United States"', *US v Mitchell*, citing *US v Sherwood* (1914) 312 US 584, 587–88. See also *US v Nordic Village, Inc* (1992) 503 US 30.

[83] *US v Dalm* (n 76), 622 (Stevens J, dissenting).

The federal or state governments' immunity from suit before their own courts, or other procedural privileges such as *nullum tempus occurrit regis* (time does not run against the king) and preference of payment—understood as a dimension of sovereign immunity—is conceptually distinct from sovereign immunity understood as a product of federalism. Feudal privileges of the king are part of the common law and, in this sense, the king's feudal privilege not to be sued in his own court without his consent is a 'familiar doctrine at common law'.[84] But the king's feudal immunity from suit became associated with *the king can do no wrong* in English legal thinking as a result of the constitutional struggles of the seventeenth century and the imperative of protecting a much less powerful king after the constitutional arrangement of parliamentary sovereignty was reached upon the Glorious Revolution—a concern alien to a republic characterized by an elected presidential mode of government. The objective of protecting the king in the constitutional order led to the subsequent development—notably in the work of Blackstone—of fictions relating to the notion of the king's perfection and ultimately, in the nineteenth century, of his incapacity to do wrong and the absence of a wrong in the king.[85] Therefore, when the doctrine of sovereign immunity is understood in American legal thinking as the 'vainest of all legal fictions' and that it has 'its origin in the ancient myth that the "[K]ing can do no wrong"',[86] it is manifest that the patchwork of various understandings of *the king can do no wrong* throughout different historical periods has not been pieced out. The recent fiction that there can be no wrong in the king is certainly traceable to the notion of perfection in Blackstone's *Commentaries*,[87] but it was most certainly not part of the feudal understanding of the king's status in relation to law and of his feudal privileges. The fiction is not, therefore, attributable to 'an ancient myth' or an ancient common law doctrine. As for the *the king can do no wrong* itself, it was coined only at the turn of the seventeenth century.[88] And regarding the later nineteenth- and early twentieth-century English judicial misconception that the crown is the government and that the latter must therefore partake from the former's feudal, personal privileges, it is a recent development which occurred after the United States were created and which cannot be attributed to an ancient common law doctrine. The American doctrine of sovereignty in its dimension relating to privileges and immunities of one level of government before its own courts and citizens is either grounded in the king's feudal privileges or

[84] *Will v Michigan Dept of State Police* (n 57) 67 (White J). See also *Beers v Arkansas* (1858) 61 US 527, 529, cited in ibid, where it is called an 'established principle of jurisprudence'.

[85] See Chapter 4, section 3.3.

[86] *US v Dalm* (n 76) 622 (Stevens J, dissenting); Stevens J frequently associated sovereign immunity with *the king can do no wrong*: see also *Will v Michigan Dept of State Police* (n 57) 87 (Stevens J, dissenting): 'The doctrine of sovereign immunity rests on the fictional premise that the "King can do no wrong"'; and *Nevada v Hall* (n 58) 415 (Stevens J): 'The king's immunity rested . . . on a fiction that the King could do no wrong'.

[87] See Chapter 4, sections 2.1 and 3.2.

[88] See Chapter 2, section 3 and Chapter 3, section 3.1.1.

in the early modern understanding that the sovereign is above the law and cannot, therefore, be subject to it.

Two interpretations of *the king can do no wrong* are derived from Matthew Hale's seventeenth-century interpretation of the three powers of the law but divorced from its nuances. The two are contradictory. The first interpretation—found in Matthew Hale's and Blackstone's thinking—was that the king is perfect, whereas the second interpretation—found in nineteenth-century petition of right cases[89]—assumed that the king was capable of issuing wrongful orders, but that they were void and were not a wrong insofar as the king was concerned.

The view that the king was perfect and incapable of doing wrong was not logically compatible with the view that the king's wrongful acts were void: if the king was perfect, he was incapable of thinking or doing wrong to begin with and there could be no wrongful orders to be invalidated. Nevertheless, both the notion of perfection underlying the king's incapacity to do wrong and the fiction that wrongful acts were not wrongs in the king became increasingly associated with *the king can do no wrong* from the second half of the nineteenth century. Both the notion of the king's perfection and the fiction that wrongful acts are not wrongs of the king can be seen as compatible with the survival of the king in the constitutional order by ensuring his immunity from both political and legal responsibility. But ensuring the king's physical and constitutional survival was no longer a concern in America in the late eighteenth and nineteenth centuries.[90] *The king can do no wrong* is now frequently understood as the king is perfect and incapable of doing wrong. These are not understandings which can logically ground sovereign immunity in American legal thinking, in a republic where the office of the president was created specifically to ensure an optimal form of executive accountability. Viewed in this light, the criticism voiced in American thought against sovereign immunity understood to protect a non-existent monarch in the republican American constitutional context is apt.

As for the fiction that there is no wrong in the king, although it was in the making throughout petition of right cases in nineteenth-century English case law, it was not clearly expressed until Cockburn CJ's speech in *Feather*, in 1865.[91] The fiction could not, chronologically speaking, have influenced the foundations of sovereign immunity as they were laid down in 1793 in the follow-up to the *Chisholm* decision. Moreover, after *Feather* was decided in 1865, the fiction that there can be no wrong in the king as applied to the federal and state governments was rejected in 1879 in *Langford v US*.[92] Miller J remarked in that case that 'we do not understand that

[89] *Tobin v The Queen*, 16 CB (NS) 356; *Feather v The Queen* (1865) 6 B&S 257 (122 ER 1191). See Chapter 3, sections 3.3.3 and 3.3.4, and Chapter 4, section 3.3.1.

[90] 'The maxim is pointless where there is no king': John J Maguire, 'State Liability for Tort' (1916) 30 Harv L Rev 20, 20. 'We have no king to whom it can be applied.': *Langford v US* (1879) 101 US 341, 343 (Miller J).

[91] *Feather v The Queen* (n 89).

[92] *Langford v US* (n 90) 342–43. See also n 30.

either in reference to the government of the United States, or of the several states, or of any of their officers, the English maxim has any existence in this country' and 'The English maxim does not declare that the Government, or those who administer it, can do no wrong'.[93] The fiction that the president or the government is incapable of doing wrong, or that there can be no wrong in the president or the government, so that the blame for their wrong should be attributed to an inferior minister or public officer, was rejected by the Supreme Court. In *Langford*, it is *the king can do no wrong*—understood as the then newly judicially minted nineteenth-century English fiction that there can be no wrong in the king—which was rejected by the American Supreme Court: '[*The king can do no wrong*] cannot apply to [the president], because the Constitution admits that he may do wrong, and has provided, by the proceeding of impeachment, for his trial for wrongdoing, and his removal from office if found guilty'.[94] The Court rejected as well, in *Langford*, *the king can do no wrong* understood as imputed ministerial responsibility—a rejection which harked back to days of the Convention in 1787:

> None of the eminent counsel who defended President Johnson on his impeachment trial asserted that by law he was incapable of doing wrong, *or that, if done, it could not, as in the case of the King, be imputed to him, but must be laid to the charge of the ministers who advised him*.[95]

The dissenters in *Seminole Tribe* were therefore mistaken when, writing of *Langford*[96] and *Nevada*,[97] they opined that 'it is clear that the idea of the sovereign, or any part of it, being above the law in this sense has not survived in American law'.[98] In *Langford*, it is the fiction that there is no wrong in the king which was rejected—including as applied to the government—and *the king can do no wrong* understood as imputed ministerial responsibility. In *Nevada*, it was *the king can do no wrong* understood as 'two quite different concepts, one applicable to suits in the sovereign's own courts and the other to suits in the courts of another sovereign' which was at stake.[99] The Court explained that '[t]he King's immunity [from suit in his own courts] rested primarily on the structure of the feudal system' and noted that this immunity shared with other feudal lords did not exempt a lesser vassal from being sued in a higher lord's courts.[100] As a result, the Supreme Court in *Nevada* denied the state of Nevada immunity from suit in another state's courts, in this case California. The Court also rejected again, as it had done in *Langford*,

93 *Langford v US* (n 90) 342–43.
94 *Langford v US* (n 87) 343.
95 ibid (emphasis added).
96 ibid 342–43.
97 *Nevada v Hall* (n 58) 415 (Stevens J).
98 *Seminole Tribe of Florida v Florida* (n 4) 131 (Souter J, dissenting).
99 *Nevada v Hall* (n 58) 414 (Stevens J).
100 ibid 415.

the king can do no wrong understood as the king's incapacity to do wrong: 'We must, of course, reject the fiction. It was rejected by the colonists when they declared their independence from the Crown, and the record in this case discloses an actual wrong committed by Nevada.'[101] Neither of the two cases, however, rejected the notion that sovereign immunity is grounded in the idea of a sovereign above the law. On the contrary, the Court, relying on Jay CJ and Holmes J's discussion of sovereignty in *Chisholm* and *Kawananakoa*, respectively, admitted that 'the notion that immunity from suit is an attribute of sovereignty is reflected in our cases'.[102]

In short, the notions of the king's (or the sovereign's) status in relation to law and of his immunity from suit coexist in American legal thinking relating to sovereign immunity. In some instances, the notion of the sovereign's status as above the law is denied, his capacity to do wrong is acknowledged, his amenability to suit is said to follow, and the notion of immunity from suit is discredited as feudal and unsuited to the American republican context. Yet in others, the sovereign's status as above the law is affirmed, with the consequence that none can command him and that he is therefore not amenable to justice without his consent.

2.3 Conclusion: a republican sovereign above the law and immune from suit

American legal thinking has significantly departed from the understandings of *the king can do no wrong* in English legal thinking taken historically. English understandings of *the king can do no wrong* are not conceptually linked to sovereign immunity in American law. *The king can do no wrong*, understood as the king is incapable of doing wrong or the legal fiction that there can be no wrong in the king, has been an important feature of English legal thinking since the nineteenth century—yet both understandings were rejected in the United States. *The king can do no wrong* understood in the Bractonian sense—that the king is under the law—escaped American thinking when the doctrine of sovereign immunity was being developed. *The king can do no wrong* understood in the English constitutional-arrangement sense—that the king is personally immune from suit but his wrongful commands are void and his ministers and servants must be held liable instead—was specifically rejected by the Founders, who did not want to adopt the flaws of a ministerial form of accountability. They provided that the president could be impeached in the Constitution[103] and the Supreme Court subsequently found that the president cannot claim any immunity that would deflect accountability unto a

[101] ibid.

[102] ibid 415–16.

[103] US Constitution, Art II, s 4: 'The President, Vice President, and all civil Officers of the United States, shall be removed from Office, on Impeachment for, and Conviction of, Treason, Bribery, or other high Crimes and Misdemeanors.'

lower public official.[104] The executive is capable of doing wrong in American legal thinking. But that substantive dimension of governmental liability, the capacity to do wrong, has not been reconciled with sovereign immunity understood as the sovereign is immune from suit because he is above the law.

As for the understanding that *the king can do no wrong* conveys an immunity from suit to the monarch because the king is deprived of any real say or power in the constitutional order, it is inapplicable in the American republic. *The king can do no wrong* understood in the Royalist, 'Stuart' seventeenth-century understanding that the divine king is above the law spurred a revolution and a civil war and was promptly abandoned in England. Yet it is the notion of the sovereign as above the law which is the conceptual foundation of sovereign immunity in American legal thinking. American thinking on sovereign immunity differs markedly from English—and Canadian and Australian—legal thinking as a result, as is further evidenced by the fact that sovereign immunity finds application in American law even in the realm of contractual liability.[105] In contrast, the crown's immunity from suit resounded in tort, but not in contract.

Criticism of sovereign immunity as a historical relic of a monarchical English feudal past as inappropriate in the American republic therefore misses the point on two accounts. First, the English king has always been subject to law, and although he is immune from ordinary actions in his own courts, he could be sued to by various other proceedings. As for the reconceptualization of *the king can do no wrong* by English courts as a legal fiction that there can be no wrong in the king, it dates to the second half of the nineteenth century—almost a century after the United States became independent—and cannot logically have grounded sovereign immunity in the early days of the republic. It was, in fact, almost immediately rejected by the United States Supreme Court. Second, the doctrine of sovereign immunity is not mainly rooted in English common law or feudal privileges, but rather in early modern conceptions of sovereignty which were also reflected in the standing of nation-states at international law. Early modern understandings of sovereignty found in the works of the likes of Bodin and Hobbes are alien to feudal understandings of the king's subjection to God and the law and the Bractonian understanding of *the king can do no wrong*. While the American concept of sovereign immunity is based on a Hobbesian-like premise that the sovereign is above the law and is consequently immune from suit, English legal thinking, on the other hand, has since the days of Bracton in the thirteenth century, conceived of the king as under the law but nevertheless immune from suit by ordinary actions—an immunity that, from a feudal privilege shared by all feudal lords, became more

[104] *Langford v US* (n 90).

[105] Harold J Krent, 'Reconceptualizing Sovereign Immunity' (1992) 45 Vand L Rev 1529, 1560–62; Gillian Hadfield, 'Of Sovereignty and Contract: Damages for Breach of Contract by Government' (1999) 8 S Cal Interdisc LJ 467, 471–72.

important to the stability of the constitutional order after the Glorious Revolution and was unique to the person of the king. In summary, in English legal thinking, the *king* was immune from suit *despite* his subjection to law. In American legal thinking, the dominant view has been that the *sovereign* is immune from suit *because* he is above the law.

If American sovereign immunity were one-dimensional and related only to one level of government's immunities before its own courts and citizens; were solely grounded in the procedural dimension of crown liability; and were tied to the king's personal, feudal, immunity from suit in his own courts, then criticisms of its anachronistic and inadequate survival in a republic would have more force.[106] But another dimension of the doctrine of sovereign immunity—perhaps the most significant—is peculiar to the American constitutional order and its federal structure. As the Supreme Court has explained, 'the notion that immunity from suit is an attribute of sovereignty is reflected in our cases'.[107] Indeed, another important dimension of the doctrine of sovereign immunity relates to federalism, and the dimension of the doctrine relating to federalism and sovereignty within the Union is entangled in American legal thinking with the constitutional compact. This is a debate as to who is the sovereign in the American federal constitutional order, and an unfortunate reliance on the work of an English jurist—Blackstone—who had himself failed to recognize the nuances of the old and new English constitutional order.

3 Ireland: birth of the republic and burial of the prerogative

Irish legal thinking, in conceiving of the state's liability, took the prerogative as its main focus. Blackstone's definition of the prerogative was relied on—as it was in the United States of America—but the outcome was markedly different. While American early thinkers rejected the monarch, the degree of significance to be granted to the people in interpreting the Constitution—specifically in what became known as sovereign immunity—was never clearly defined as paramount. The people who created the American republic saw their thunder stolen by the states, who claimed a sovereign status and the inheritance of the former English sovereign's prerogatives. The prevarication between the states and the people's status as sovereign under the American Constitution is apparent from the text of the Tenth Amendment itself: 'The powers not delegated to the United States by the

[106] For academic critical analysis of sovereign immunity, see eg Amar (n 10); Vicki C Jackson, 'The Supreme Court, the Eleventh Amendment, and State Sovereign Immunity' (1988) 88 Yale LJ 1; Daniel J Meltzer, 'The Seminole Decision and State Sovereign Immunity' (1996) 40 Sup Ct Rev 1; Erwin Chemerinsky, 'Against Sovereign Immunity' (2001) 53 Stanford L Rev 1201; Mark Strasser, 'Chisholm, the Eleventh Amendment, and Sovereign Immunity: On Alden's Return to Confederation Principles' (2001) 28 Fla St U L Rev 605; Louise Weinberg, 'Of Sovereignty and Union: The Legends of Alden' (2001) 76 Notre Dame L Rev 1113.

[107] *Nevada v Hall* (n 58) 415 (Stevens J).

Constitution, nor prohibited by it to the States, are reserved *to the States respectively, or to the people*' (my emphasis).

By contrast, while Irish courts also cited Blackstone and conferred on the Irish Free State, after 1922, the king's prerogatives, the 1937 Constitution and the birth of the Republic of Ireland was interpreted by Irish courts, post 1937, as a breaking point that saw the death of the king's prerogatives—a death foretold in 1922, according to the Irish Supreme Court fifty years later, in the 1972 seminal case of *Byrne v Ireland*.

Free of competing claims from federated entities within the republic, the Irish people, the only constituent power, were given pride of place in the courts' interpretation of the Irish Constitution and of the state's liability and constitutional duty to vindicate personal rights and freedoms granted by the Constitution to the Irish people. The Irish courts' interpretation of the social contract in the 1937 Constitution did not give rise to a Leviathan sovereign above others or the law, or to an unidentified sovereign benefitting from what is understood as feudal kingly prerogatives as is the case of the American sovereign and sovereign immunity under the American Constitution.

The king can do no wrong in Irish legal thinking is understood as the relic of a feudal monarchical past and conceived of as incompatible with the idea of a democratic, independent, and modern republic found in the text of the Constitution. In addition to American legal thinking, Ireland's approach will also be put in relation with Australian approaches in section 4.

3.1 The rejection of *the king can do no wrong* in the Irish republican state

The island of Ireland was home to waves of peoples of various origin from as far back as ten thousand years ago, during the Mesolithic era.[108] Perhaps the most famous of these newcomers were the Celts, who arrived in Ireland from the seventh century BE.[109] Then, in early medieval Ireland, Irish kings ruled over the island and commercial and political ties with Britain were an important feature of Irish people's lives.[110] External invasions were rare before the arrival of the raiding Vikings at the end of the eighth century.[111] The Scandinavian pillagers then settled on the island and built prosperous commercial port towns, among which were Dublin and Cork.[112] Irish kings and the descendants of the Viking kings who

[108] JP Mallory, *The Origins of the Irish* (Thames & Hudson 2013) 37, 40.

[109] ibid 157.

[110] Edel Bhreathnach, 'Communities and Their Landscape' in Brendan Smith (ed), *The Cambridge History of Ireland*, vol 1, 600–1550 (1st edn, CUP 2018) 16–19.

[111] ibid 18; Alex Woolf, 'The Scandinavian Intervention' in Brendan Smith (ed), *The Cambridge History of Ireland*, vol 1, 600–1550 (1st edn, CUP 2018).

[112] Woolf (n 111) 108.

settled in Ireland fought over the dominance of the island and the title of High King—the kingship of Ireland.[113]

In 1169, an alliance between one such defeated king and English noblemen led to the Anglo-Norman invasion, soon thereafter co-opted by the king of England, Henry II, who claimed as his own his vassals' territorial gains in Ireland.[114] While Angevin Ireland thereafter saw its Anglo-Norman Earls adopting Gaelic culture, due in part to intermarriage, the Reformation and Henry VIII's and Elizabeth I's desire to tighten their rule over Ireland in the sixteenth and early seventeenth centuries led to the 'Tudor conquest of Ireland'.[115] After the defeat of Irish Earls at the Battle of Kinsale in 1601, English plantations were created, mainly in the North of the island. Battles and rebellions against the English monarchs became recurrent over the next hundred years, until the rebellious Irish forces led by Michael Collins signed the Anglo-Irish Treaty in 1922. This pivotal moment is associated with the Irish Civil War between pro- and anti-Treaty factions. It led to the creation of the Irish Free State and the adoption of the 1922 Constitution of Saorstát Éireann.[116] The creation of the Irish Free State marked the partition of the island of Ireland between the six counties in the North—which form part of Northern Ireland—and the twenty-six counties that later became the Republic of Ireland with the adoption of a new Constitution in 1937.[117]

3.1.1 Rejection of the law governing the Dominion of Canada

According to Article 2 of the 1922 Articles of Agreement for a Treaty Between Great Britain and Ireland,[118] the law governing the Irish Free State in relation to

[113] ibid 109.

[114] Nicholas Vincent, 'Angevin Ireland' in Brendan Smith (ed), *The Cambridge History of Ireland*, vol 1, 600–1550 (1st edn, CUP 2018) 185–87.

[115] Christopher Maginn, 'Contintuity and Change: 1470–1550' in Brendan Smith (ed), *The Cambridge History of Ireland*, vol 1, 600–1550 (1st edn, CUP 2018) 300.

[116] The Anglo-Irish Treaty was adopted by the Imperial Parliament by way of statute, to which it was added as a schedule: Irish Free State (Agreement) Act, 1922, 12 & 13 Geo 5 c 4, sch, cl 1 (UK); see also, on the creation of the Irish Free State, Irish Free State (Consequential Provisions) Act 1922, 13 Geo 5 sess 2, c 2. The 1922 Constitution's official title as adopted by the Dáil was Constitution of the Irish Free State (Saorstát Éireann) Act, 1922, No 1/1922; it was also adopted by the Imperial Parliament as Irish Free State (Constitution) Act, 1922, 13 Geo 5 sess 2, c 3. On the context relating to the ratification of the Treaty, see Liam Weeks and Mícheál Ó Fathartaigh, *The Treaty: Debating and Establishing the Irish State* (Irish Academic Press 2018). On the drafting and adoption of the 1922 Constitution of Saorstát Éireann, see Barra Ó Briain, *The Irish Constitution* (Talbot Press 1929); Laura Cahillane, *Drafting the Irish Free State Constitution* (Manchester UP 2016); Laura Cahillane, 'Popular Sovereignty under the 1922 Constitution' in Maria Cahill and others (eds), *Constitutional Change and Popular Sovereignty: Populism, Politics and the Law in Ireland* (Routledge 2021) 22. References to contemporary works can also be found in VTH Delany, 'The Constitution of Ireland: Its Origins and Development' (1957) 12 UTLJ 1, fn 7.

[117] The 1937 Constitution's official name, in Irish, is Bunreacht na hÉirann. The 1937 Irish Constitution created a republic, but did not say it expressly. Ireland was declared a republic in the Republic of Ireland Act, 1948, No 22, s 2: 'It is hereby declared that the description of the State shall be the Republic of Ireland'; see James O'Reilly and Mary Redmond, *Cases and Materials on the Irish Constitution* (Incorporated Law Society of Ireland 1980) 168.

[118] Also commonly known as the Anglo-Irish Treaty, it was concluded following the Irish war of independence: see n 116.

the crown and the Imperial Parliament was to be that of the then Dominion of Canada.[119] Article 51 of the Constitution of the Irish Free State (1922) provided that executive authority of the Irish Free State vested in the king, and 'shall be exercisable, in accordance with the law, practice and constitutional usage governing the exercise of the Executive Authority in the case of the Dominion of Canada, by the Representative of the Crown'.[120] Indeed, under the Canadian Constitution, executive authority was, and is still to this day, vested in the king.[121] Canadian constitutional law, for a short period from 1922 to 1937, was to guide Irish constitutional law. Indeed, at first, Irish courts found that the general policy of the 1922 Constitution was to establish a transition as smooth as possible, with little departure from previous law as possible.[122] The Irish Supreme Court, however, soon departed from Canadian law on the issue of the crown's prerogatives after the adoption of the 1937 Constitution. Irish legal thinking was to chart its own unique path in relation to *the king can do no wrong*.

In 1951, recounting the state of the law in Canada as it was incorporated by Article 2 of the Articles of Agreement for a Treaty Between Great Britain and Ireland and what he perceived as Canada's limited legislative autonomy, Kingsmill Moore J opined that the reference to Canadian law in the Articles 'did not purpose in any other way to restrict the autonomy or legislative power of Saorstát Éireann'.[123] As Kingsmill Moore J explained, the Quebec Resolutions of 1866—which proved to be the blueprint for the British North America Act 1867 and the creation of the Dominion of Canada—provided that the new country's Constitution was to be enacted 'with a view to the perpetuation of the connection with the Mother Country'.[124] The historical background of the Saorstát Éireann Constitution, on the other hand, was 'very different' and 'arose out of an armed revolt against British rule and the terms of a Treaty to put an end to hostilities': to Kinsgmill Moore J, 'There is not the slightest reason to suppose that "with a view to the perpetuation of the connection with the Mother Country" [those who

[119] Irish Free State (Consequential Provisions) Act 1922 (n 116). Section 2 of the Act provided that: 'Subject to the provisions hereinafter set out the position of the Irish Free State in relation to the Imperial Parliament and Government and otherwise shall be that of the Dominion of Canada, and the law, practice and constitutional usage governing the relationship of the Crown or the representative of the Crown and of the Imperial Parliament to the Dominion of Canada shall govern their relationship to the Irish Free State.'

[120] Constitution of the Irish Free State (Saorstát Éireann) Act, 1922 (n 116).

[121] The Constitution Act, 1867, 30 & 31 Vict c 3, s 9 (UK).

[122] Indeed, O'Byrne J had found in *The State (Kennedy) v Little* [1931] IR 39 that the general policy of the 1922 Constitution was to establish a transition as smooth as possible, with as little departure from previous law as possible. See John M Kelly, 'Hidden Treasure and the Constitution' (1988) 10 DULJ 5, 10. Irish courts from the second half of the twentieth century took quite a different view. The House of Lords also ruled as early as 1925 that the creation of the Irish Free State changed the law in relation to the petition of right, which became unavailable against the king in Ireland after 1922: *Attorney General v Great Southern and Western Railway Company of Ireland* (1925) AC 754.

[123] *In Re Irish Employers Mutual Insurance Association Ltd* [1955] IR 176, 217.

[124] ibid 222.

enacted it] desired "to follow the model of the British Constitution so far as circumstances permit"'.[125]

In the landmark case of *Byrne v Ireland*,[126] in 1972, the Irish Supreme Court also expressed very strong disapproval of the wholesale adoption of Canadian law on the prerogatives of the crown that had occurred prior to the adoption of the 1937 Constitution—even that of priority of payment. Kingsmill Moore J's decision was cited with approval by Budd J, who also recounted the various ways in which the Dominion's constitutional subjection to the Imperial Parliament and the king's ministers in the United Kingdom made the law relating to Canada incompatible with the Irish Constitution:

> Now, in 1921 the autonomy of the Dominion of Canada was restricted in various ways. It was subject to the supremacy of the Imperial Parliament by the Colonial Laws Validity Act, 1865; its Parliament could not pass laws having an extra-territorial effect; an appeal lay from its Courts to the Privy Council; the Governor General could refuse to assent to a bill and reserve it for the consideration of the king, and the king in giving or refusing his consent would be bound to act on the advice of his ministers in the United Kingdom; the Governor General was a representative of the king and took his instructions from the king, but those instructions would also ultimately have to conform with the advice given to the king by his ministers in the United Kingdom. Lastly, the king, on the advice of his ministers in the United Kingdom might disallow a law to which his Governor General had already given consent—although this restriction was probably already extinguished by constitutional usage. It seems to me that Article 2 was intended to impose on the new Free State those limitations on autonomy and restrictions of status at least until the law practice and constitutional usage of Canada was changed. But it was not intended to do more. It did not purpose in any other way to restrict the autonomy or legislative power of Saorstát Éireann and it was quite competent for the new state either by its Constitution, or by subsequent enactment, or by its procedure and the forms it adopted, to regulate its own finances and control its own property in any way it wished. It might adopt the British procedure of vesting property and finances in the king, with certain consequent advantages, but on the other hand, it might not; and in my view it did not.[127]

Revisiting cases from that short period spanning from 1922 to 1937,[128] Walsh J, also writing for the majority of the Supreme Court in *Byrne v Ireland*, expressed

[125] ibid 222–23.

[126] *Byrne v Ireland* [1972] 1 IR 214.

[127] *In Re Irish Employers* (n 123) 217 (Kingsmill Moore J), referred to in *Byrne v Ireland* (n 126) 296 (Budd J).

[128] Walsh J revisited in particular *In re Maloney* [1926] IR 202, where it had been found that the Irish Land Commission—thought to be akin to the crown by Johnson J in that case—could rely on the crown's prerogative of priority of payment, on the ground that its prerogative rights exempted it from

the view that 'the reference to the constitutional usage of Canada, in addition to being the basis of a concession, was used too generally in the context because it did not follow that, because in the law of Canada the Crown had the prerogative right to claim priority in the payment of debt, the right necessarily existed also in the Irish Free State'.[129] Walsh J also rejected the conclusions reached in *Galway County Council*, where the court had cited with approval the Privy Council's decision in relation to the application of crown prerogatives in Canada.[130]

The *Byrne* principle now stands for the idea that immunities belonging to the crown did not survive the Irish Free State in 1922, and that the only immunities to exist are those expressly provided for in the Constitution.[131] To Doyle J, relying on *Byrne v Ireland*, for example, the survival of an immunity against mandamus that belonged to the crown was inconsistent with the Constitution. He accordingly granted an order of mandamus against the Minister to direct the Commissioners of Public Works to conduct repair of a courthouse.[132]

In fact, the king was referred to on many occasions in the 1922 Constitution, but no trace remained of him following the adoption of the 1936 Constitution (Amendment No 27) Act, 1936, which provided in section 1 that all references to

the application of the statutory priorities of s 4(1) of the Preferential Payments in Bankruptcy (Ireland) Act, 1889. *In re Maloney* was said to raise 'highly interesting questions of constitutional law' by Gavan Duffy J in *Irish Land Commission v Ruane* [1938] IR 148, 159, but he ultimately decided that the statute bound the Land Commissioners on other grounds; for a discussion of *In re Maloney*, see also John M Kelly, *The Irish Constitution* (2nd edn, Jurist 1984) 696. See also *In Re K* [1927] IR 260, 269–70, where Kennedy CJ found that the issue of the applicability of the prerogative of priority of payment when statutory priorities are in force implied two distinct common law prerogatives rights—immunity from statute and the king's preference of payment. The prerogative of preference of payment having an ancillary procedural prerogative that the crown's claim must be preferred against the subject's, if the former was displaced by statute, so was the latter. See also *In Re PC, an Arranging Debtor* [1939] IR 306 (73 ILTR 84), where it was decided that the prerogative of priority of payment requires the existence of some royal fund or exchequer, and that the latter would have been unconstitutional in light of Art 61 of the Saorstát Éireann Constitution, which provided that the Central Fund was a state fund; and *In re The Irish Aero Club; Gillic v Minister for Industry and Commerce* [1939] IR 204, where Gavan Duffy J opined that the prerogative of payment was personal to the king: '[t]he common law prerogative of prior payment of his debts belonged to the king, not because he was the supreme executive authority, but because of the personal pre-eminence over all subjects which attached to him at common law, on the principle expressed in the phrase *detur digniori*'.

[129] *Byrne v Ireland* (n 126) 269–70.

[130] *Galway County Council v Minister for Finance* [1931] IR 215, 232 where Jonhson J had relied on the Privy Council's decision in *The Liquidators of the Maritime Bank of Canada v The Receiver General of New Brunswick* [1892] AC 437 (PC), regarding the application of crown prerogative in Canada, including Canadian provinces, to conclude that '[t]here can be no doubt, and it has not been argued in the present case to the contrary, that the Prerogative and prerogative right can be relied upon by the Irish Free State, and is part of the law of the land'; see Laura Cahillane, 'The Prerogative and Its Survival in Ireland: Dusty Antique or Positively Useful?' (2010) 1 IJLS 1, 11.

[131] As such, the ruling in *Pesca Valentia Ltd v Minister for Fisheries* [1985] IR 193 that there can be no injunction against Ireland is a strange ruling post *Byrne*, particularly knowing that mandamus orders can be obtained: see Gerard Hogan and Tony Kerr, 'The Law of Ireland' in John Bell and AW Bradley (eds), *Governmental Liability: A Comparative Study* (United Kingdom National Committee of Comparative Law 1991) 165–66.

[132] *The State (King) v Minister for Justice* [1984] IR 169, 176.

the king or his representatives in all provisions of the Irish Free State Constitution identified in the schedule to that Act were to be removed. The amendment occurred alongside the abdication of King Edward VIII, and Walsh J recounts in *Byrne v Ireland* the joint effect the amendment, along with the Executive Authority (External Relations) Act, 1936, had on the Irish Free State Constitution—which was to remove the king entirely from it, and take away from him all executive or governmental power.[133] The 1937 Constitution followed suit in establishing a republic. A contextual interpretation of the 1922 Constitution, which was adopted after the Easter Risings of 1916 and the Anglo-Irish War—and resulted in the Civil War of 1922–1923 after the signing of the Anglo-Irish treaty—led to the rejection of the law of the Dominion of Canada, perceived as inadequate because founded on very different objectives of continued close bounds with and imitation of the constitution of the United Kingdom.

In short, Irish courts have expressly departed from Canadian law on the crown's prerogatives. They relied instead on their republican brethren, American courts, in defining Irish constitutional law. But, free from the contingencies of federalism, Irish courts arrived at a different result from their American counterparts.

3.1.2 American influence

Cork County Council & Burke v Commissioners of Public Works, overturned by Walsh J in *Byrne*, had marked an early attempt by an Irish court to uphold what it conceived of as a 'prerogative' in the context of a republican state by turning to American cases.[134]

At issue in *Cork County* was the rule of statutory interpretation that statutes do not bind the crown.[135] O'Byrne and Black JJ in *Cork County* relied on Story J's reasons in *US v Hoar*: 'It [is] a safe rule, founded in the principles of the Common Law, that the general words of a statute ought not to include the Government, or affect its rights, unless that construction be clear and indisputable upon the text of the Act.'[136] Story J opined that the federal government was privileged not to be bound by the legislature of the state of Massachusetts's with regard to limitations, unless a federal statute waived the privilege. There was, therefore, an important federalism dimension to the case of *United States v Hoar*, but the Irish judges in *Cork County* relied on Story J's reasoning to ground their position that the prerogative

[133] *Byrne v Ireland* (n 126) 282–84.

[134] *Cork County Council & Burke v Commissioners of Public Works* [1945] IR 561.

[135] The rule, later defined by Lord du Parcq for the Board in *Province of Bombay v Municipal Corporation of the City of Bombay* (n 7), is a presumption that statutes do not bind the crown unless the crown is expressly mentioned or by necessary implication. It is not a prerogative, although it is often treated as such: Fortin, 'Revisiting the Application of Statutes to the Crown' (n 8) 276–83. Story J, however, noted that the rule was in the nature of a presumption, not a prerogative, in *US v Hoar* (1821) 26 Fed Cas 329: 'And though this is sometimes called a prerogative right, it is in fact nothing more than a reservation, or exception, introduced for the public benefit, and equally applicable to all governments.'

[136] *US v Hoar* (n 135). Story J was a US Supreme Court justice acting in this case as a circuit court judge for the state of Massachusetts.

could survive even in the absence of kingship. Being part of the common law, the prerogative then passes on to the government. O'Byrne J upheld the state's defence that general statutes providing for ratings on houses did not bind the state and, citing to the continuation provisions of Article 73 of the 1922 Constitution, wrote that he could 'see no reason for holding that the prerogative, with which I am dealing, was not transferred to the Irish Free State. It was part of the common law, which was applied to the Irish Free State by Article 73 . . . [And in view of Articles 49 and 50 of the 1937 Constitution] it seems to me clear that the State is now entitled to the benefit of the Prerogative in question.'[137]

If the prerogative survived for more than a hundred years in the American republic, Black J concluded, it can be conceived of as separate from the institution of kingship, and it can equally be passed on to the Irish government.[138] This view was ultimately rejected in *Byrne*, where Walsh J explained that American legal thinking had mistakenly adopted the concept of sovereign immunity 'as basic to the common law without, perhaps, a proper recognition of the nature of its origin'.[139] To Walsh J, the king's feudal immunity was personal to him only, because he was the sole personification of the state, and it could not be conceived of as attaching to the state itself.[140] The notion of perfection ascribed to the king, Walsh J added, could only be granted to him as a person: it did not extend to the state.[141] Budd J, also writing for the majority in *Byrne v Ireland*, agreed: 'I can find no suggestion in the Constitution of anything in the nature of perfection in the State.'[142] Walsh J also rejected the conclusions reached by the US Supreme Court in *US v Lee* and by Holmes J in *Kawananakoa* v *Polyblank* that sovereign immunity is the result of a necessary policy choice and is 'vital for an efficient working of government'.[143] A comparative analysis of the law of state liability in other jurisdictions, including French and German law, but also the United Kingdom's Crown Proceedings Act 1947 and Canada's now defunct Canada Petition of Right Act 1875, convinced Walsh J that, contrary to the conclusion reached by American courts, 'immunity from suit for wrong is not a necessary ingredient of State sovereignty'.[144]

As for the application of statute to the state, more specifically, it was found in *Howard v The Commissioners of Public Works in Ireland*[145] that the crown's

[137] *Cork County Council & Burke v Commissioners of Public Works* (n 134) 578. See Kelly, *The Irish Constitution* (n 128) 697.
[138] *Cork County Council & Burke v Commissioners of Public Works* (n 134) 587 (Black J).
[139] *Byrne v Ireland* (n 126) 266.
[140] ibid.
[141] ibid 272.
[142] ibid 298 (Budd J).
[143] ibid 267, citing *Kawananakoa v Polyblank* (n 62); *US v Lee* (n 12).
[144] *Byrne v Ireland* (n 126) 269; see Crown Proceedings Act 1947, 10 & 11 Geo 6 c 44 (UK); Petition of Right Act, 38 Vict c 12 (Canada) (the latter was modified in 1876: Canada Petition of Right Act, 39 Vict c 27).
[145] *Howard v Commissioners of Public Works in Ireland* [1994] 1 IR 101.

prerogative to be exempt from the application of statutes 'had not survived the enactment of the Constitution'.[146]

Irish courts also departed from American thinking in their different treatment of Blackstone. In *In Re Irish Employers Mutual Insurance*, Kingsmill Moore J stated that the prerogative of priority of payment of crown debts was incompatible with the 1922 Constitution. Interestingly, he relied on Blackstone to further explain his reasoning that direct prerogatives which belonged to the king now belonged to the people and are exercisable by the government. Direct prerogatives as defined by Blackstone are powers such as declaring war and peace.[147] But in relation to what Blackstone referred to as incidental prerogatives—privileges such as priority of payment—Kingsmill Moore J concluded that they are exceptions to the equal application of the law, and are therefore incompatible with the Constitution:

> Blackstone divides the prerogatives of the king into two classes, the 'direct' and the 'incidental'. The direct prerogative he defines as 'such positive substantial parts of the royal character and authority, as are rooted in and spring from the king's political person', and such prerogatives would, in general have been preserved by the Saorstát Éireann constitution, which vested executive authority in the king, and would now (by Article 49 of our Constitution) belong to the People and be exercisable by the Government. The incidental prerogatives on the other hand are defined as 'exceptions in favour of the crown, to those general rules that are established for the rest of the community', and the right to priority payment of debts is given as an exam [*sic*] of such prerogatives.[148]

Kingsmill Moore revisited Blackstone to adapt his writings to a modern republic, where the people is central. His decision was affirmed by Murnaghan J at the Supreme Court.

Despite Irish courts' reliance on American precedents, Irish legal thinking in relation to sovereignty is markedly different from American legal thinking. While, in American legal thinking, the identity of the sovereign is nebulous and sovereign immunity rests on the premise that the states cannot be sued at the will of any citizen without their consent, in Irish legal thinking, the people is the true holder of ultimate sovereignty. Early cases even entertained the idea that the people are the master of state employees,[149] and in *Byrne v Ireland*, although it is the state

[146] Gerard Hogan, David Gwynn Morgan, and Paul Daly, *Administrative Law in Ireland* (5th edn, Round Hall 2019) 28.

[147] Blackstone (n 42) 232–33.

[148] *In Re Irish Employers* (n 123) 198.

[149] See *Attorney General v CIÉ* (1956) 90 ILTR 139; *Attorney General v Dublin United Tramways Co* [1939] IR 590 (74 ILTR 46); and *Minister for Public Expenditure and Reform v O'Brien* [1949] IR 91; the idea that the people could be vicariously liable for the wrong of state employees on the basis that the people could be conceived of as their master was subsequently put to rest in *Attorney General v Ryan's Car Hire* [1965] IR 642: see Kelly (n 128) 740; Hogan, Morgan, and Daly (n 146) 132.

that was ultimately held liable, it was the people which had been the initial plaintiff before the claim was amended. The state was created by the people, and by virtue of the equality that the democratic principle enounced under Article 5 of the Constitution entails, is equal to individuals. The Irish state cannot, therefore, benefit from prerogatives that would put it above them. The Constitution also imposes a duty on the state to vindicate individuals' personal rights. The Irish state is but a trustee of government to the benefit of the people.

On the contrary, American legal thinking on sovereign immunity borrowed from Blackstone's definition of the prerogative and granted the sovereign—an unidentified entity that could be an abstract entity, the federal government, or the states—a prerogative immunity from suit that belonged to the king. American legal thinking is exemplified in the following excerpt from *Briggs v Light-Boat*, dating to 1865. It is clear from it that the sovereign is a being above the people, who must not be allowed to disturb the sovereign in the conduct of public government:

> It is an elementary and familiar principle of English and American constitutional law, that no direct suit can be brought against the sovereign in his own courts without his consent. In the older books, this is often put upon the technical ground that, all judicial writs being in the name of the king as the fountain of justice, the king cannot by his own writ command himself. But the broader reason is, that it would be inconsisten[t] with the very idea of supreme executive power, and would endanger the performance of the public duties of the sovereign, to subject him to repeated suits as a matter of right, at the will of any citizen, and to submit to the judicial tribunals the control and disposition of his public property, his instruments and means of carrying on the government in war and peace, and the money in his treasury.[150]

In short, the central role the people play in Irish legal thinking in conceiving of the state, the latter's status in relation to law and the people, and its capacity to be sued in light of the text of the Irish Constitution are still but aspirations in American legal thinking.[151]

3.1.3 Rejection of Ireland's feudal ties

The king can do no wrong in twentieth-century Irish legal thinking has predominantly been understood, in light of nineteenth-century English case law, as the fiction that there is no wrong in the king or that the king, being incapable of doing wrong, could not have ordered a wrong. *Carolan v Minister of Defence* offers an example where *the king can do no wrong* is seemingly understood as the king's incapacity to do wrong, and where other understandings are conceived of as distinct,

[150] *Briggs v Light-Boats* (1865) 93 Mass (11 Allen) 157, 162–63 (Gray J).
[151] See Amar (n 10).

such as 'the fact that the King could not be sued in his own court; being a superior feudal lord in the early days of the common law' and 'the King's legal disability to command himself to appear in his own Court'.[152] *Carolan* was later reversed—the High Court's finding in that case that the minister for defence could not be held liable for the negligent driving of a military lorry by a soldier is not compatible with current Irish legal thinking under the 1937 Constitution—but it offers a window into Irish legal thinking on *the king can do no wrong* under the Constitution of the Irish Free State. The appellant's submission that the Privy Council's conclusion in *Farnell v Bowman*, dating to 1887 and discussed in section 4, should apply just as much in the Australian context as in the Irish Free State is also evidence of an early dialogue between Irish and Australian legal thinking on state liability.[153]

That *the king can do no wrong* in the Bractonian sense meant that the king was not entitled to do wrong did not, however, escape Walsh J in the seminal Irish Supreme Court case of *Byrne v Ireland*:

> The suggestion advanced in this case that the State cannot be made amenable for civil wrong stems from the English feudal concept that 'the King can do no wrong'. There is some authority for believing that this phrase originally meant precisely the contrary to what it now means, and that its original meaning was that the King must not, and was not allowed to, and was not entitled to, do wrong.[154]

Although he confused time periods, defining *the king can do no wrong* as an English feudal concept, Walsh J offers in *Byrne v Ireland* perhaps a unique occurrence in judicial discussion and analysis across the common law world of *the king can do no wrong*'s origins, meanings, and scope. His analysis confuses the sequencing, timewise, of the evolution of the concept, but his insights are accurate. He correctly concluded, for instance, '[t]hat the grant of a petition of right was based precisely on the proposition that the King had acted contrary to law'.[155] Walsh J's conclusion reflects understandings of *the king can do no wrong* where the king is not conceived of as perfect, is subject to law, and has an obligation to remedy a wrong, which all grounded the petition of right and reflected the understanding that the king was capable of doing wrong. Although he accepted the contemporary, nineteenth-century view, that '[i]n the sphere of tort the petition of right did not

[152] *Carolan v Minister for Defence* [1927] IR 62, 70 (Hanna J). Ultimately the High Court in that case found that the minister was not liable for the soldier's negligent driving of a military lorry because the Constitution of the Irish Free State and relevant statutes did not change the state of the law which prevailed under English law, *viz* that both were servants of the crown, and a servant is not liable for a fellow servant's wrong.

[153] Plaintiff's submissions read as follows: '*Farnell v Bowman* turned on the wording of a Colonial statute, but considerations such as those referred to in the judgment of Sir Barnes Peacock, at p. 649, apply in the Irish Free State'; ibid 63.

[154] *Byrne v Ireland* (n 126) 265.

[155] ibid 266.

normally lie outside real actions', Walsh J concluded rightly that '[t]ortious immunity was a judge-made rule'.[156] Walsh J even identified the logical justification often invoked to explain that judge-made immunity: 'it would be a logical anomaly for the King to issue or enforce a writ against himself'.[157] This justification, as we have seen, was surmised by no less than Maitland,[158] but Walsh J kept a healthy scepticism in relation to it.[159] He was right to do so, as the impossibility for the king to issue a writ against himself has often been invoked in relation to the absence of ordinary actions against the king since the Middle Ages, but it had no connection with the nineteenth-century cases that narrowed the scope of the petition of right. This latter judge-made immunity in the realm of torts is a much more recent construct. Walsh J also perceptively associated the judge-made immunity with the notion of perfection of the king, and with the king's consequent incapacity to commit a wrong: 'The theory was that the King, as the source of all justice, was incapable of committing a wrong.'[160] In short, Walsh J attempts in *Byrne v Ireland* to disentangle the various explanations and justifications often associated with *the king can do no wrong*. He may have been confused in relation to the concept's historical evolution—his affirmation that 'for many centuries past there has been no doubt as to the meaning of the phrase'[161] would be correct if one were to assume that the phrase in its Bractonian sense was in use during the Middle Ages, which it was not—but Walsh J very aptly distinguished between the substantive and procedural dimensions of crown liability: ' "the King can do no wrong", . . . is a concept which differs from the concept that he was immune from suit'.[162] Walsh J's dubious stance in relation to the justifications to explain the king's immunity from suit is a refreshing trait of critical thinking in relation to *the king can do no wrong* which is rarely found even in twentieth- and twenty-first-century cases in common law jurisdictions.

The Irish Supreme Court's rejection and retention of elements of the prerogative after the Constitution came into force have been skillfully debated, notably on textual and historical grounds.[163] Justice Walsh's core argument in *Byrne v Ireland*,

[156] ibid.
[157] ibid.
[158] See Chapter 2, section 2.3.3.
[159] 'It would appear to have been based on the view that it would be a logical anomaly', *Byrne v Ireland* (n 126) 266 (Walsh J).
[160] ibid.
[161] ibid 265.
[162] ibid.
[163] See eg Kelly, 'Hidden Treasure' (n 122); Niall Lenihan, 'Royal Prerogatives and the Constitution' (1989) 24 Irish Jurist 1; Kevin Costello, 'The Expulsion of Prerogative Doctrine from Irish Law: Quantifying and Remedying the Loss of the Royal Prerogative' [1997] Irish Jurist 145; Cahillane, 'Dusty Antique' (n 130); Paul Daly, 'The Constitutionalisation of English Judicial Review in Ireland: Continuity and Change' in Swati Jhaveri and Michael Ramsden (eds), *Judicial Review of Administrative Action Across the Common Law World* (1st edn, CUP 2021) 104–05. As Casey explains, 'J. M. Kelly doubted the major premises of the Supreme Court's reasoning [in *Webb*]—that the Irish Free State, as established in 1922, was sovereign': James P Casey, *Constitutional Law in Ireland* (3rd edn, Round Hall Sweet & Maxwell 2000) 51.

dating to the early 1970s, was that the legal remainder of a feudal past does not accord with constitutional and democratic imperatives. His opinion as to the inadequacy of English constitutional law in framing constitutional law under the new Irish Constitution found echo in previous cases.

The survival of the prerogative of priority of payment had already been cast into doubt as early as 1939 by Gavan Duffy J in *In re The Irish Aero Club*: 'the State would be entitled to enjoy the prerogative which has accorded to the British Crown a right to a payment in full in priority to its subjects', a proposition which 'would be hard to reconcile with the Constitution'.[164] A year later, Article 28 of the Constitution—which provides that '[t]he executive power of the State shall, subject to the provisions of this Constitution, be exercised by or on the authority of the Government'—was relied upon to conclude that there remained no trace of the crown in the Constitution after the constitutional changes brought forth in 1937.[165] Then, in 1951, in *In Re Tilson*, Murnaghan J expressed the view that would later be at the core of Irish legal thinking, that the Irish Constitution is the hallmark of a modern, democratic, state and cannot therefore allow the survival of legal elements of feudal origins: 'The archaic law of England rapidly disintegrating under modern conditions need not be a guide for the fundamental principles of a modern state. It is not a proper method of construing a new constitution of a modern state to make an approach in the light of legal survivals of an earlier law.'[166]

In 1955, in *In Re Irish Employers Mutual Insurance Association Ltd*, Kingsmill Moore J also pointed the finger at the feudal origins of the prerogative of payment, which took form at a time when royal revenues were personal to the king:

> The prerogative originated in a period when modern conceptions of the nature of sovereignty and government had not yet arisen. The structure of society was still feudal; property law was built on a feudal skeleton; loyalty was an essentially personal matter; the king was looked on more as a feudal overlord than as the embodiment of national power and aspiration; and the royal revenues, feudal by nature, were regarded as the king's personal possession, which could be spent by him according to his personal desires and without restriction by ministerial or parliamentary interference.[167]

Kingsmill Moore J was keen to highlight the feudal origins of the British Constitution, for he had also described it as a feudal castle in *Comyn's Case* a few years earlier:

[164] *In re The Irish Aero Club; Gillic v Minister for Industry and Commerce* (n 128) 209.

[165] *Attorney General v Crawford* [1940] IR 335.

[166] *In Re Tilson* [1951] IR 1, 32 (Murnaghan J). This excerpt was cited with approval by Walsh J in *Byrne v Ireland* (n 126) 281–82.

[167] *In Re Irish Employers* (n 123) 214.

> That Constitution was built up on a framework of feudal land tenure and absolute monarchy. The British people, conservative by nature, averse to revolution, distrustful of abstract theory, were loath to annihilate that framework; yet, they never shrank from recognising manifest abuses or adopting practical subterfuges to remedy them. . . . Yet the forms and language of feudalism are still there. The facade and structure remain that of a fortified Tudor manor house, though within is to be found 'every modern convenience' and a liberal assortment of all modern luxuries. The King is still the executive; the Departments of the executive are organised bodies of his servants.[168]

To Walsh J in *Byrne v Ireland* in 1972, the conclusion previously reached by the court in 1945 in *Galway County Council* and *Cork County Council & Burke v Commissioners of Public Works*[169] that the law of England was simply carried over into the Irish Free State by operation of Article 73 of the 1922 Constitution[170] 'was an erroneous over-simplification of the issues'.[171] Walsh J's conclusion that the 1937 Constitution contained no trace of a theory of immunity from suit of the state 'stemming from or based upon the immunity of a personal sovereign who was the keystone of a feudal edifice'[172] is another leading example of judicial rejection of feudal elements in the republican constitutional order.

In *Byrne v Ireland*, the plaintiff, Ms Byrne, sued the people of Ireland (later amended to 'Ireland') and the Attorney General for the physical damage she suffered as a result of walking on a footpath which had been excavated and refilled by employees of the Department of Posts and Telegraphs, and which subsided. The plaintiff's action against Ireland and the Attorney General was grounded in vicarious liability for their employees' breach of statutory duty, negligence, and, alternatively, nuisance. The Irish Supreme Court in *Byrne v Ireland* abolished what it perceived as the king's feudal prerogative of immunity from suit. The Supreme Court in *Byrne* also found the king's prerogative of immunity from suit to be inconsistent with Article 40, section 3, of the Constitution, 'whereby the State guarantees in its laws to defend and vindicate the personal rights of the citizen and

[168] *Comyn v The Attorney General* [1950] IR 142, 151 (*Comyn's Case*).

[169] *Cork County Council & Burke v Commissioners of Public Works* (n 134). O'Byrne J cited the continuation provisions of Art 73 of the 1922 Constitution and said he could 'see no reason for holding that the prerogative, with which I am dealing, was not transferred to the Irish Free State. It was part of the common law, which was applied to the Irish Free State by Article 73 . . . [and in view of Arts 49 and 50 of the 1937 Constitution] it seems to me clear that the State is now entitled to the benefit of the Prerogative in question': ibid 578.

[170] Art 73 of the 1922 Constitution read: 'Subject to this Constitution and to the extent to which they are not inconsistent therewith, the laws in force in the Irish Free State . . . at the date of the coming into force of this Constitution shall continue to be of full force and effect until the same or any of them shall have been repealed or amended by enactment of the Oireachtas.'

[171] *Byrne v Ireland* (n 126) 272 (Walsh J); see also 301 (Budd J). See also *Cooper v Attorney General &Ors* [1935] IR 425, where Art 73 was thought to have carried over the prerogative of fishing rights reserved to the crown.

[172] *Byrne v Ireland* (n 126) 281.

to protect and vindicate the life, person, good name and property rights of every citizen'.[173] The Court had similarly found, in a habeas corpus case, that the text of the Constitution could not be pre-empted by past practices under the common law, and that rights of appeal and the courts' jurisdiction under the Constitution should prevail.[174] Citing this precedent, the Court in *Byrne* said 'English common-law practices, doctrines, or immunities cannot qualify or dilute the provisions of the Constitution'.[175] The prerogative had not survived the Constitution of the Irish Free State in 1922,[176] it could not therefore have carried over in 1937 to the current Constitution, and the common law could not displace constitutional supremacy. If the Irish state had any power, it was given to it by the Constitution alone.

Walsh J subsequently decided a year later, in *The State (O) v O'Brien*,[177] that although the English king may have personally administered justice under the English Constitution, and that the English courts' jurisdiction was derived from him as fountain of justice, the king was not given such power under the Constitution of the Irish Free State. To Walsh J, because 'all powers of government and all authority, legislative, executive and judicial, in Ireland were derived from the people of Ireland' under Article 2 of the 1922 Constitution of Saorstát Éireann, and that 'the same shall be exercised in the Irish Free State (Saorstát Éireann) through the organisations established by or under, and in accord with, this Constitution', the Constitution quite clearly did not accept the crown as the fountain of justice. The king's prerogative of mercy was consequently denied and found to vest as a judicial function in the courts only.

Although it buried *the king can do no wrong* understood as an archaic, ancient feudal procedural privilege, as well as the prerogative of mercy and the rule that statutes do not bind the state, the Irish Supreme Court nevertheless maintained other aspects of the prerogative. When the Derrynaflan Hoard—exquisite pieces of Irish metal craftsmanship of the eighth century—was found by Irish treasure hunters in the 1980s, the Irish Supreme Court in *Webb* dug out the crown's prerogative right to treasure trove and passed it on—reborn as a necessary component of sovereignty—to the Irish state.[178] Nevertheless, Finlay CJ, writing for the Court in *Webb*, adopted Walsh J's view in *Byrne v Ireland* that the king's 'royal prerogatives'—'any royal prerogative'—died upon the birth of the Irish Free State in 1922

[173] ibid 303.

[174] *The State (Browne) v Feran* [1967] IR 147.

[175] *Byrne v Ireland* (n 126) 281.

[176] Kelly was critical of this revisionist stance in relation to the 1922 Constitution; he was of the view 'that the Crown and its prerogative were understood to have survived into the newly independent Irish Free State, as part of the common law, under Article 73, so far as such survival was not, in letter or in spirit, inconsistent with some specific dimension of the new Constitution': Kelly, 'Hidden Treasure' (n 122) 14.

[177] *The State (O) v O'Brien* [1973] IR 50.

[178] *Webb v Ireland* [1988] 1 IR 353. The right to treasure trove is conceived of by the Supreme Court, following *Webb*, as 'a right latent in the Constitution': Costello (n 163) 183. It had been found, prior to Ireland's independence, that treasure trove vested in the crown: *R v O'Toole* (1867) IR 2CL 36.

and could not, as a result, have been carried over in the 1937 Constitution.[179] The state's right to treasure trove exists in the Irish republic 'not as a right derived from the Crown but rather as an inherent attribute of the sovereignty of the State'.[180]

That any royal prerogatives of the king—understood as the king's feudal privileges and immunities—are now extinguished in the Irish Constitution was maintained again in *Howard v Commissioners of Public Works* in 1994. There, the Supreme Court found that the rule of statutory interpretation that the king is presumed not to be bound by statutes that do not expressly name him or bind him by necessary implication is a rule 'in fact so rooted in the prerogative and the Crown as the personification of the State that it is, in fact, inseparable from that concept'.[181] The rule of statutory construction being associated, in Irish legal thinking, with the prerogative, it followed the same fate. It could not, therefore, have survived the enactment of the 1937 Constitution.

3.2 The Irish state as a juristic person

In his seminal opinion in *Byrne v Ireland*, Walsh J wrote that 'the King was the personification of the State' in the English constitutional order, while already in 1922, he opined, 'Article 2 of the Constitution of the Irish Free State declared that all the powers of government and all authority, legislative, executive and judicial, in Ireland were derived from the People of Ireland'.[182] Walsh J crossed out from the 1922 Constitution of the Irish Free State Articles 41, 51, 55, 60, 66, and 68, which vested executive authority in the king; Article 12, which made the king an integral part of the Oireachtas; and Article 66, which provided for a petition to the king for special leave to appeal from the Supreme Court to King in Council. Walsh J's rewriting of Irish constitutional history was in line with the new narrative set out by the 1937 Constitution, which further clarified that, in the Irish constitutional order, the main actors are 'the people of Éire' mentioned in the preamble, the 'Nation' (Arts 1–3), the 'State' (Arts 4–11), the 'Government' (Art 28), as well as, notably, the 'President', the 'National Parliament', 'Dáil Éireann', 'Seanad Éireann', and the 'Courts'.[183] In Ireland's constitutional history, the English king, a person representing the state, was replaced by the state, a person representing the Irish people.

[179] *Webb* (n 178) [53]: 'As is also set out in the decision in *Byrne v Ireland* it must follow from this conclusion that the royal prerogatives were not prerogatives exercisable in Saorstát Éireann immediately before 11 December 1936 and were therefore not captured by Article 49.1 of the Constitution.'

[180] ibid 383 (Finlay CJ).

[181] *Howard v Commissioners of Public Works in Ireland* (n 145) 136–37 (Denman J).

[182] *Byrne v Ireland* (n 126) 272 (Walsh J).

[183] The President (Arts 12–14), the National Parliament (Arts 15–27), Dáil Éireann (Arts 16–17), Seanad Éireann (Arts 18–19), the Courts (Arts 34–37).

Fifty years after the adoption of the Constitution of the Irish Free State, the country's highest court sounded the death knell for the king's prerogative. The Irish state was granted legal personhood and liability to be sued, at first vicariously and later directly. Despite these changes and evolution, Ireland's cultural heritage was maintained, and the prerogative right to treasure trove was reborn as an inherent attribute of statehood crucial to the preservation of Ireland's past.

3.2.1 Change and continuity

Ireland's independence from the United Kingdom and its new existence as a republic with the adoption of the present Constitution resulted in the king having 'no place' in the Irish constitutional order.[184] Under the 1937 Irish Constitution, executive power is granted to the government, as distinct from ministers.[185] The government is also distinct from the state, which has legal personality and was created by the people, as the Constitution clearly states under Article 6:

> 1 All powers of government, legislative, executive and judicial, derive, under God, from the people, whose right it is to designate the rulers of the State and, in final appeal, to decide all questions of national policy, according to the requirements of the common good.
> 2 These powers of government are exercisable only by or on the authority of the organs of State established by this Constitution.

A first phase in the evolution of Irish legal thinking in relation to state liability saw the courts ascribing great significance to the democratic dimension of the Irish state enounced in Article 5 of the 1937 Constitution,[186] and its legal consequence in granting equality to all, including the state *vis-à-vis* individuals. In the 1960s, in *O'Donovan v Attorney General*, Budd J opined that 'a "democratic State" denotes one in which all citizens have equal political rights' and 'That the words should be given such a meaning in our Constitution seems to be supported by [Articles 16.1.4 and 40.1] as to the restriction of voting power to one vote per person and the equality of all before the law'.[187] Likewise, in 1965, in *Ryan v Attorney General*, Article 5 of the Constitution and its declaring Ireland as a democratic state was conceived of

[184] *Byrne v Ireland* (n 126) 282 (Walsh J).

[185] Art 28.2, under 'The Government' reads: '2 The executive power of the State shall, subject to the provisions of this Constitution, be exercised by or on the authority of the Government.'
Art 29.4 (1), under 'International Relations' reads: 'The executive power of the State in or in connection with its external relations shall in accordance with Article 28 of this Constitution be exercised by or on the authority of the Government.'

[186] Art 5: 'Ireland is a sovereign, independent, democratic state.' See *The State (Burke) v Lennon* [1940] IR 136, 144 (Gavan Duffy J): 'The architects of the Constitution were alive to the need for protecting the rights declared in the Constitution; accordingly, in Article 5, they characterised the State as a democratic State . . . '; and *The State (M.) v Attorney General* [1979] IR 73, in relation to the granting of passport and the right to travel outside the state.

[187] *O'Donovan v Attorney General* [1961] IR 114, 139.

as grounding an interpretation of Article 40.3 as conferring fundamental personal rights other than those specifically enumerated in the Constitution.[188] In the Irish republic, a democracy, 'the sovereign power resides in the people as a whole'.[189]

The state was also gradually recognized as a juristic person.[190] In *Comyn's Case*,[191] it was held that the state is a juristic person capable of holding property. The government was also identified as the executive organ exercising the supreme executive power of the state by virtue of Article 28 of the Constitution. The government was also found to be distinct from the departments of government, for which the government is collectively responsible.[192] Kingsmill Moore J also decided in that case that the state is an entity distinct from the people and the government.[193] His decision was upheld by the Supreme Court and reiterated in *Commissioners of Public Works v Kavanagh*, where Ó Dálaigh J held that the word 'person' in a statute should not be construed as being limited to human persons, and is general enough to encompass the state as a juristic person—either under Article 11 of the Constitution of Saorstát Éireann or, following the supplanting of the Free State by the Republic of Ireland, under Article 10.2 of the Constitution of Ireland.[194]

Finally, in 1966, in *Macauley*, Kenny J used *Comyn's Case* and *Kavanagh* to further conclude that the state could be sued:

> [The] ... Republic of Ireland (or the People) is, and ... Saorstát Éireann was, a legally recognised juristic person capable of holding property. In my view, the State may now be sued in the courts whenever it is necessary to vindicate or assert the rights of a citizen.[195]

Kenny J's equating the state and the people in this quote is further evidence of the central role the Irish people play in the Constitution.[196]

But amongst this fundamental change brought about by the existence of the Irish state and its liability to be sued, there is also continuity, albeit with a period of interruption. The Irish were not foreign to feudal structures of society: medieval Irish kings were not different from other medieval lords and kings. Post Irish independence and the adoption of the 1922 and 1937 Constitutions, the Irish Supreme

[188] *Ryan v Attorney General* [1965] IR 294, 313 (Kenny J).
[189] *de Burcá v Attorney General* [1976] IR 36, 47 (Pringle J)(High Court), reversed on other grounds by the Supreme Court: *de Burcá v Attorney General* [1976] IR 36, 57.
[190] Budd J recounted the evolution of the legal nature of the state in *Byrne v Ireland* (n 126) 290–91. See Hogan, Morgan, and Daly (n 146) 1290–91.
[191] *Comyn v The Attorney General* (n 168).
[192] ibid 156.
[193] ibid 158–61.
[194] *Commissioners of Public Works v Kavanagh* [1962] IR 216, 226–27.
[195] *Macauley v Minister for Posts and Telegraphs* [1966] IR 345, 353.
[196] Ó Dálaigh J had also associated the state with the citizens taken as a corporation in *Kavanagh*: 'It is not necessary for me to say whether the State as a juristic person is to be looked upon as an abstract concept or viewed rather as the body of the citizens in a corporate capacity.': *Kavanagh* (n 194) 226–27.

Court's rejection in 1972 in *Byrne v Ireland* of what it perceived as feudal privileges and prerogatives of the English king was not a wholesale rejection of Ireland's history. On the contrary, the fundamental reason the Supreme Court gave in the 1988 case of *Webb* for granting the Irish state the prerogative to treasure trove was 'that one of the most important national assets belonging to the people is their heritage and knowledge of its true origins and the buildings and objects which constitute keys to their ancient history'.[197]

Both Walsh J in *Byrne* and Finlay CJ in *Webb* found that it is an inherent ingredient of sovereignty of a modern state to be able to claim possession of artifacts of importance as they relate to the origins and comprehension thereof of the people of that state, just as both Walsh and Budd JJ agreed in *Byrne* that immunity could not be associated with the idea of a modern state. In *Webb*, Finlay CJ rejected the Blackstone-like distinction between prerogatives incidental to the person of the king and those traced to his position as sovereign ruler.[198] To Finlay CJ, such a distinction appeared to skew the crucial feature of the 1922 Constitution, which was to create a new sovereign state where the monarch's role or functions existed only insofar as the provisions of the Constitution and the state it created allowed and vested in him.[199] *Byrne v Ireland* and *Webb* are an effort by the Irish Supreme Court to realign Irish constitutional law with its new republican structure—and pave the way for a modern Irish state while preserving its history.[200]

3.2.2 Vicarious and direct liability

The Irish state can now be sued in tort as a result of Article 40.3 and the 1972 case of *Byrne v Ireland*.[201] In the decades that preceded *Byrne v Ireland*, reforms of the Irish law of state liability were suggested, and increasingly so after the UK Parliament enacted the Crown Proceedings Act 1947: it became harder to justify maintaining in Ireland an immunity which originated in England, and which had since been

[197] *Webb v Ireland* (n 178) 383 (Finlay CJ).

[198] Blackstone distinguished between direct and incidental prerogatives of the king: Blackstone (n 42) 232–33. Kelly also adopted a dual conception of the prerogative in interpreting the Supreme Court's reasons in *Byrne* and *Webb* and read the Supreme Court's seminal cases as maintaining, in Irish constitutional law, only those prerogatives which are 'broad-based upon the public interest', and which were passed on to the state, but not those that 'were the appendages of the person of the sovereign': Kelly, 'Hidden Treasure' (n 122) 7; Lenihan (n 163) 11.

[199] *Webb v Ireland* (n 178).

[200] See also recent attempts by the Supreme Court to preserve the Irish constitution's integrity as against European law and international trade agreements in *Costello v Ireland* (2022) IESC 44.

[201] *Byrne v Ireland* (n 126). See Hogan, Morgan, and Daly (n 146) 1290–91. Art 40.3, found under 'Personal rights' provides:

> 40.3
> 1° The State guarantees in its laws to respect, and, as far as practicable, by its laws to defend and vindicate the personal rights of the citizen.
> 2° The State shall, in particular, by its laws protect as best it may from unjust attack and, in the case of injustice done, vindicate the life, person, good name, and property rights of every citizen.
> 3° Provision may be made by law for the regulation of termination of pregnancy.

curtailed by legislation. Cases were brought forth by imaginative counsel to obtain compensation from the state for the wrong done to individuals.[202] These previous (unsuccessful) attempts at suing the state or state officials were grounded in vicarious liability, which contributed to the liability of the state being conceived of as vicarious in *Byrne v Ireland*.

For instance, the courts had refused to find that the warder of a prison was the agent of that prison's governor in *O'Connell v Kavanagh* in 1958.[203] In *O'Hanlon v Minister for Posts and Telegraph*, dating to 1960, the minister was also let off the hook for the negligence of the employees of the department in a case where the plaintiff's yacht was damaged as a result of its entanglement in telegraph wires straddling the Shannon River.[204] The courts concluded that the plaintiff brought the misfortune on himself by choosing to proceed down the waterway despite the presence of the wires.

The wind turned in *Byrne v Ireland*, where the state was found to be liable for the wrong done by its employees of the Department of Post and Telegraph. The employees' negligent work caused the footpath to subside and Ms Byrne to be injured as a result. *Byrne v Ireland* can therefore be conceived of as a vicarious liability case: to Budd J, employees of the department were public servants of the state, and the state as employer can be sued for the wrong done by its employees.[205] Walsh J further opined in *Byrne* that an organ of the state can be liable, and so can the state itself as the principal.[206] But vicarious liability of the state was not the sole possible outcome after *Byrne*: the state as a juristic person could also be conceived of as liable, a departure from English legal thinking on the liability of governmental departments at common law since the turn of the twentieth century.[207] To Walsh J, even if one were to accept the argument that the state can only act through its organs—and therefore that it is vicariously liable—that would not prevent a finding of liability against the state, for the doctrine of *respondeat superior* applies. Note that Walsh J's understanding of the doctrine of *respondeat superior*

[202] The context that preceded *Byrne v Ireland* is recounted in Nial Osborough, 'The Demise of the State's Immunity in Tort' 8 Irish Jurist 275, 284–89.

[203] *O'Connell v Kavanagh* (1958) 92 ITLR 10, referred to in ibid 285.

[204] *O'Hanlon v Minister for Posts and Telegraphs* [1960] Ir Jur Rep 25; see Osborough (n 202) 285–86.

[205] *Byrne v Ireland* (n 126) 304–05 (Budd J). Budd J relied on *McLoughlin v Minister for Social Welfare* [1958] IR 1, 16 (Kingsmill Moore J), 25–26 (Ó Dálaigh J), for the proposition that civil servants are in the public service of the state.

[206] *Byrne v Ireland* (n 126) 280–81 (Walsh J).

[207] For a finding of direct liability of the state for a wrong done by another organ, see *O'Keefe v Ireland* (2014) 59 EHRR 15. Note, however, that it is on the basis of vicarious liability that the case had been pleaded on appeal, and the Supreme Court had not found the state liable: *O'Keefe v Hickey* [2009] 2 IR 302, although that decision was strongly criticized as allowing the state to escape liability for systemic failure, in this case by outsourcing education: Conor O'Mahony, 'State Liability for Abuse in Primary Schools: Systemic Failure and *O'Keefe v. Hickey*' (2009) 28 Ir Ed St 315. The Supreme Court in *O'Keefe* significantly dampened Walsh J's broadening of the scope of vicarious liability in *Moynihan v Moynihan* [1975] IR 192. The Supreme Court in *O'Keefe* implicitly endorsed instead Henchy J's dissent in *Moynihan*: see William Binchy, 'Tort Law in Ireland: A Half-Century Review' (2016) 56 Irish Jurist 199.

is that the principal is liable to make good the damage done by his servants, regardless of whether the principal can or cannot commit the particular tort.[208] The doctrine does not rest on the principal's own wrong, but on the principal's duty to compensate for the wrong done by the servant carrying on the principal's affairs. When Walsh J wrote his opinion in *Byrne*, he had the benefit of the evolution, over the course of the twentieth century, of the doctrine of *respondeat superior*. He was not tied, as were English courts in the nineteenth century, by the doctrine as it was then understood, and which rested on the principal's own wrong.[209] As was explained before in Chapter 4, in relation to the 1865 English case of *Feather*,[210] 'a master is only liable for the acts of his servants on the principle that their wrongdoing is his wrongdoing'.[211] It was that aspect of the doctrine which had led English courts to reconceive of *the king can do no wrong* as there is no wrong in the king, and that he cannot, therefore, be held responsible for the wrongs done by his servants. The doctrine had changed by the second half of the twentieth century, and the principal's own wrong was not a bar anymore to the state's vicarious liability for the wrong of state servants when Walsh J wrote his majority opinion in *Byrne*.

3.3 Conclusion: a modern republican view of state liability

In *Byrne v Ireland*, Walsh J recounted how '[f]or many years in this country, like the American experience, the notion of sovereign immunity of the State seems to have been accepted as part of the common law, without full regard to its true origin in the common law'.[212] In this seminal case, it was the historically inaccurate understanding of *the king can do no wrong* as conferring procedural immunity from suit on the English king as feudal overlord which was rejected in Irish legal thinking, as well as sovereign immunity as it is understood in America. 'There is no basis, theoretical or otherwise, for a claim that the State can do no wrong.'[213] This quote captures well Irish legal thinking on state liability.

Irish legal thinking is also grounded in the conception that if 'the People by the Constitution create rights against the State or impose duties upon the State, a remedy to enforce these must be deemed to be also available'.[214] If there is a right enshrined by virtue of the people's will in the Constitution, a remedy must be

[208] *Byrne v Ireland* (n 126) 280 (Walsh J).
[209] See Chapter 5, section 4.3.1. The understanding of *the king can do no wrong* that the crown cannot commit a tort and cannot be liable in tort for the wrong of its servant because the principle of respondeat superior did not apply to it can be found in Lord Dunedin's speech in *Attorney-General v De Keyser's Royal Hotel Ltd* [1920] AC 508 (HL) 523, 532.
[210] *Feather v The Queen* (1865) 6 B&S 257, 297 (Cockburn CJ); see Chapter 4, section 3.3.1.
[211] William Reynell Anson, *The Law and Custom of the Constitution*, vol 2 part 1 (A Berriedale Keith ed, 4th edn, Clarendon Press 1935) 20.
[212] *Byrne v Ireland* (n 126) 269 (Walsh J).
[213] ibid 279 (Walsh J).
[214] ibid 281 (Walsh J).

deemed to exist to give effect to it. Irish legal thinking differs from Blackstone's procedurally focussed notion that if there is no wrong, there is no remedy.[215] The Irish Constitution creates rights, therefore there must be a remedy.

In Ireland, the state is subject to law. The Irish view, first expounded by Walsh J, that the 'whole tenor of the Constitution is to the effect that there is no power, institution, or person in the land free of the law'[216] is in essence very Bractonian. Article 40.1 of the Constitution—which provides for equality before the law—was relied on to support the Supreme Court's ruling that the rule of interpretation that statutes do not bind the state unless expressly named or by necessary application was contrary to the Constitution.[217] The notion of equality before the law extending to the Irish state achieves a greater reach in Irish legal thinking than Dicey's focus on individual officers contemplated.[218]

Sovereign immunity is as much a product of the American Constitution creating a federal structure and of the Eleventh Amendment, as the denial of any immunity from suit benefiting the Irish state is a product of the Irish Constitution. In conceiving of state liability, both American and Irish legal thinking relied on Blackstone, but with very different outcomes. American courts and legal thinkers relied on Blackstone's famed *Commentaries* in devising the concept of sovereign immunity. That reliance entailed chaining sovereign immunity in American legal thinking to the very un-English notion that the sovereign is above the law. The notion that the Irish state is above the law because Article 5 of the Constitution declares Ireland to be a sovereign, independent, democratic state, was firmly rejected in *Byrne*.[219] The notion of perfection of the monarch and 'feudal theories' associated with *the king can do no wrong* were also cast aside: 'All these conceptions and theories, which are dealt with in Blackstone, are conceptions which seem quite irreconcilable with modern ideas.'[220]

As for the prerogative, a defining feature of Blackstone's work, it was also used as a focal point in Irish legal thinking. The Irish Supreme Court, for example, conceives of the rule of statutory construction that the crown is not presumed to be bound by a statute to be part of the prerogative (a position which was also implicitly adopted in Canada, but rejected in Australia and, belatedly, in the United Kingdom).[221] Although Irish courts used the prerogative as a focal point, they

[215] See Chapter 4, section 2.1.

[216] *Byrne v Ireland* (n 126) 281 (Walsh J).

[217] *Howard v Commissioners of Public Works in Ireland* (n 145) 136–37 (Denman J).

[218] See Chapter 4, section 3.3.3.

[219] 'In the first place I think that the learned trial judge misconstrued the intent of Article 5 if he construed it as a constitutional declaration that the State is above the law': *Byrne v Ireland* (n 126) 264 (Walsh J); '[T]he general trend is to put obligations on the state' and 'the State is not internally sovereign but, in internal affairs, subject to the Constitution which limits, confines and restricts its power': ibid 299 (Budd J).

[220] ibid 298 (Budd J).

[221] *R v Eldorado Nuclear Ltd* [1983] 2 SCR 551, 556 (Dickson J); *Alberta Government Telephones v (Canada) Canadian Radio-television and Telecommunications Commission* [1989] 2 SCR 225, 291 (Dickson CJ); *Bropho v Western Australia* (1990) 171 CLR 1, 15 (Mason CJ, Deane, Dawson, Toohey,

rejected *the king can do no wrong* understood as conferring immunity from suit on the state, unlike their American counterparts, and have wholeheartedly adopted the Constitution's conferral of sovereignty on the people:

> It appears to me abundantly clear from those provisions that the State is the creation of the People and is to be governed in accordance with the provisions of the Constitution which was enacted by the People and which can be amended by the People only, and that in the last analysis the sovereign authority is the People.[222]

The Irish state cannot claim sovereign immunity before the courts in Ireland because under the Constitution, the sovereign is the people.[223] In Irish legal thinking, therefore, there is no equivocation as to the locus of sovereignty under the Constitution, unlike, as Walsh J opined, 'the position in the United States of America where Chief Justice John Marshall initially established the basic premise that the United States was created by the States and the people of the States, and not by the people separated from the States'.[224] Free of the constraints and debates occurring in America as to the identity of the sovereign in a federal structure, Irish legal thinking has conferred on the Irish state juristic personhood and, in the name of and to the benefit of the people, various prerogatives which belonged to the English king, but which are now conceived of as flowing from the text of the Constitution and state sovereignty in a modern world. English common law immunities cannot defeat the provisions of the Irish Constitution.[225] *The king can do no wrong* understood as a feudal immunity from suit was buried, and the prerogative which was dug out by Irish courts post *Byrne* was not that of the king, but that of the state, to the benefit of the people. Under the Irish Constitution, the king is dead, long live the state.[226]

Ireland's evolution into an independent republic has allowed it to lift the veil surrounding the notion of the crown more efficiently than in other Commonwealth jurisdictions, such as Canada and the United Kingdom itself. Already in 1927, the Irish Supreme Court reasoned that 'The Crown is in each Dominion the permanent symbol of executive government, but the actual government is in fact and in constitutional reality in the hands of national ministers responsible to, and

Gaudron, and McHugh JJ); *ACCC v Baxter Healthcare Pty Ltd* (2007) 232 CLR 1, 27 (Gleeson CJ, Gummow, Hayne, Heydon, and Crennan JJ), 48–49 (Kirby J); *R(on the application of Black) v Secretary of State for Justice* (2017) UKSC 81, [2018] AC 215 [36] (Lady Hale); Anthony Gray, 'Immunity of the Crown from Statute and Suit' (2010) Canb LR 1; Fortin (n 8) 275–80.

222 *Byrne v Ireland* (n 126) 262 (Walsh J).
223 ibid 295–96, 302 (Budd J).
224 ibid.
225 ibid 281 (Walsh J).
226 '[T]he King has gone from the Constitution and with him any feudal theories of immunity from suit based on the royal prerogative': ibid 303 (Budd J).

changeable at the will of, the national parliament'.[227] Likewise, the appellant's submission in *Carolan v Minister for Defence* that the Minister for Defence 'must be deemed to be the employer of the soldier, because there is no other legal person to be employer'[228] illustrates just how profound a change occurred when British ministers of the crown were replaced with ministers of state, corporations sole created by statute to run governmental departments.

'The State may be a person known to international law, but it is not a person known to its own municipal law'.[229] This observation by the appellant in *Carolan* is an accurate depiction of the state of the law in the United Kingdom and many other members of the Commonwealth, including Canada, almost a century later. As Kingsmill Moore J wrote in *Comyn's Case*, 'English law avoided the necessity of considering the juristic nature of the State by the expedient of regarding the King (or Crown) as a corporation sole . . . but the King has now disappeared from our Constitution, and . . . Irish lawyers can no longer shut their eyes to the problems involved in the conception of a State'.[230] Once the all-encompassing role the king plays in the English Constitution was removed from the Irish constitution, the vacuum it left had to be filled in. The 1937 Constitution firmly grounded constituting power in the Irish people and expressly created a distinct entity—the state. 'Gradually', recounts Budd J in *Byrne v Ireland*, 'the results and effects of having a written Constitution have been borne in on us'.[231] Ultimately, Irish legal thinking reached the conclusion that the nature and attributes of the state must be found in the wording of the constitution itself. Irish cases from the twentieth century nevertheless offer a rich mine—a treasure trove, in fact—from which modern ideas about the state and its liability for a wrong can be extracted, a conclusion which did not escape the Australian High Court, as will be explained in section 4.[232]

4 Avant-garde Australia: colonial context and liability at common law

In the early twentieth century, famed Australian scholar Evatt gave the royal prerogative pride of place in his analysis of Australian constitutional law.[233] The prerogative was Evatt's focal point, as it has been in Irish legal thinking under the 1937 Constitution, but with a different outcome (see section 3). While Irish courts have used the prerogative as a trope to evict the king and feudalism from

[227] *In Re Reade* [1927] IR 31(Kennedy CJ) cited in Costello (n 163) 171.
[228] *Carolan v Minister for Defence* (n 152) 63.
[229] ibid.
[230] *Comyn v The Attorney General* (n 168) 157.
[231] *Byrne v Ireland* (n 126) 294.
[232] See Kirby J's reasons in *Baxter* (n 221).
[233] Herbert Vere Evatt, *The Royal Prerogative* (Leslie Zines ed, Law Book Company 1987).

the Irish constitutional order, Evatt used the prerogative as a source of power for the colonial government in Australia in its own right, independent from the United Kingdom. Evatt's aim was also independence, albeit of a different kind, and the trend in freeing Australian law from English influences has endured in Australian legal thinking on crown liability. Gaudron, Gummow, and Kirby JJ, for instance, cautioned that in relation to *the king can do no wrong*, 'care is required in translating to the legal structure and practical circumstances applying in Australia doctrines which in England have been identified as "constitutional" . . . [t]he inapplicability in federal jurisdiction of the maxim that the Crown can do no wrong is one example'.[234] Kirby J also reasoned that 'the specificities and juxtapositions in the Australian Constitution . . . rendered it inapposite to import into our constitutional institutions, without significant adjustment, notions of governmental immunities and prerogatives that earlier existed in the United Kingdom'.[235]

With the adoption of the Constitution in 1901, the new state of Australia was created with a federal constitutional architecture distinguishing the Commonwealth from the states. The crown proceedings legislation of the colonies that preceded the creation of Australia will be discussed in this section, but given that the Commonwealth's and the state governments' respective civil liability differ both as to their scope and nature,[236] the focus of the analysis is Australian legal thinking on *the king can do no wrong* at the federal level.

Unlike English legal thinking—where the crown understood as the governmental apparatus has been conceived of as immune from suit at common law since the turn of the twentieth century—and unlike American legal thinking—where the sovereign is conceived of as inherently immune from suit—Australian legal thinking has abandoned the view that the common law controls the Commonwealth's immunity from suit. Over the last decades, it is to Irish legal thinking and the Irish Supreme Court's reasoning in *Byrne v Ireland* that Australian judges have looked in order to conclude that 'the starting point' in developing their understanding of crown immunity must be the text of the Constitution itself, and not 'the immunities, privileges and prerogatives of the Crown, as traditionally enjoyed in ancient times and as expressed in previous common law doctrine'.[237]

[234] *Bateman's Bay Local Aboriginal Land Council v Aboriginal Community Benefit Fund Pty Ltd* (1998) 155 ALR 684, 694, cited in Greg Weeks, 'Private Law Litigation Against the Government: Are Public Authorities and Private Actors Really "the Same"?' (2010) 68 UNSW LR 1, 8. See also *Jarratt v Commissioner of Police* (NSW) (2005) 221 ALR 95; 79 ALJR 1581, [7], [68], [75]; Mark Leeming, 'The Liability of the Government under the Constitution' (1998) 17 Aust Bar Rev 214.

[235] *Australian Consumer and Competition Commission v Baxter Healthcare Pty Ltd* (2007) 232 CLR 1, 48.

[236] Leeming (n 234) 215.

[237] *Australian Consumer and Competition Commission v Baxter Healthcare Pty Ltd* (2007) 232 CLR 1, 45, 53 (Kirby J). On the differences, in the realm of governmental liability, between the American and Australian constitutions, see Leeming (n 234) 232–36; Bradley Selway, 'The Source and Nature of the Liability in Tort of Australian Governments' (2002) 10 Tort L Rev 14, 30–32.

Australian legal thinking on crown liability offers a rich product of comparative analysis, built on the history of the common law world's earliest legislation on crown liability. Australian legal thinking on crown liability inherited (and rejected) aspects of English legal thinking on *the king can do no wrong*, and Australia's written Constitution has fostered a remarkable influence of American law on constitutional review, as well as of Irish legal thinking on state liability. Australian legal thinking on crown liability also echoes the two dimensions of crown liability explored in this book: the plurality of the High Court in *Mewett* found that the Constitution of the Commonwealth grounds the procedural dimension of crown liability—allowing for a legal remedy to exist against the Commonwealth by virtue of section 75 (iii)—while the substantive dimension of crown liability was found to reside in the common law.[238]

4.1 Early rejection of crown immunity

The history of crown proceeding legislation in what is now Australia dates to the middle of the nineteenth century, an innovation across the common law world which is still noted with pride by Australian scholars: 'The distance of the tyranny of English ways of thinking together with the need, in a frontier society, for new systems and roles of government combined to make Australia the pioneer of Crown proceedings legislation.'[239] Already in the early days of the federation, Australian courts were prone to highlight that history and the modernity of the former colonies' legislative innovations, as is evidenced in the following reasons of O'Connor J in *Baume*, dating to 1906:

> Long before the passing of the Constitution Act the several States of Australia had brought the law with regard to claims against the Government more into conformity with modern notions of fairness and common sense than those which prevailed in the days when the maxim was strictly upheld; and in all the States, in some form or other, it was possible to bring an action of tort against the Crown.[240]

Almost a century after *Baume*, Australian pride at the states' legislative acumen in the realm of governmental liability was still apparent from Gummow J's reasons in *Pyrenees Shire Council v Day*, where he emphasized that the removal of 'sovereign immunity' in Australia long predated the enactment of the Crown Proceedings Act 1947 in the United Kingdom and the Federal Tort Claims Act of 1946 in the United

[238] *Commonwealth v Mewett* (1997) 191 CLR 471, 502 (Dawson J), 513 (Toohey J), 532 (McHugh J), 550–51 (Gummow and Kirby JJ).
[239] Nick Seddon, 'The Crown' (2000) 28 FL Rev 245, 257.
[240] *Baume v Commonwealth* (1906) 4 CLR 97, 118 (O'Connor J).

States.[241] The history of crown immunity in colonial and post federation Australia is surveyed in this section.

4.1.1 Crown proceeding legislation in the colonies

Crown proceeding legislation was adopted to allow suits against the crown—in contract and in tort—as early as the middle of the nineteenth century in South Australia (1853)[242] and New South Wales (1857),[243] with the shared objective of remedying the limited scope of the petition of right.[244] The two colonies' legislation preceded the adoption of the Petitions of Right Act 1860 by the UK Parliament. Inexplicably, a reversal occurred in New South Wales, where the English Petition of Rights Act 1860 was adopted in the 1861 New South Wales Claims Against the Crown Act[245]—thereby letting the innovative 1857 Act lapse in that colony.[246] But the same 1857 Act lived on in Queensland—separated from New South Wales in 1859—and there a 'legal revolution' occurred in the form of the 1866 statute allowing 'any just claim or demand' against the 'Government'.[247] The Queensland revolution eventually reached New South Wales again in 1876.[248] Western Australia and Victoria opted for a more conservative route, and Victoria later modelled its legislation in 1955 on the UK Parliament's Crown Proceeding Act 1947.[249]

The colonies' legislative innovations were initially hampered by colonial courts' reliance on a more conservative English case law. It was the Board's decision in *Farnell v Bowman*, dating to 1887, that marked the rejection of *the king can do no wrong* understood as governmental immunity from suit in the Australian colonial context.[250] At the end of the nineteenth century, just as the Victorian English courts had recently revisited *the king can do no wrong* to create a fiction that there is no wrong in the king in order to deny actions in tort against the monarch in

[241] *Pyrenees Shire Council v Day* (1998) 192 CLR 330, 375 (Gummow J). On the distinctive evolution of the law of public authority liability in Australia in the first half of the twentieth century, see Geoffrey Sawer, 'Shield of the Crown Revisited' (1958) 1 Melb ULR 137, 139–40.

[242] Claimants' Relief Act, No 6, 1853. Aronson notes that the act was essentially procedural and that 'London disallowed an earlier South Australian "Act", which it feared would lead to further subsidies from the British Treasury': Mark Aronson, 'Government Liability in Negligence' (2008) 32 Melb ULR 44, 44 citing Greg Taylor, 'John Baker's Act: The South Australian Origins of Australian Claims-against-the-Government Legislation' (2004) 27 UNSWLJ 736, 755.

[243] 20 Vict No 15.

[244] Paul D Finn, *Law and Government in Colonial Australia* (OUP 1987) 141–43. In addition to Finn's seminal work, detailed accounts of the history of crown proceedings legislation in Australia can be found in Susan Kneebone, *Tort Liability of Public Authorities* (LBC Information Services 1998) 297–301; Leeming (n 234) 215–18.

[245] Claims Against the Crown Act 1861, 24 Vict No 27 (NSW).

[246] Finn (n 244) 143.

[247] Claims Against the Government Act 1866, 29 Vict 238 (Queensland); Finn (n 244) 144–45.

[248] Claims Against the Government Act 1876, 39 Vict 38 (NSW); it was mirrored in Tasmania in the Crown Redress Act 1891, 55 Vict 24; Finn (n 244) 145; Leeming (n 234) 217.

[249] Claims Against Government, Petition of Right 1867, 31 Vict 7 (WA); An Act for the enforcement of Claims against the Crown 1858, 21 Vict 49 (Victoria); Finn (n 244) 155–59; Peter W Hogg, 'Victoria's Crown Proceeding Act' (1970) 7 Melb ULR 342; Leeming (n 234) 217; Weeks (n 234) 11.

[250] *Farnell v Bowman* (1887) 12 App Cas 643 (PC).

petition of right cases,[251] the Privy Council was doing just the opposite with regard to the colonies which would eventually become Australia. In *Farnell v Bowman*, the Board found that colonial legislation allowed the colonial governments to be sued in tort and in contract.

The case arose in New South Wales and the action was brought under a special colonial statute,[252] under which the government of the colony was held liable to be sued in an action for tort. The colonial government—Australia as we now know it was not yet in existence—while undertaking public work, caused damage to the plaintiff through its trespassing government servants, who destroyed by fire the plaintiff's grass, trees, and fences. The Board found that the particular context which prevailed in the colonies, including that of the various commercial activities undertaken by the colonial governments, could only mean that the law in relation to crown liability had to be different:

> It must be borne in mind that the local governments in the Colonies, as pioneers of improvements, are frequently obliged to embark in undertakings which in other countries are left to private enterprise, such, for instance, as the construction of railways, canals, and other works for the construction of which it is necessary to employ many inferior officers and workmen. If, therefore, the maxim that 'the king can do no wrong' were applied to Colonial governments in the way now contended for by the appellants, it would work much greater hardship than it does in England.[253]

The Board justified its distinctive treatment of the law in Australia in relation to immunity from suit of the government on the factual basis that colonial governments were far more invested in developing public services and infrastructure. Depriving individuals of any form of recourse against it would amount to a grave frustration of one's rights.

The Board was in fact justifying its lifting of the immunity in nineteenth-century Australia on grounds which also became true of most western post-war governments since the second half of the twentieth century. As Laski observed as early as 1919, in his study of the responsibility of the state in England, the modern state is 'a great public-service corporation' which now undertakes a myriad of functions—'education, police, poor-law, defense, insurance against ill-health and unemployment'.[254] The arrival of this modern welfare state and its acknowledgement by the courts struck sooner in Australia than it did in England.[255]

[251] In *Tobin* and *Feather* (n 89); see Chapter 4, section 3.3.

[252] The New South Wales Act 1876, 39 Vict No 38.

[253] *Farnell v Bowman* (n 250) 649.

[254] Laski (n 61) 452.

[255] To Maguire, 'The opinion indicates that so long as a state confines itself to old fashioned, customary functions, it is subject to no liability for tort' but when acting in their 'civil capacity', courts

4.1.2 Crown immunity post federation

After federation in 1901, the ruling in *Farnell v Bowman* was applied at the Australian federal level. The Commonwealth Constitution gave Parliament, under section 78, the power to make laws regulating proceedings by subjects against the Commonwealth and against a state. Parliament exercised that power by enacting the Judiciary Act 1903, which provides under section 64 that 'In any suit to which the Commonwealth or a State is a party, the rights of parties shall as nearly as possible be the same, and judgment may be given and costs awarded on either side, as in a suit between subject and subject'.

Soon after the enactment of the Judiciary Act 1903, Australian courts noted the resemblance in language with that of the previous crown proceeding legislation of New South Wales, which had been under consideration in 1887 in *Farnell v Bowman*.[256] They concluded that the Privy Council's decision in the latter case still stood, and that the Commonwealth was in the same position in relation to tort actions as the colony had been in prior to federation,[257] resulting in the crown being liable in tort both directly and vicariously.[258]

Until the end of the twentieth century, as is discussed further in section 4.2.2, the crown's incapacity to do wrong was conceived of in Australian legal thinking as a prerogative at common law, with the result that it 'could not be liable in tort'.[259] The Australian governments could be sued in tort only because the relevant provisions of the Judiciary Act 1903 (Cth) and the states' respective crown proceeding legislation, as interpreted by the Board in *Farnell v Bowman*, allowed such actions before Australian courts.[260] There was a disconnect, however, between the theory that the crown's liability was imposed by the various statutory provisions at both state and federal level, and the courts' practice in deciding crown liability cases as if the crown was liable at common law, sometimes even ignoring statutory language.[261] The reconciliation between the court's practice and legal thinking on crown liability occurred at the end of the twentieth century, as is discussed in section 4.2.

have found colonial governments liable 'for negligently operating telegraphs, railways, and trading vessels': Maguire (n 90) 29.

256 *Farnell v Bowman* (n 250).

257 *Asiatic Steam Navigation Co Ltd v The Commonwealth* (1956) 96 CLR 397, 427 (Kitto J); *Baume v Commonwealth* (1906) 4 CLR 97, 110 (Griffith CJ), 118–19 (O'Connor J); see Leeming (n 234) 221; Weeks (n 234) 8. The clarification was necessary for, as Kirby J explained in *Baxter*, the Commonwealth, the territories and the states were created by the Constitution 'as integral parts of a new Commonwealth, a distinct and "indissoluble" federal entity' and, in the particular case of the states, these new polities 'are not merely a continuation of pre-existing colonies under a different appellation': *Baxter* (n 221) [93]–[94] (Kirby J). See also *Bank of NSW v The Commonwealth* (1948) 76 CLR 1, 363 (Dixon J); Sebastian Howard Hartford Davis, 'The Legal Personality of the Commonwealth of Australia' (2019) 47 FL Rev 3.

258 Selway (n 237) 18, 20.

259 ibid 15.

260 ibid 21.

261 ibid 21–22, 26.

4.2 Commonwealth's liability

Australian legal thinking presents its own understanding of the Commonwealth's liability: 'In Australia, several respected sources have concurred with earlier authority that the understanding that the sovereign had a common law "immunity" from suit is misconceived.'[262] The Commonwealth and the states were denied the status of the sovereign in a monarchy, and were instead found to be 'amenable to the jurisdiction' of the Australian courts, 'upon which the responsibility of enforcing the Constitution rests'.[263] *Marbury v Madison* has successfully migrated to the Australian federation's constitutional law, but *the king can do no wrong* understood as sovereign immunity was thrown overboard. These two aspects are analysed in turn.

4.2.1 A constitutional difference

As is the case under the American[264] and Irish Constitutions,[265] executive power is considered, in Australian legal thought, to find its source in the Constitution, and more specifically in section 61.[266] The Commonwealth itself is conceived of as owing its existence to the Constitution that creates it and grants it legal authority.[267]

The Australian federal Constitution has been read to imply that the crown is divisible in the Australian federation, and that the states were 'separate bodies politic with separate legal personality'[268]—as is the case in America. American constitutional law acted as a guide for Australian courts in adapting English common law rules to a federal state with a written constitution.[269] Australia's High Court

[262] Greg Weeks, *Soft Law and Public Authorities: Remedies and Reform* (Hart Publishing 2016) 183. Weeks cites G Hill, 'Private Law Actions Against the Government (Part 1)—Removing the Government's Immunity from Suit in Federal Cases' (2007) 30 Melb ULR 716, 725; Mark Leeming, 'The Liability of the Government under the Constitution' (1998) 17 Australian Bar Review 215, 216.

[263] *Bank of NSW v The Commonwealth* (1948) 76 CLR 1, 363 (Dixon J).

[264] The Constitution of the United States of America vests executive power in the 'President' under Art II, s 1.

[265] The 1937 Constitution of Ireland, *Bunreacht na hÉireann*, creates the 'State' (Arts 4–11), the 'President' (Arts 12–14), and the 'Government' (Art 28).

[266] s 61, 'Executive power', is found under Chapter II, titled 'The Executive Government', and reads: 'The executive power of the Commonwealth is vested in the Queen and is exercisable by the Governor-General as the Queen's representative, and extends to the execution and maintenance of this Constitution, and of the laws of the Commonwealth.' See Bradley Selway, 'All at Sea—Constitutional Assumptions and "The Executive Power of the Commonwealth"' (2003) 31 FL Rev 495; Mark Aronson, Matthew Groves, and Greg Weeks, *Judicial Review of Administrative Action and Government Liability* (6th edn, Lawbook Company 2017) 1089. s 61, however, does not define executive power, and therefore, the original source of the Commonwealth's executive power 'can include other provisions of the Constitution, statute or the prerogative': Anne Twomey, 'The Prerogative and the Courts in Australia' (2021) 3 J CommonwL 55, 58.

[267] *Lamshed v Lake* (1958) 99 CLR 132, 141–42 (Dixon CJ), cited in Aronson, Groves, and Weeks (n 266) 1090.

[268] *Sue v Hill* (1999) 199 CLR 462, 525–26, [165] (Gaudron J). The separation between the Commonwealth and the states' legal personalities was found to be particularly manifest in ss 75(iii), 75(iv), and 78 of the Commonwealth Constitution: Davis (n 257) 12.

[269] *Lange v Australian Broadcasting Corporation* (1997) 189 CLR 520, 562. On the influence of the American Constitution on the drafting of the Australian Constitution, see eg John Reynolds, 'Andrew

also accepted as 'axiomatic'[270] the principle laid down by the Supreme Court of the United States in *Marbury v Madison* that it is the judicial branch's role to determine controversies relating to the constitutionality of the legislative and executive branches' actions.[271] Under section 75(iii) of the Australian Constitution, the judiciary is tasked with ensuring compliance with the Constitution.[272] But unlike in America, the judiciary's role in ensuring constitutional supremacy was interpreted to have 'placed a fundamental limitation upon any general acceptance in the exercise of federal jurisdiction of the maxim that the Sovereign could do no wrong.'[273]

As did Canadian courts, colonial courts and later Australian courts adopted English courts' understanding of *the king can do no wrong*—and in particular the understanding, dating to *Feather* in the second half of the nineteenth century—that the crown was incapable of committing of a wrong.[274] For example, in the following excerpt from *The Commonwealth v New South Wales*, dating to 1923, the majority of the High Court of Australia understood *the king can do no wrong* to convey immunity from suit, the fiction that there is no wrong in the king, imputed ministerial responsibility, and the constitutional understanding that the king is immune from suit but that his ministers and servants are liable instead:

> There is undoubtedly in our common law a principle that the Sovereign cannot be sued in his own Courts. A tort by the Sovereign is impossible at common law; the fault, if any, being attributed to the subject who actually committed or authorised it the Sovereign being assumed never to authorise a breach of the law.[275]

Inglis Clark's American Sympathies and His Influence on Australian Federation' (1958) 32 ALJ 62; JM Neasey, 'Andrew Inglis Clark Senior and Australian Federation' (1969) 15 AJPH 1.

[270] *Australian Communist Party v The Commonwealth* (1951) 83 CLR 1, 262.

[271] *Marbury v Madison* (1803) 5 US 137.

[272] s 75(iii) reads as follows:

> Original jurisdiction of High Court
> In all matters: . . .
> (iii) in which the Commonwealth, or a person suing or being sued on behalf of the Commonwealth, is a party; . . .
> the High Court shall have original jurisdiction.

The High Court also has jurisdiction, under s 75(iv), to hear disputes 'between States, or between residents of different States, or between a State and a resident of another State'. The High Court's jurisdiction under s 75(iv) is similar to federal courts' diversity jurisdiction under Art III, s 2 of the American Constitution. On the influence Art III of the American Constitution had over the drafting of the Australian Constitution on the federal judicial power, see William G Buss, 'Andrew Inglis Clark's Draft Constitution, Chapter III of the Australian Constitution, and the Assist from Article III of the Constitution of the United States' (2009) 33 Melb ULR 718.

[273] *Commonwealth v Mewett* (1997) 191 CLR 471, 547 (Gummow, Kirby JJ).

[274] *Feather* (n 89); Selway (n 237) 15. The phenomenon was termed 'legal colonialism': Paul D Finn, *Law and Government in Colonial Australia* (OUP 1987) 165–66. On English courts' revisited understanding of *the king can do no wrong* in the nineteenth century, see Chapter 4, section 3.3.

[275] *The Commonwealth v New South Wales* (1923) 32 CLR 200, 211 (Isaacs, Rich, and Starke JJ).

In the joint reasons of the majority in *The Commonwealth v New South Wales*, the crown was thought not to be liable at common law, but the concept of a sovereign's immunity before his own courts was found not to stand in relation to disputes between constitutional actors. The High Court adopted the view in *The Commonwealth v New South Wales* that it has original jurisdiction under section 75—even without the consent of the defendant—to decide issues between states, between states and the federal government, and between states and the residents of other states.[276] As Gummow and Kirby JJ later found in *Mewett*, commenting on *The Commonwealth v New South Wales*, 'in this Court a State might be sued in tort by the Commonwealth without the consent of that State' and 'the Constitution itself denies any operation of either of the maxims which together stated the immunity doctrine as developed in England'.[277] Although the Commonwealth was plaintiff in *The Commonwealth v New South Wales*—its boat having been damaged by a vessel belonging to the state of New South Wales—Gummow and Kirby JJ found that the reasoning equally supported the conclusion that section 75(iii) of the Constitution submitted the Commonwealth to liability.

The Constitution's fundamental role in the Australian constitutional order was also emphasized in Kirby J's concurring reasons in *Baxter*. Kirby J looked not only to the text of the Australian Constitution itself, but also to *Byrne v Ireland*[278] as 'the starting point'[279] in elaborating a constitutional interpretive approach grounded in the Constitution. He adopted the view expressed by Walsh J in the seminal Irish case that in light of the creation of the Irish republic as a new state by way of 'a written constitution securing its authority ultimately from the *people* of Ireland whose will gave it birth, it was a basic error of legal principle to treat as applicable to the new State all of the pre-existing *Crown* immunities and prerogatives'.[280] To Kirby J, the conclusion reached by Irish judges in *Byrne v Ireland* applied equally in Australia, where the new state resulted from the adoption of its written Constitution following a referendum: 'It is a basic legal mistake to consider that common law Crown immunities and prerogatives can be picked up holus-bolus and transferred to our antipodean constitutional setting without serious reconsideration, and adjustment, appropriate to the Australian constitutional text.'[281] The High Court had already emphasized the importance of relying on the constitutional text in interpreting the 'compact made by the people of Australia in founding their wider citizenship';[282] Kirby J's reasons in *Baxter* are part of a longer trend in

[276] ibid 213 (Isaacs, Rich, and Starke JJ). Disputes between the government and Parliament, as well as injunctions against ministers and claims made by an aggrieved individual suing a governmental agent relying on unlawful legislation to justify her actions are also justiciable before the High Court.
[277] *Commonwealth v Mewett* (n 238).
[278] *Byrne v Ireland* (n 126). See section 3.
[279] *Baxter* (n 237) 53, 56.
[280] ibid 49.
[281] ibid 48.
[282] *The Commonwealth v New South Wales* (n 275) 210 (Isaacs, Rich, and Starke JJ), citing *Amalgamated Society of Engineers v Adelaide Steamship Co* (1920) 28 CLR 129.

Australian legal thinking of defining its own governing principles in the realm of crown liability in light of the Constitution.

4.2.2 Substantive and procedural dimensions of crown liability

Australian legal thinking offers an illustration of the two dimensions of crown liability: the Commonwealth is liable in tort at common law—substantive liability—while section 75 of the Australian Constitution simply created a remedy—a procedural dimension. Australian legal thinking supports a distinction between the two dimensions of crown liability, found in in the case law as well as in Australian legal literature.[283] The seminal case of *Commonweath v Mewett*, in particular, acts as a beacon of light in the confused darkness that has surrounded *the king can do no wrong* in legal thinking ever since Blackstone wrote his *Commentaries on the Laws of England* in the eighteenth century.[284] Although Australia was a pioneer in the realm of crown proceedings legislation, Australian legal thinking had not escaped unscathed the confusion surrounding the understandings of *the king can do no wrong* and their historical evolution.[285] The majority of the High Court's reasoning in *Mewett*, its relation to the historical evolution of Australian legal thinking on crown liability, and its consequence for our understanding of the two dimensions of crown liability is explored in this section.

The king can do no wrong understood as the crown's incapacity to do wrong at common law, so that it 'could not be liable in tort', was prevalent in Australian legal thinking for most of the twentieth century. Crown liability had two dimensions, and the procedural dimension was conceived of as flowing from the crown's incapacity to do wrong at common law—the substantive dimension. If the English nineteenth-century understanding of *the king can do no wrong* as the legal fiction that there can be no wrong in the crown at common law was prevalent in Australia for most of the twentieth century, the Bractonian view, adopted for instance by the Law Commission of New South Wales, that *the king can do no wrong* 'did not mean that the Crown could not commit a wrong, but rather that the Crown was under the same obligation as his or her subjects to act lawfully' ultimately prevailed.[286]

Already in 1938, in *Werrin v The Commonwealth*, Dixon J explained how section 75 of the Constitution was not itself the source of the substantive liability of the

[283] See eg Mark Aronson and Harry Whitmore, *Public Torts and Contracts* (Law Book Company 1982) 7; Susan Kneebone, 'Claims Against the Commonwealth and States and Their Instrumentalities in Federal Jurisdiction: Section 64 of the Judiciary Act' (1996) 24 FL Rev 93; Aronson, Groves, and Weeks (n 266) 1094; Mark Aronson, 'Government Liability in Negligence' (2008) 32 Melb ULR 44, 45; Weeks, 'Private Law Liability' (n 234) 7.

[284] Blackstone (n 42); see Chapter 4.

[285] See *R v Toohey; Ex parte Northern Land Council* (1981) 151 CLR 170, 220, 230, where Mason J understood the 'doctrine' and 'principle' of *the king can do no wrong* to have 'evolved' from the 'earlier rule' that the sovereign cannot be sued in his own courts, and confused these 'ideals' with those grounded in the divine right of kings and advanced by 'royal sycophants' in Stuart England.

[286] Selway (n 237) 15; citing Law Reform Commission of New South Wales, *Proceedings By and Against the Crown* (LRC 24, 1976) 135–36.

Commonwealth, but 'treats the liability as already existing in abstracto as a duty of imperfect obligation and made perfect by the creation of a jurisdiction in which the Crown may be sued without its consent'.[287] To Dixon J, 'it would not mean that the substantive liability was itself created and imposed by the Constitution', but that section 75 allowed for that 'substantive liability' to become 'the subject of a legal remedy'.[288] In *Werrin*, Dixon J adopted a Bractonian understanding of *the king can do no wrong* when he concluded—disagreeing on this point with the majority of the High Court in the 1923 case of *Commonwealth v New South Wales*—that section 75 itself could not be the source of the substantive liability of the Commonwealth. To Dixon J, the two dimensions of crown liability had not been sufficiently grasped, and the crown should be conceived of as liable at common law, although there was no legal remedy at common law to enforce that substantive dimension.[289]

After Dixon J's reasons in *Werrin*, the joint judgments in *Commonwealth v New South Wales* were quietly ignored.[290] Then, in 1995, in *Northern Territory v Mengel*, the principle that the crown's liability should be the same as its subjects' was conceived of as a common law principle by the High Court.[291] The issue was definitively settled in 1997 in *Commonwealth v Mewett*: by virtue of section 75 of the Constitution, any immunity of the crown is procedural rather than substantive.[292] In *Mewett*, after having observed that the generalized crown immunity that developed in English and Australian law was based on a misunderstanding of historical legal writers—namely Bracton and what it understood as a 'medieval' maxim that *the king can do no wrong*—the Commonwealth of Australia was found to be liable at common law.[293] The same fate befell the states thereafter.[294]

Gummow and Kirby JJ's reasons in *Mewett* (with whom Brennan CJ and Gaudron J agreed) are pivotal to our understanding of *the king can do no wrong* and crown liability. At issue in that case was a federal statute that created a no-fault statutory compensation scheme for government employees who suffered injuries at work, but which also abolished any other action which may have arisen from the injury sustained by the employee. The issue, put another way, was whether crown immunity as it developed in English common law not only denied adjudication of claims against the crown in tort and contract, but went further and denied the very existence of the contract and any wrongful act or omission. In short, did English common law deny the king's capacity to do wrong? Gummow and Kirby

[287] *Werrin v The Commonwealth* (1938) 59 CLR 150, 168 (Dixon J).

[288] ibid.

[289] ibid 167–68; Selway (n 237) 29.

[290] Selway (n 237) 30. cf Lee Aitken, 'The Liability of the Commonwealth under section 75(III) and Related Questions' (1992) 15 UNSWLJ 483, to whom liability of the Commonwealth flowed from s 75 of the Commonwealth Constitution as described in *Commonwealth v New South Wales*.

[291] *Northern Territory v Mengel* (1995) 185 CLR 307, 348; Selway (n 237) 22.

[292] *Commonwealth v Mewett* (n 238); Greg Weeks, *Soft Law and Public Authorities: Remedies and Reform* (Hart Publishing 2016) 183.

[293] *Commonwealth v Mewett* (n 238) 543–44.

[294] *British American Tobacco Australia Ltd v Western Australia* (2003) 217 CLR 30.

JJ noted in *Mewett* that before 1947, there were equitable remedies against the crown in the Court of the Exchequer, as well as enforcement procedures against the crown as trustee; the petition of right could also be resorted to for actions in contract, and they cited Holdsworth's observation that the petition of right did lie in the Middle Ages for real actions before the modern distinctions between tort and contract were made.[295] They observed that it was recognized even by the Privy Council in *Farnell v Bowman* that in all Australian colonies—save for Victoria—the state could be sued in tort and in contract pursuant to legislation.[296] In light of that historical context, they reasoned, the fact that the state was liable to be sued must be taken into account when interpreting the Commonwealth Constitution. The majority adopted Dixon J's view in *Werrin* that the Commonwealth is liable at common law, and that its 'immunity from liability' was abrogated by section 75(iii) of the Constitution.[297] In other words, the Commonwealth is capable of doing wrong at common law, and the procedural immunity from suit which the English feudal king has enjoyed before his own courts was removed by section 75(iii) of the Australian Constitution, resulting in the Commonwealth being amenable to justice.

In a conclusion that is not dissimilar to that reached by Irish courts, Gummow and Kirby JJ concluded in *Mewett* that in Australia, the courts are not the 'king's courts': the Commonwealth Constitution vests the judicial power not in the king, but in the High Court of Australia and other courts invested with federal jurisdictions, and, as a result, the king's privilege not to be sued in his own courts does not apply in Australia.[298] *Byrne v Ireland* and *Mewett* marked a revolution in legal thinking on *the king can do no wrong* and state liability in common law legal thinking. The two cases mark a revolution in the sense of a major change in legal thinking, but also in the sense that they complete a return, in a movement of continuity, to the Bractonian understanding of *the king can do no wrong*.

4.3 Conclusion: a pioneering bi-dimensional conception of crown liability

The two dimensions of crown liability—substantive and procedural—are now a feature of Australian legal thinking. At common law, in Australia, the Commonwealth is capable of committing a wrong (substantive dimension) and is conceived of as amenable to justice (procedural dimension). The Commonwealth is liable; the Constitution and the Judiciary Act 1903 adopted in pursuance of it simply provided

[295] *Commonwealth v Mewett* (n 238) 544.
[296] ibid 544–45.
[297] ibid 550–51.
[298] ibid 546.

the remedy.[299] The High Court's view in *Mewett* has elements of continuity with the Bractonian understanding that the king is capable of committing of wrong but that he is not entitled to do so, being equally under the law. The king is capable of doing wrong and a wrong can be ascribed to the king. His non-amenability to suit is not substantive—denying any liability—it is instead procedural. The two dimensions of crown liability which eluded Cockburn CJ in the nineteenth-century English case of *Feather*[300] are evident to Australian scholars: 'the Crown's general common law immunity from the *procedure* of a suit being issued in a tort action was misunderstood as a common law immunity from *substantive* tort liability'.[301]

5 Conclusion: *the king can do no wrong* in America, Ireland, and Australia

The model developed in this book to better grasp the evolution of English legal thinking on *the king can do no wrong* shows additional comparative utility, although its application to other jurisdictions in comparative historical work requires caution: not all aspects of the model will be relevant in each jurisdiction. The possibly drastic departure from previous understandings of *the king can do no wrong* mandated by the constitutional text—or interpreted by the courts as such—or by other external considerations at play in given jurisdictions may, however, also render the model useful in keeping a cautionary approach against generalizations or assumptions based only on superficial similarities, and the notions and two dimensions of the model may act as guideposts in assessing the degree of divergence.

In Chapter 1, I described how three notions underpin the two dimensions of crown liability—the procedural and substantive dimensions. Those three notions, associated with various understandings of *the king can do no wrong* in the historical evolution of the English legal thinking, are the king's status in relation to law, the notion of perfection of the king, and the king's immunity from suit. In the United States, it is the notion of the king's status in relation to law that is determinative of the doctrine of sovereign immunity: the American sovereign is conceived of—as with Hobbes or Austin—as the ultimate authority, and therefore as above the law that that sovereign makes. In Ireland, it is rather the rejection of the notion that the state is above the Constitution which shaped Irish legal thinking, along with the rejection of the king's immunity from suit, deemed incompatible with a

[299] Although there was criticism of the plurality's reasons in *Mewett*, it was followed by the High Court in *British American Tobacco Australia Ltd v Western Australia* (n 294) 57–58 (McHugh, Gummow, and Hayne JJ). For commentaries on *Mewett*, see Leeming (n 262); Selway (n 237); Graeme Hill, 'Private Law Actions Against the Government (Part 1)—Removing the Government's Immunity from Suit in Federal Cases' (2007) 30 Melb ULR 716.

[300] *Feather* (n 89); see Chapter 4, section 3.3.

[301] Weeks (n 234) 7.

republican constitutional order. Irish jurists and judges aimed for modernity in developing a new republican understanding of state liability, and the subjection of the Irish state to law and to the Constitution, as well as the amenability to justice of the state and all governmental officials and entities, are core features of Irish legal thinking on *the king can do no wrong*. What is remarkable in Australia is rather the conception—adopted early on in the twentieth century and maintained thereafter—that there are two dimensions to crown liability. Australian legal thinking distinguishes between the substantive dimension—the crown's capacity to do wrong—and the procedural dimension—allowing or barring a remedy—of crown liability. If Irish legal thinking ultimately departed from American legal thinking on sovereign immunity despite their shared republican mode of government, Australian legal thinking has kept an open dialogue with Irish cases post *Byrne v Ireland* on the fundamental role the constitutional text plays in defining the law of crown liability, and shares with famed American scholar Louis Jaffe and this book's heuristic model a bi-dimensional view of the law of governmental liability.

Conclusion

From a fundamental medieval principle memorialised by Bracton and conveying limitations imposed on the king by the law, *the king can do no wrong* was coined by Edward Coke at the turn of the seventeenth century to encapsulate the Bractonian understanding that the king is not entitled to do wrong. *The king can do no wrong* subsequently became associated with the king's immunity from suit and with ministerial responsibility after the constitutional struggles of the seventeenth century. Over the course of the eighteenth century, legal thinking in relation to *the king can do no wrong* was influenced by Blackstone's emphasis on the notion of perfection of the king, after which *the king can do no wrong* became a fiction that there can be no wrong in the king in the nineteenth century. The influence of Dicey's work and ignorance of the constitutional pact which conferred immunity on the king—both politically and legally—in exchange for his ministers' and servants' liability after the seventeenth century led the courts, at the turn of the twentieth century, to extend immunity from suit to ministers and government departments, who became associated with a new notion of the 'crown'. Yet ministers and their government departments were expressly excluded from the notion of crown in the seminal case of *M v Home Office*, based on constitutional principles expounded after the Civil War.[1] *The king can do no wrong* has therefore recovered its seventeenth-century constitutional understanding in the realm of judicial review following *M v Home Office* and, following *Miller 2*, in the realm of the prerogative, where the monarch is not held liable for following the Prime Minister's unlawful advice to prorogue Parliament.[2] Yet understandings of *the king can do no wrong* are still mired in confusion in the realm of crown liability. Close attention to constitutional fundamentals, however, allows us to develop an intellectual history of *the king can do no wrong*, identifying significant continuity which can help legal scholars and practitioners to revisit contemporary law.

The medieval origins of the king's immunity from suit were rooted in a feudal privilege not to be sued in one's own court and the theological justification of the king's role as God's vicar. As was discussed in Chapter 2, late medieval English thinkers conceived of the king as below the law and, in the then-prevailing Christian and theological legal mindset, they were content that the king took an oath to administer justice, was subject to justice through the petition of right and

[1] *M v Home Office* [1994] 1 AC 377 (HL).
[2] ibid; *R(Miller) v Prime Minister* (2019) UKSC 41 (*Miller 2*).

The King Can Do No Wrong. Marie-France Fortin, Oxford University Press. © Marie-France Fortin 2024.
DOI: 10.1093/9780191994487.003.0008

other remedies, and could ultimately be punished by God. In the seventeenth century, English Parliamentarians rejected the Royalist position that there was no right of resistance against the king. They set out to remedy what is now anachronistically considered to have been a flaw—a 'great constitutional problem'[3]—in the English medieval constitution: the lack of legal coercion against the king. The subjection of Charles I to capital punishment, however, set a traumatic constitutional precedent never to be replicated. The seventeenth-century constitutional understanding of *the king can do no wrong* that ensued endowed the monarch with absolute immunity from suit in exchange for the liability of every other minister and servant of the crown.

In Bracton's thinking, the king's wrongful act could not be judged, but it could be questioned.[4] It could not be judged because the king, in Bracton's theory, had no superior on earth. Bracton's understanding that the king was capable of committing a wrong and that the king was not entitled to commit a wrong was also found in Plowden's and Coke's understanding, in the sixteenth and seventeenth centuries, that the king is under the law and not entitled to do wrong. This Bractonian understanding of *the king can do no wrong* was followed by Matthew Hale in the seventeenth century. At the time Hale wrote his work, Bracton's understanding that the king is under the law was still widely viewed as the common law position.[5] Hale interpreted *the king can do no wrong* and the three powers of the law as meaning that the king was below the directive and invalidating powers of the law, although not the coercive power, from which he was immune. Yet Hale thought that the king was nonetheless suable to by petition of right, an indication that the Bractonian understanding that the king had to remedy his wrong was not altogether rejected. To Hale, the directive and invalidating powers of the law applied to the king's wrongful command and rendered it invalid. The effect of the invalidating power of the law on the king's wrongful command was to deny it any legal standing.[6] The act or command could not therefore be relied on as an excuse by the minister or servant who executed it. Were the king entitled to do wrong in Hale's thinking, the law would not have applied to qualify the king's command as 'wrongful' and would not have invalidated it. In Hale's exposition of the three powers of the law in connection with *the king can do no wrong*, therefore, the king was not entitled to do wrong—as was the case in Bracton's and Coke's thinking.

Hale also wrote that the king's wrongful act being void, it was not the act of the king. The idea that the king's wrongful act was not a wrong in the eyes of the law

[3] Margaret Judson, *The Crisis of the Constitution: An Essay in Constitutional and Political Thought in England, 1603–1645* (1st edn, Rutgers UP 1949) 53.

[4] See Chapter 2, section 2.1.1.

[5] Gerald Postema, 'Introduction' in Matthew Hale, *On the Law of Nature, Reason, and Common Law: Selected Jurisprudential Writings* (Gerald Postema ed, OUP 2017) xxvii.

[6] ibid lvi.

was later adopted by Cockburn CJ in *Feather*.[7] But that the king's wrongful act was void and was not the act of the king in Hale's work could also be interpreted—in accordance with the common law Bractonian position prevalent at the time Hale wrote[8]—as the king's wrongful act exceeding the king's jurisdiction.[9] Given Hale's deep commitment to the common law and his conviction that any ruling power must be accountable to law,[10] the interpretation that the king was not entitled to do wrong in Hale's understanding of *the king can do no wrong* appears to be in line with his constitutional thinking. Hale's interpretation of *the king can do no wrong* should be understood as the king not having the power to act wrongfully. If the king did act wrongfully, his act was not the act of a king because it exceeded the power the law gave to the king. To act wrongfully exceeded the jurisdiction of the king, who was not entitled to do wrong.[11] Hale followed on this point medieval thinkers who preceded him.

In Hale's thinking, the directive and invalidating powers of the law 'oblige' and 'bind' the king.[12] The directive and the invalidating powers of the law 'bind the king's acts and mak[e] them void if they are against law'.[13] The king in Hale's thinking is in fact capable of doing wrong: 'though he do[es] things contrary to [the law], he cannot be sued but by petition'.[14] The king was the sole person not to be subject to the coercive power of the law: Hale was clear that it extended to all the king's subjects.[15]

Hale's interpretation of *the king can do no wrong* (including its Bractonian influence) was followed in part by William Blackstone in the eighteenth century. The latter's treatment of *the king can do no wrong* was not, however, consistent. As was discussed in Chapter 4, while Blackstone's king was under the law and not entitled to do wrong, he was nevertheless also said to be perfect and incapable of thinking wrong. The notion of the king's perfection could be found in Hale's interpretation of *the king can do no wrong*. It was the king's perfection—his sublimity—which to Hale justified the king's exemption from the coercive power of the law. Hale had attempted to provide an interpretation of *the king can do no wrong* which rendered the king immune from suit and yet maintained the Bractonian understanding that the king was under the law and not entitled to do wrong. But Blackstone referred to the notion of perfection to negate the king's capacity of doing or thinking wrong. Blackstone's use of the notion of perfection in interpreting *the king can do no wrong*

[7] *Feather v The Queen* (1865) 6 B&S 257 (122 ER 1191); see Chapter 4, section 3.3.
[8] Postema (n 5) xxiv–xxv.
[9] See Chapter 3, section 3.4.4, and Chapter 4, section 3.3.1.
[10] Postema (n 5) xvii.
[11] Denis Baranger, *Parlementarisme Des Origines* (Presses Universitaires de France 1999) 55, 57–58.
[12] Matthew Hale, *On the Law of Nature, Reason, and Common Law: Selected Jurisprudential Writings* (Gerald Postema ed, OUP 2017) 197.
[13] ibid.
[14] ibid 221.
[15] ibid 197.

magnified the inconsistency present in his famous and influential *Commentaries on the Laws of England*, where he also wrote that the king was not entitled to act contrary to law or to use his prerogative to do wrong.[16]

Dicey's interpretation of *the king can do no wrong* was also based on Hale's. As was the case for Hale, Dicey interpreted *the king can do no wrong* as the king's immunity from suit and as the king's orders are not a valid defence. That the king's wrongful command could not be invoked as a justification meant that it was invalid. An implication of Dicey's work is that the king is subject to the invalidating power of the law. Dicey conceived of the king as capable of doing a wrong—and even of murdering the Prime Minister—although Dicey chose to emphasize the king's immunity from suit in interpreting *the king can do no wrong*.[17]

The omission from Dicey's work of the idea that the king is not entitled to do wrong reflected cases dating from the second half of the nineteenth century. While the Bractonian understanding that the king is not entitled to do wrong could still be traced in Erle CJ's speech in *Tobin*,[18] *the king can do no wrong* was reinterpreted in the nineteenth century in *Tobin* and *Feather* in a way that obfuscated the issue of the king's capacity to do wrong. The courts in *Tobin* and *Feather* adopted an interpretation of *the king can do no wrong* otherwise divorced from its Bractonian context. In *Tobin* and *Feather*, the king's wrongful act was not the king's. If it was wrongful, the king's wrongful act or command fictitiously ceased to originate with the king and was not attributed to him. The wrongful act's origins became unexplained. Hale had submitted, in the seventeenth century, that *the king can do no wrong* meant that the 'king's act in such case being void . . . is not the act of the king'.[19] What Hale can be taken to have meant was—in a Bractonian sense—that the king's wrongful act, being unlawful, was invalidated by the force of the law and was devoid of the legal status of a kingly act. It was a nullity and could not constitute a valid defence. In contrast, the king's wrongful act or command, in *Tobin* and *Feather*, was fictitiously not a wrong: 'That which the sovereign does personally, the law presumes will not be wrong: that which the sovereign does by command to his servants, cannot be a wrong in the sovereign',[20] and 'in the eye of the law no such wrong can be done'.[21] Since the second half of the nineteenth century, in the eyes of the law, the king's wrong has not been a wrong. That innovation, which amounted to the king not being under the law and being immune from suit was, therefore, much more recent than has previously been suggested.[22] *The king can do no wrong*

[16] See Chapter 4, sections 2.1 and 2.2, and Chapter 6, section 2.1.2.

[17] AV Dicey, *Lectures Introductory to the Study of the Law of the Constitution: The Oxford Edition of Dicey*, vol 1 (JWF Allison ed, OUP 2013) 21.

[18] See Chapter 4, section 3.3.1.

[19] Matthew Hale, *The Prerogatives of the King*, vol 92 (DEC Yale ed, Selden Society 1976) 15.

[20] *Tobin v The Queen* (1864) 16 CB NS 310, 353–54.

[21] *Feather v The Queen* (n 7), 295.

[22] See Chapter 4. Harold J Laski, 'The Responsibility of the State in England' (1919) 32 Harv L Rev 447, 448; Edwin Borchard, 'Governmental Responsibility in Tort, VI' (1926) 36-1 YLJ 1, 30–31;

conveying the king's absolute immunity dates only to the cases of *Tobin* and *Feather* and to Dicey's work in the second half of the nineteenth century. Combined with the extension of the king's immunity from suit to the formal notion of the crown understood as central government—high public officers in their representative capacity and government departments—the revisiting of *the king can do no wrong* by Victorian English courts and scholars marked a reversal of the seventeenth-century constitutional settlement.

In nineteenth-century cases on the petition of right discussed in Chapter 4, the objective was to shield the person of the king from the remedy of the petition of right. It was thought impossible that the monarch who had no effective control over an ever-increasing governmental machinery should be personally liable to compensate individuals—out of her private funds—for the wrongs of her servants. To achieve the objective of shielding the monarch personally, nineteenth-century courts—in particular, Erle CJ in *Tobin* and Cockburn CJ in *Feather*—reinterpreted *the king can do no wrong* as the fiction that there is no wrong in the king in the eyes of the law. This new fiction of the absence of a wrong in the king operated a reversal of the two dimensions of crown liability, as the king's amenability to justice became the prevalent concern, and his capacity to do wrong was obfuscated. It also constituted a reversal of the seventeenth-century constitutional settlement understanding of *the king can do no wrong*, reflected in Hale's work, that the king was capable of doing and ordering a wrong, that the petition of right was available against him, and that his ministers and servants could not invoke the wrongful kingly order as a defence.

What Erle CJ and Cockburn CJ could not anticipate, however, was that their new interpretation of *the king can do no wrong* would be applied, this time in the context of ordinary actions, to the formal notion of the crown understood as central government following the *Mersey Docks* cases.[23] The result was that, at common law, the amenability to justice of high public officers in their representative capacity and of government departments themselves was denied. Their capacity to do wrong was obfuscated, as was the king's in *Tobin* and *Feather*. *The king can do no wrong* became *the crown can do no wrong*, with the 'crown' taken to represent the expanding apparatus of government, which was granted the benefit of the nineteenth-century fiction that there is no wrong in the king. There is, as a result, no wrong in the government, and it is accordingly immune from liability in tort at common law.

Current legal thinking in relation to crown liability—as defined in this book as the crown's capacity to do wrong and its amenability to justice for a wrong—is the

Robert Dorsey Watkins, *The State as a Party Litigant* (Johns Hopkins Press 1927) 11; David L Keir and FH Lawson, *Cases in Constitutional Law* (FH Lawson and DJ Bentley eds, 6th edn, Clarendon Press 1979) 72.

[23] *Mersey Docks Trustees v Cameron* (1864) 11 HLC 443; *Mersey Docks Trustees v Gibbs* (1866) 1 LR 93 (HL). See Chapter 4, section 3.3, and Chapter 5.

result of the combination of the analytical confusion of the two dimensions of crown liability since the second half of the nineteenth century, the influence of Dicey's notion of equality before the law, and the confusion surrounding the notion of the crown itself. As a result of the cases on the petition of right in the nineteenth century, *the king can do no wrong* came to be understood as a wrong cannot be the king's in law and he was not amenable to justice for it. The formal notion of the crown—the central government—elaborated in the nineteenth century came to partake of the king's various immunities and privileges because of the confusion surrounding the term 'crown' and its association with both king and central government. The formal notion of the crown—high public officers in their representative capacity and central government departments—became immune from suit because 'the crown can do no wrong'. The king's unequal status *vis-à-vis* his subjects was passed on to the central government as both became referred to as the 'crown'. Central government departments, like the king, were, as a result, not equal to ordinary individuals. Their amenability to justice and their capacity to do wrong were denied. An illogicality ensued, as government departments were conceived of as both crown servants and as the crown itself.[24] Relying on that illogicality, government departments, in their capacity as crown servants, could not be sued vicariously for another crown servant's wrong. In their capacity as the formal notion of the crown, they relied on *the king can do no wrong* understood as immunity from suit.

If, as Sedley rightly points out,[25] ministers never benefitted from any immunity as the result of the Civil War—whether they acted in their representative capacity or not—then it must follow that government departments headed by ministers are no more immune. In addition to the 'distinction between Ministers of the Crown (who enjoy no immunity) and the Crown (which is immune)',[26] there is also a distinction to be made between the crown—understood as the king—and government departments. The immunity from suit conferred on the monarch by the seventeenth-century constitutional settlement understanding of *the king can do no wrong* expressly did not extend to anyone else than the king. The servants executing the king's wrongful commands were liable. Just as the ministers' representative role cannot shield them from liability—as *M v Home Office* illustrates[27]—neither can that representative role shield government departments.

[24] For an example of the confusion, see *Baron de Bode's Case* (1845) 8 QB 208, where 'the Lords of the Treasury took the money as mere servants of the crown, and it was settled law that mandamus did not lie against the crown': Michael Lobban, 'The Commissioners for Claims on France and the Case of the Baron de Bode, 1815–1861' in Mark Godfrey (ed), *Law and Authority in British Legal History, 1200–1900* (CUP 2016) 238.

[25] Stephen Sedley, 'The Crown in Its Own Courts' in Christopher F Forsyth and Ivan Hare (eds), *The Golden Metwand and the Crooked Cord: Essays in Honour of Sir William Wade QC* (OUP 1999) 256–57.

[26] Christopher Forsyth, '*M v The Home Office* [1992]: Ministers and Injunctions' in Satvinder Juss and Maurice Sunkin (eds), *Landmark Cases in Public Law* (Hart Publishing 2017) 150. See also William Wade, Christopher Forsyth, and Julian Ghosh, *Administrative Law* (12th edn, OUP 2022) 35–39, 651–54, 664–65.

[27] *M v Home Office* (n 1) 395 (Lord Templeman).

The result of the elaboration in the nineteenth century of a formal notion of the crown—understood as central government—and of the reinterpretation of *the king can do no wrong*, was a fundamental modification of the constitutional settlement reached in the seventeenth century. Maitland captured the essence of that seventeenth-century constitutional settlement understanding of *the king can do no wrong* as follows: 'our modern doctrine' of *the king can do no wrong* is that 'though the king can neither be punished nor sued, no other person, no other servant of the king, is protected against the ordinary legal consequences of an unlawful act by the king's command'.[28] No person other than the king is immune from suit. In contrast, nineteenth- and twentieth-century courts, as a result of a reinterpretation of *the king can do no wrong* and the confusion surrounding the term 'crown', crowned the government departments king, granted them the king's immunity from suit, and obfuscated the issue of their capacity to do wrong to emphasize instead their non-amenability to justice. High public officers in their representative capacity of the crown, while they would have been liable following the seventeenth-century constitutional settlement understanding of *the king can do no wrong* precisely because they are acting for the king, were instead found not to be liable in their representative capacity.

The king can do no wrong's evolution in legal thinking shows that the understanding of the king's capacity to do wrong impacted the king's amenability to justice until the nineteenth century. In *Tobin* and *Feather*, the reversal of the analysis of the two dimensions—an early indication of which could be found in Blackstone's interpretation of *the king can do no wrong*—was adopted. The king's amenability to justice—the second, procedural dimension of crown liability—became the primary concern. The substantive dimension of crown liability—the issue of the king's capacity to do wrong—was obfuscated. As a result, the lack of direct liability of government departments themselves is still an issue in common law jurisdictions such as England and Canada, where the crown's liability rests on a finding of a tortious conduct by its individual servant. The absence of direct liability of governmental departments under the Crown Proceedings Act 1947 (CPA) and similar statutes is the result of a confusion in conceiving of the crown and of the sovereign, and the tendency in common law, captured by Dicey's notion of equality before the law, to focus on the individual liability of a given civil servant. From *the king can do no wrong* understood in the nineteenth century as the king cannot authorize a wrong and cannot, therefore, be ascribed a wrong committed by a servant in his name, a further mistaken understanding emerged that government departments are the crown, that they cannot command a wrong, and that they cannot, as a consequence, be imputed the wrong committed by a crown servant—even if that servant was following governmental orders.

[28] FW Maitland, *The Constitutional History of England* (CUP 1963) 102–03.

The emphasis on the procedural dimension of crown liability in legal thinking since the second half of the nineteenth century has brought the notion of the crown's immunity from suit at common law to the forefront. But the focus on the procedural dimension has led to the obfuscation of the substantive dimension of crown liability—whether the king, and the now the crown understood as the central government, are capable of issuing wrongful commands. Can the government do wrong? Is the government capable of issuing wrongful orders to individual officers and crown servants? Who is the crown issuing the wrongful orders? Is it fictitiously the king, who cannot be sued but whose unlawful order is invalidated by the law, or is it the government, an instrument of the king who must be held liable because all others but the king are amenable to justice? Those issues have not been resolved because the substantive dimension of crown liability was omitted from legal discourse since nineteenth-century English courts negated the king's capacity to do wrong by developing the fiction that there is no wrong in the king. By addressing the issue of the government's capacity to do wrong and removing the ahistorical use of *the king can do no wrong* as a justification for the government's non-amenability to justice at common law, the debate as to the normative justifications for governmental immunity from suit becomes possible. Once the veil of confusion surrounding *the king can do no wrong* is lifted and its constitutional understanding is properly grasped, the procedural dimension of crown liability and the policy reasons for conferring immunity on the governmental apparatus can be scrutinized and conceived of in light of the substantive dimension of crown liability, the government's capacity to do wrong.

The comparative study of American, Irish, and Australian legal thinking on governmental liability offers an instructive counterpoint. Sovereign immunity in American legal thinking is associated with immunity from suit and is a political product of federalism as a novel form of constitutional design and what is conceived of as a deeply historically entrenched feature of the common law. Perhaps for that reason and because of the absence of the aura surrounding a royal crown in the American and Irish republics, the fiction that governmental departments can do no wrong could more easily be identified as deeply flawed and rights-threatening. The fiction that government departments—and, in America, the president—or the state are incapable of doing wrong was rejected in America, Ireland, and Australia, while it has gained traction in the realm of tortious liability of the crown in England and in Canada since the second half of the nineteenth century. The fiction that government departments are incapable of doing wrong—that they *can do no wrong*—was rejected in American legal thinking early in the twentieth century in the realm of constitutional rights violation.[29] American legal thinking may still be grappling with the theoretical groundings of sovereign

[29] Akhil Reed Amar, 'Of Sovereignty and Federalism' (1987) 96 YLJ 1425, 1490. See *Home Tel & Tel Co v City of Los Angeles* (1913) 227 US 278.

immunity in constitutional law and the scope of the discretionary function exception under the Federal Tort Claims Act,[30] but the liability of governmental entities for the violation of constitutional rights is a more clear-cut issue. The state of the law in America mirrors that of other jurisdictions: concepts similar to the discretionary function exception—either the issue of justiciability in English law or that of the policy-operation distinction in Canadian law—still causes much ink to be spilled, but the readiness to conceive of governmental entities as liable themselves for rights violations can be found just as much in Canada[31] and the United Kingdom[32] as in the United States and Ireland under their respective constitutions. The direct constitutional liability of governmental entities—and a willingness to consider the Commonwealth liable in Australia—is in stark contrast with governmental departments' vicarious liability in tort, where an individual tortfeasor crown servant has to be identified as a *sine qua none* criterion for the action to proceed. Equally, much is still to be learned from a comparative study of the emerging fields of social and environmental responsibility of private corporations, and of the study of corporate liability for criminal conduct in revisiting our understanding of the law of crown liability.[33]

While it is indisputable that English legal historians have claimed that the king could not issue a writ to command himself and that the idea of a sovereign above the law can be traced to Hobbes' *Leviathan* and found in Austin's thinking, the idea that the king is above the law is not a feature of English legal thinking, at least when viewed from a historical constitutional perspective. In many common law jurisdictions, the government's privileged status in the realm of crown liability is historically phenomenal. The critique is particularly apt in England and Canada, where governmental departments benefit from an absolute immunity from suit at common law. Under crown proceedings legislation, they are liable only vicariously for the wrongs of individual servants carrying their orders on the ground that *the crown can do no wrong*. Central government departments' claim to a supra-legal status has been bolstered since the middle of the twentieth century by a rule of statutory interpretation that begins from the starting point that statutes do not bind the government. Governmental departments cannot claim to be the sovereign in

[30] The distinction between officials' personal liability and their official capacity is also a feature of American case law: see *Larson v Domestic & Foreign Commerce Corp* (1949) 337 US 682, 687–88; *Brandon v Holt* (1985) 469 US 464, 471; *Kentucky v Graham* (1985) 473 US 159, 165–66.

[31] Under s 32 of the Canadian Charter of Rights and Freedoms, being Part I of the Constitution Act 1982, Sch B to the Canada Act 1982 (UK), 1982, c 11.

[32] Under the Human Rights Act 1998, c 42.

[33] See eg Orla Kelleher, 'Incorporating Climate Justice into Legal Reasoning: Shifting Towards a Risk-Based Approach to Causation in Climate Litigation' (2022) 13 JHRE 290; Orla Kelleher, 'Systemic Climate Change Litigation, Standing Rules and the Aarhus Convention: A Purposive Approach' (2022) 34 JEL 107; 'Carlos Gómez-Jara Díez, 'Corporate Criminal Liability in the Twenty-First Century: Are All Corporations Equally Capable of Wrongdoing?' (2011) 41 Stetson LR 41; Sylvia Rich, 'Can Corporations Experience Duress? An Examination of Emotion-Based Excuses and Group Agents' (2019) 13 CLPH 149.

their respective constitutional orders, yet the privileged status in relation to law they enjoy in contemporary legal thinking resemble the Leviathan's—and surpass the one enjoyed by English medieval kings.

American and Irish legal thinking's focus on the locus of sovereignty in conceiving of governmental liability can offer a useful perspective for self-reflection in other common law jurisdictions. Although the American concept of sovereign immunity is intertwined with federalism and the particulars of American constitutional history, analysing the concept can nevertheless be useful, as is the study of Irish law of state liability, because they beg the question 'who is the sovereign?'. Whether the sovereign should enjoy absolute immunity from suit and a status as above the law in a given constitutional order is a separate question, but if one is not even the sovereign to begin with—and government departments and other public officials are most definitely not—then their enjoyment of supra-legal attributes on grounds of sovereignty logically should fall. The continued existence of governmental departments' immunity from suit at common law and other privileges such as the non-application of statutes can only rest on other unexpressed normative considerations. The separation of powers and the courts' reluctance to encroach on the democratic will embodied by governmental policy decisions belong to such normative considerations. As Lord Wilberforce wrote in *Anns v Merton London Borough Council*, 'public authorities have to strike a balance between the claims of efficiency and thrift: whether they get the balance right can only be decided through the ballot box, not in the courts'.[34] The legitimacy of the privileges and of the judicial deference governments enjoy in the realm of civil liability throughout the common law world depends on the normative underpinnings of these privileges and deference being assessed in the light of day, once obfuscating, ahistorical claims are removed. As Street wisely wrote, individuals cannot rely on their government to fulfil their utmost well-being, and the benefits of living in an organized society come at a cost—but not at all costs, and transparent rules must be devised to allow us to determine when one individual has paid too high a price for our collective action:

> The point is that individual well-being is not in itself absolutely assured by any government, and that whenever private interest conflicts with public good, the former must be subordinated to the latter. The individual must pay for the privilege of living in an ordered society. Rules must be framed which, in the light of economic conditions, administrative needs and juristic considerations, will determine when the citizen is paying too high a price. When he suffers a bad bargain let him be compensated for his loss.[35]

[34] *Anns v Merton London Borough Council* [1978] AC 728, 754 (Lord Wilberforce).

[35] Harry Street, 'Tort Liability of the State: The Federal Tort Claims Act and the Crown Proceedings Act' (1948) 47 Mich L Rev 341, 366–67.

Viewed from a historical constitutional perspective, *the king can do no wrong* does not clothe governmental departments with feudal robes of immunity from suit: governmental departments appearing before the courts under the guise of the emperor are in fact naked. The only person who—despite being subject to law and capable of being and doing wrong—can nevertheless claim immunity from suit as a historical constitutional tenet is the sole bearer of the crown: the king himself.

Properly understood in its historical constitutional evolution, *the king can do no wrong* is not a historically rooted immunity from suit. It does not mandate high public officers'—in their representative capacity—or government departments' immunity from suit at common law. Our current understanding of crown liability is due to the obfuscation of the first dimension of crown liability—the king's capacity to do wrong—in the nineteenth century, in conjunction with the development of a formal notion of the crown. The king's personal exemption from the coercive power of the law in Hale's thinking became, in the nineteenth century, the legal fiction that there is no wrong in the king. The reinterpretation of *the king can do no wrong* in petition of right cases of the nineteenth century against the king personally was applied in the very different context of ordinary actions against high public officers and government departments at the turn of the twentieth century. As a result, the king's personal exemption from the coercive power of the law and the fiction that there is no wrong in the king in the eyes of the law were passed on to the formal notion of the crown understood as central government.

Removing the ahistorical premise of *the king can do no wrong*, understood erroneously as a constitutional dogma of the crown's immunity from suit and irresponsibility grounded in a mythical feudal past, may allow for a discussion of the crown's absolute immunity from suit at common law and for policy issues to be addressed openly. *The king can do no wrong* and the notion of the crown, because of the confusion and misunderstanding surrounding them, currently serve improperly as opaque covers preventing a debate as to the policy underpinning crown liability. Adopting a historical constitutional approach to *the king can do no wrong* in revisiting our understanding of crown liability would prevent, for instance, the easy casting aside of reports of the Law Commission on possible avenues of reform of crown liability.[36] The removal of *the king can do no wrong* used—falsely—as a

[36] Editorial, 'Damages for Maladministration: The Commission Debacle' (2012) 17 JR 211. Policy reasons in support of government departments' immunity in current legal literature include the risk of a chilling effect on decision-making, the possible subversion of the political nature of decisions on allocation of resources, and the financial implications for departments and ultimately, for taxpayers: Duncan Fairgrieve, 'Pushing Back the Boundaries of Public Authority Liability: Tort Law Enters the Classroom' [2002] PL 288; Duncan Fairgrieve, *State Liability in Tort: A Comparative Law Study* (OUP 2003) 32–33; The Hon David W Stratas, 'The Liability of Public Authorities: New Horizons' (2015) 69 SCLR (2d) 1, 6. See also UK Law Commission, 'Remedies against Public Bodies: A Scoping Report' (UK Law Commission 2006) [2.24]–[2.26]; UK Law Commission, 'Consultation Paper (No 187), Administrative Redress: Public Bodies and the Citizen' (UK Law Commission 2008) [2.2], [2.6], [2.7], [6.1], [6.2]; UK Law Commission, 'Administrative Redress: Public Bodies and the Citizen' (UK Law Commission 2010) 322 [1.18].

historical basis for governmental immunity in tort could contribute to fostering policy discussions across the common law world as to governmental liability in tort at common law and suggestions for reform.[37]

One such avenue for reform could be grounded in reviving the petition of right. In addition to courts adopting in the realm of crown liability the same historical constitutional understanding that they have adopted in other seminal public law cases, this avenue would offer an alternative option should legislative interventions prove improbable in the context of parliamentary democracies where legislative agendas are predominantly controlled by the same executive that benefits from crown immunity. The old procedure of the petition of right was historically conceived of as a common law remedy in legal thinking and would fill in the gap where the current crown proceedings legislation does not provide a remedy, such as in cases of institutional failures. Indeed, while the CPA and crown proceedings statutes in other common law jurisdictions render an unidentified 'crown' vicariously liable for the wrongs of individual crown servants, they do not create direct liability for government departments.[38] Under the CPA and similar crown proceedings legislation, the undefined notion of crown is vicariously liable for the wrongs of individual civil servants working for government departments. But the same undefined crown (all we know for certain is that it is not the person of the king) is not liable for the wrongs committed at an institutional level by government departments themselves. Yet we live in a complex twenty-first-century regulatory environment administered by highly developed, professional, expert, departmentalized administrative structures governing diverse economies and societies. Institutional wrongdoing understood as a wrong committed by the collective action of many individuals and departments within the governmental apparatus is more likely and potentially far more damaging than a wrong done by a rogue nineteenth-century local collector of taxes riding a horse in the English countryside. But it is that

[37] In addition to the numerous reports of the UK Law Commission in n 36, suggestions and reports by law commissions also abound across the common law world: see eg in New Zealand, *The Crown in Court: A Review of the Crown Proceedings Act and National Security Information in Proceedings the Commission recommends a new statute to replace the Crown Proceedings Act 1950* (Law Commission 2015) (the Law Commission recommended, *inter alia*, that the current crown proceedings legislation be amended to allow for the crown's direct liability in tort); in Australia, *Traditional Rights and Freedoms—Encroachments by Commonwealth Laws* (ALRC Report 129 2016) c 16; and in Canada, 'The Legal Status of the Federal Administration' (Law Reform Commission of Canada Working Paper 40 1985) 69, where the need to reform the law of crown liability in tort was noted almost forty years ago:

> A general reform better suited to the direction in which contemporary law is moving seems essential. The complexity and confusion which are characteristic of the present situation require that a simpler and more consistent system be adopted. It also seems essential that such a system should be better adapted to certain types of damage or damaging acts for which it is at present difficult to obtain compensation.

[38] The crown is not directly liable under crown proceedings legislation modelled on the United Kingdom's CPA, except for defined situations such as occupiers' liability: s 2(1)(a), (c) CPA. Crown proceedings legislation does not confer legal personhood on government departments lacking such personhood either. See Chapter 5.

law of a bygone era, based on Victorian Diceyan views of individual crown servant liability, that still acts as the cornerstone of the law of crown liability in many common law jurisdictions today.

Reviving the petition of right understood as a common law remedy has been suggested before in the realm of contractual liability of the crown. The Petitions of Right Act 1860 provided that a petition of right could be instituted against the king in his private capacity for a contract entered into by the king on his own personal behalf or on behalf of his household. Moreover, section 14 of the Petition of Right Act 1860 made a distinction between petitions of right which 'relate to any public matter' and those which 'relate to any private property enjoyed by Her Majesty in her private capacity'; the former were to be satisfied out of the Treasury.[39] The CPA abolished that possibility and repealed the king's private liability in contract.[40] Importantly, however, the CPA repealed the Petitions of Right Act 1860, not the old procedure of the petition of right. Williams and Street have argued that it may be possible, using that old common law procedure, to sue to the king, in his private capacity, in contract.[41] In the same vein, Craig suggests that whether the petition of right may still be used in claims other than in relation to the UK government is debatable, and points to the possibility that it may still be available against the king personally.[42]

Masters' vicarious liability for the wrong of their servants is now a strict liability issue and no fault on the part of the master is presumed.[43] When the CPA was enacted, however, developments in the law of vicarious liability were ignored and so the crown's vicarious liability under the Act is based on the older doctrine of vicarious liability, which conceived of the master's liability for the wrong of the servant as being grounded in the master's own fault.[44] As was discussed in Chapter 6, Irish courts understood, when they charted a new course for the law of state liability, the evolution of the law in the realm of vicarious liability and took onboard those developments.[45] Should the same be done in relation to the CPA, the wrong complained of in proceedings against the crown would not be conceived of under the CPA as the crown's own wrong, in line with the more recent law of vicarious liability.

Taken together, the possibility of a revival of the petition of right and the evolution of the law of vicarious liability allow the old, common law petition of right

[39] Harrison Moore, 'The Crown as Corporation' (1904) 20 LQR 351, 353–54; Martin Loughlin, 'The State, the Crown and the Law' in Maurice Sunkin and Sebastian Payne (eds), *The Nature of the Crown: A Legal and Political Analysis* (OUP 1999) 60.

[40] See Harry Street, 'Crown Proceedings Act, 1947' (1948) 11 MLR 129, 132–33.

[41] ibid; Glanville Llewelyn Williams, *Crown Proceedings: An Account of Civil Proceedings by and Against the Crown as Affected by the Crown Proceedings Act, 1947* (Stevens 1948) 8. See also Wade and Forsyth (n 26) 664.

[42] Paul Craig, *Administrative Law* (9th edn, Sweet & Maxwell 2021) 147.

[43] Peter W Hogg, Patrick Monahan, and Wade K Wright, *Liability of the Crown* (Carswell 2011) 159.

[44] Carol Harlow, *Compensation and Government Torts* (Sweet & Maxwell 1982) 21–23.

[45] See Chapter 6, section 3.2.2.

to be resorted to in order to sue to the king in his political capacity for a wrong committed not by the king or under the king's command, but for the wrong of his government departments, for example in cases of institutional failures. The wrong complained of would not be conceived of as the king's, but as that of a government department. The perfect king, holder of the office of the crown and fountain of justice, would remedy the wrong done in his name. Such a revival of the petition of right conceived of as a common law residual remedy would be grounded in a historical constitutional approach to crown liability based on the medieval, Bractonian foundations of the petition of right and on the king's duty to remedy a wrong, as well as on the seventeenth-century constitutional settlement understanding of *the king can do no wrong* whereby all are liable but the king. The proposed revival of the petition of right would also be grounded in other elements of continuity in English legal thinking, such as the eighteenth- and nineteenth-century notion of the king's perfection which underpinned the prerogative writs and equitable remedies. As was the case under section 14 of the Petitions of Right Act 1860, such petitions of right which 'relate to any public matter' would have to be satisfied out of the Treasury—and not out of the monarch's civil list—pursuant to a statutory basis for that appropriation.[46]

A petition of right to the king as holder of the crown to remedy a wrong in cases of institutional wrongs not otherwise contemplated by crown proceedings legislation would admittedly equally rest on a legal fiction—that of a perfect king—but would address procedural difficulties when government departments do not have legal personhood or the capacity to be sued. Indeed, prior to the adoption of the CPA, not all government departments had corporate status or the capacity to sue or be sued, and the fact that government departments and ministerial offices did not have legal capacity was found to constitute a bar to actions in tort against them at common law.[47] A petition of right to the office of the crown, a corporation sole—or to its holder, the king—would also remedy the absence of corporate status of certain government departments.

The procedural suggestion of reform that the common law petition of right be revived marks continuity with legal thinking in relation to *the king can do no wrong*. Hale recognized that the petition of right was available against the king. Blackstone conceived of the king as perfect and incapable of doing wrong. The possibility of suing to the office of the crown by petition of right for a wrong committed by a government department—especially where the latter's corporate status is an issue—would be in line with both Hale and Blackstone's thinking. The perfect king occupying the office of the crown would not, if the suggestion of a revival of the petition of right were to be followed, have to be conceived of as having done wrong,

[46] But liability itself would not be contingent on Parliament voting to appropriate the funds: Wade and Forsyth (n 26) 653–54.

[47] See eg *Trawnik v Gordon* (1985) 1 WLR 532 (CA); Sedley (n 25) 264–65.

and the wrong would not have to be attributed to the king or to the office of the crown, thereby avoiding overturning nineteenth-century cases. The notion of perfection of the king which has been part of legal thinking since Hale and Blackstone would instead support the revival of the petition of right. The perfect, benevolent king would see to it that institutional wrongs done in the name of the crown by government departments be remedied.

Regardless of suggestions of revival of the petition of right, a historical constitutional approach to rethinking crown liability by relying on a revisited understanding of *the king can do no wrong* can have an important impact on the interpretation of crown proceedings legislation. The adoption of a seventeenth-century constitutional settlement understanding of *the king can do no wrong* allows for a clearer understanding of the notion of crown and a greater achievement of the notion of equality before the law. It has frequently been noted that the current understanding of *the king can do no wrong* as a justification for the crown's blanket immunity does not sit well with current constitutional principles—and in particular the rule of law.[48] To Wade and Forsyth, 'It is fundamental to the rule of law that the Crown, like other public authorities, should bear its fair share of legal liability and be answerable for wrongs done to its subjects'.[49] Rethinking crown liability from a historically informed approach in adopting the seventeenth-century constitutional settlement understanding of *the king can do no wrong* and thereby conceiving of government departments as liable at common law would achieve equality before the law to a greater extent than Dicey's and the courts' traditionally Diceyan[50] application of equality before the law to individual servants only.

A historically informed understanding of *the king can do no wrong* also supports a teleological interpretation of the crown proceedings legislation and the assumption that it simply facilitates recourses against a government which is liable at common law. The CPA was adopted in an attempt to achieve greater equality before the law.[51] By enacting liability—albeit vicariously only—for the formal notion of crown understood as government departments, the CPA can be read as maintaining the essence of Hale's interpretation of *the king can do no wrong* by limiting immunity from the coercive power of the law to the person of the king only. Under the seventeenth-century constitutional understanding of *the king can do no wrong*, while the king is immune from suit for issuing wrongful commands, the instruments executing the command are not. Ministers, government departments, and crown servants are liable for executing the crown's unlawful command. A historically informed reading

[48] William Wade, 'The Crown, Ministers and Officials: Legal Status and Liability' in Maurice Sunkin and Sebastian Payne (eds), *The Nature of the Crown* (OUP 1999) 23–26; JWF Allison, *A Continental Distinction in the Common Law: A Historical and Comparative Perspective on English Public Law* (revised edn, OUP 2000) 107; Maurice Sunkin, 'Crown Immunity from Criminal Liability in English Law' [2003] PL 716, 716; *R v Eldorado Nuclear Ltd* [1983] 2 SCR 551, 558 (Dickson J).

[49] Wade and Forsyth (n 26) 651.

[50] Allison (n 48) 107.

[51] Williams (n 41); Hogg, Monahan, and Wright (n 43) 10–11; Wade and Forsyth (n 26) 651.

of section 2(3) and (4) of the CPA, for instance,[52] supports a seventeenth-century constitutional settlement understanding of *the king can do no wrong* where the king is immune from suit for issuing wrongful commands but the instruments executing them—ministers, government departments, and servants—are liable. As was achieved partly with the adoption of crown proceedings legislation providing for vicarious liability of the formal notion of crown understood as government departments, adopting the constitutional settlement understanding of *the king can do no wrong* in interpreting crown proceedings legislation would achieve greater equality before the law in providing theoretical support for the formal notion of crown's direct liability at common law. Revisiting our understanding of crown liability from a historical constitutional approach grounded in a historically informed understanding of *the king can do no wrong* can also inform an analysis of the constitutionality of statutory immunities and of their conformity with the rule of law.[53]

Historically in legal thought, *the king can do no wrong* raised issues relating to the two dimensions—substantive and procedural—of crown liability. Grounding our understanding of crown liability on two dimensions—capacity to do wrong and amenability to justice—in a similar fashion to Australian legal thinking, allows for a more generous notion of equality before the law than Dicey's. Dicey focussed on the relationship between the king's officers and wronged individuals in developing his notion of equality before the law. He addressed the procedural dimension of crown liability, but not the substantive dimension of crown liability—the crown's capacity to do wrong. Including the concept of the crown's capacity to do wrong—meaning the governmental apparatus's capacity to do wrong—in a historically informed understanding of *the king can do no wrong* can allow for a fuller application of the notion of equality before the law in the law of crown liability. It would also bring the law of crown liability in alignment with that of other public bodies since *Robinson*, of judicial review since *M v Home Office*, and of constitutional law in the realm of the prerogative since *Miller 2*.[54]

The king can do no wrong is not a medieval maxim, but it has a uniquely long history in common law legal thinking. Digging through layers of its history results in a core sample of the evolution of crown liability in English legal thinking. The study of its travels and travails across the common law world also allows for an enriching analysis of the transplant of *the king can do no wrong* in different legal soils, where its different understandings have withered or adapted depending on the constitutional text and context. Perhaps the lesson the story *the king can do no wrong* teaches us is best told in the words of the monarchs who answered petitions of right themselves: *que droit soit fait*. Let right be done.

[52] See Chapter 5, section 4.3.2.

[53] On the inconsistency of statutory immunities with the rule of law, see Mark Elliott and Jason Varuhas, *Administrative Law: Text and Materials* (5th edn, OUP 2017) 588.

[54] *Robinson v Chief Constable of West Yorkshire Police* [2018] UKSC 4; *M v Home Office* (n 1); *Miller 2* (n 2); see Chapter 5, section 5.

Index

For the benefit of digital users, indexed terms that span two pages (e.g., 52–53) may, on occasion, appear on only one of those pages.

The manufacturer's authorised representative in the EU for product safety is Oxford University Press España S.A. of el Parque Empresarial San Fernando de Henares, Avenida de Castilla, 2 – 28830 Madrid (www.oup.es/en or product.safety@oup.com). OUP España S.A. also acts as importer into Spain of products made by the manufacturer.

www.ingramcontent.com/pod-product-compliance
Lightning Source LLC
LaVergne TN
LVHW011821200926
848484LV00005B/1266
9780198886914